I ENVY YOU
I. N. V. U.
Innocent   Nice   Vivid   Unique

ALSO AVAILABLE FROM 🐱 TOKYOPOP®

MANGA

ACTION

ANGELIC LAYER*
CLAMP SCHOOL DETECTIVES* (April 2003)
DIGIMON (March 2003)
DUKLYON: CLAMP SCHOOL DEFENDERS* (September 2003)
GATEKEEPERS* (March 2003)
GTO*
HARLEM BEAT
INITIAL D*
ISLAND
JING: KING OF BANDITS* (June 2003)
JULINE
LUPIN III*
MONSTERS, INC.
PRIEST
RAVE*
REAL BOUT HIGH SCHOOL*
REBOUND* (April 2003)
SAMURAI DEEPER KYO* (June 2003)
SCRYED* (March 2003)
SHAOLIN SISTERS* (February 2003)
THE SKULL MAN*

FANTASY

CHRONICLES OF THE CURSED SWORD (July 2003)
DEMON DIARY (May 2003)
DRAGON HUNTER (June 2003)
DRAGON KNIGHTS*
KING OF HELL (June 2003)
PLANET LADDER*
RAGNAROK
REBIRTH (March 2003)
SHIRAHIME:TALES OF THE SNOW PRINCESS* (December 2003)
SORCERER HUNTERS
WISH*

CINE-MANGA™

AKIRA*
CARDCAPTORS
KIM POSSIBLE (March 2003)
LIZZIE McGUIRE (March 2003)
POWER RANGERS (May 2003)
SPY KIDS 2 (March 2003)

ANIME GUIDES

GUNDAM TECHNICAL MANUALS
COWBOY BEBOP
SAILOR MOON SCOUT GUIDES

ROMANCE

HAPPY MANIA* (April 2003)
I.N.V.U. (February 2003)
LOVE HINA*
KARE KANO*
KODOCHA*
MAN OF MANY FACES* (May 2003)
MARMALADE BOY*
MARS*
PARADISE KISS*
PEACH GIRL
UNDER A GLASS MOON (June 2003)

SCIENCE FICTION

CHOBITS*
CLOVER
COWBOY BEBOP*
COWBOY BEBOP: SHOOTING STAR* (June 2003)
G-GUNDAM*
GUNDAM WING
GUNDAM WING: ENDLESS WALTZ*
GUNDAM: THE LAST OUTPOST*
PARASYTE
REALITY CHECK (March 2003)

MAGICAL GIRLS

CARDCAPTOR SAKURA
CARDCAPTOR SAKURA: MASTER OF THE CLOW*
CORRECTOR YUI
MAGIC KNIGHT RAYEARTH* (August 2003)
MIRACLE GIRLS
SAILOR MOON
SAINT TAIL
TOKYO MEW MEW* (April 2003)

NOVELS

SAILOR MOON
SUSHI SQUAD (April 2003)

ART BOOKS

CARDCAPTOR SAKURA*
MAGIC KNIGHT RAYEARTH*

TOKYOPOP KIDS

STRAY SHEEP (September 2003)

I.N.V.U.

1

by
Kim Kang Won

TOKYOPOP®
Los Angeles • Tokyo

Translator - Lauren Na
English Adaptation - Bailey Murphy
Associate Editor - Bryce Coleman & Paul Morrissey
Retouch & Lettering - Mark Paniccia, Kevin McCall,
Monalisa de Asis & Paul Morrissey
Graphic Design - Mark Paniccia
Cover Layout - Anna Kernbaum

Senior Editor - Mark Paniccia
Managing Editor - Jill Freshney
Production Manager - Jennifer Miller
Art Director - Matthew Alford
VP of Production & Manufacturing - Ron Klamert
President & C.O.O. - John Parker
Publisher - Stuart Levy

Email: editor@TOKYOPOP.com
Come visit us online at www.TOKYOPOP.com

A **TOKYOPOP** Manga

TOKYOPOP® is an imprint of Mixx Entertainment Inc.
5900 Wilshire Blvd. Suite 2000, Los Angeles, CA 90036

ISBN: 1-59182-001-4

First TOKYOPOP® printing: February 2003

10 9 8 7 6 5 4 3 2 1
Printed in Canada

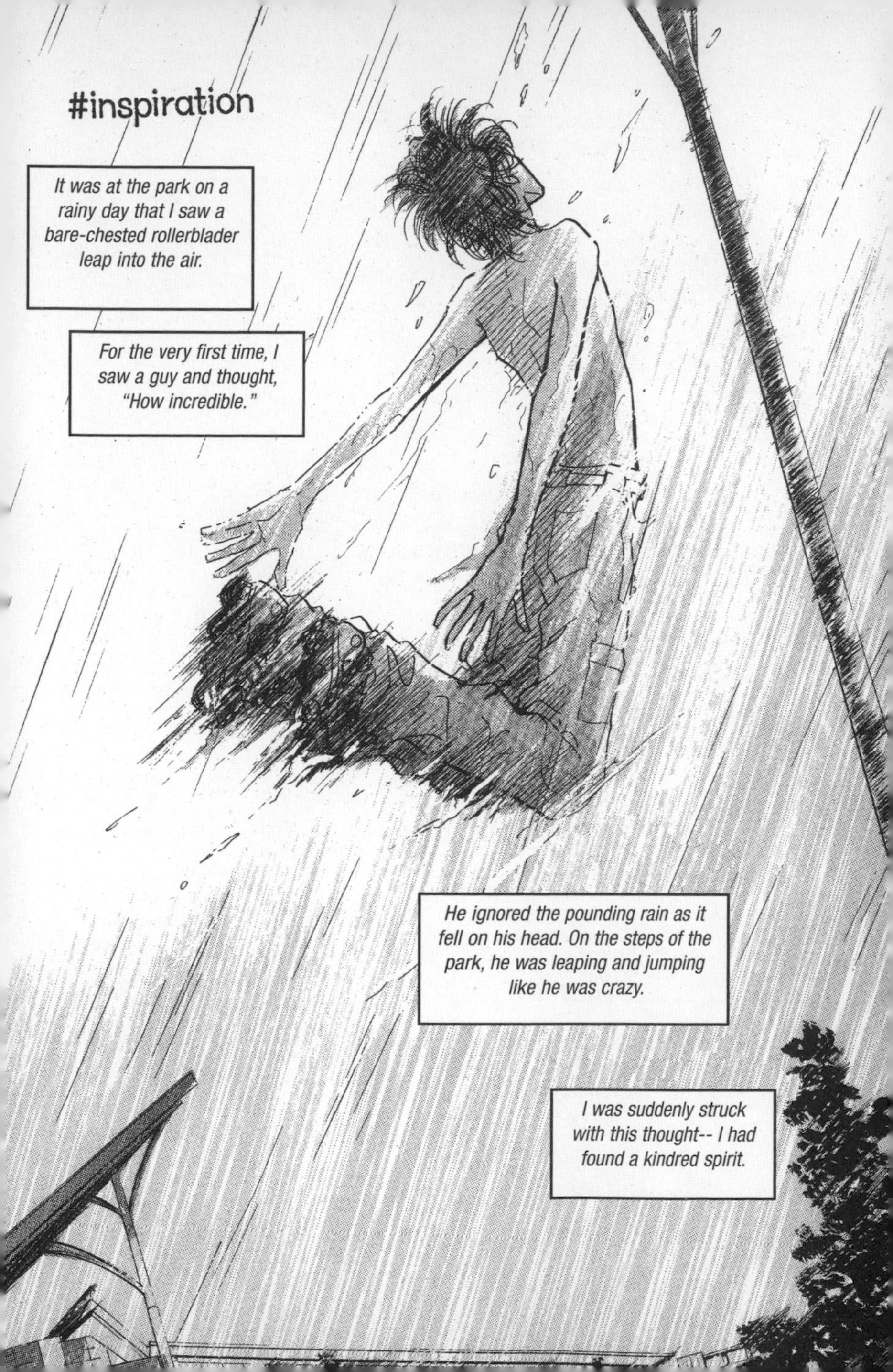
#inspiration
It was at the park on a rainy day that I saw a bare-chested rollerblader leap into the air.
For the very first time, I saw a guy and thought, "How incredible."
He ignored the pounding rain as it fell on his head. On the steps of the park, he was leaping and jumping like he was crazy.
I was suddenly struck with this thought-- I had found a kindred spirit.

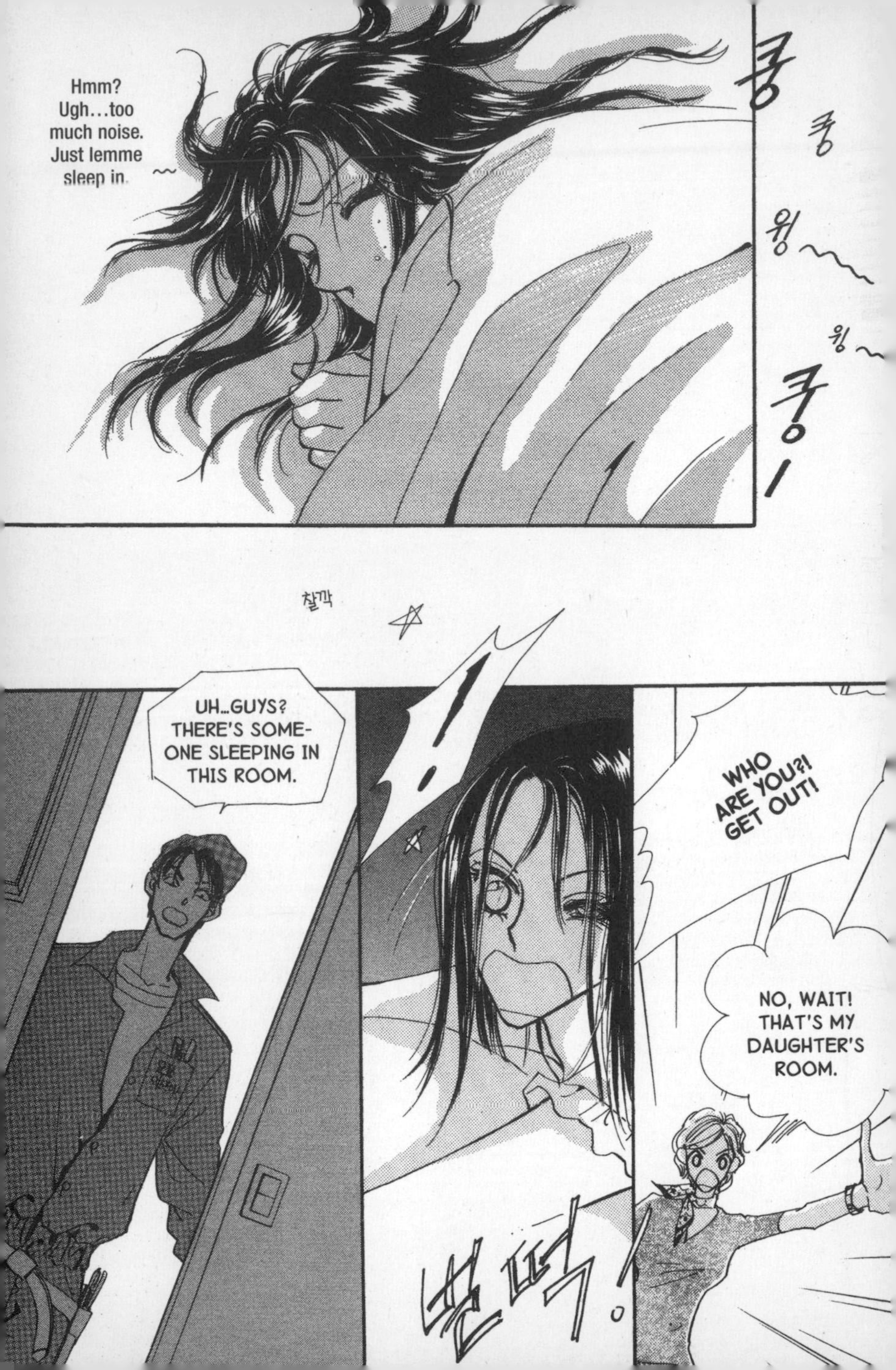
Hmm? Ugh…too much noise. Just lemme sleep in. ~
쿵
쿵
윙~
윙~
쿵!
찰칵
UH...GUYS? THERE'S SOME-ONE SLEEPING IN THIS ROOM.
!
WHO ARE YOU?! GET OUT!
NO, WAIT! THAT'S MY DAUGHTER'S ROOM.
벌떡!

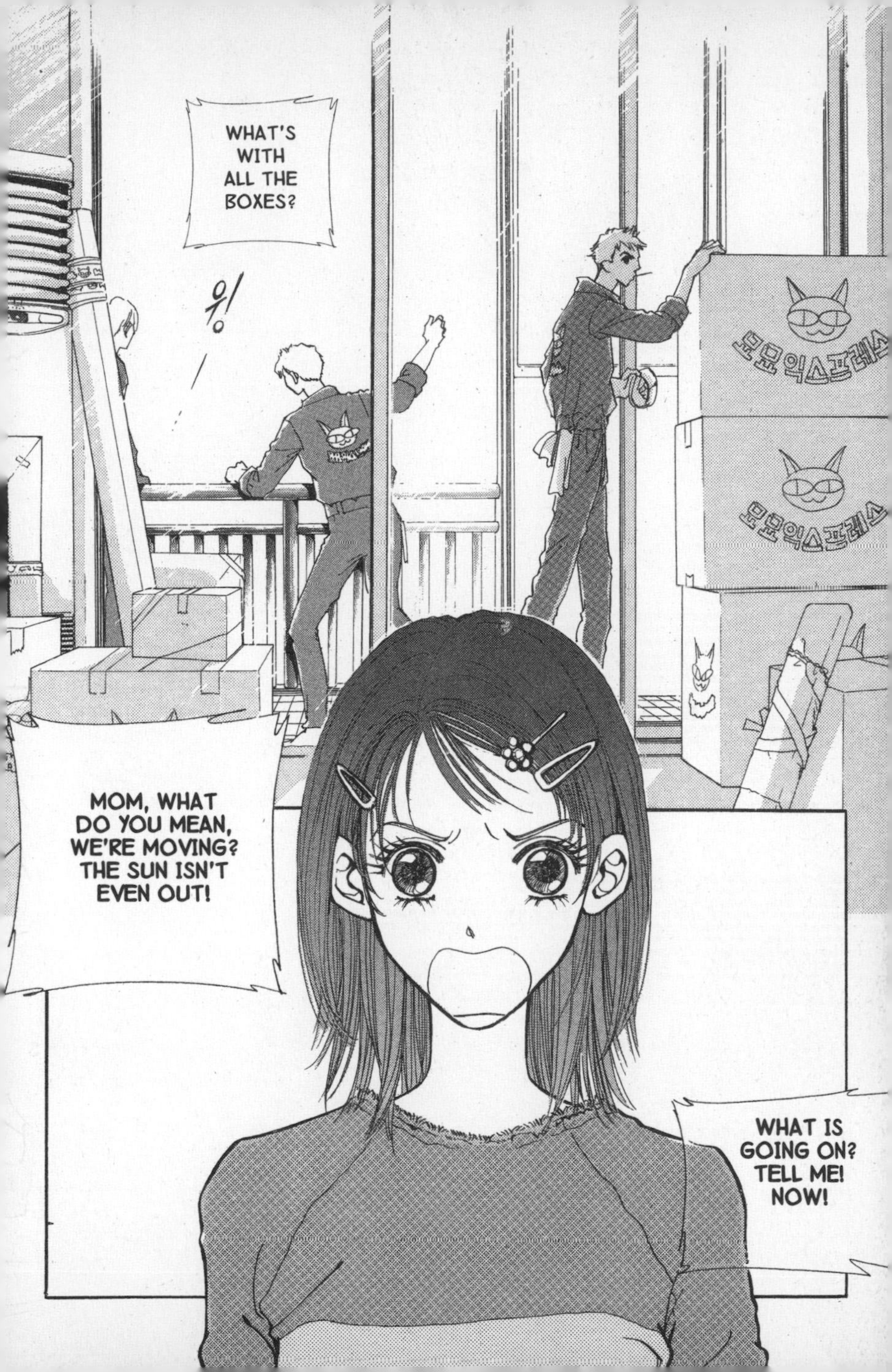
WHAT'S WITH ALL THE BOXES?
MOM, WHAT DO YOU MEAN, WE'RE MOVING? THE SUN ISN'T EVEN OUT!
WHAT IS GOING ON? TELL ME! NOW!

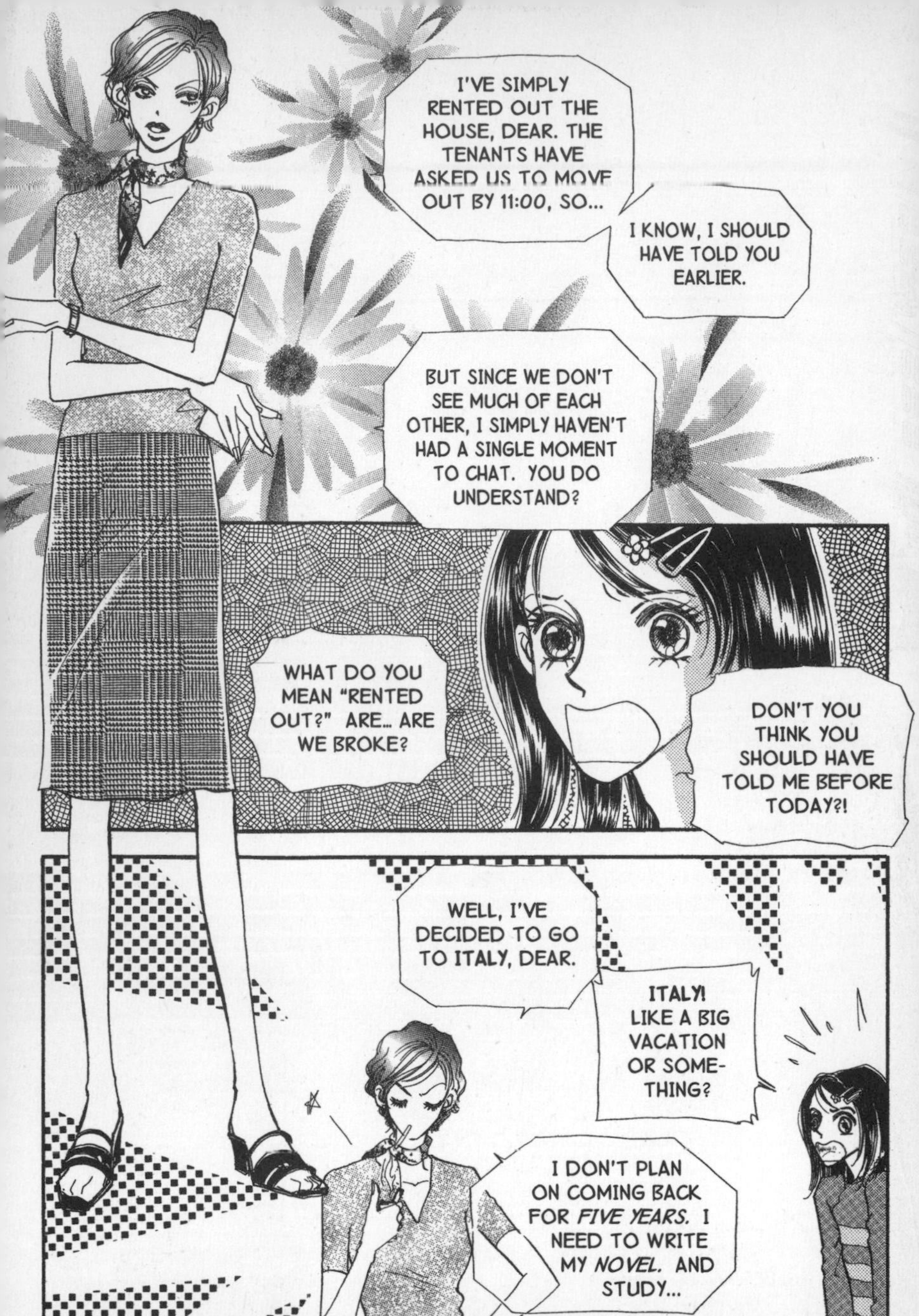
I'VE SIMPLY RENTED OUT THE HOUSE, DEAR. THE TENANTS HAVE ASKED US TO MOVE OUT BY 11:00, SO...
I KNOW, I SHOULD HAVE TOLD YOU EARLIER.
BUT SINCE WE DON'T SEE MUCH OF EACH OTHER, I SIMPLY HAVEN'T HAD A SINGLE MOMENT TO CHAT. YOU DO UNDERSTAND?
WHAT DO YOU MEAN "RENTED OUT?" ARE... ARE WE BROKE?
DON'T YOU THINK YOU SHOULD HAVE TOLD ME BEFORE TODAY?!
WELL, I'VE DECIDED TO GO TO ITALY, DEAR.
ITALY! LIKE A BIG VACATION OR SOME-THING?
I DON'T PLAN ON COMING BACK FOR *FIVE YEARS.* I NEED TO WRITE MY *NOVEL.* AND STUDY...

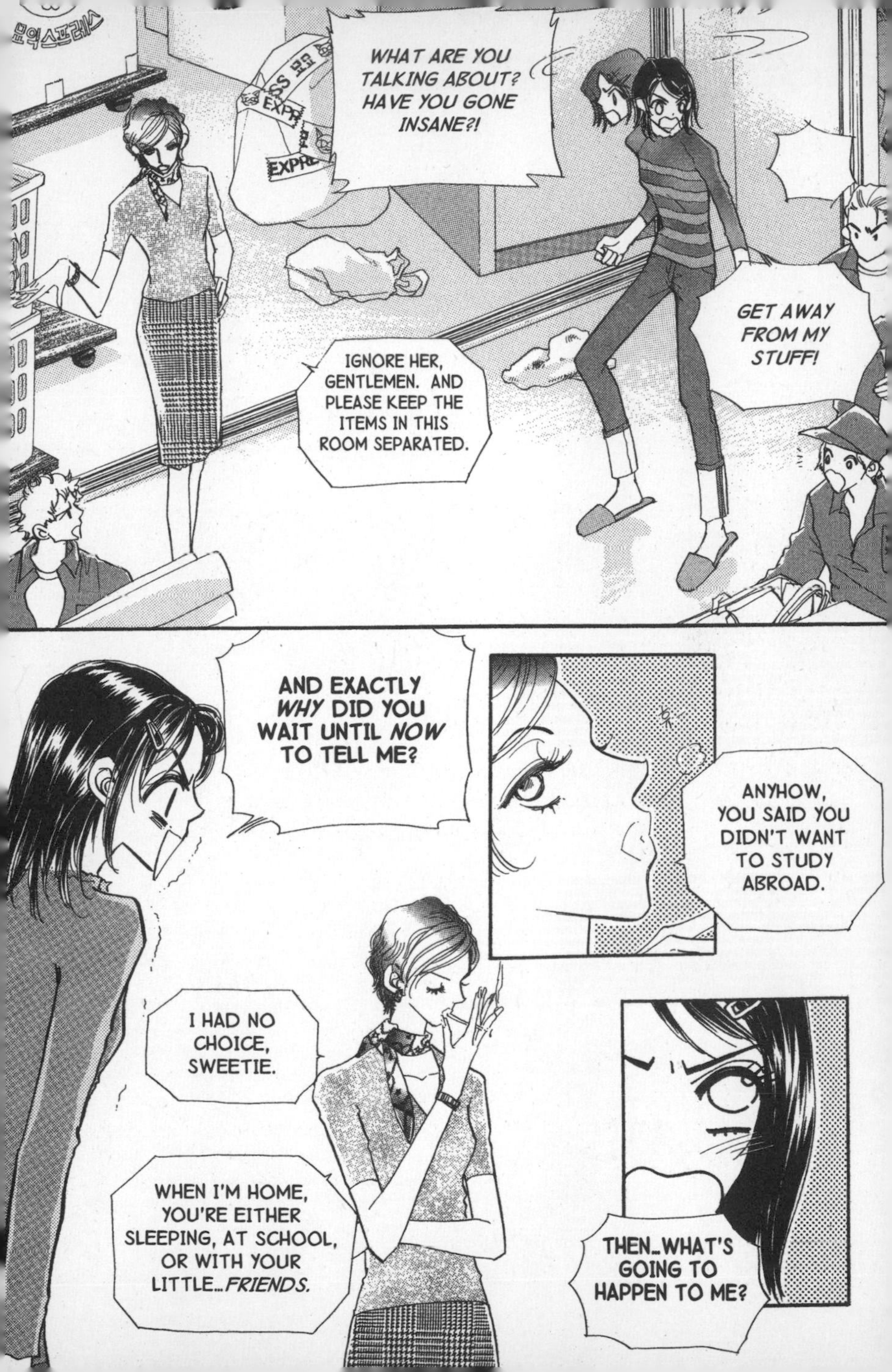
묘익스프레스
WHAT ARE YOU TALKING ABOUT? HAVE YOU GONE INSANE?!
GET AWAY FROM MY STUFF!
IGNORE HER, GENTLEMEN. AND PLEASE KEEP THE ITEMS IN THIS ROOM SEPARATED.
AND EXACTLY *WHY* DID YOU WAIT UNTIL *NOW* TO TELL ME?
ANYHOW, YOU SAID YOU DIDN'T WANT TO STUDY ABROAD.
I HAD NO CHOICE, SWEETIE.
WHEN I'M HOME, YOU'RE EITHER SLEEPING, AT SCHOOL, OR WITH YOUR LITTLE...*FRIENDS.*
THEN...WHAT'S GOING TO HAPPEN TO ME?

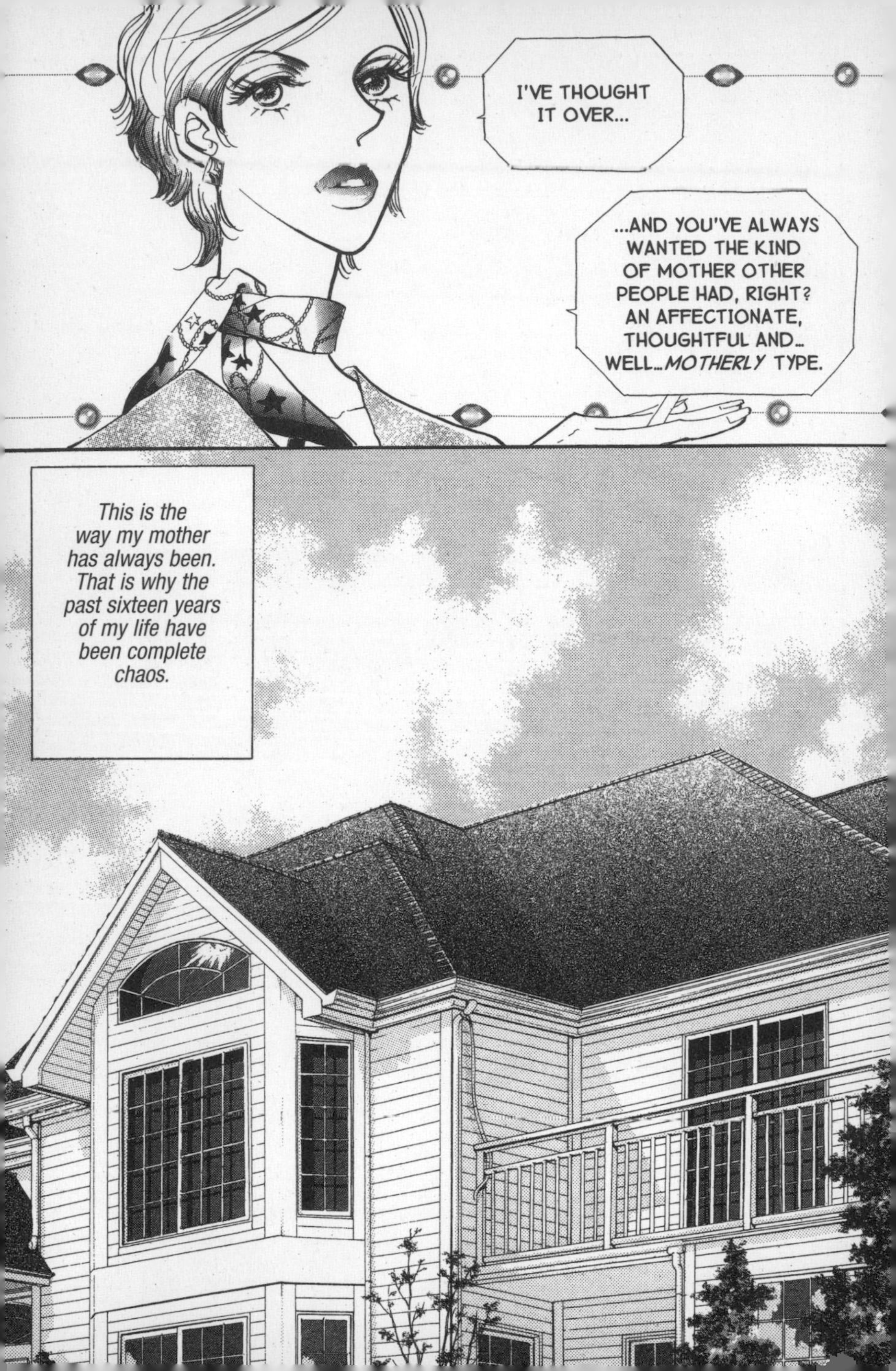
I'VE THOUGHT IT OVER...
...AND YOU'VE ALWAYS WANTED THE KIND OF MOTHER OTHER PEOPLE HAD, RIGHT? AN AFFECTIONATE, THOUGHTFUL AND... WELL...*MOTHERLY* TYPE.
This is the way my mother has always been. That is why the past sixteen years of my life have been complete chaos.

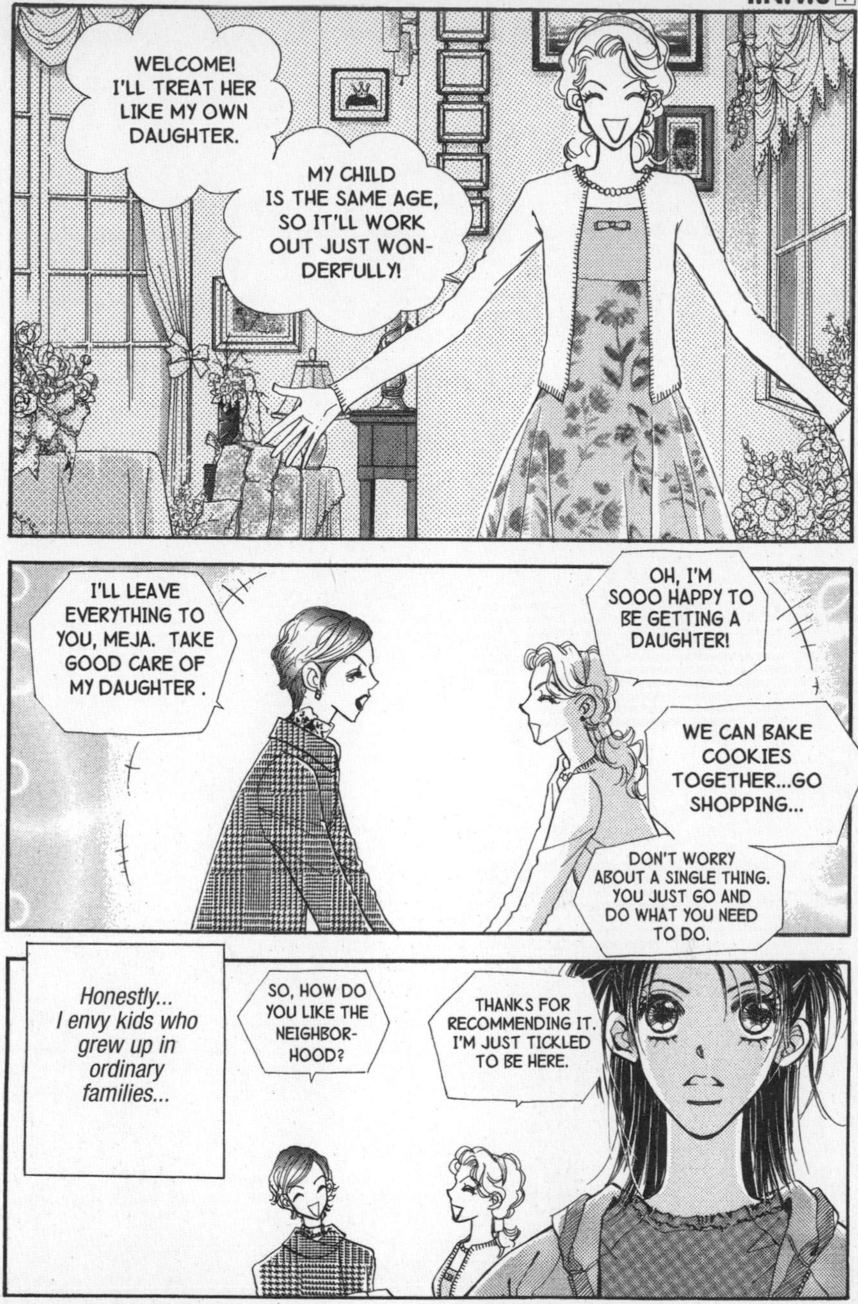
WELCOME! I'LL TREAT HER LIKE MY OWN DAUGHTER.
MY CHILD IS THE SAME AGE, SO IT'LL WORK OUT JUST WON-DERFULLY!
I'LL LEAVE EVERYTHING TO YOU, MEJA. TAKE GOOD CARE OF MY DAUGHTER .
OH, I'M SOOO HAPPY TO BE GETTING A DAUGHTER!
WE CAN BAKE COOKIES TOGETHER...GO SHOPPING...
DON'T WORRY ABOUT A SINGLE THING. YOU JUST GO AND DO WHAT YOU NEED TO DO.
Honestly... I envy kids who grew up in ordinary families...
SO, HOW DO YOU LIKE THE NEIGHBOR-HOOD?
THANKS FOR RECOMMENDING IT. I'M JUST TICKLED TO BE HERE.

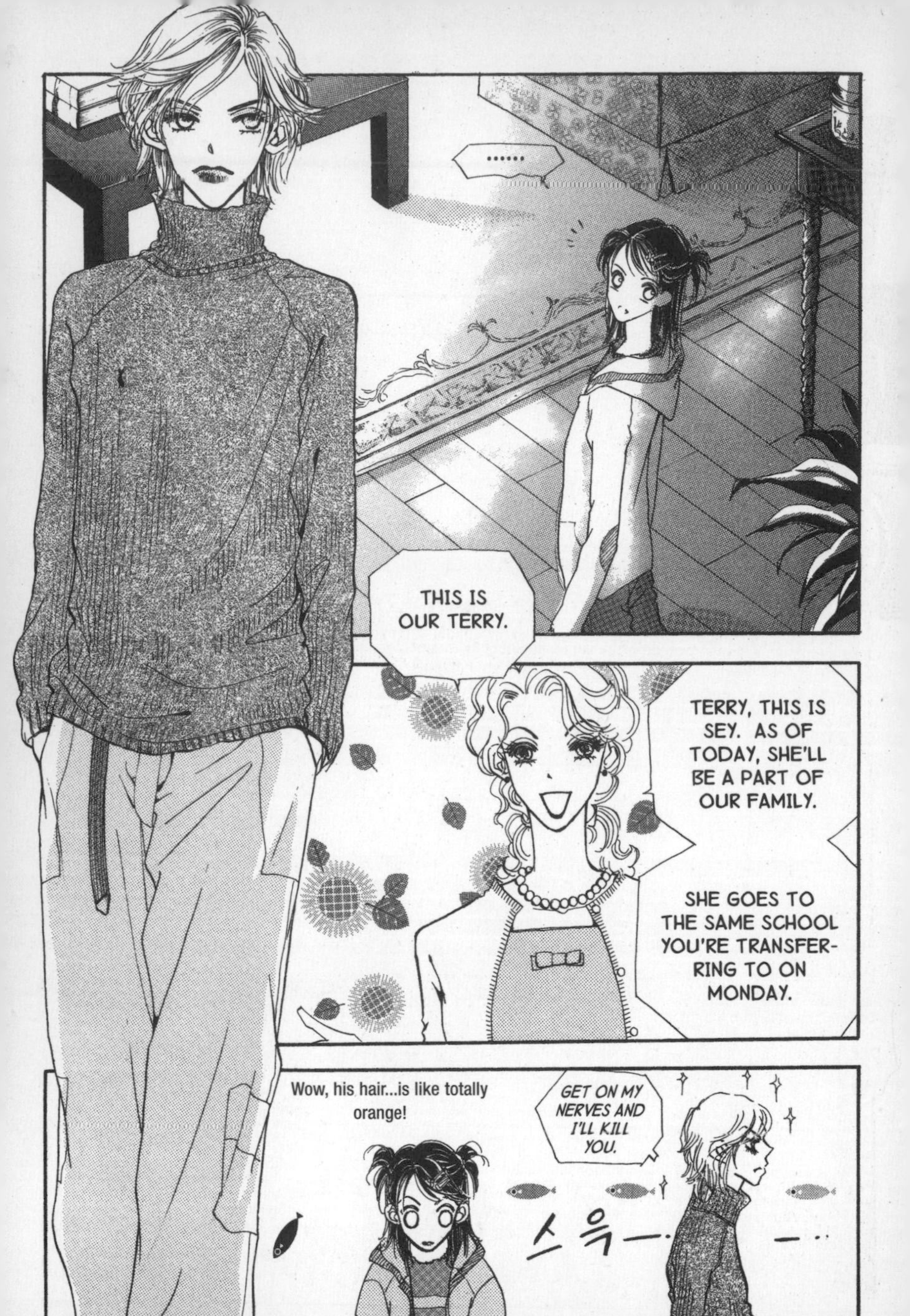
......
THIS IS OUR TERRY.
TERRY, THIS IS SEY. AS OF TODAY, SHE'LL BE A PART OF OUR FAMILY.
SHE GOES TO THE SAME SCHOOL YOU'RE TRANSFERRING TO ON MONDAY.
Wow, his hair...is like totally orange!
GET ON MY NERVES AND I'LL KILL YOU.
스윽—

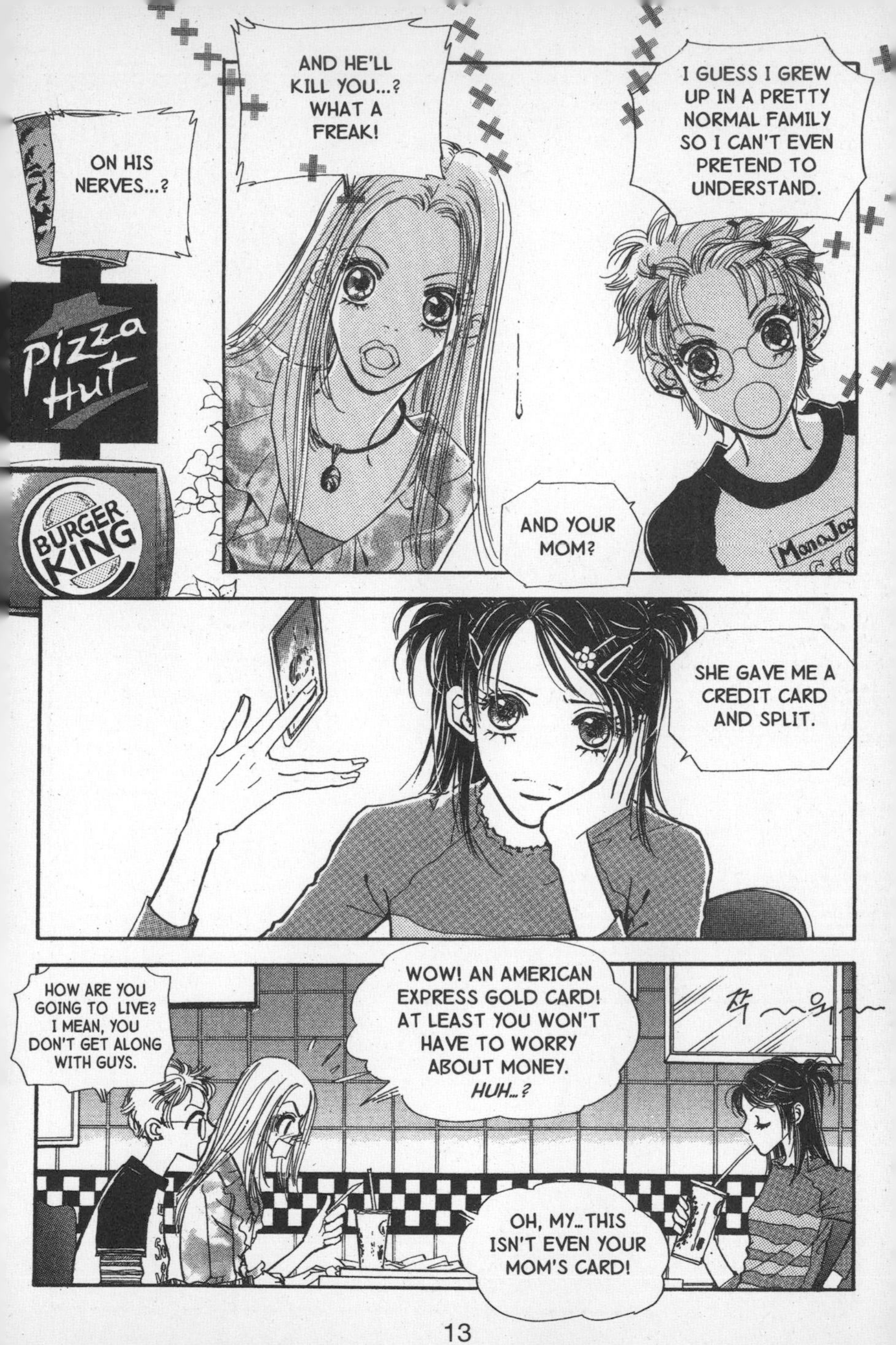
ON HIS NERVES...?
AND HE'LL KILL YOU...? WHAT A FREAK!
I GUESS I GREW UP IN A PRETTY NORMAL FAMILY SO I CAN'T EVEN PRETEND TO UNDERSTAND.
AND YOUR MOM?
SHE GAVE ME A CREDIT CARD AND SPLIT.
HOW ARE YOU GOING TO LIVE? I MEAN, YOU DON'T GET ALONG WITH GUYS.
WOW! AN AMERICAN EXPRESS GOLD CARD! AT LEAST YOU WON'T HAVE TO WORRY ABOUT MONEY. *HUH...?*
쭈~~욱~~
OH, MY...THIS ISN'T EVEN YOUR MOM'S CARD!

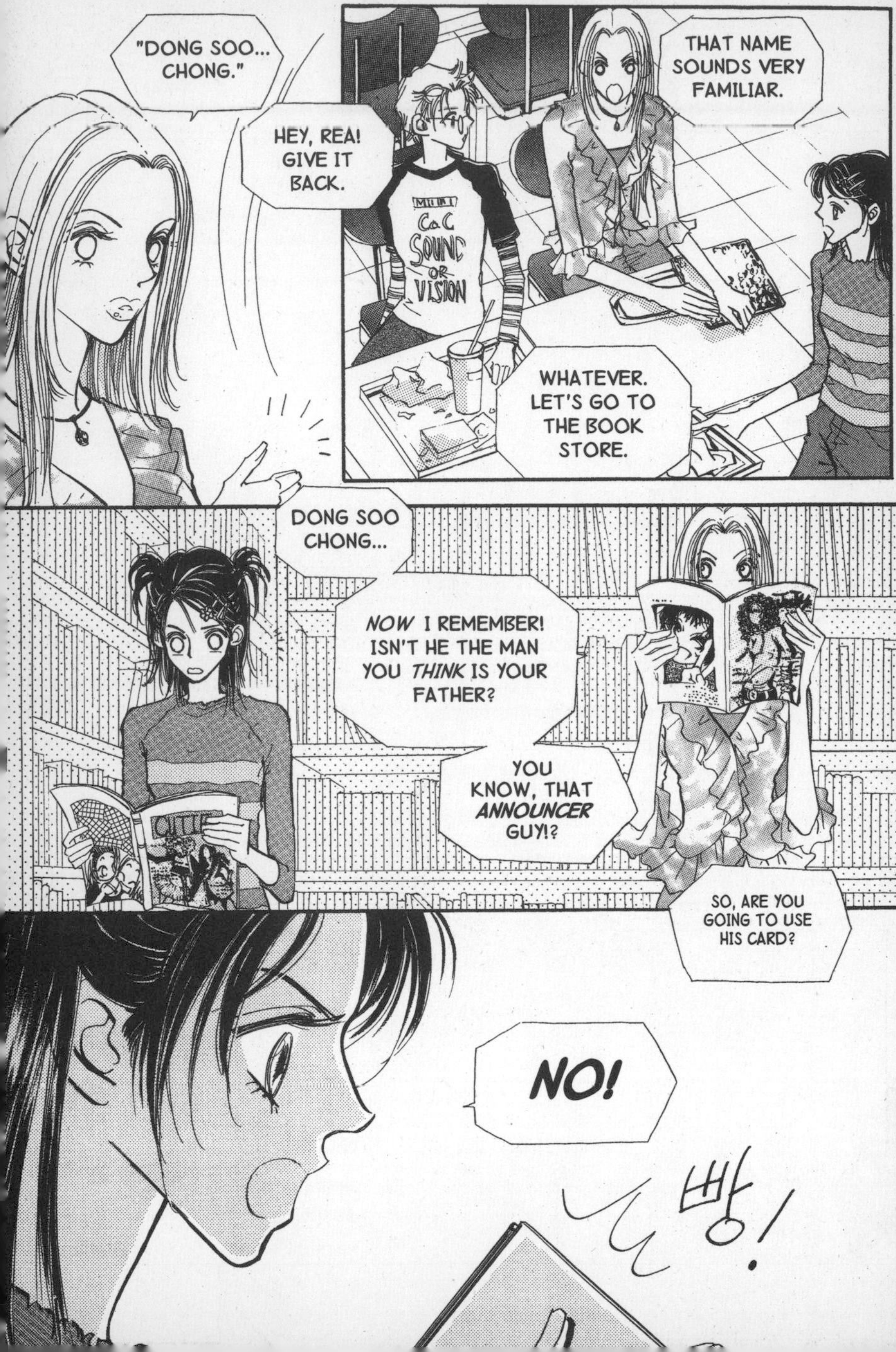
"DONG SOO... CHONG."
HEY, REA! GIVE IT BACK.
THAT NAME SOUNDS VERY FAMILIAR.
WHATEVER. LET'S GO TO THE BOOK STORE.
DONG SOO CHONG...
NOW I REMEMBER! ISN'T HE THE MAN YOU *THINK* IS YOUR FATHER?
YOU KNOW, THAT *ANNOUNCER* GUY!?
SO, ARE YOU GOING TO USE HIS CARD?
NO!
빵!

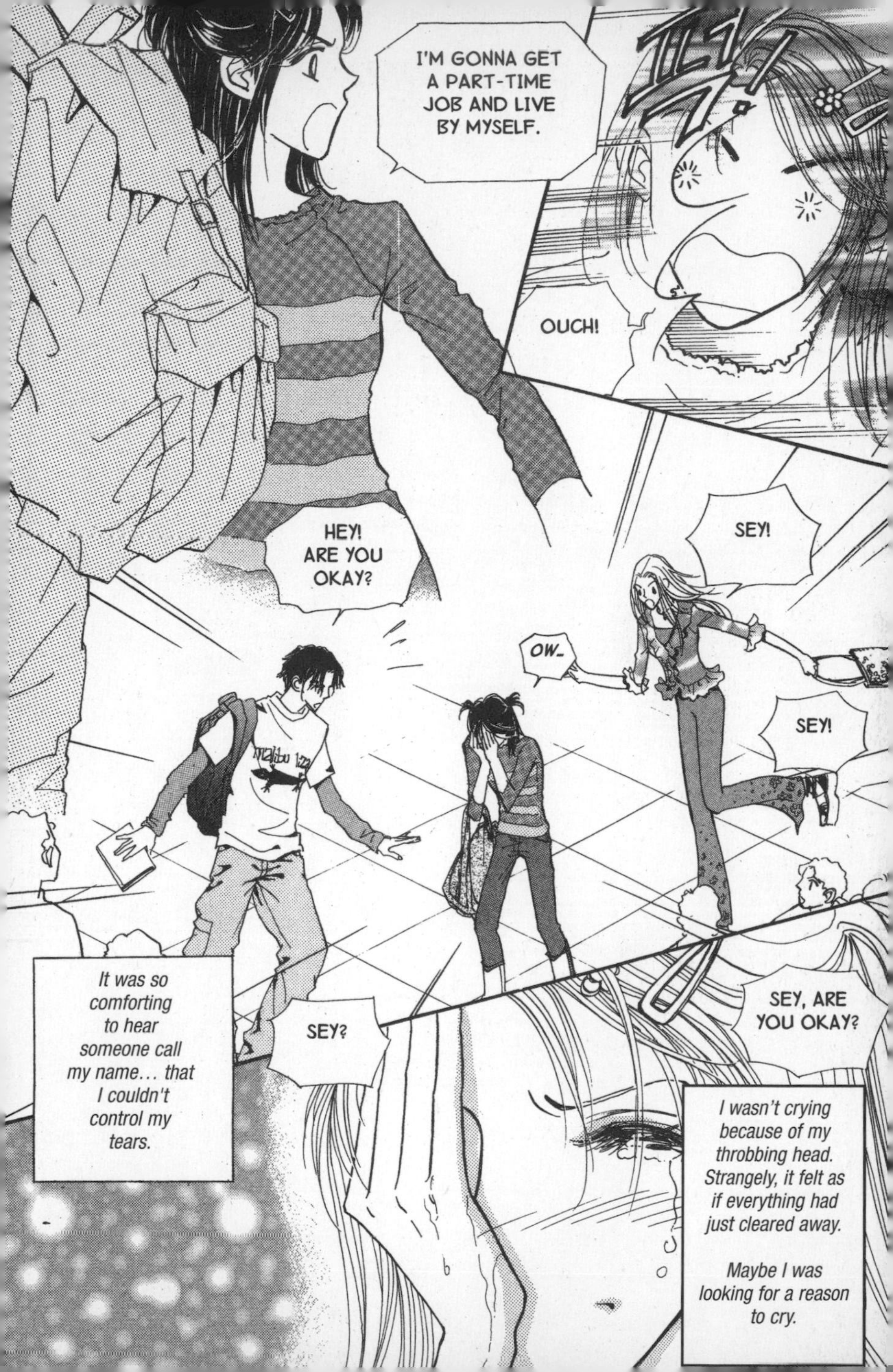
I'M GONNA GET A PART-TIME JOB AND LIVE BY MYSELF.
OUCH!
HEY! ARE YOU OKAY?
SEY!
OW..
SEY!
It was so comforting to hear someone call my name… that I couldn't control my tears.
SEY?
SEY, ARE YOU OKAY?
I wasn't crying because of my throbbing head. Strangely, it felt as if everything had just cleared away.
Maybe I was looking for a reason to cry.

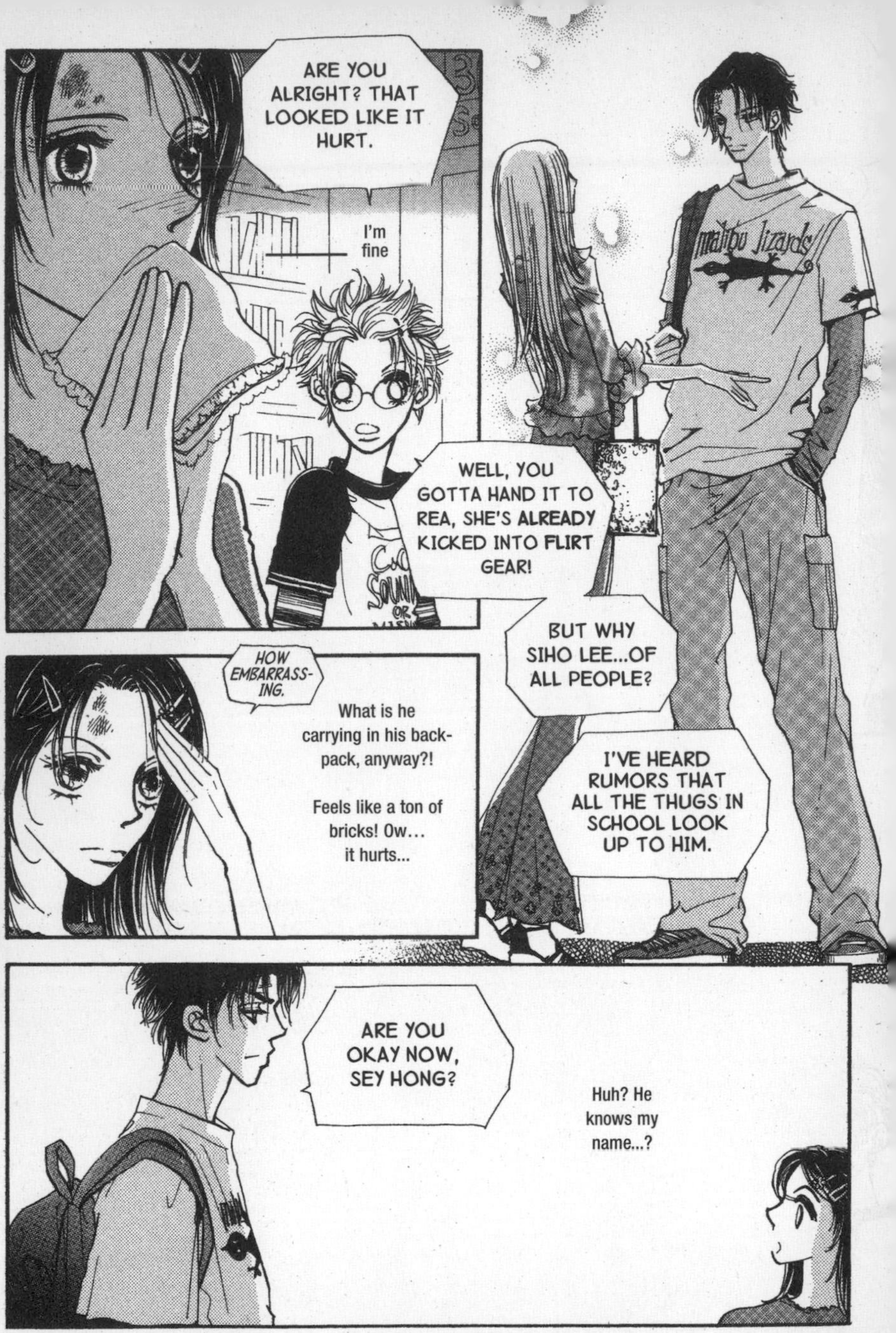
ARE YOU ALRIGHT? THAT LOOKED LIKE IT HURT.
I'm fine
WELL, YOU GOTTA HAND IT TO REA, SHE'S ALREADY KICKED INTO FLIRT GEAR!
HOW EMBARRASS-ING.
What is he carrying in his back-pack, anyway?!
Feels like a ton of bricks! Ow... it hurts...
BUT WHY SIHO LEE...OF ALL PEOPLE?
I'VE HEARD RUMORS THAT ALL THE THUGS IN SCHOOL LOOK UP TO HIM.
ARE YOU OKAY NOW, SEY HONG?
Huh? He knows my name...?

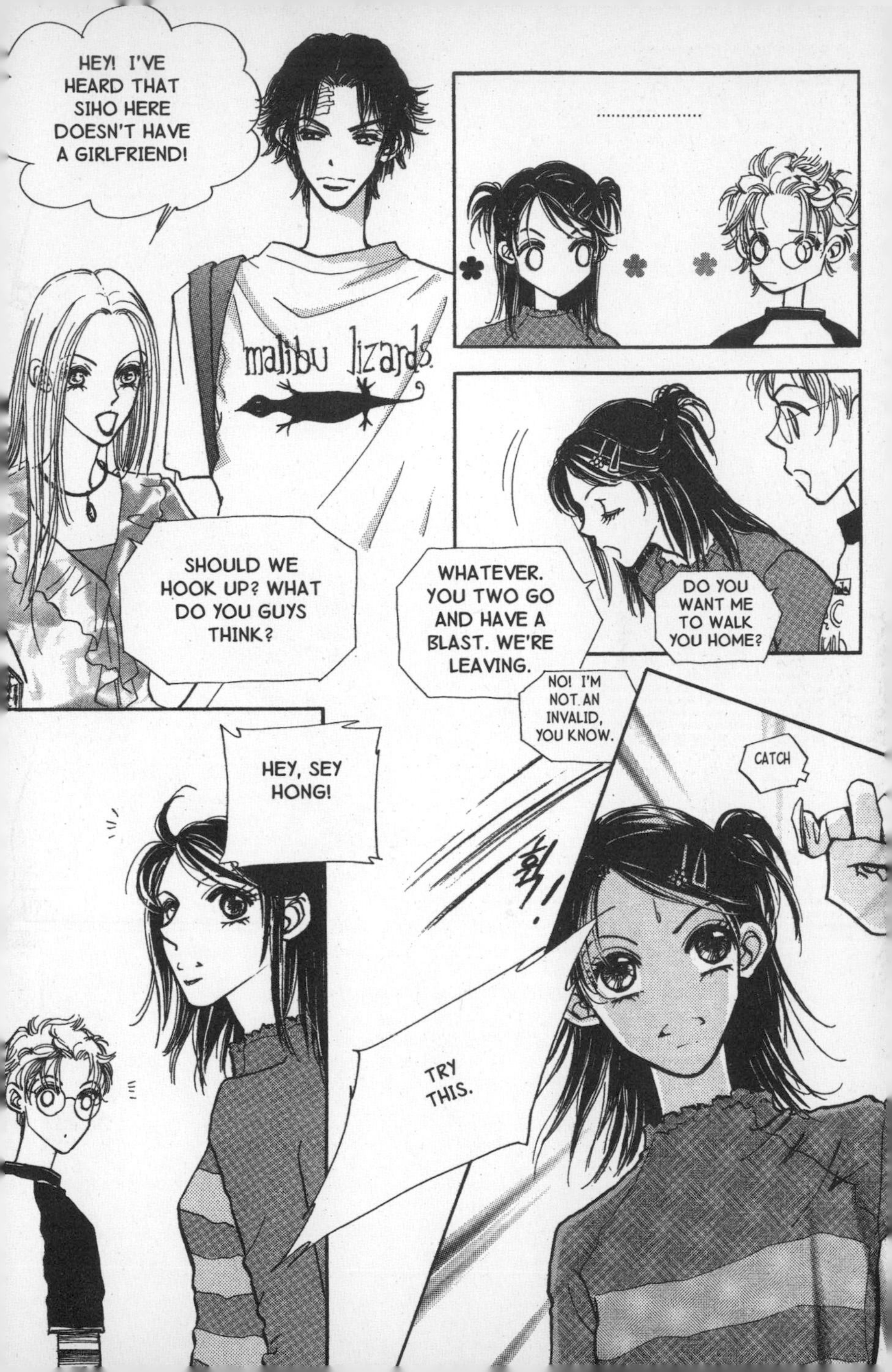
HEY! I'VE HEARD THAT SIHO HERE DOESN'T HAVE A GIRLFRIEND!
malibu lizards
SHOULD WE HOOK UP? WHAT DO YOU GUYS THINK?
....
WHATEVER. YOU TWO GO AND HAVE A BLAST. WE'RE LEAVING.
DO YOU WANT ME TO WALK YOU HOME?
NO! I'M NOT AN INVALID, YOU KNOW.
HEY, SEY HONG!
CATCH
TRY THIS.

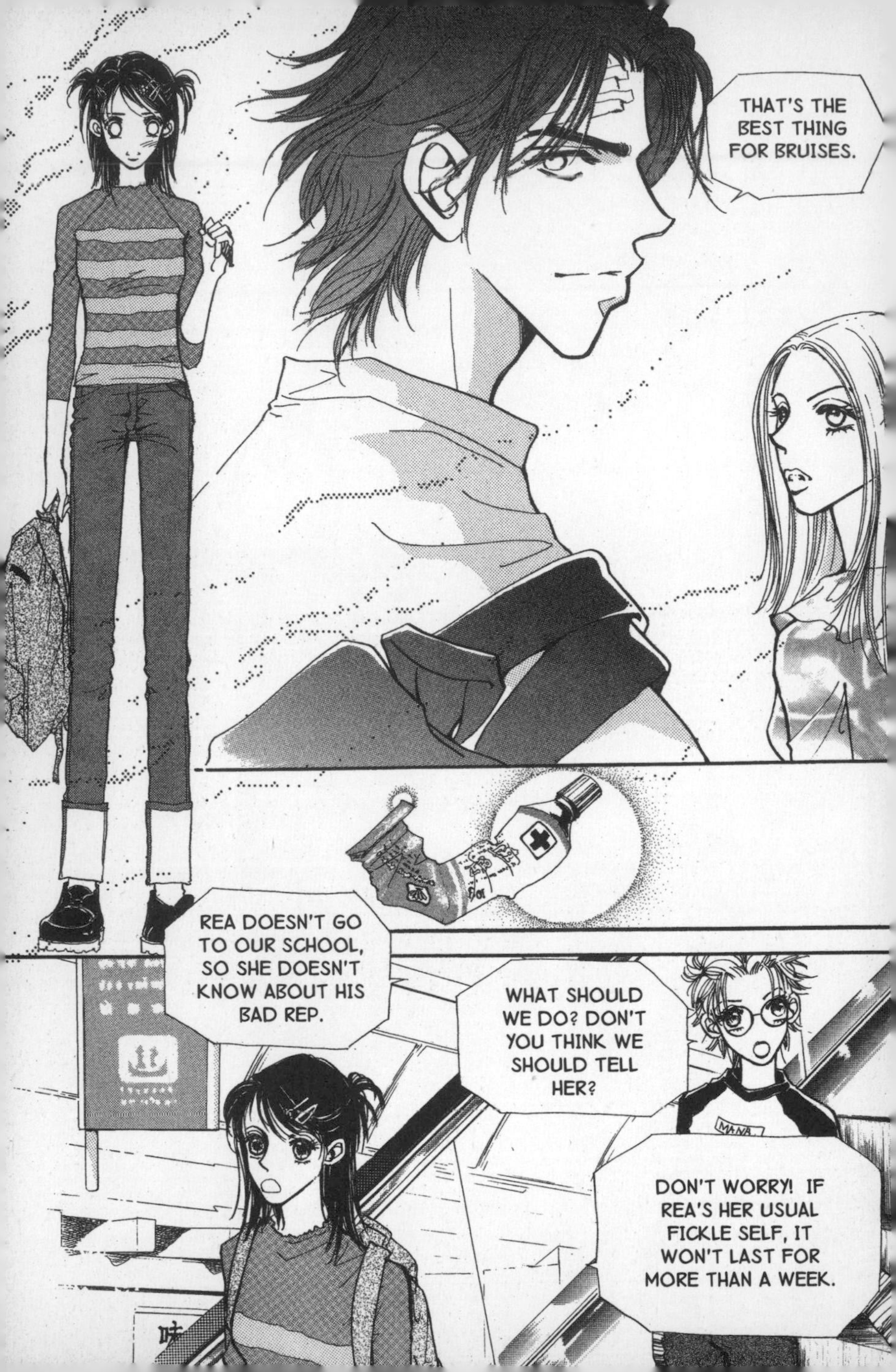
THAT'S THE BEST THING FOR BRUISES.
REA DOESN'T GO TO OUR SCHOOL, SO SHE DOESN'T KNOW ABOUT HIS BAD REP.
WHAT SHOULD WE DO? DON'T YOU THINK WE SHOULD TELL HER?
DON'T WORRY! IF REA'S HER USUAL FICKLE SELF, IT WON'T LAST FOR MORE THAN A WEEK.

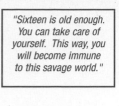

"Sixteen is old enough. You can take care of yourself. This way, you will become immune to this savage world."

Those were my mom's parting words as she took off for her new life. How sweet.

YOU'RE HOME LATE, SEY.

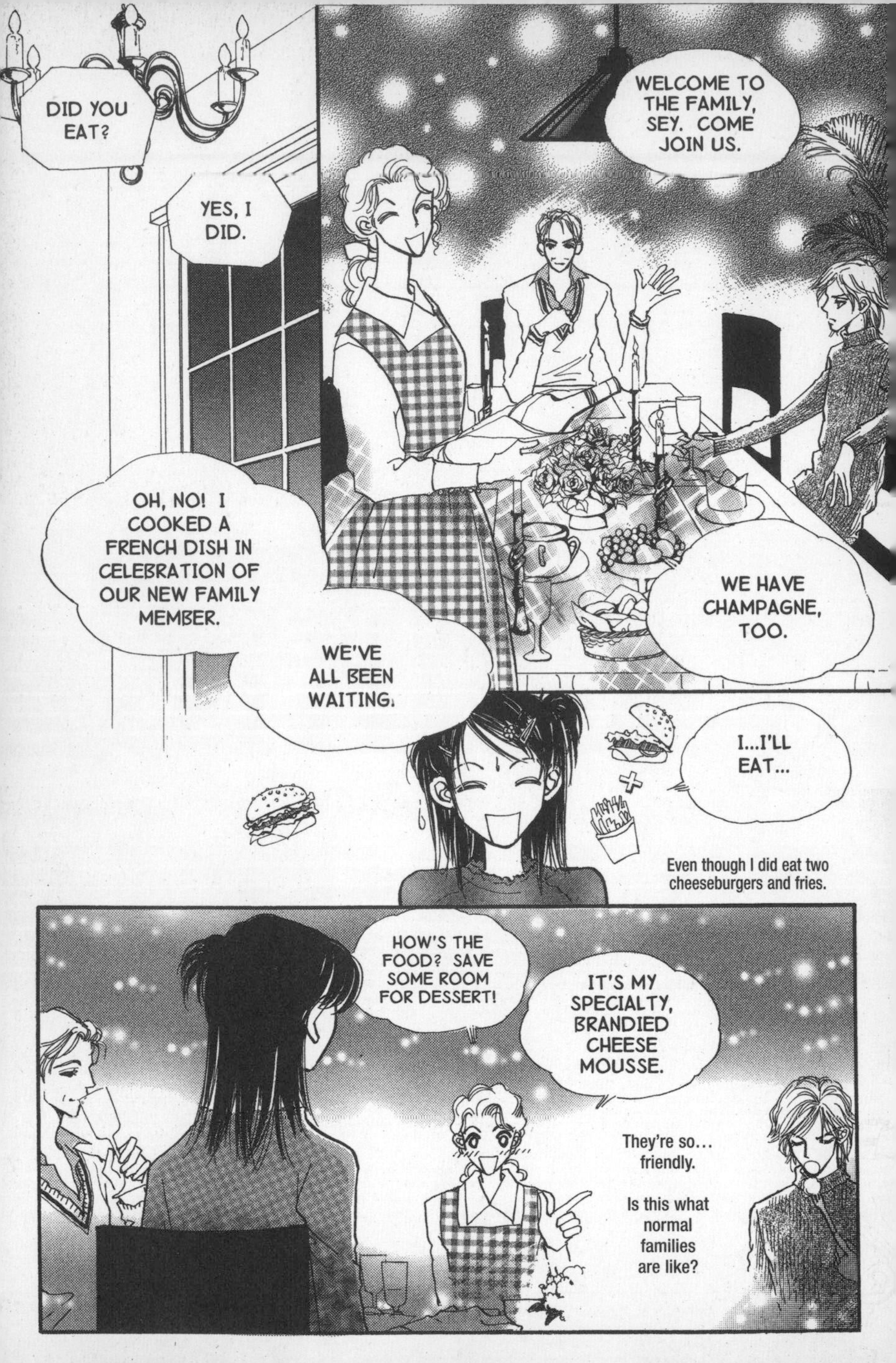
DID YOU EAT?
YES, I DID.
WELCOME TO THE FAMILY, SEY. COME JOIN US.
OH, NO! I COOKED A FRENCH DISH IN CELEBRATION OF OUR NEW FAMILY MEMBER.
WE'VE ALL BEEN WAITING.
WE HAVE CHAMPAGNE, TOO.
I...I'LL EAT...
Even though I did eat two cheeseburgers and fries.
HOW'S THE FOOD? SAVE SOME ROOM FOR DESSERT!
IT'S MY SPECIALTY, BRANDIED CHEESE MOUSSE.
They're so… friendly.
Is this what normal families are like?

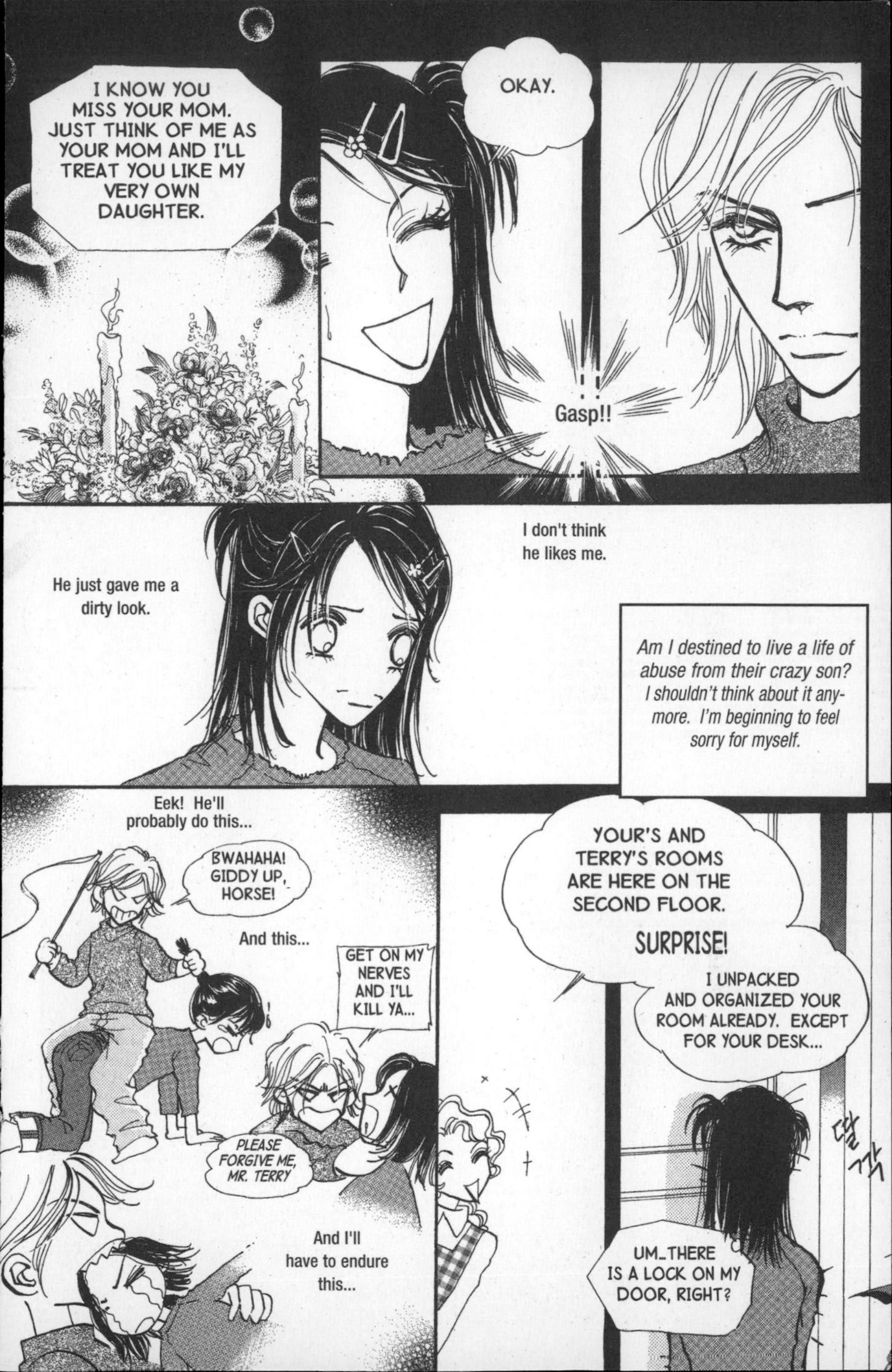

I KNOW YOU MISS YOUR MOM. JUST THINK OF ME AS YOUR MOM AND I'LL TREAT YOU LIKE MY VERY OWN DAUGHTER.
OKAY.
Gasp!!
He just gave me a dirty look.
I don't think he likes me.
Am I destined to live a life of abuse from their crazy son? I shouldn't think about it any-more. I'm beginning to feel sorry for myself.
Eek! He'll probably do this...
BWAHAHA! GIDDY UP, HORSE!
And this...
GET ON MY NERVES AND I'LL KILL YA...
PLEASE FORGIVE ME, MR. TERRY
And I'll have to endure this...
YOUR'S AND TERRY'S ROOMS ARE HERE ON THE SECOND FLOOR.
SURPRISE!
I UNPACKED AND ORGANIZED YOUR ROOM ALREADY. EXCEPT FOR YOUR DESK...
딸깍
UM...THERE IS A LOCK ON MY DOOR, RIGHT?

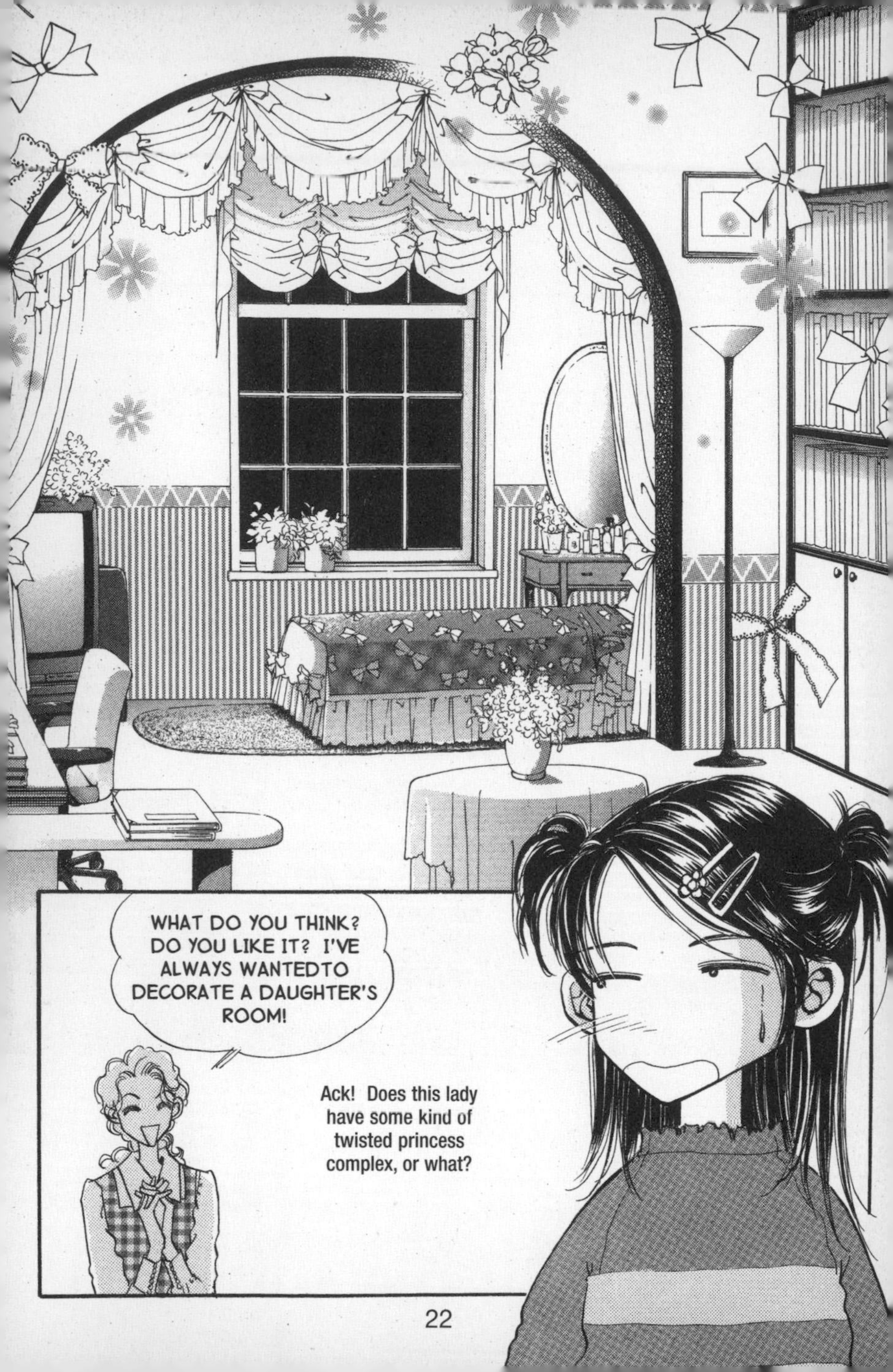
WHAT DO YOU THINK? DO YOU LIKE IT? I'VE ALWAYS WANTEDTO DECORATE A DAUGHTER'S ROOM!
Ack! Does this lady have some kind of twisted princess complex, or what?

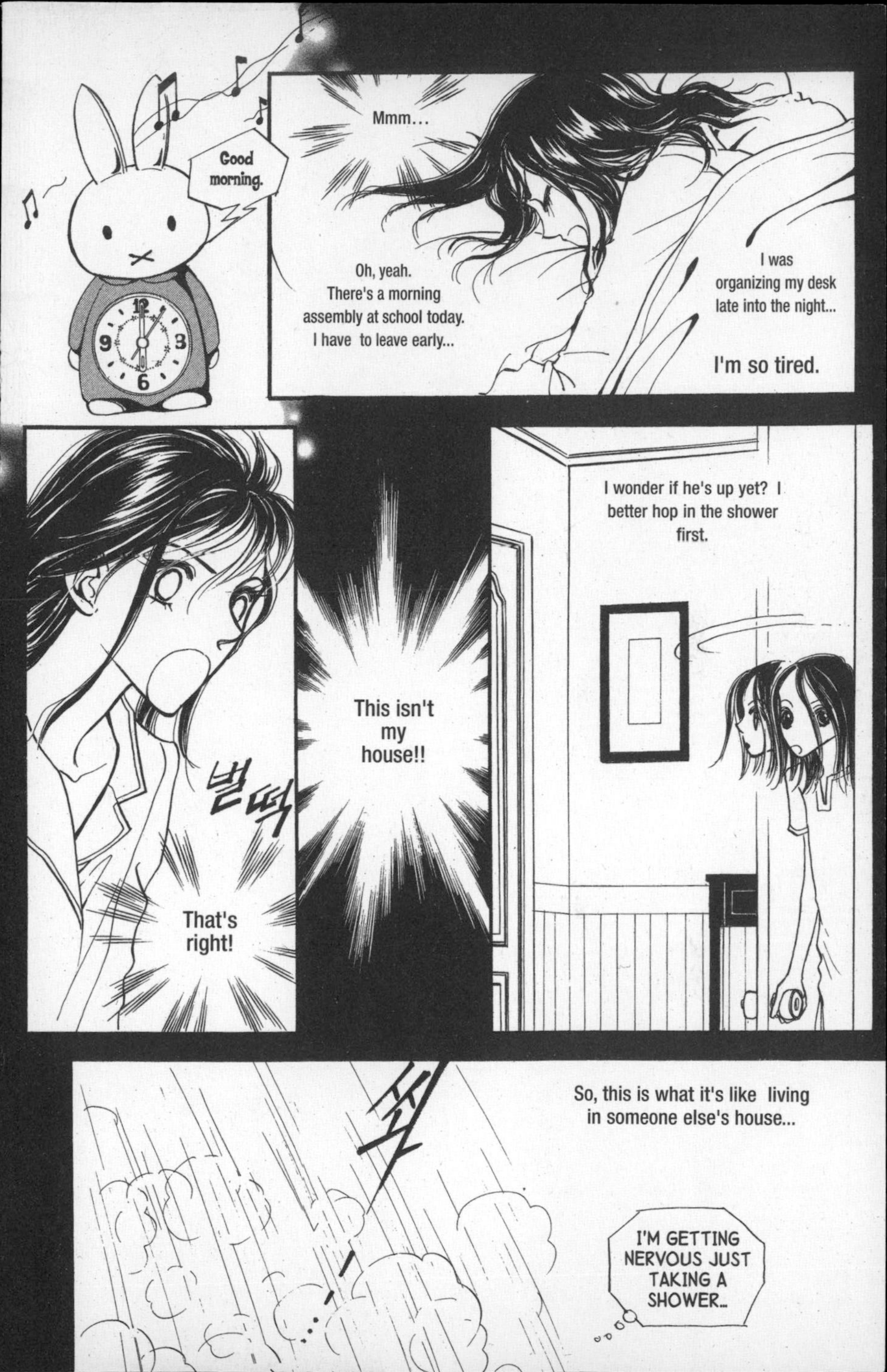
Good morning.
Mmm...
Oh, yeah. There's a morning assembly at school today. I have to leave early...
I was organizing my desk late into the night...
I'm so tired.
벌떡
That's right!
This isn't my house!!
I wonder if he's up yet? I better hop in the shower first.
So, this is what it's like living in someone else's house...
I'M GETTING NERVOUS JUST TAKING A SHOWER...

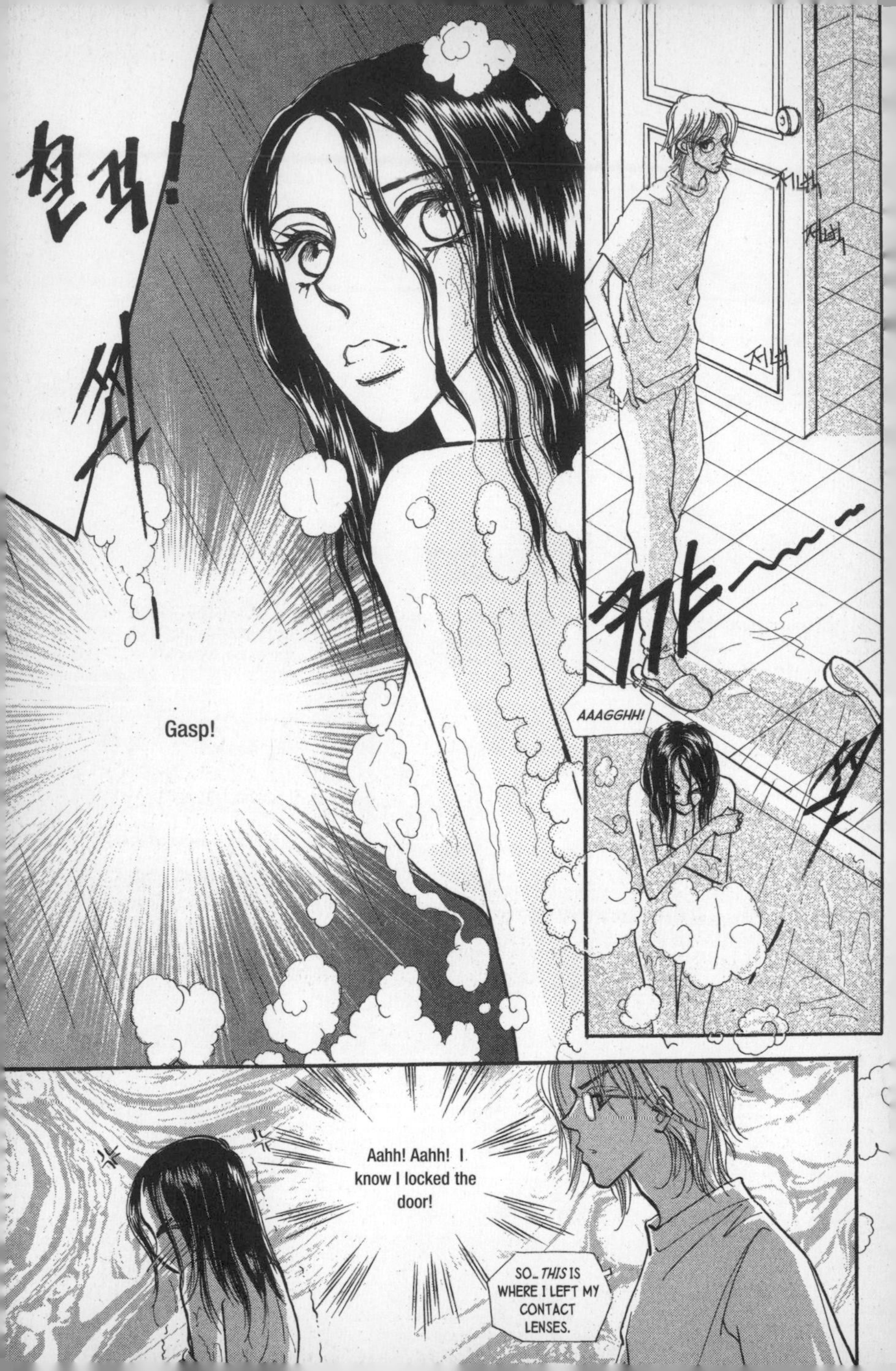

철컥!
Gasp!
꺄~~~
AAAGGHH!
Aahh! Aahh! I know I locked the door!
SO... *THIS* IS WHERE I LEFT MY CONTACT LENSES.

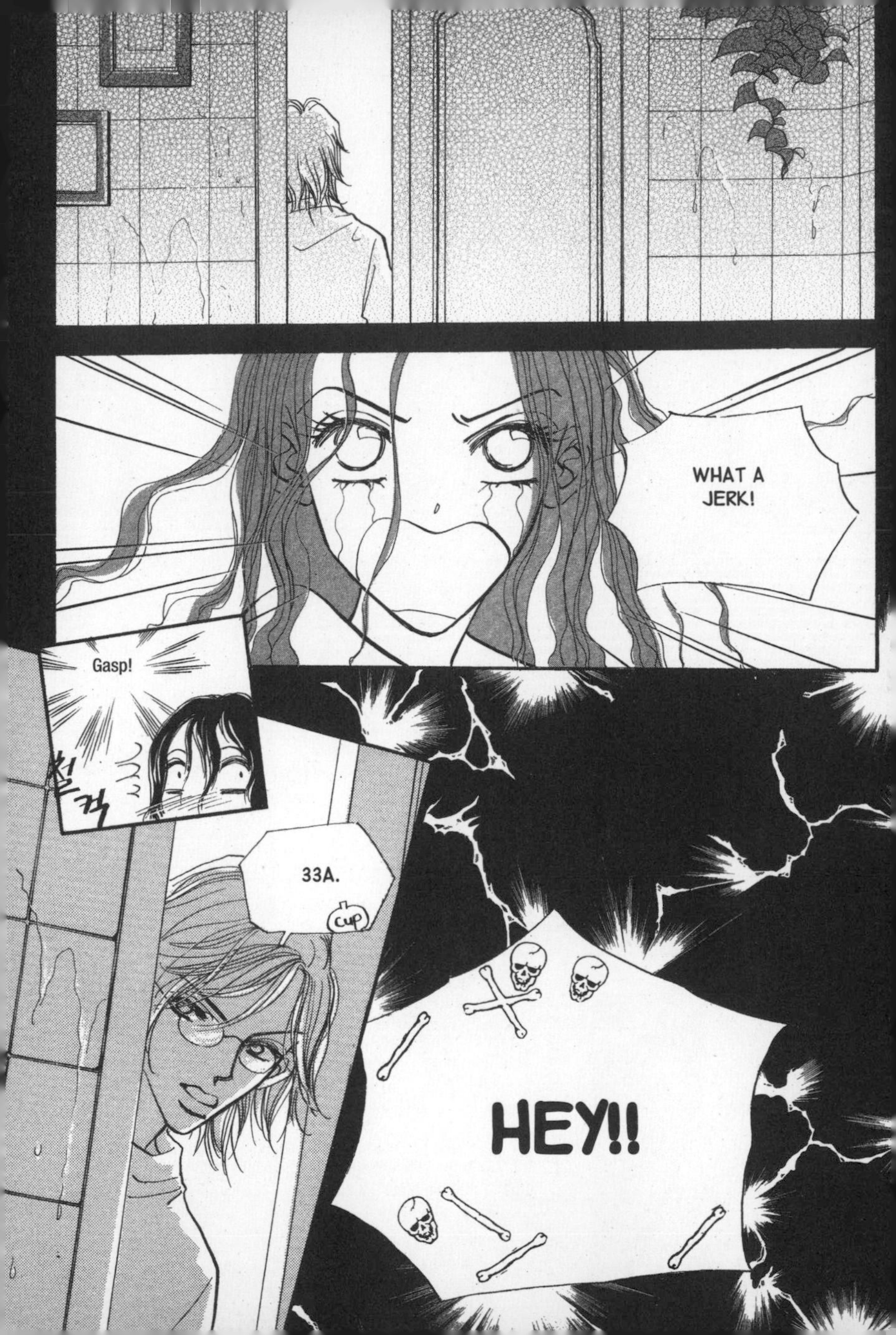
WHAT A JERK!
Gasp!
철컥
33A.
cup
HEY!!

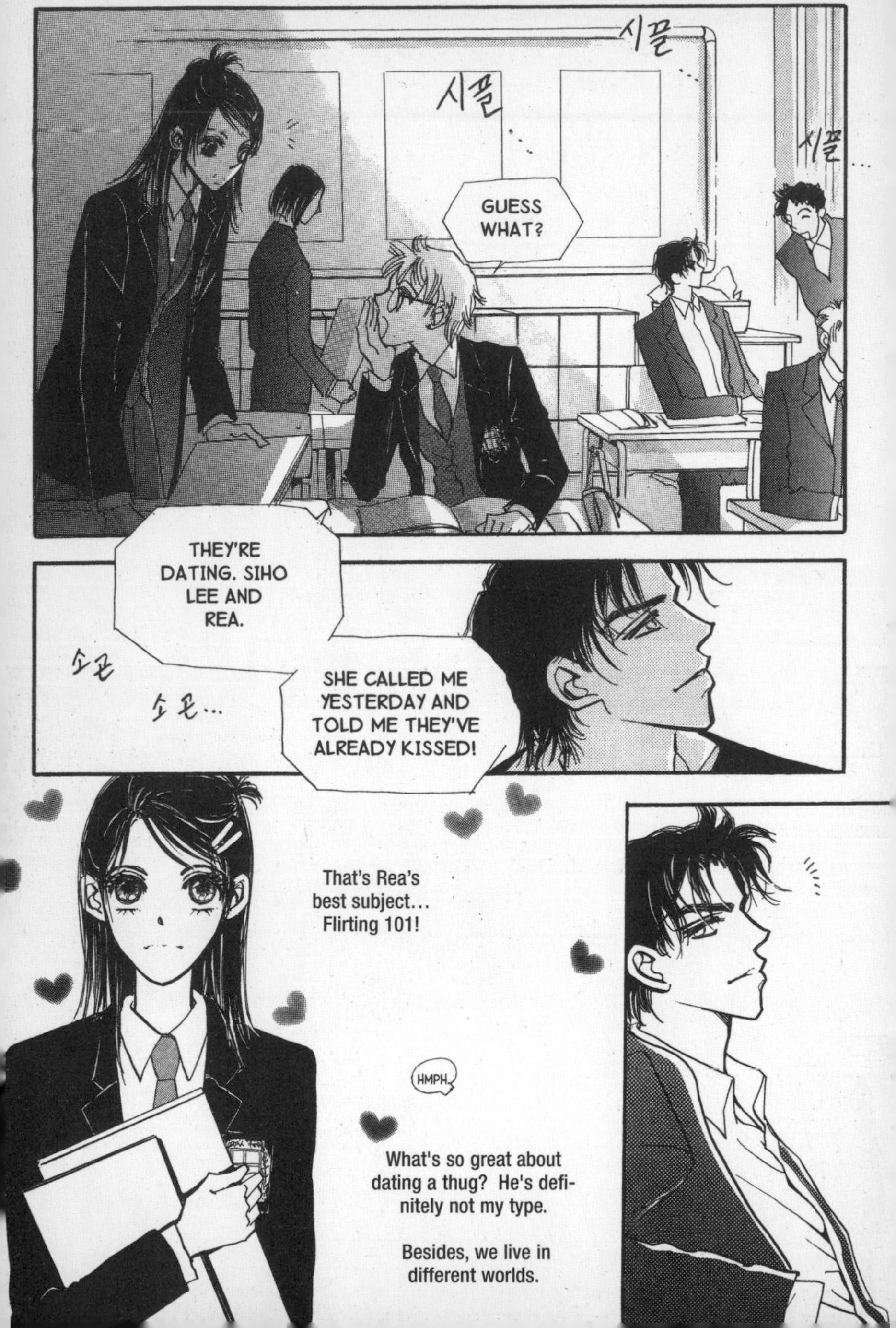
시끌
시끌
시끌...
GUESS WHAT?
THEY'RE DATING. SIHO LEE AND REA.
소곤
소곤...
SHE CALLED ME YESTERDAY AND TOLD ME THEY'VE ALREADY KISSED!
That's Rea's best subject... Flirting 101!
HMPH.
What's so great about dating a thug? He's definitely not my type.
Besides, we live in different worlds.

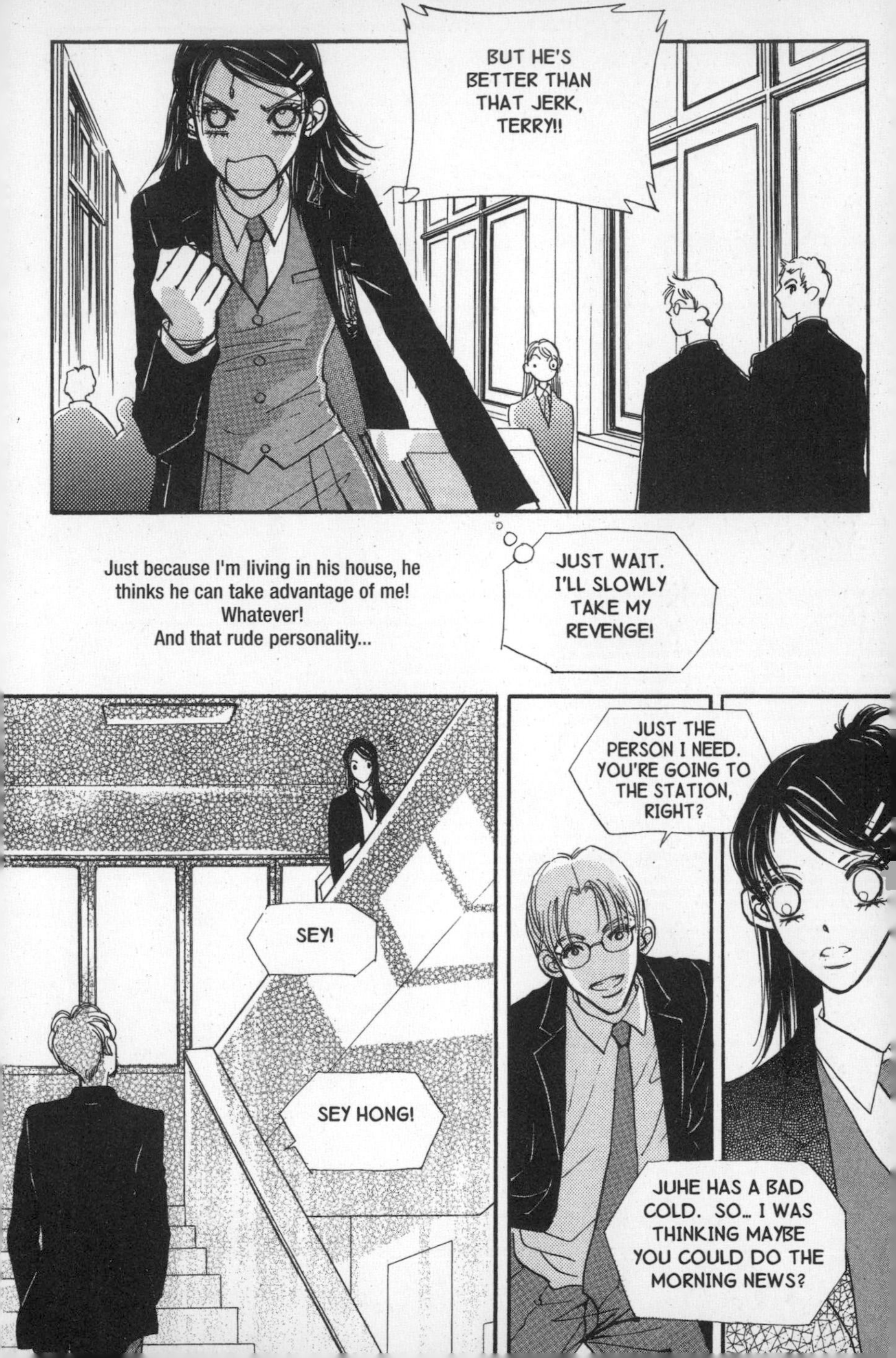
BUT HE'S BETTER THAN THAT JERK, TERRY!!
Just because I'm living in his house, he thinks he can take advantage of me! Whatever! And that rude personality...
JUST WAIT. I'LL SLOWLY TAKE MY REVENGE!
SEY!
SEY HONG!
JUST THE PERSON I NEED. YOU'RE GOING TO THE STATION, RIGHT?
JUHE HAS A BAD COLD. SO... I WAS THINKING MAYBE YOU COULD DO THE MORNING NEWS?

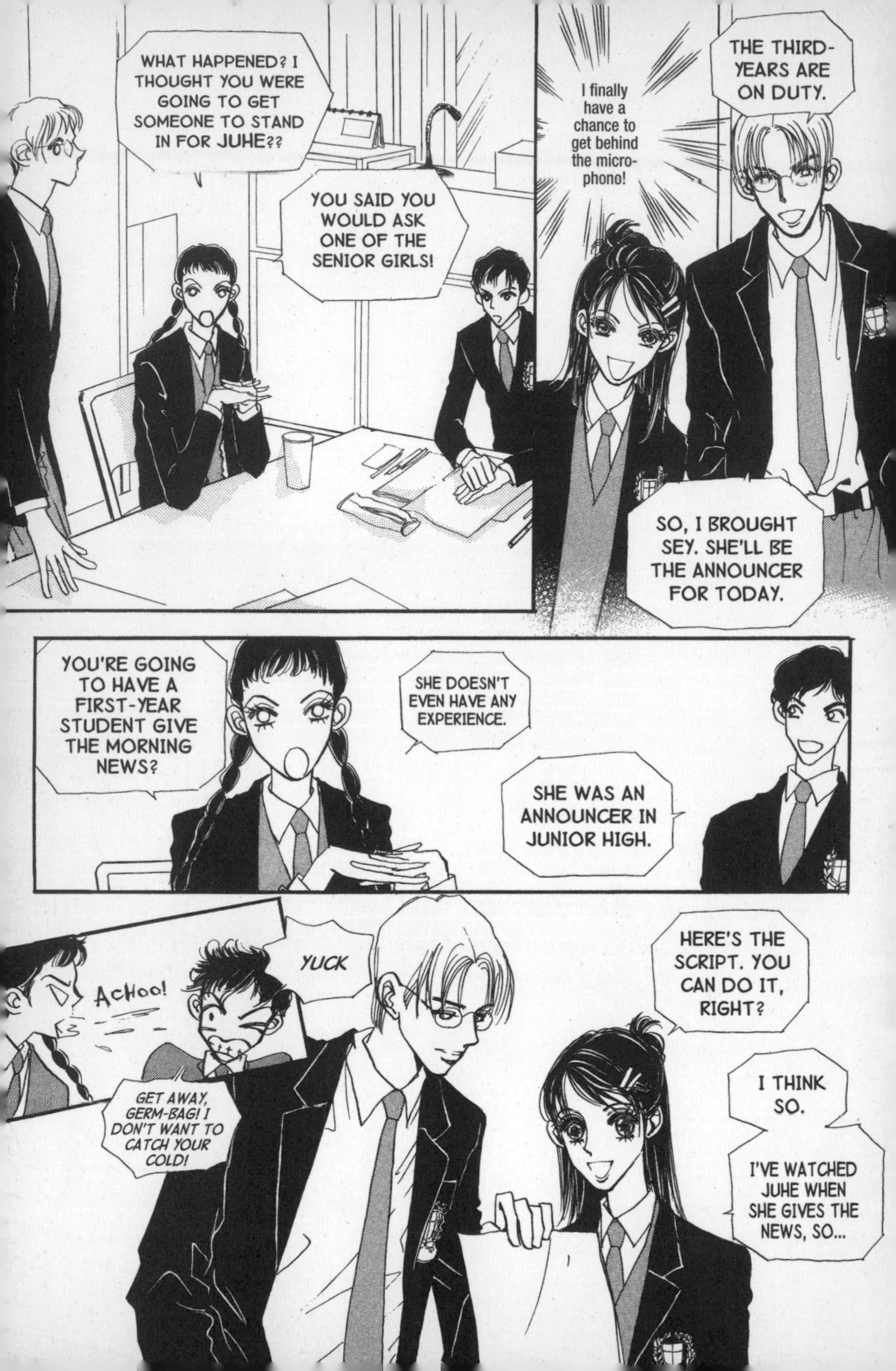
WHAT HAPPENED? I THOUGHT YOU WERE GOING TO GET SOMEONE TO STAND IN FOR JUHE??
YOU SAID YOU WOULD ASK ONE OF THE SENIOR GIRLS!
I finally have a chance to get behind the micro-phono!
THE THIRD-YEARS ARE ON DUTY.
SO, I BROUGHT SEY. SHE'LL BE THE ANNOUNCER FOR TODAY.
YOU'RE GOING TO HAVE A FIRST-YEAR STUDENT GIVE THE MORNING NEWS?
SHE DOESN'T EVEN HAVE ANY EXPERIENCE.
SHE WAS AN ANNOUNCER IN JUNIOR HIGH.
AcHoo!
YUCK
GET AWAY, GERM-BAG! I DON'T WANT TO CATCH YOUR COLD!
HERE'S THE SCRIPT. YOU CAN DO IT, RIGHT?
I THINK SO.
I'VE WATCHED JUHE WHEN SHE GIVES THE NEWS, SO...

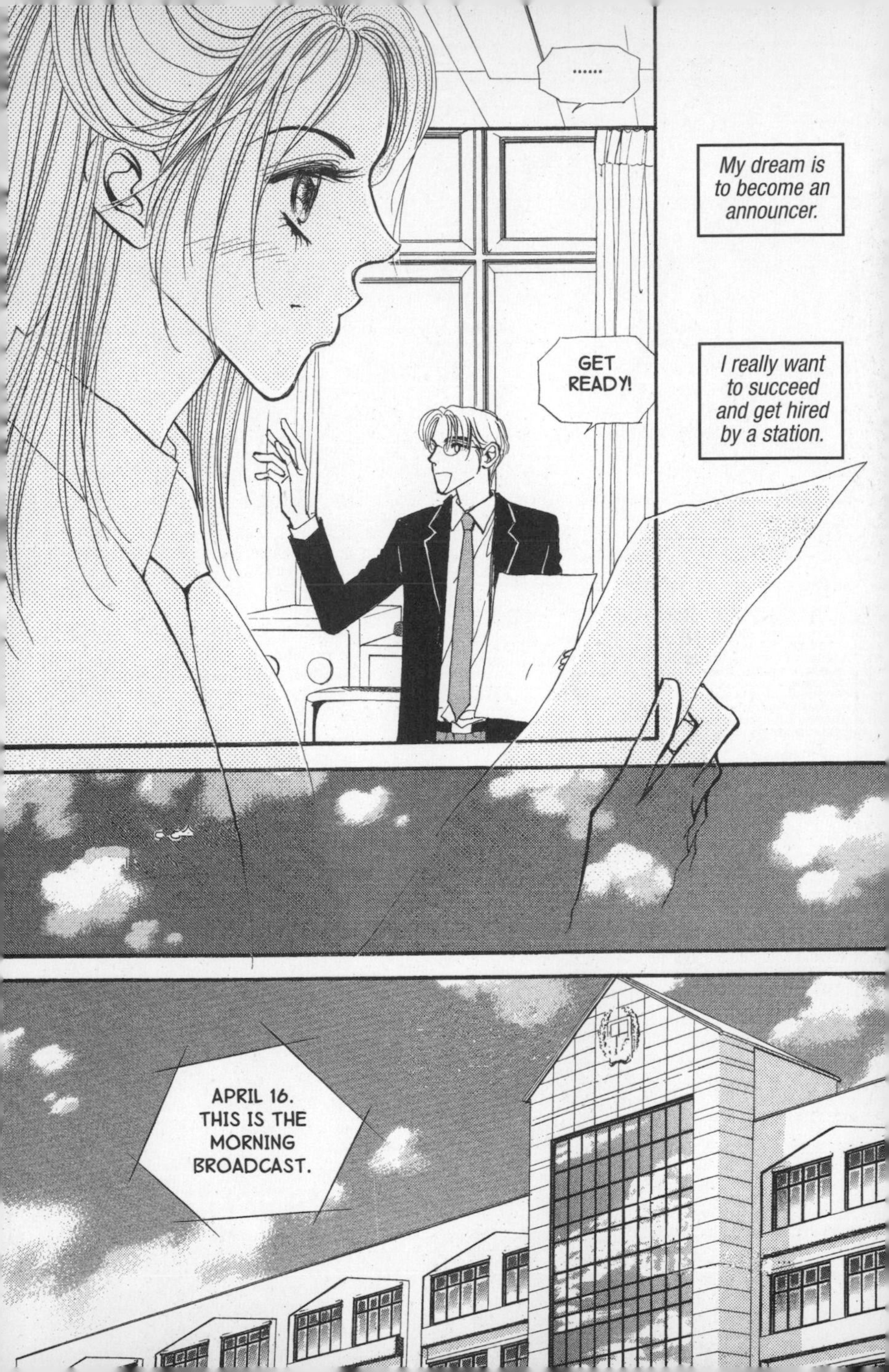
......
GET READY!
My dream is to become an announcer.
I really want to succeed and get hired by a station.
APRIL 16. THIS IS THE MORNING BROADCAST.

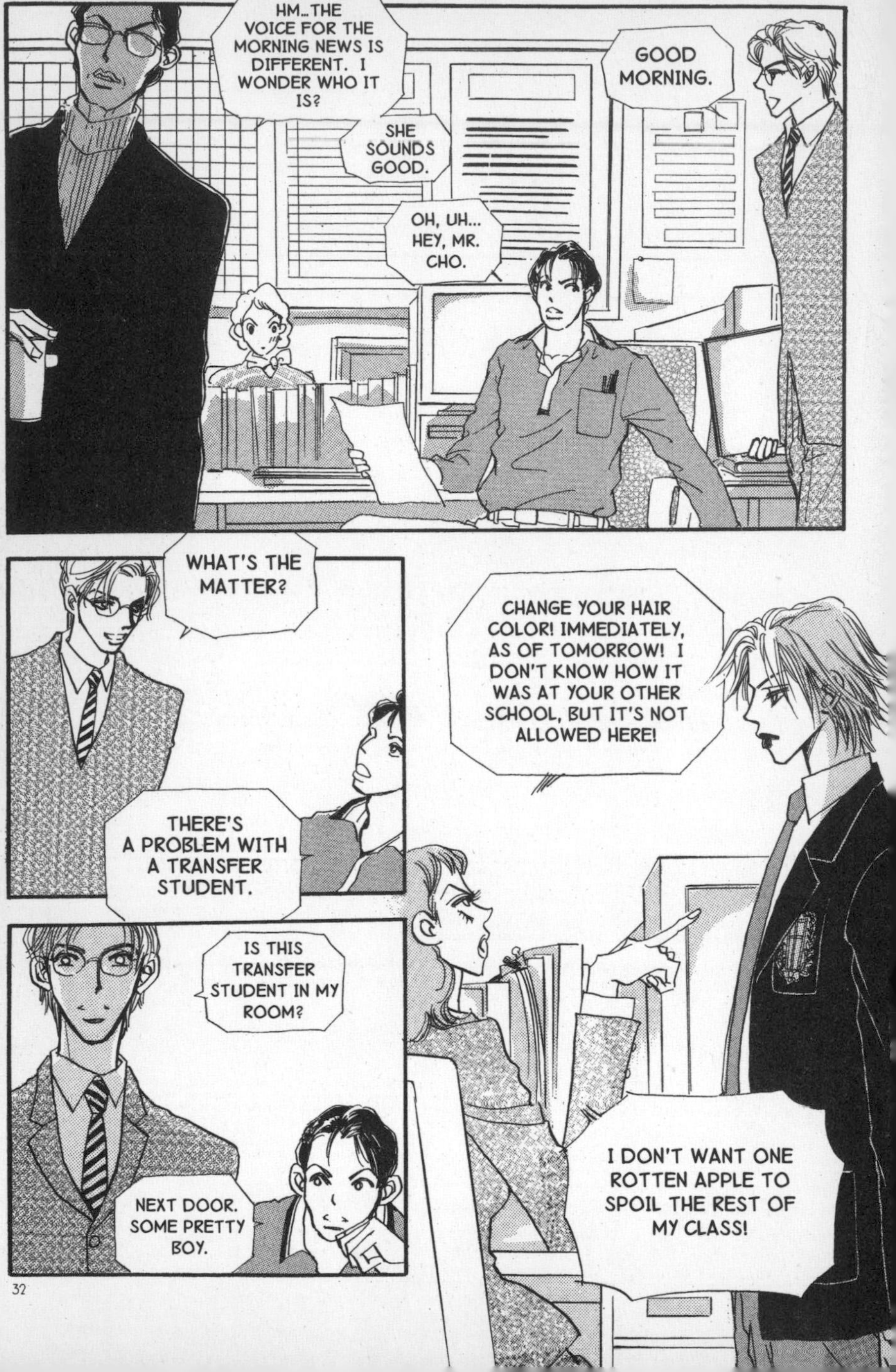
HM...THE VOICE FOR THE MORNING NEWS IS DIFFERENT. I WONDER WHO IT IS?
GOOD MORNING.
SHE SOUNDS GOOD.
OH, UH... HEY, MR. CHO.
WHAT'S THE MATTER?
THERE'S A PROBLEM WITH A TRANSFER STUDENT.
IS THIS TRANSFER STUDENT IN MY ROOM?
NEXT DOOR. SOME PRETTY BOY.
CHANGE YOUR HAIR COLOR! IMMEDIATELY, AS OF TOMORROW! I DON'T KNOW HOW IT WAS AT YOUR OTHER SCHOOL, BUT IT'S NOT ALLOWED HERE!
I DON'T WANT ONE ROTTEN APPLE TO SPOIL THE REST OF MY CLASS!

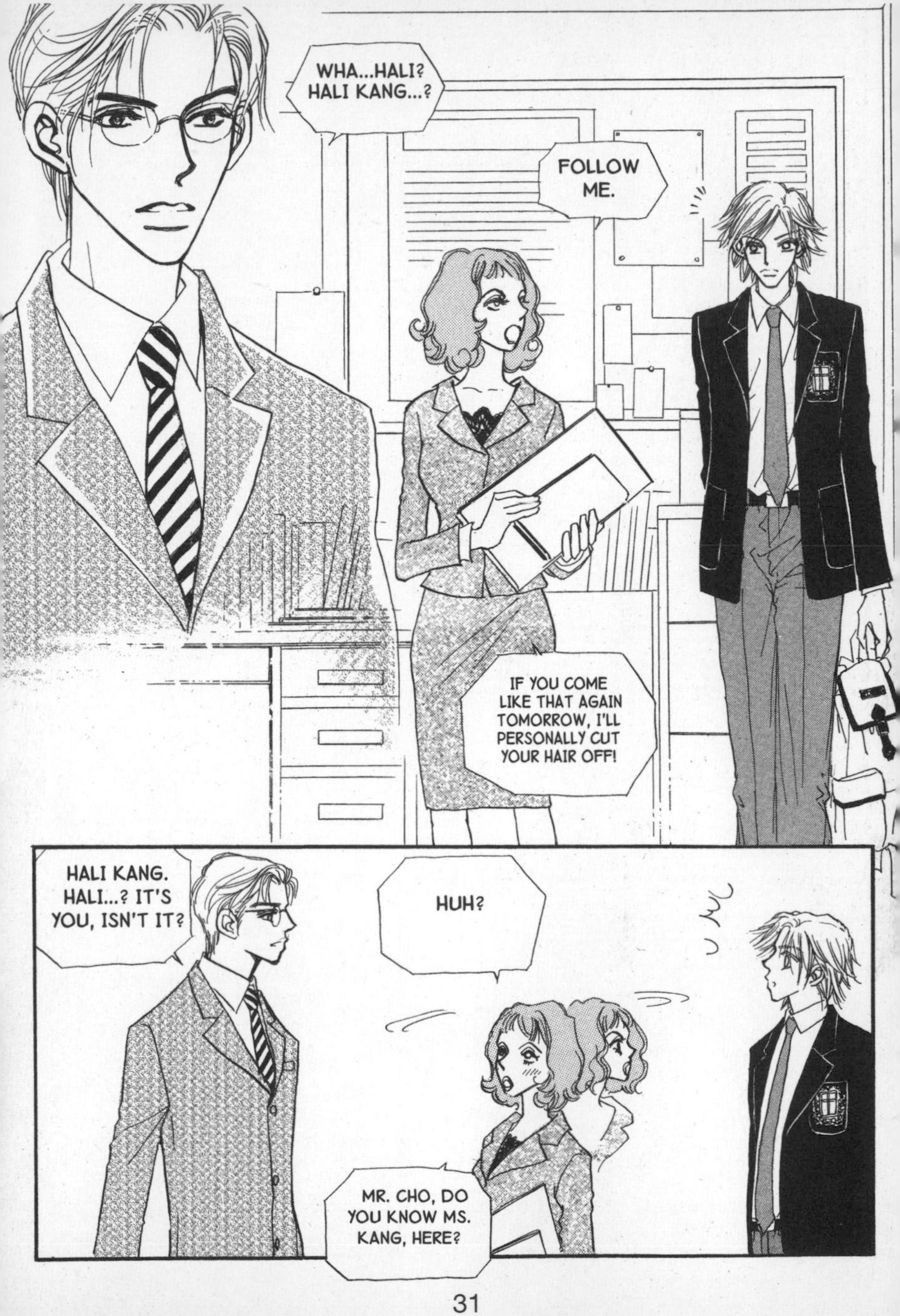
WHA...HALI? HALI KANG...?
FOLLOW ME.
IF YOU COME LIKE THAT AGAIN TOMORROW, I'LL PERSONALLY CUT YOUR HAIR OFF!
HALI KANG. HALI...? IT'S YOU, ISN'T IT?
HUH?
MR. CHO, DO YOU KNOW MS. KANG, HERE?

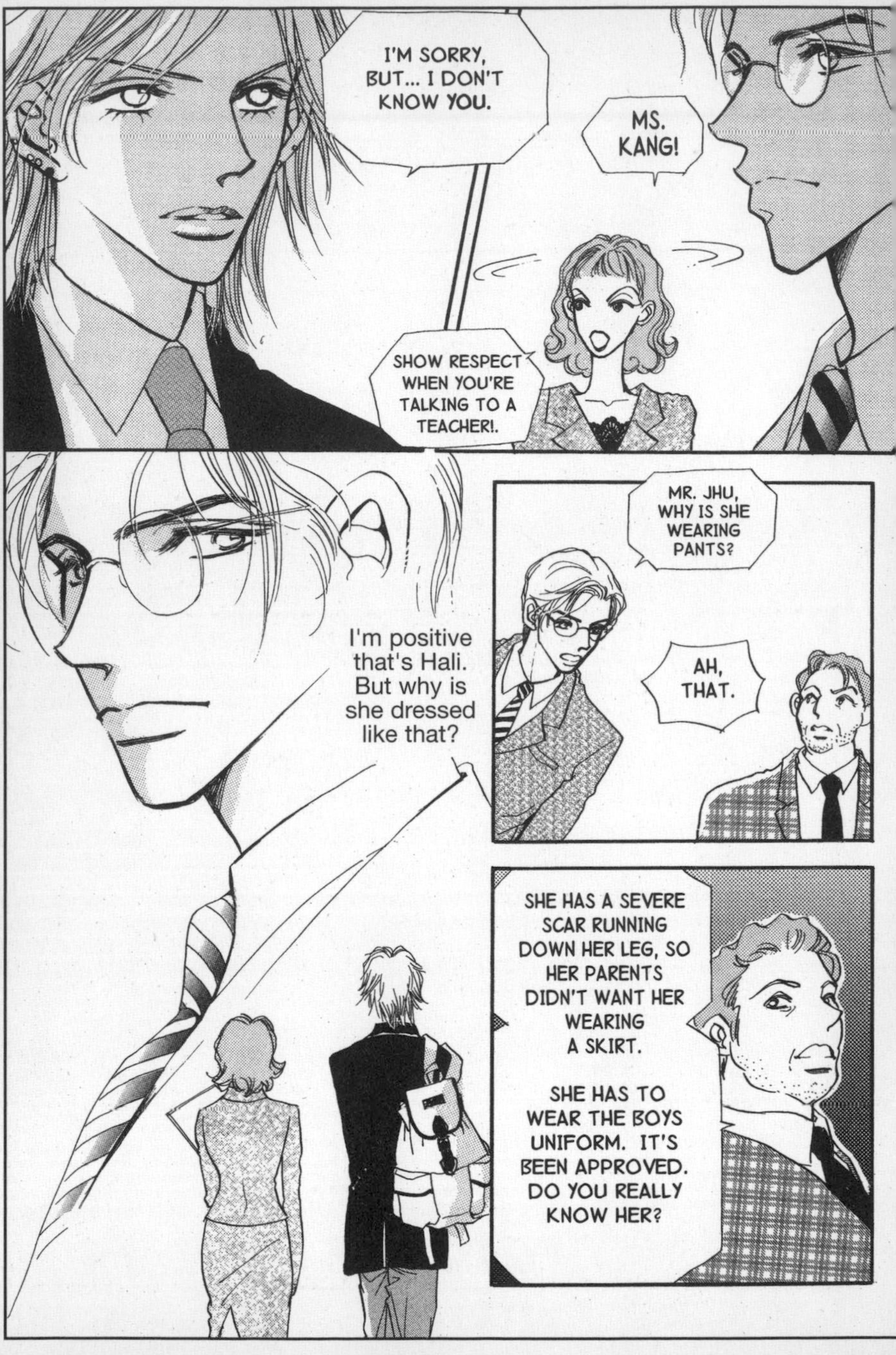
I'M SORRY, BUT... I DON'T KNOW YOU.
MS. KANG!
SHOW RESPECT WHEN YOU'RE TALKING TO A TEACHER!.
I'm positive that's Hali. But why is she dressed like that?
MR. JHU, WHY IS SHE WEARING PANTS?
AH, THAT.
SHE HAS A SEVERE SCAR RUNNING DOWN HER LEG, SO HER PARENTS DIDN'T WANT HER WEARING A SKIRT.
SHE HAS TO WEAR THE BOYS UNIFORM. IT'S BEEN APPROVED. DO YOU REALLY KNOW HER?

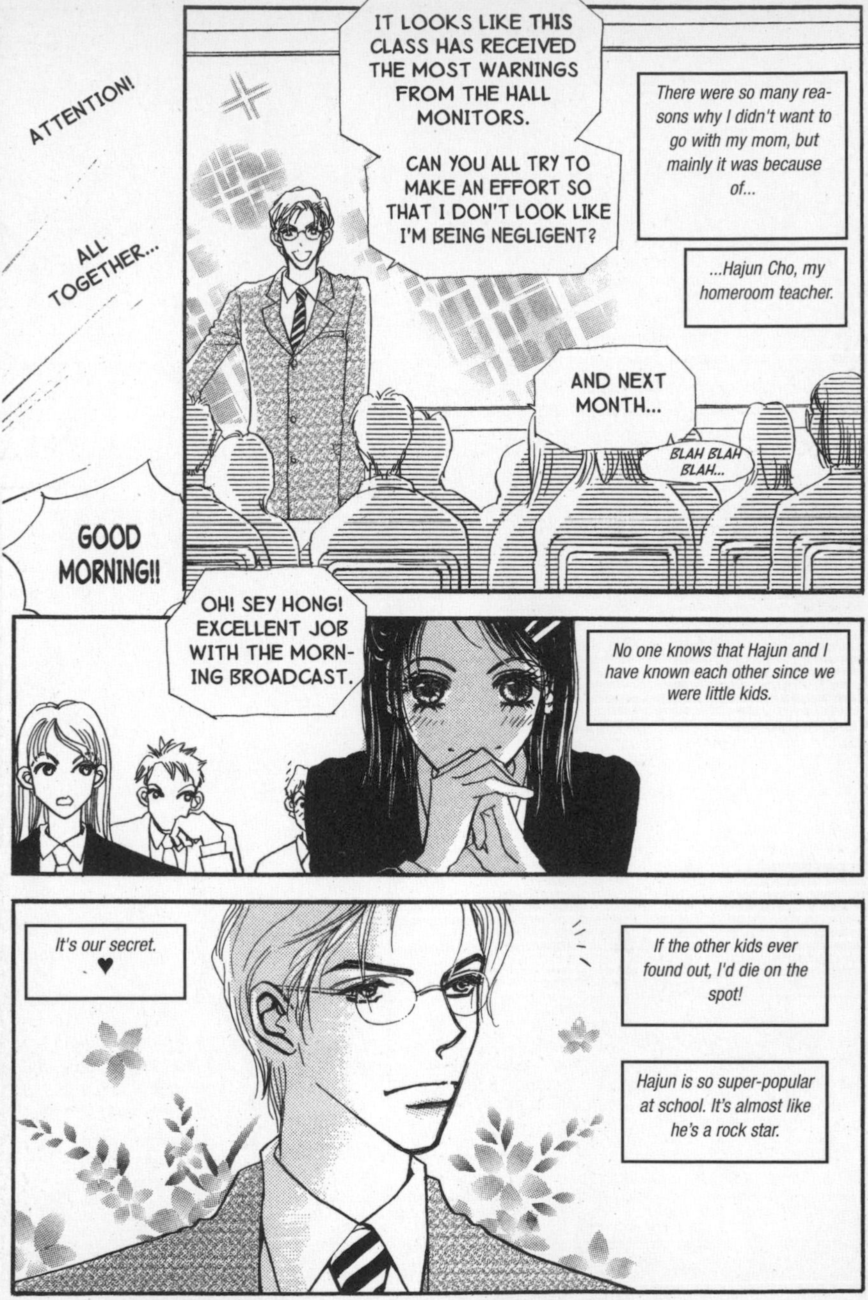
ATTENTION!
ALL TOGETHER...
GOOD MORNING!!
IT LOOKS LIKE THIS CLASS HAS RECEIVED THE MOST WARNINGS FROM THE HALL MONITORS.
CAN YOU ALL TRY TO MAKE AN EFFORT SO THAT I DON'T LOOK LIKE I'M BEING NEGLIGENT?
There were so many reasons why I didn't want to go with my mom, but mainly it was because of...
...Hajun Cho, my homeroom teacher.
AND NEXT MONTH...
BLAH BLAH BLAH...
OH! SEY HONG! EXCELLENT JOB WITH THE MORNING BROADCAST.
No one knows that Hajun and I have known each other since we were little kids.
It's our secret. ♥
If the other kids ever found out, I'd die on the spot!
Hajun is so super-popular at school. It's almost like he's a rock star.

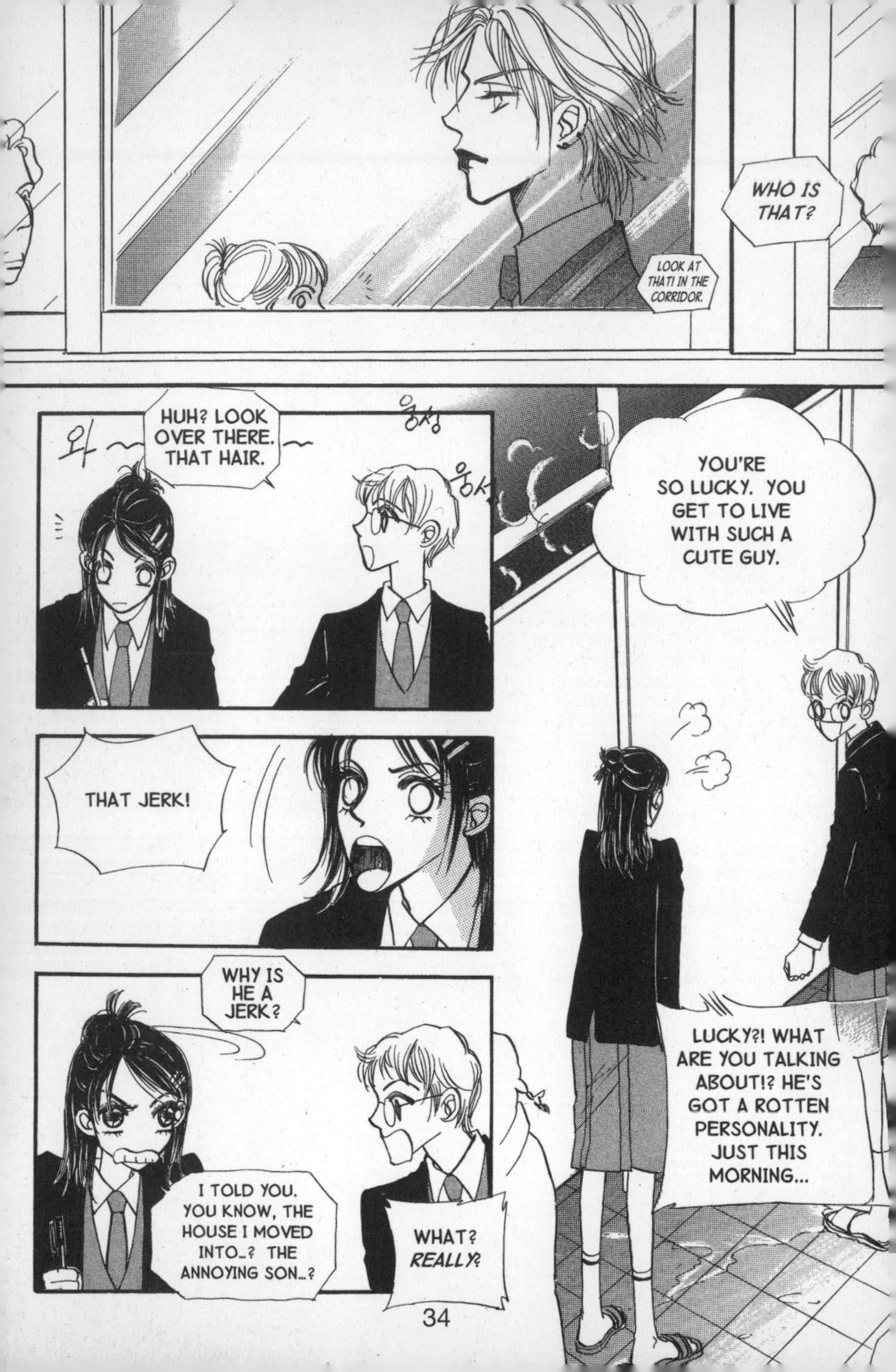

LOOK AT THAT! IN THE CORRIDOR.
WHO IS THAT?
와~
HUH? LOOK OVER THERE. THAT HAIR.
웅성
웅성
THAT JERK!
WHY IS HE A JERK?
I TOLD YOU. YOU KNOW, THE HOUSE I MOVED INTO...? THE ANNOYING SON...?
WHAT? *REALLY?*
YOU'RE SO LUCKY. YOU GET TO LIVE WITH SUCH A CUTE GUY.
LUCKY?! WHAT ARE YOU TALKING ABOUT!? HE'S GOT A ROTTEN PERSONALITY. JUST THIS MORNING...

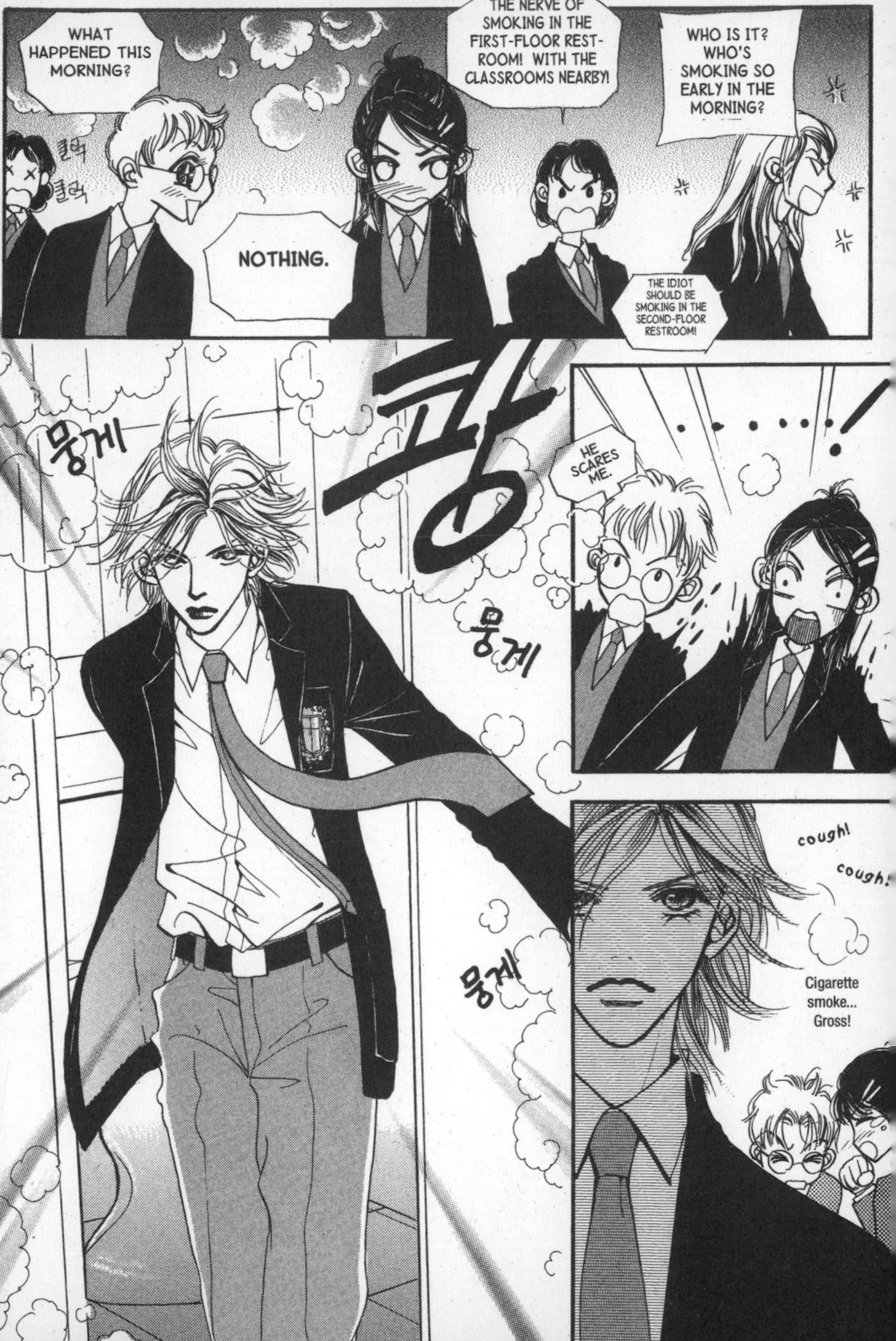

WHAT HAPPENED THIS MORNING?
NOTHING.
THE NERVE OF SMOKING IN THE FIRST-FLOOR REST-ROOM! WITH THE CLASSROOMS NEARBY!
WHO IS IT? WHO'S SMOKING SO EARLY IN THE MORNING?
THE IDIOT SHOULD BE SMOKING IN THE SECOND-FLOOR RESTROOM!
뭉게
쾅
뭉게
뭉게
......!
HE SCARES ME.
cough!
cough!
Cigarette smoke... Gross!

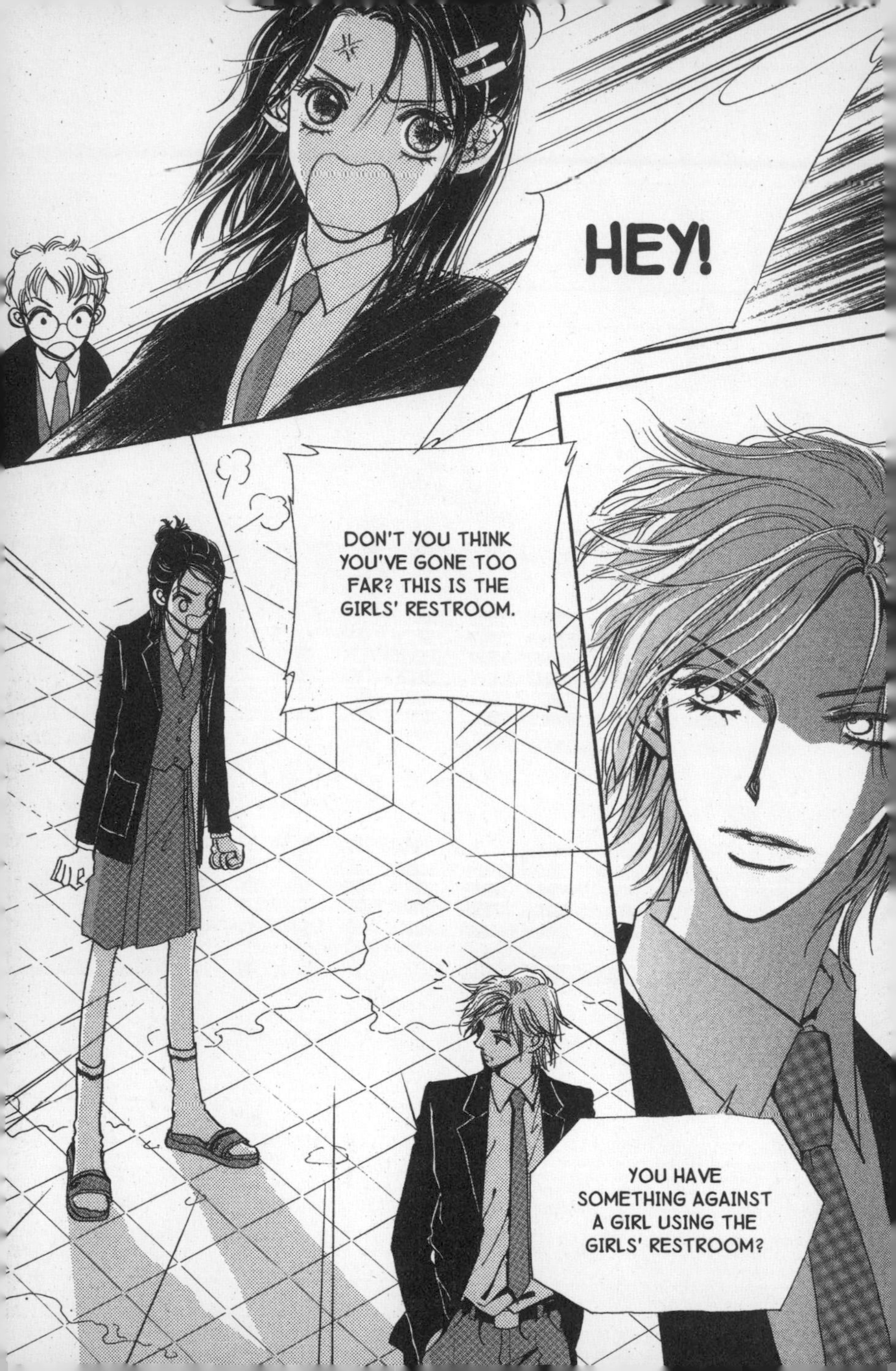
HEY!
DON'T YOU THINK YOU'VE GONE TOO FAR? THIS IS THE GIRLS' RESTROOM.
YOU HAVE SOMETHING AGAINST A GIRL USING THE GIRLS' RESTROOM?

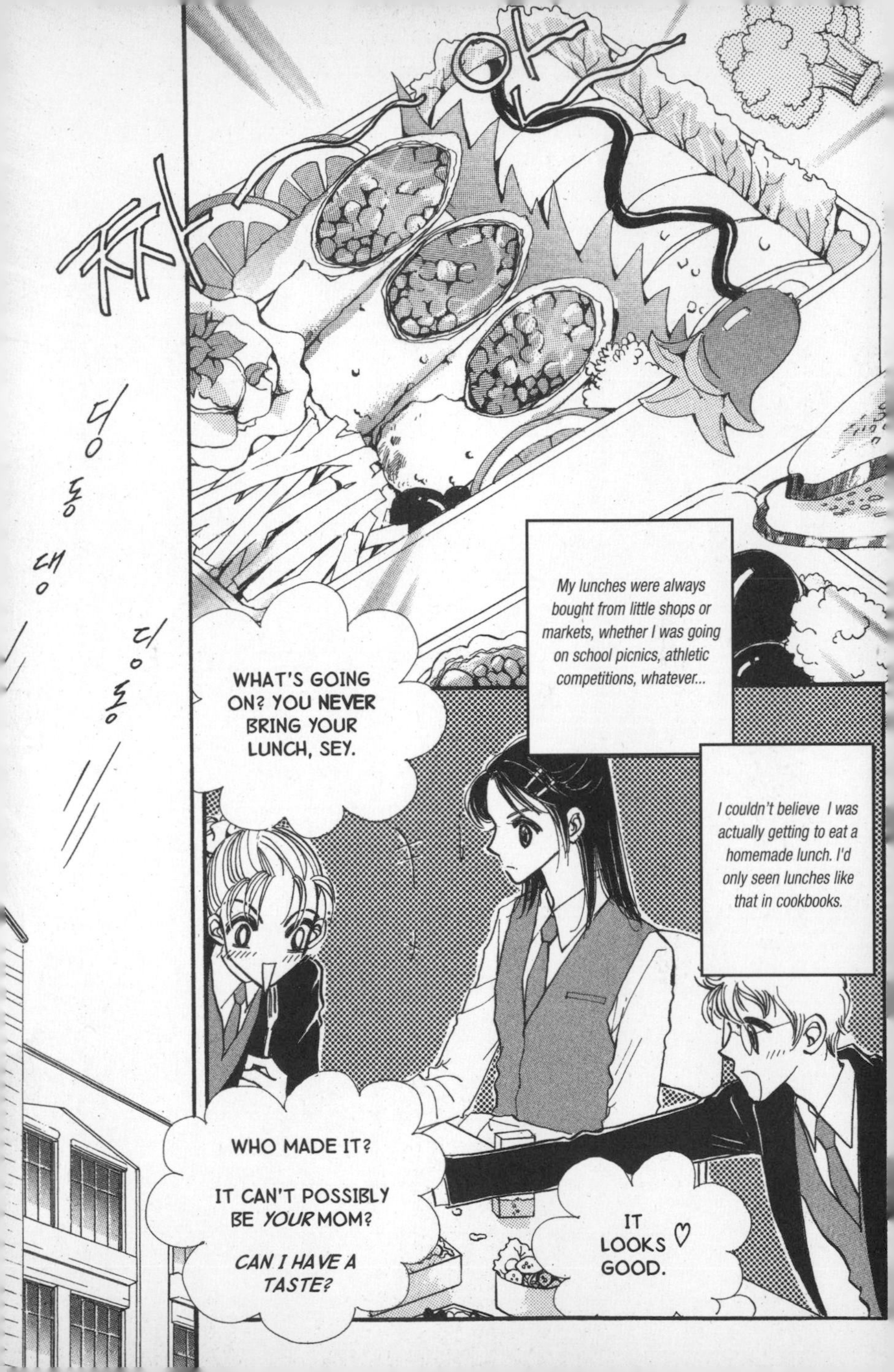

딩 동 댕
딩 동
My lunches were always bought from little shops or markets, whether I was going on school picnics, athletic competitions, whatever...
WHAT'S GOING ON? YOU NEVER BRING YOUR LUNCH, SEY.
I couldn't believe I was actually getting to eat a homemade lunch. I'd only seen lunches like that in cookbooks.
WHO MADE IT?
IT CAN'T POSSIBLY BE YOUR MOM?
CAN I HAVE A TASTE?
IT LOOKS GOOD. ♡

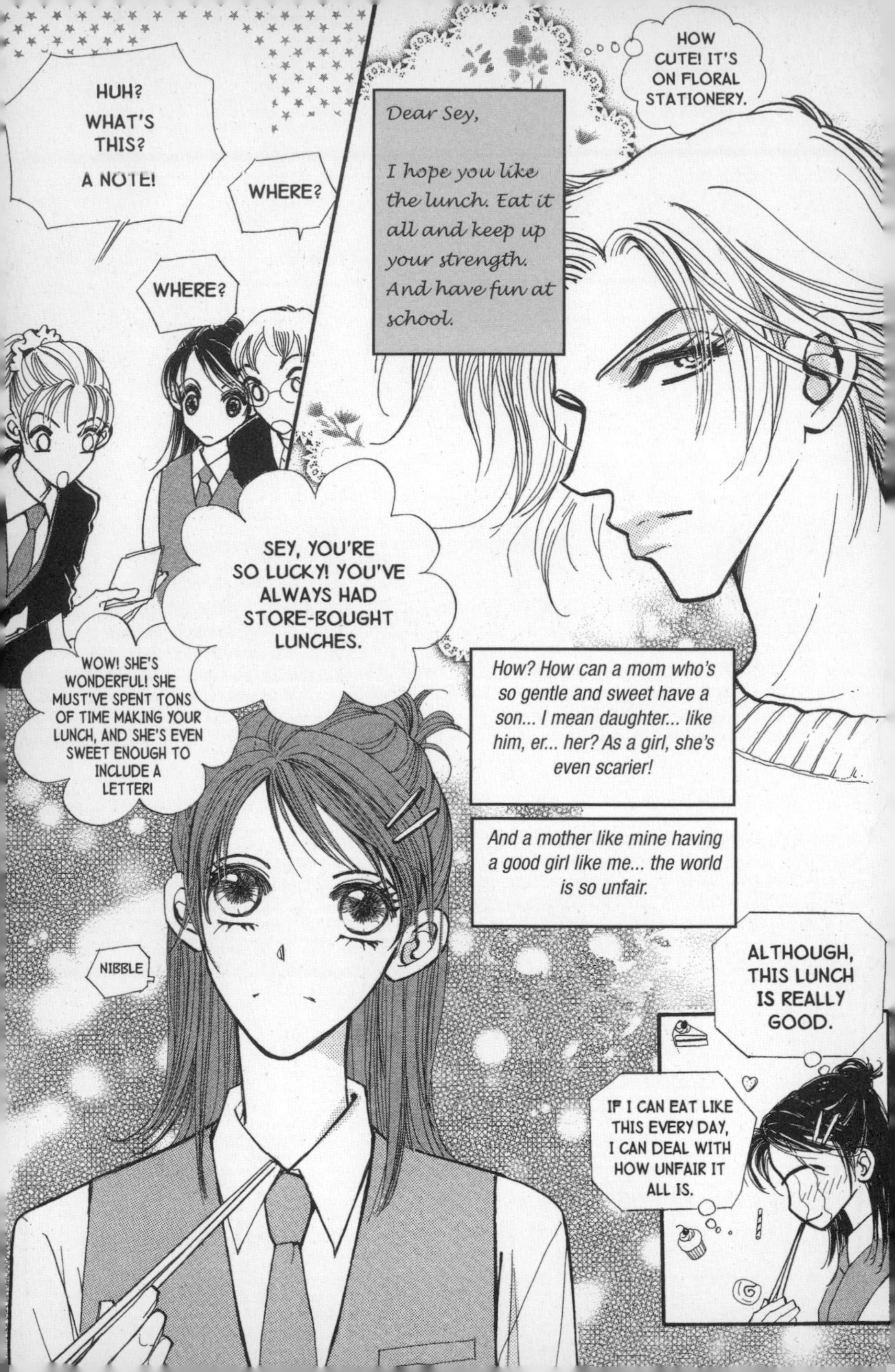

HUH? WHAT'S THIS? A NOTE!
WHERE?
WHERE?
HOW CUTE! IT'S ON FLORAL STATIONERY.
Dear Sey,
I hope you like the lunch. Eat it all and keep up your strength. And have fun at school.
SEY, YOU'RE SO LUCKY! YOU'VE ALWAYS HAD STORE-BOUGHT LUNCHES.
WOW! SHE'S WONDERFUL! SHE MUST'VE SPENT TONS OF TIME MAKING YOUR LUNCH, AND SHE'S EVEN SWEET ENOUGH TO INCLUDE A LETTER!
How? How can a mom who's so gentle and sweet have a son... I mean daughter... like him, er... her? As a girl, she's even scarier!
And a mother like mine having a good girl like me... the world is so unfair.
NIBBLE
ALTHOUGH, THIS LUNCH IS REALLY GOOD.
IF I CAN EAT LIKE THIS EVERY DAY, I CAN DEAL WITH HOW UNFAIR IT ALL IS.

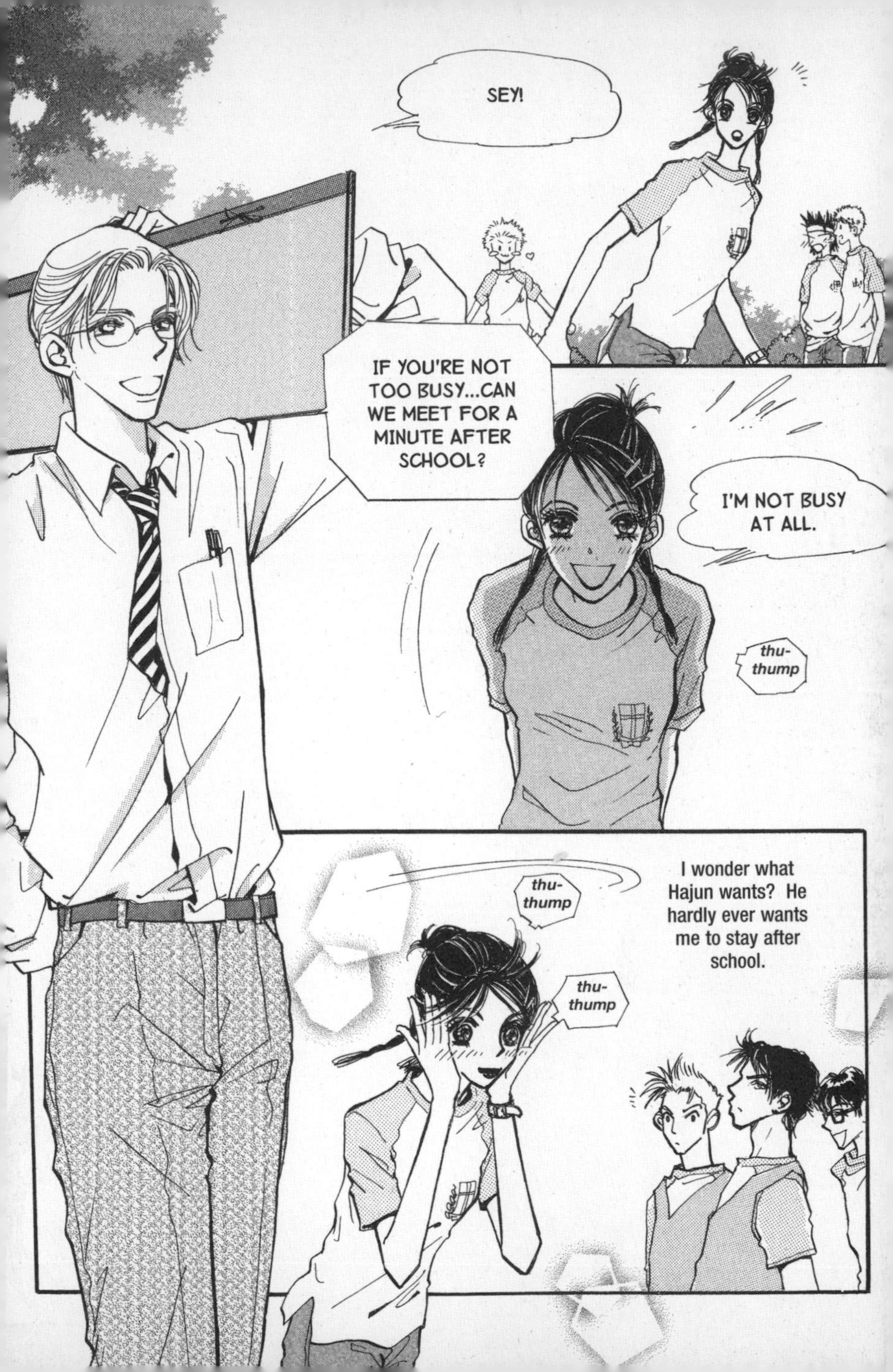
SEY!
IF YOU'RE NOT TOO BUSY...CAN WE MEET FOR A MINUTE AFTER SCHOOL?
I'M NOT BUSY AT ALL.
thu-thump
thu-thump
I wonder what Hajun wants? He hardly ever wants me to stay after school.
thu-thump

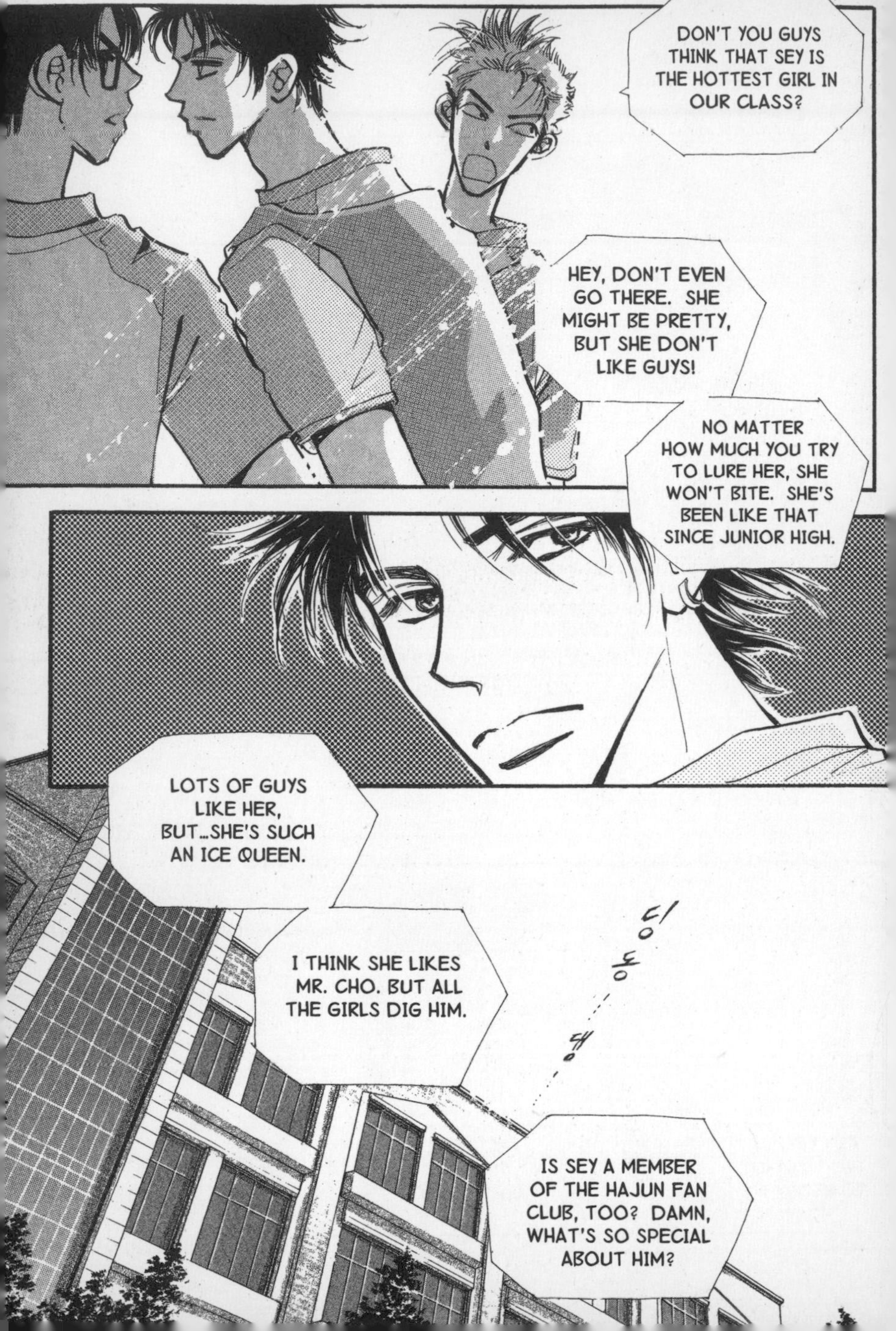
DON'T YOU GUYS THINK THAT SEY IS THE HOTTEST GIRL IN OUR CLASS?
HEY, DON'T EVEN GO THERE. SHE MIGHT BE PRETTY, BUT SHE DON'T LIKE GUYS!
NO MATTER HOW MUCH YOU TRY TO LURE HER, SHE WON'T BITE. SHE'S BEEN LIKE THAT SINCE JUNIOR HIGH.
LOTS OF GUYS LIKE HER, BUT...SHE'S SUCH AN ICE QUEEN.
I THINK SHE LIKES MR. CHO. BUT ALL THE GIRLS DIG HIM.
IS SEY A MEMBER OF THE HAJUN FAN CLUB, TOO? DAMN, WHAT'S SO SPECIAL ABOUT HIM?

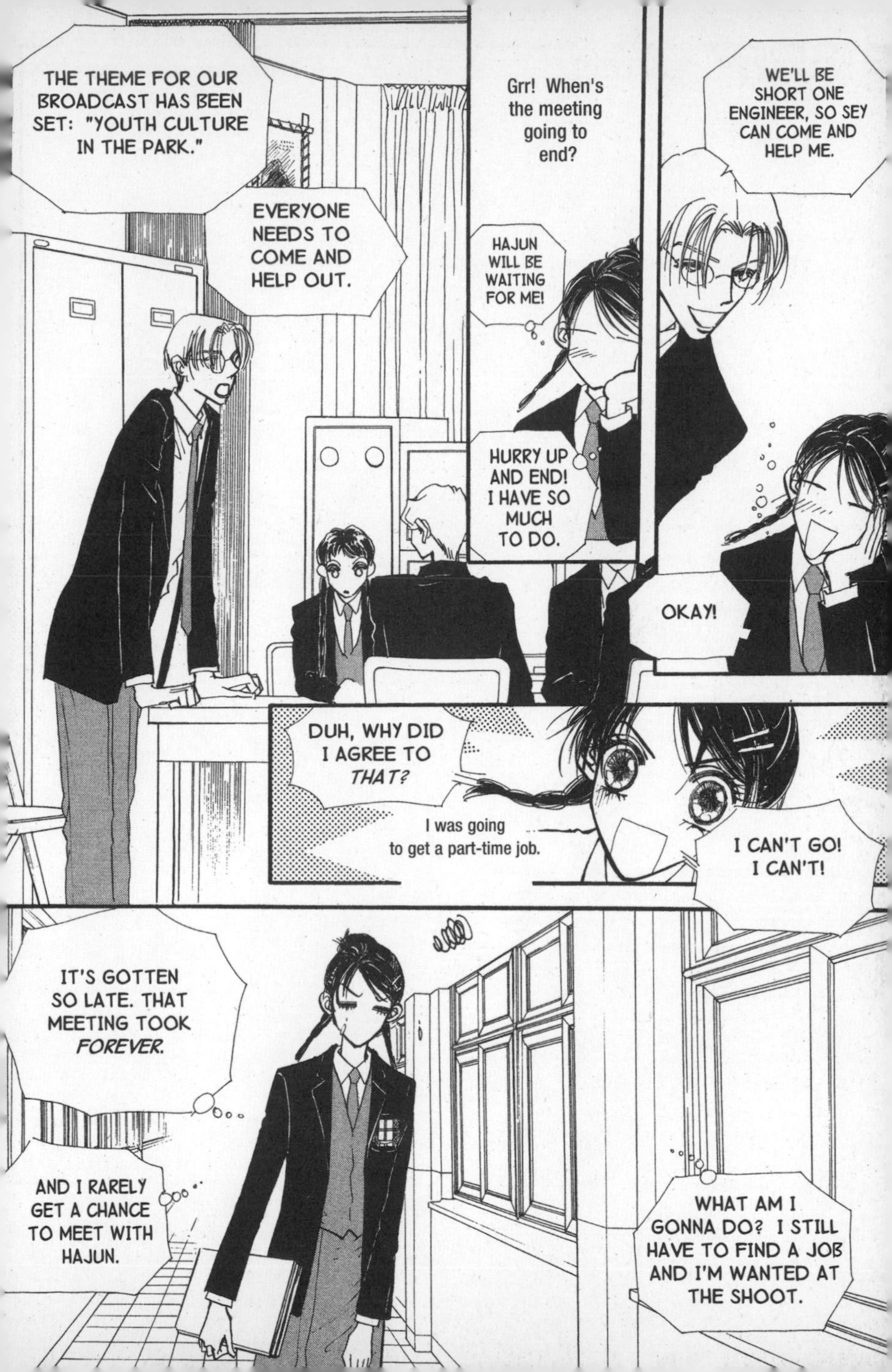
THE THEME FOR OUR BROADCAST HAS BEEN SET: "YOUTH CULTURE IN THE PARK."
EVERYONE NEEDS TO COME AND HELP OUT.
Grr! When's the meeting going to end?
HAJUN WILL BE WAITING FOR ME!
HURRY UP AND END! I HAVE SO MUCH TO DO.
WE'LL BE SHORT ONE ENGINEER, SO SEY CAN COME AND HELP ME.
OKAY!
DUH, WHY DID I AGREE TO *THAT?*
I was going to get a part-time job.
I CAN'T GO! I CAN'T!
IT'S GOTTEN SO LATE. THAT MEETING TOOK *FOREVER.*
AND I RARELY GET A CHANCE TO MEET WITH HAJUN.
WHAT AM I GONNA DO? I STILL HAVE TO FIND A JOB AND I'M WANTED AT THE SHOOT.

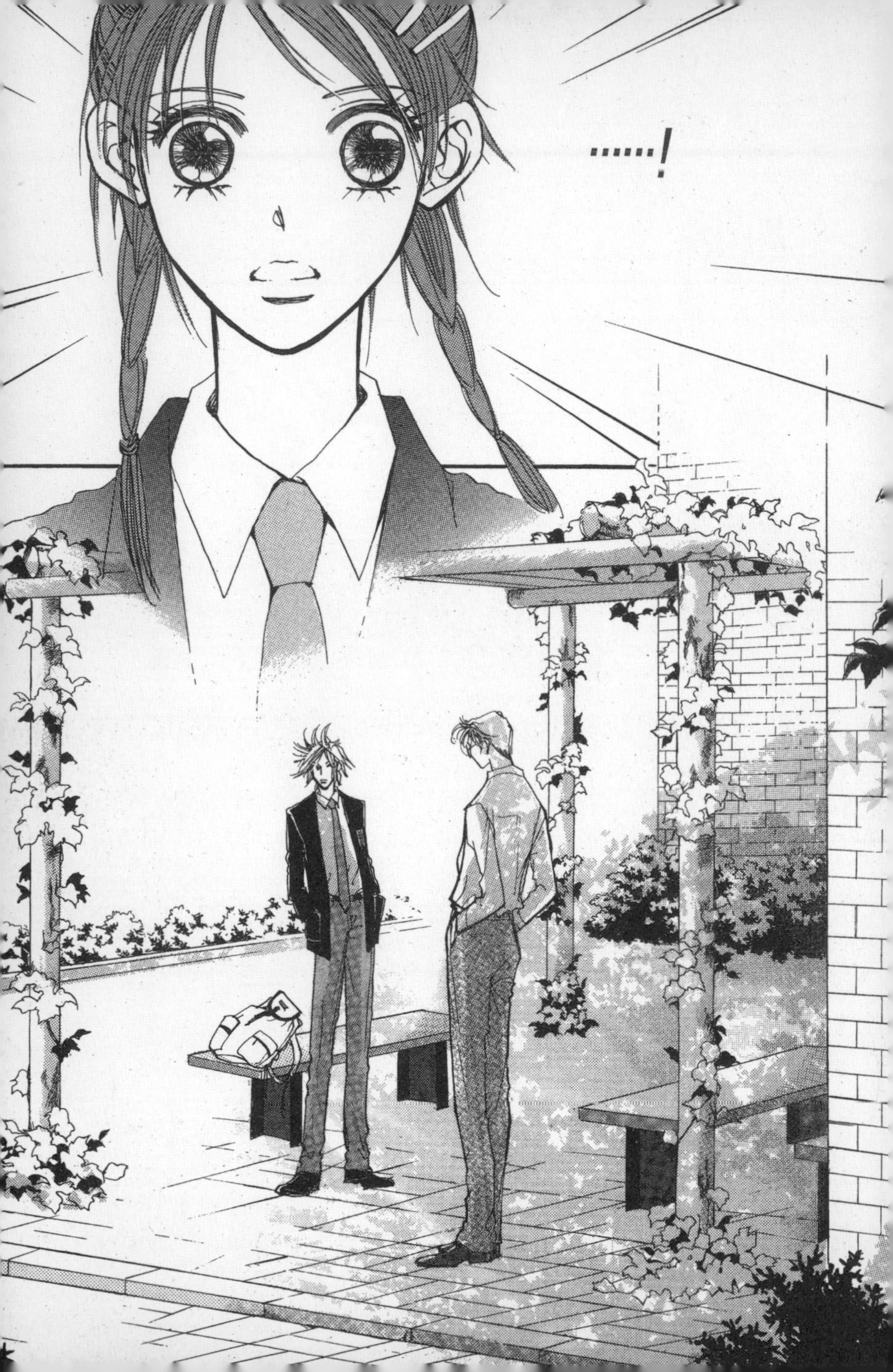
……!

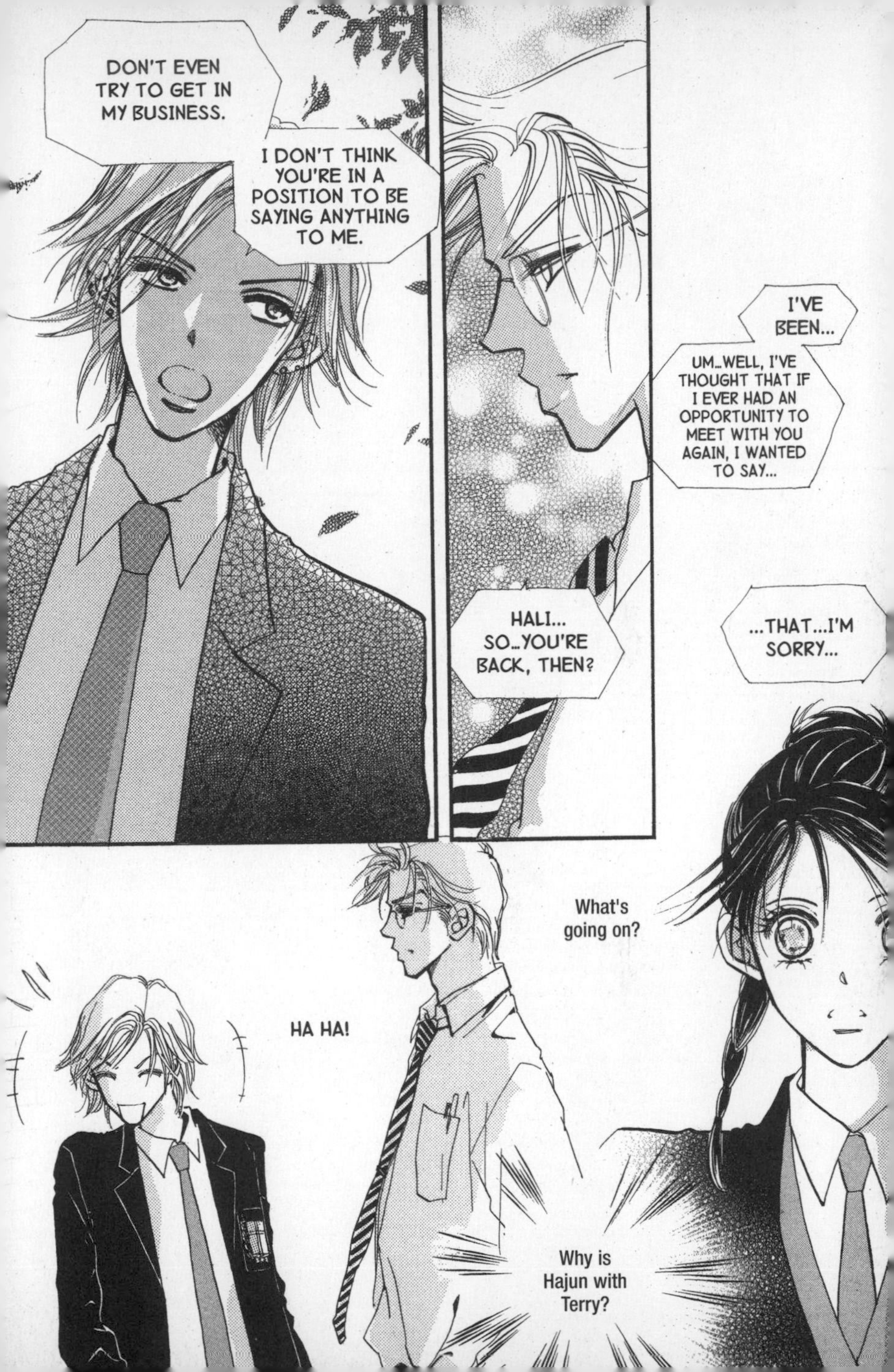
DON'T EVEN TRY TO GET IN MY BUSINESS.
I DON'T THINK YOU'RE IN A POSITION TO BE SAYING ANYTHING TO ME.
HALI... SO...YOU'RE BACK, THEN?
I'VE BEEN...
UM...WELL, I'VE THOUGHT THAT IF I EVER HAD AN OPPORTUNITY TO MEET WITH YOU AGAIN, I WANTED TO SAY...
...THAT...I'M SORRY...
What's going on?
HA HA!
Why is Hajun with Terry?

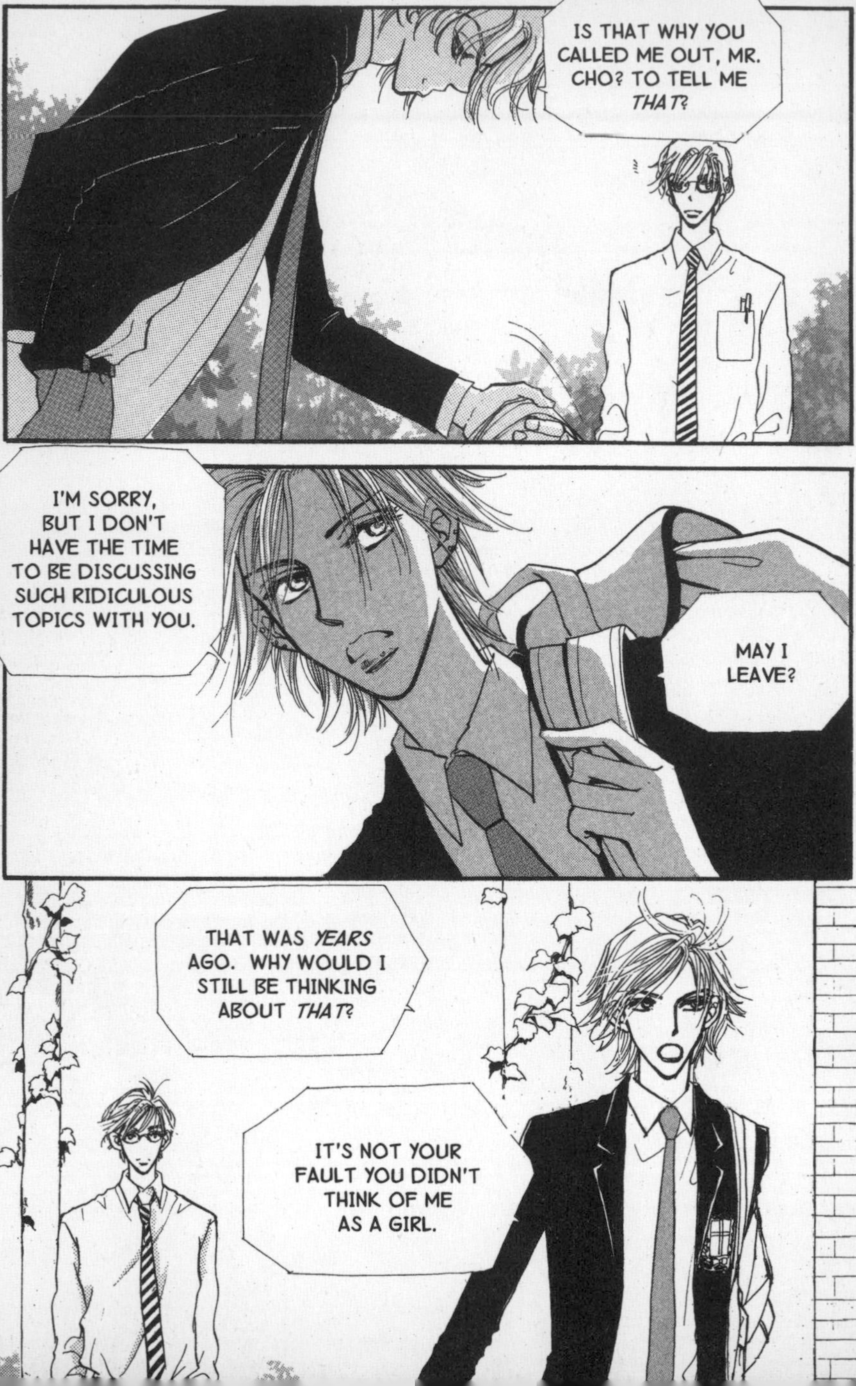
IS THAT WHY YOU CALLED ME OUT, MR. CHO? TO TELL ME *THAT*?
I'M SORRY, BUT I DON'T HAVE THE TIME TO BE DISCUSSING SUCH RIDICULOUS TOPICS WITH YOU.
MAY I LEAVE?
THAT WAS *YEARS* AGO. WHY WOULD I STILL BE THINKING ABOUT *THAT*?
IT'S NOT YOUR FAULT YOU DIDN'T THINK OF ME AS A GIRL.

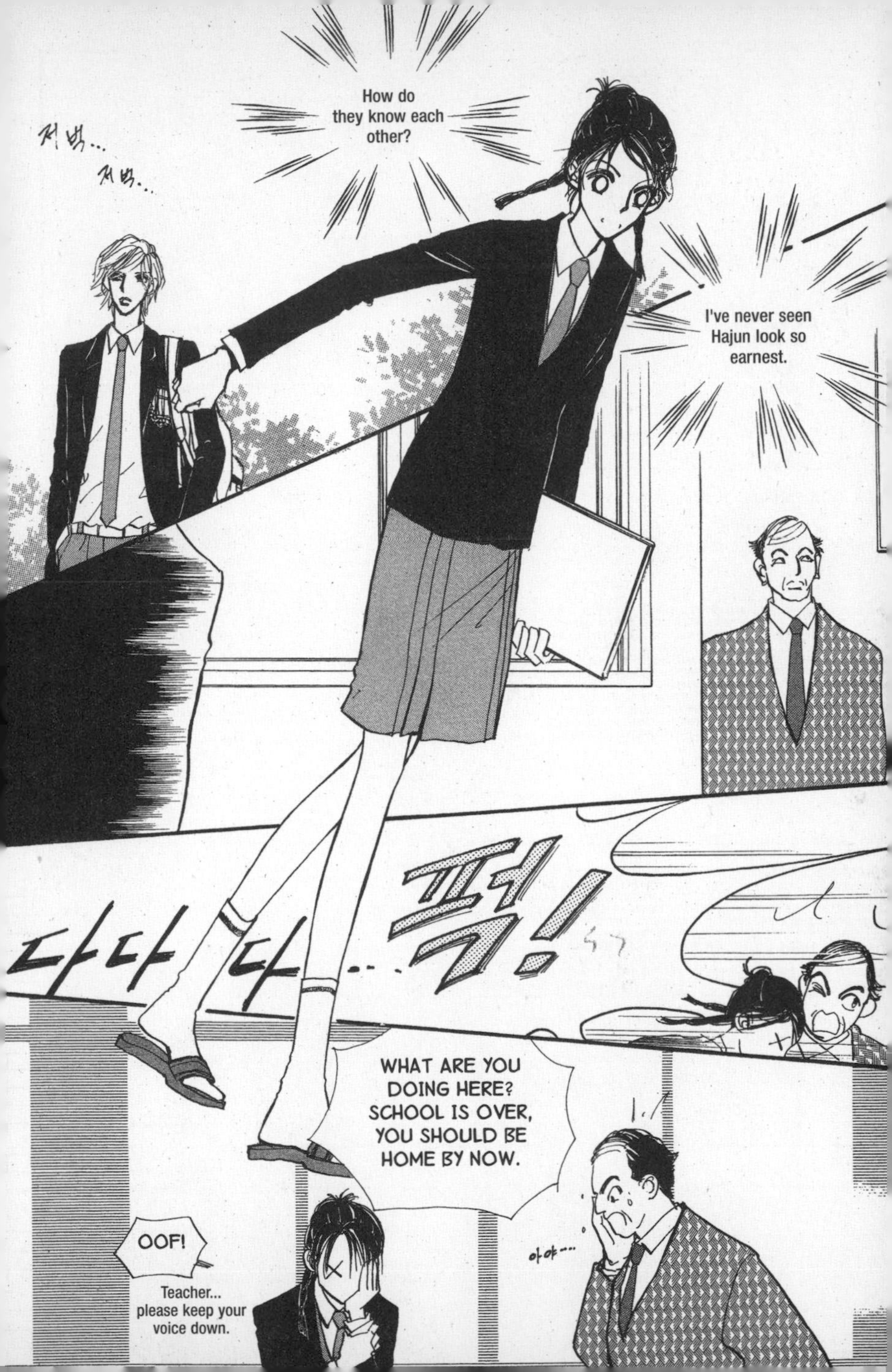
저벅...
저벅...
How do they know each other?
I've never seen Hajun look so earnest.
다다다 다...
퍽!
OOF!
Teacher... please keep your voice down.
WHAT ARE YOU DOING HERE? SCHOOL IS OVER, YOU SHOULD BE HOME BY NOW.
아야...

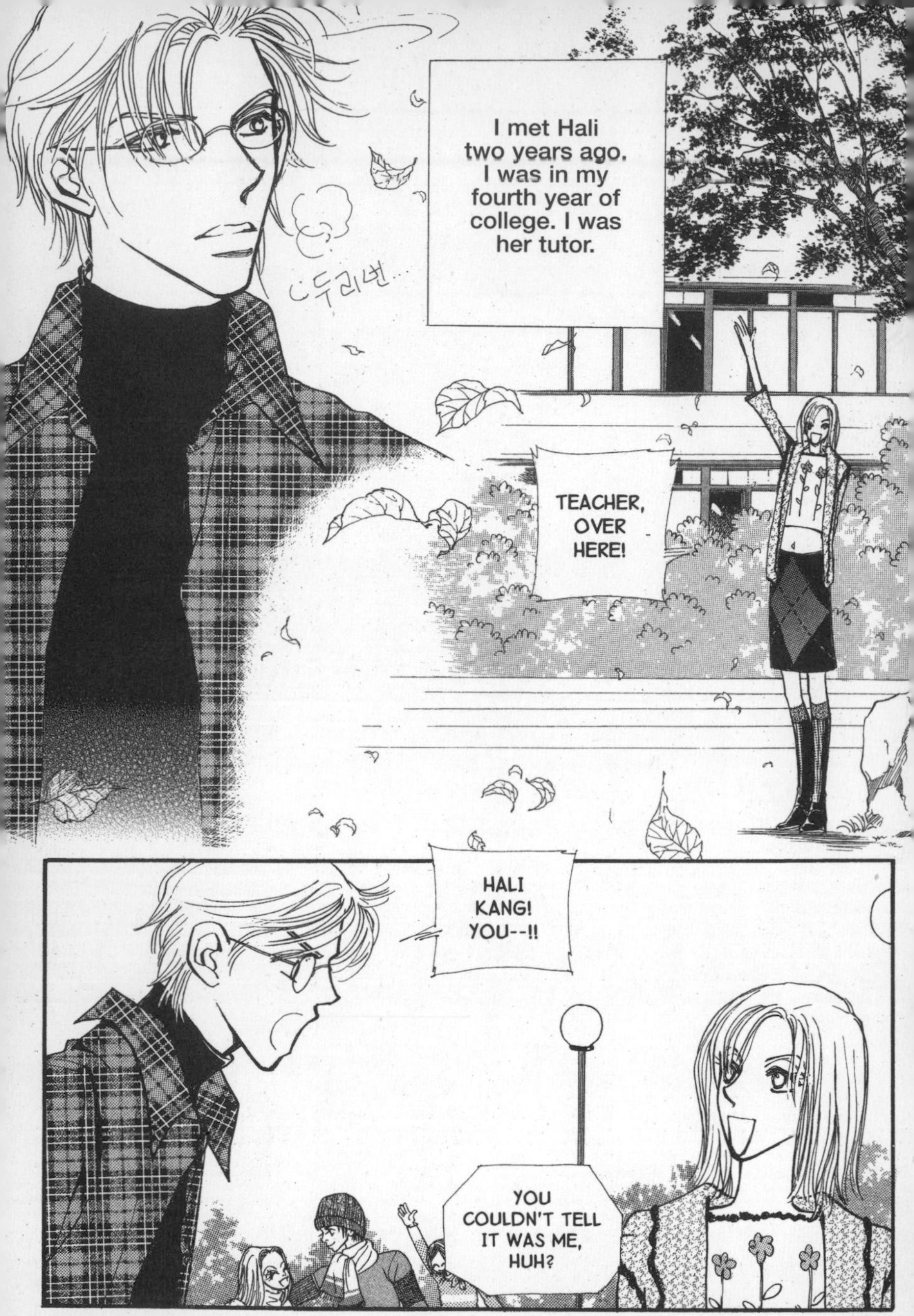
두리번…
I met Hali two years ago. I was in my fourth year of college. I was her tutor.
TEACHER, OVER HERE!
HALI KANG! YOU--!!
YOU COULDN'T TELL IT WAS ME, HUH?

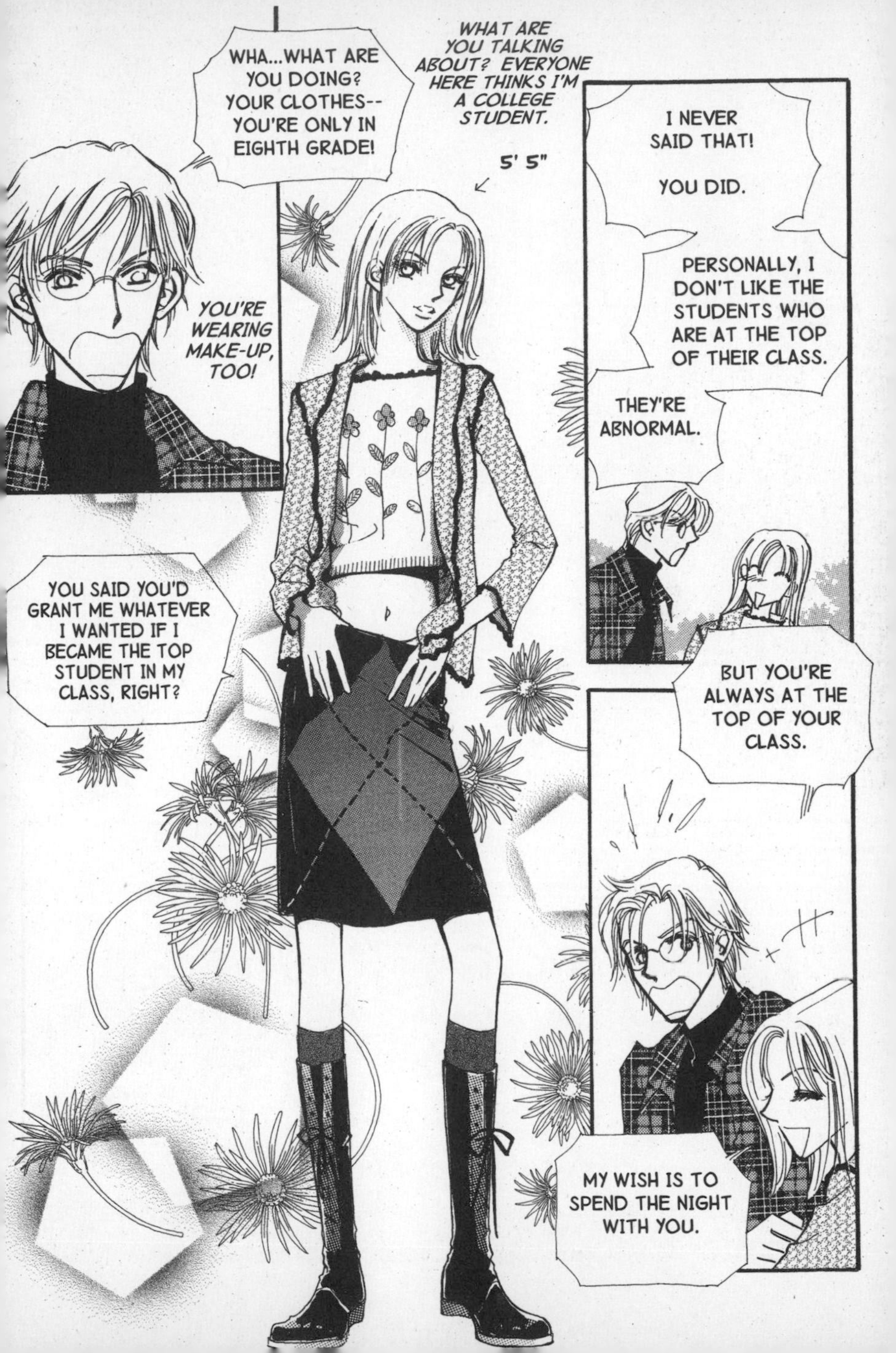
WHA...WHAT ARE YOU DOING? YOUR CLOTHES--YOU'RE ONLY IN EIGHTH GRADE!
WHAT ARE YOU TALKING ABOUT? EVERYONE HERE THINKS I'M A COLLEGE STUDENT.
5' 5"
YOU'RE WEARING MAKE-UP, TOO!
YOU SAID YOU'D GRANT ME WHATEVER I WANTED IF I BECAME THE TOP STUDENT IN MY CLASS, RIGHT?
I NEVER SAID THAT!
YOU DID.
PERSONALLY, I DON'T LIKE THE STUDENTS WHO ARE AT THE TOP OF THEIR CLASS.
THEY'RE ABNORMAL.
BUT YOU'RE ALWAYS AT THE TOP OF YOUR CLASS.
MY WISH IS TO SPEND THE NIGHT WITH YOU.

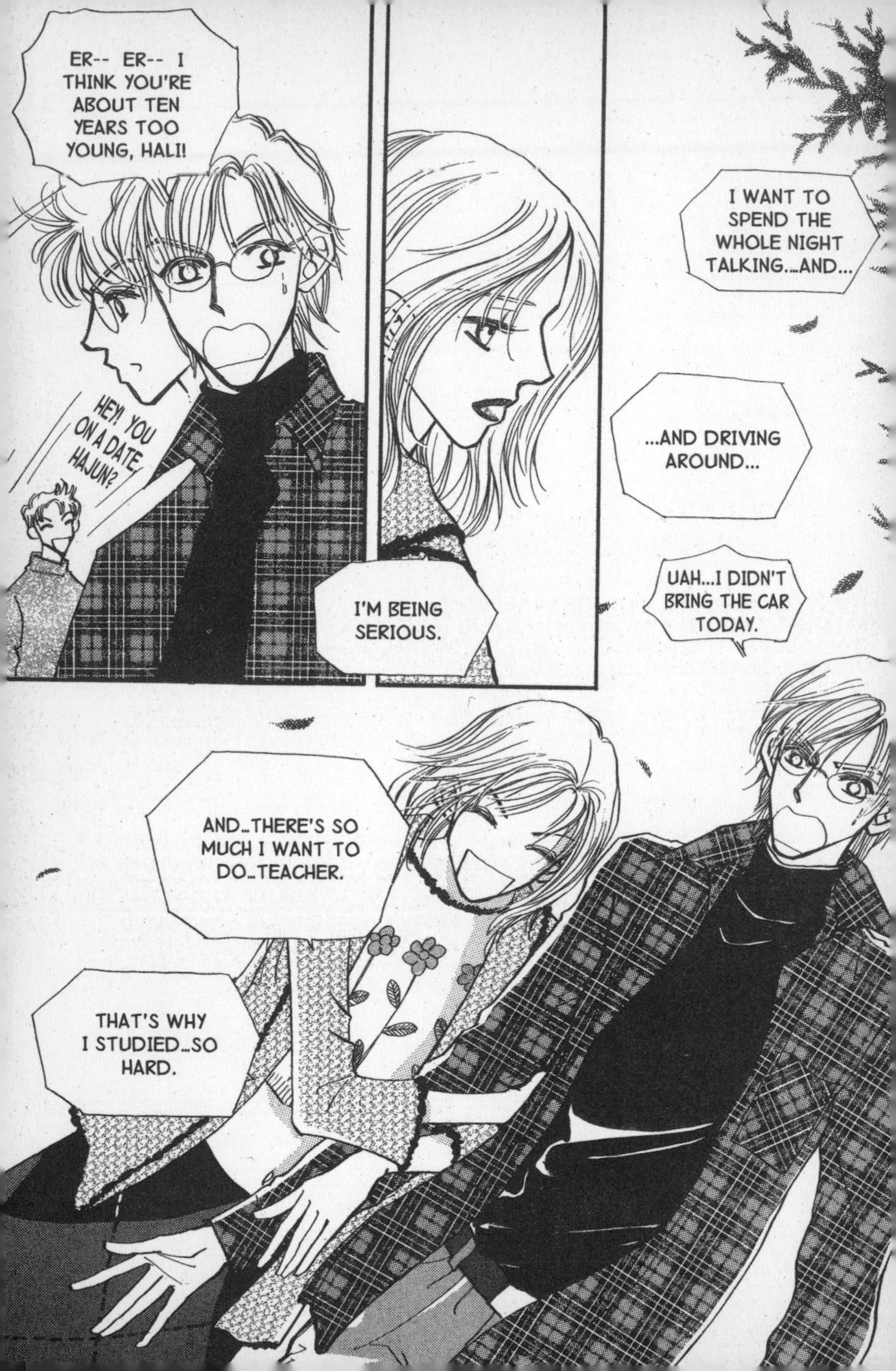
ER-- ER-- I THINK YOU'RE ABOUT TEN YEARS TOO YOUNG, HALI!
HEY! YOU ON A DATE, HAJUN?
I'M BEING SERIOUS.
I WANT TO SPEND THE WHOLE NIGHT TALKING....AND...
...AND DRIVING AROUND...
UAH...I DIDN'T BRING THE CAR TODAY.
AND...THERE'S SO MUCH I WANT TO DO...TEACHER.
THAT'S WHY I STUDIED...SO HARD.

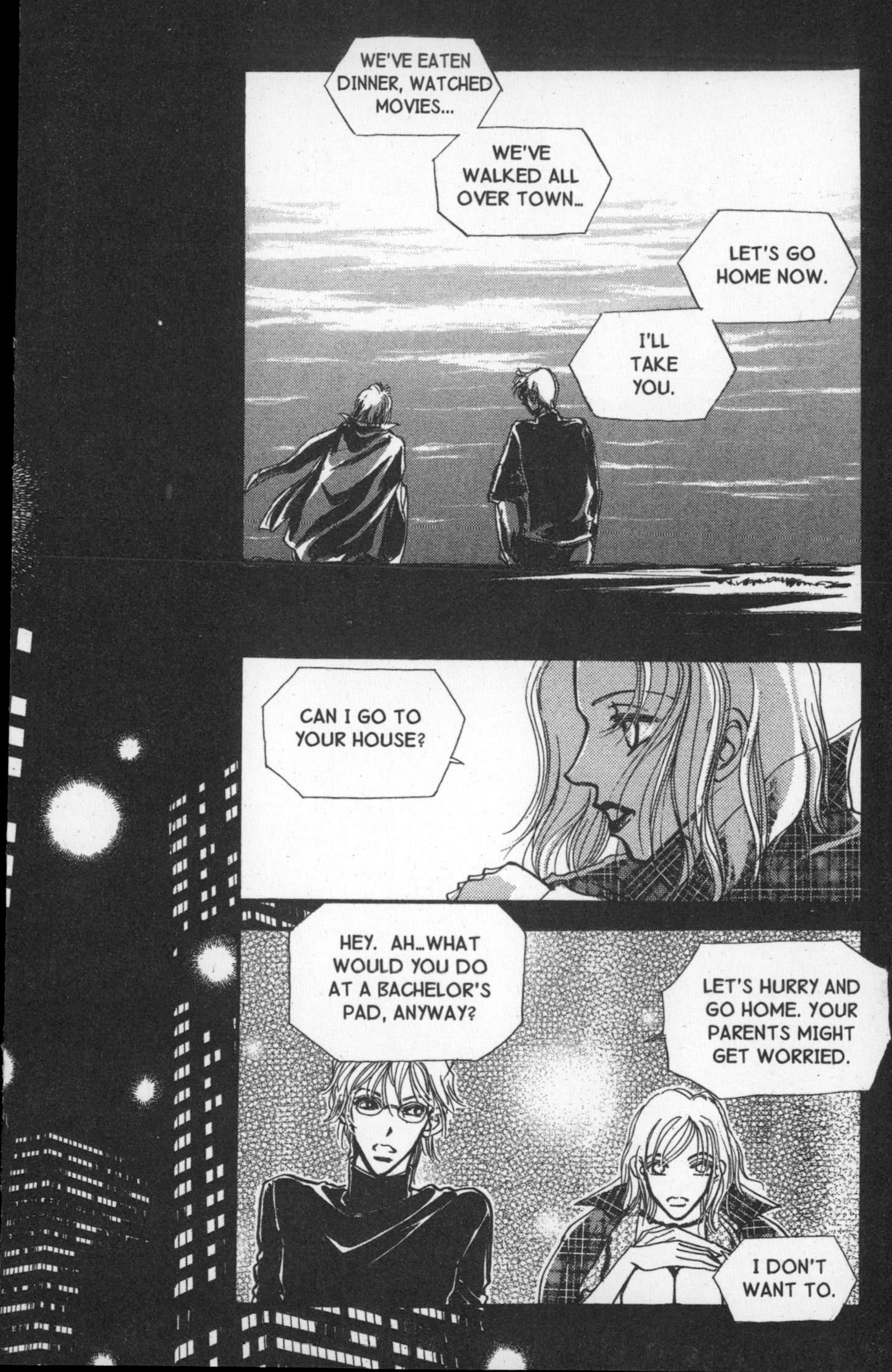
WE'VE EATEN DINNER, WATCHED MOVIES...
WE'VE WALKED ALL OVER TOWN...
LET'S GO HOME NOW.
I'LL TAKE YOU.
CAN I GO TO YOUR HOUSE?
HEY. AH...WHAT WOULD YOU DO AT A BACHELOR'S PAD, ANYWAY?
LET'S HURRY AND GO HOME. YOUR PARENTS MIGHT GET WORRIED.
I DON'T WANT TO.

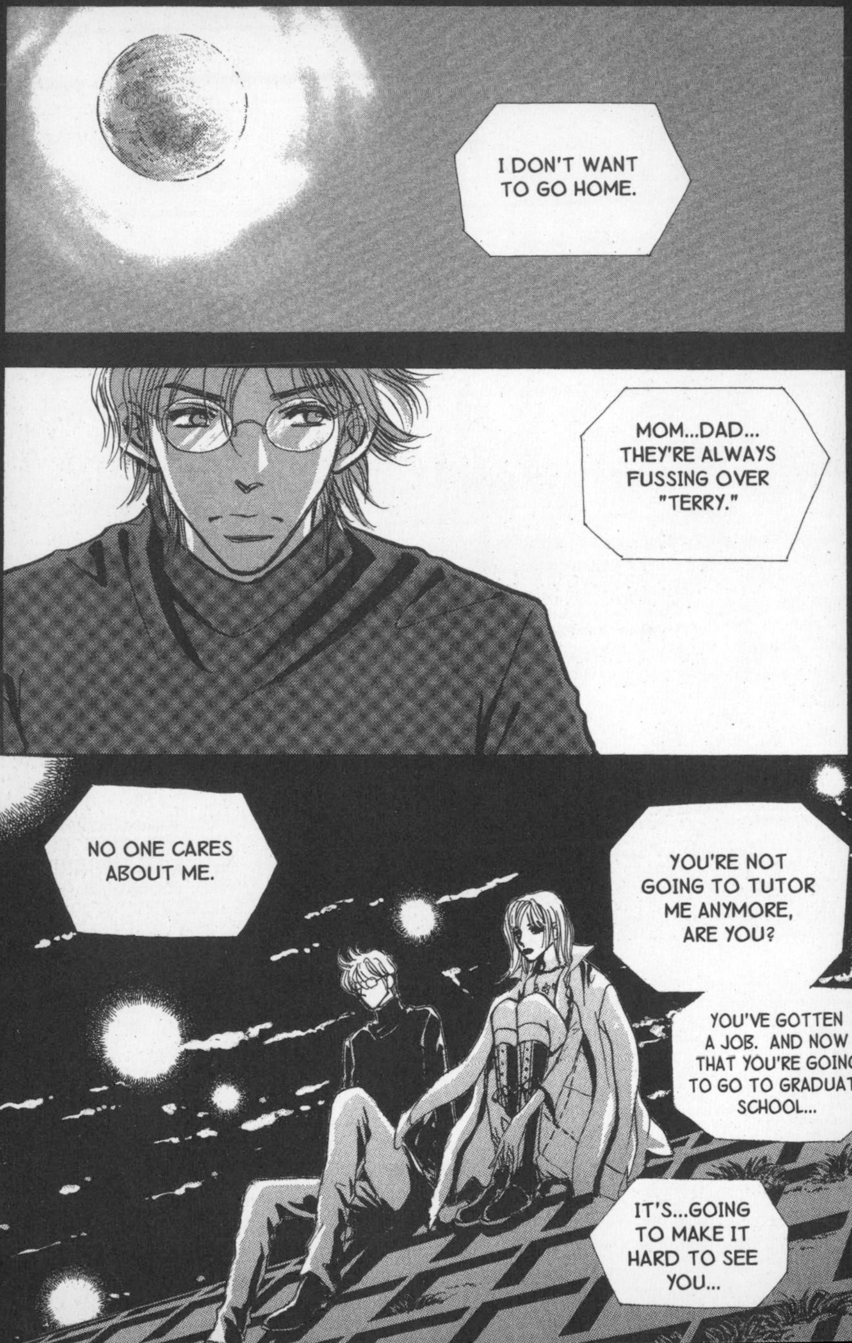
I DON'T WANT TO GO HOME.
MOM...DAD... THEY'RE ALWAYS FUSSING OVER "TERRY."
NO ONE CARES ABOUT ME.
YOU'RE NOT GOING TO TUTOR ME ANYMORE, ARE YOU?
YOU'VE GOTTEN A JOB. AND NOW THAT YOU'RE GOING TO GO TO GRADUATE SCHOOL...
IT'S...GOING TO MAKE IT HARD TO SEE YOU...

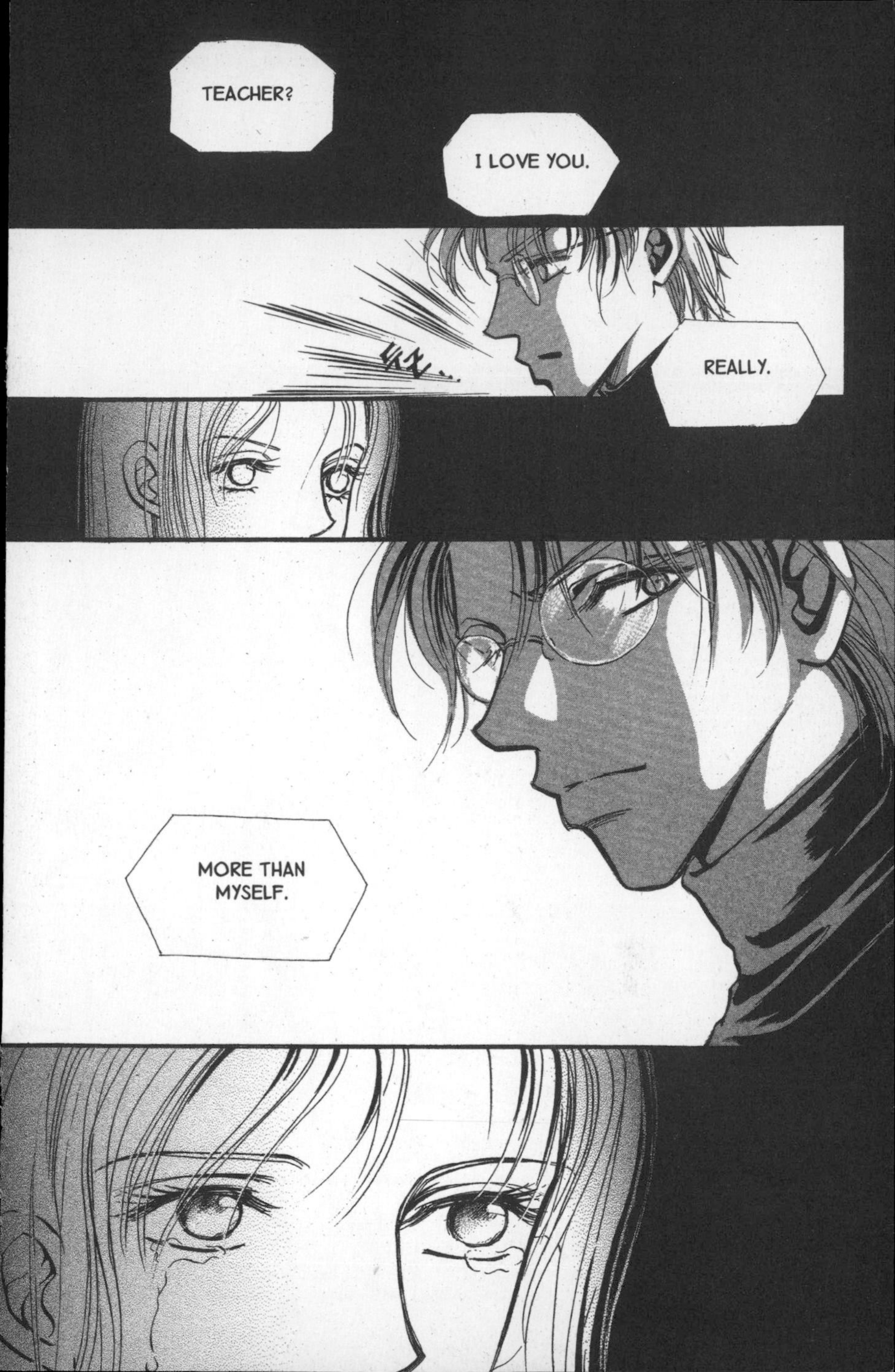
TEACHER?
I LOVE YOU.
REALLY.
MORE THAN
MYSELF.

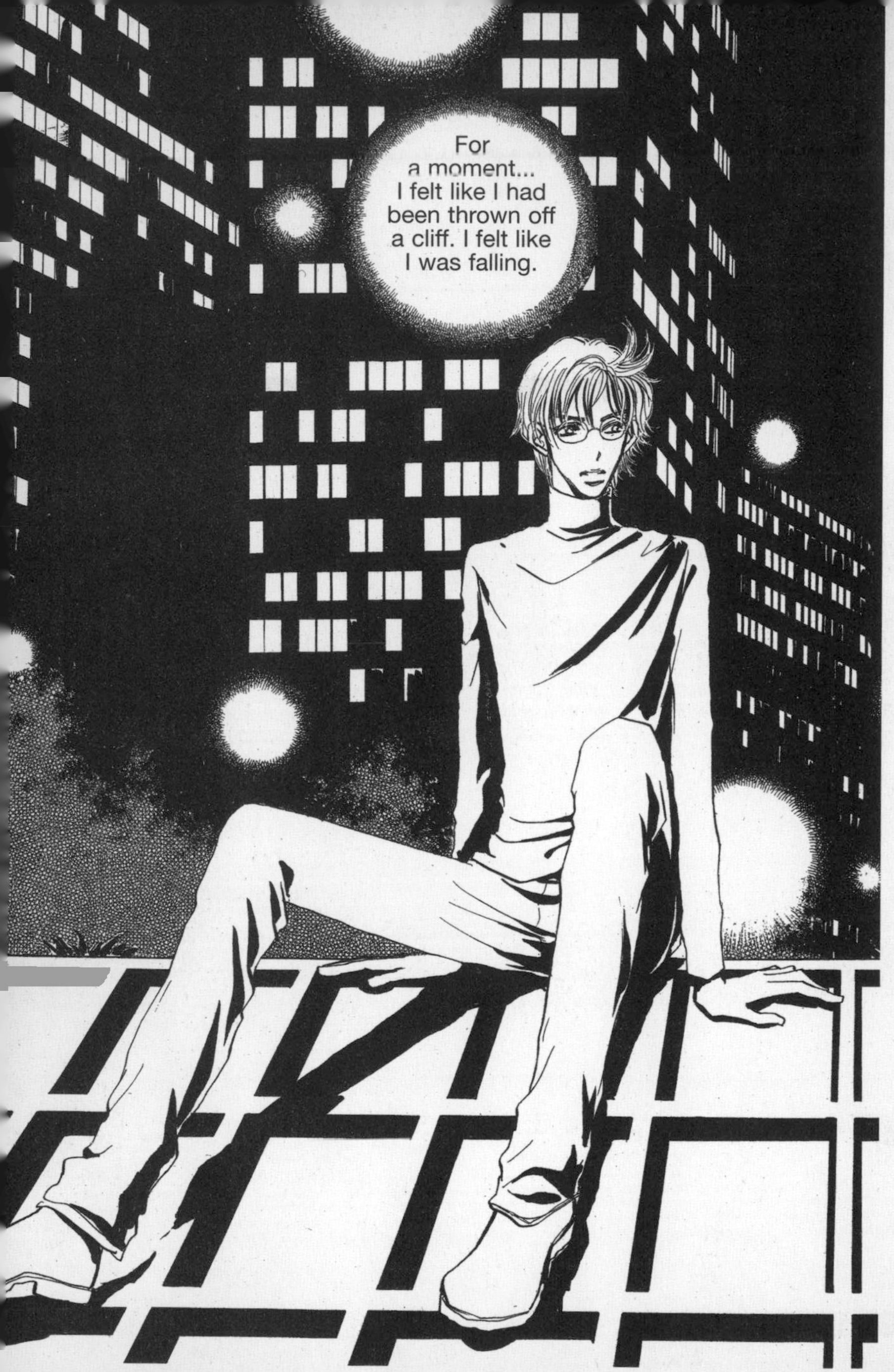
For a moment... I felt like I had been thrown off a cliff. I felt like I was falling.

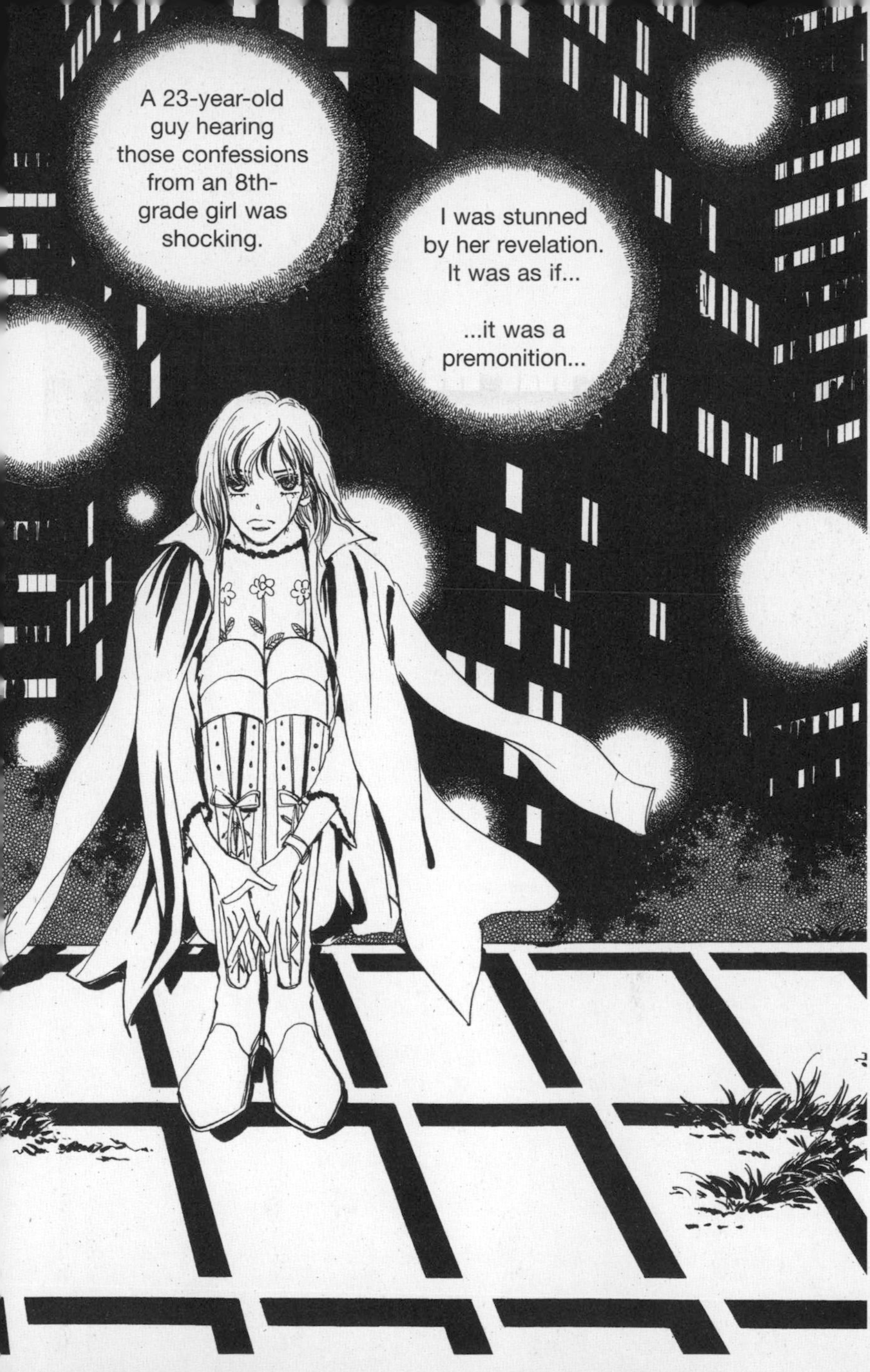
A 23-year-old guy hearing those confessions from an 8th-grade girl was shocking.
I was stunned by her revelation. It was as if...
...it was a premonition...

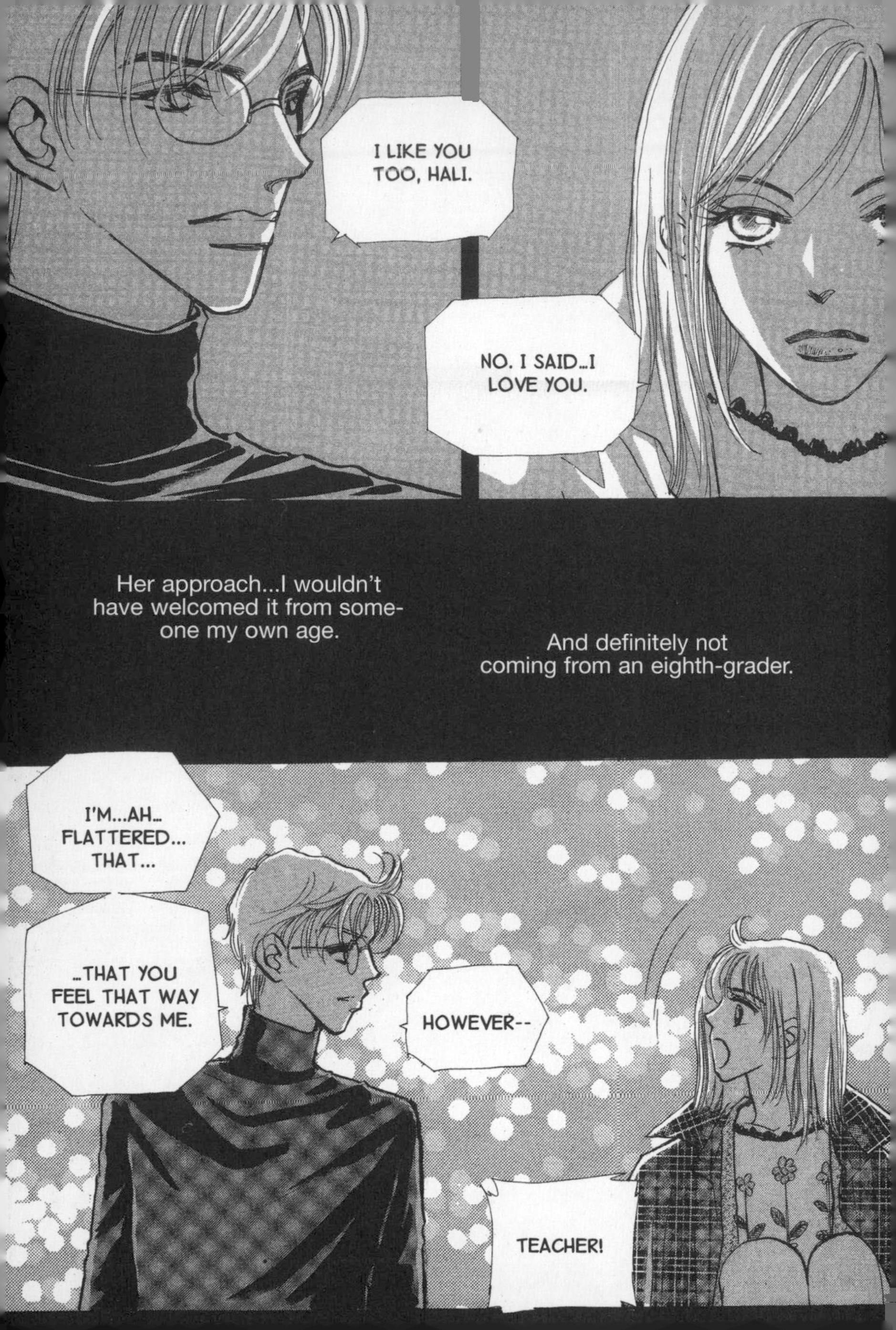
I LIKE YOU TOO, HALI.
NO. I SAID...I LOVE YOU.
Her approach...I wouldn't have welcomed it from some-one my own age.
And definitely not coming from an eighth-grader.
I'M...AH... FLATTERED... THAT...
...THAT YOU FEEL THAT WAY TOWARDS ME.
HOWEVER--
TEACHER!

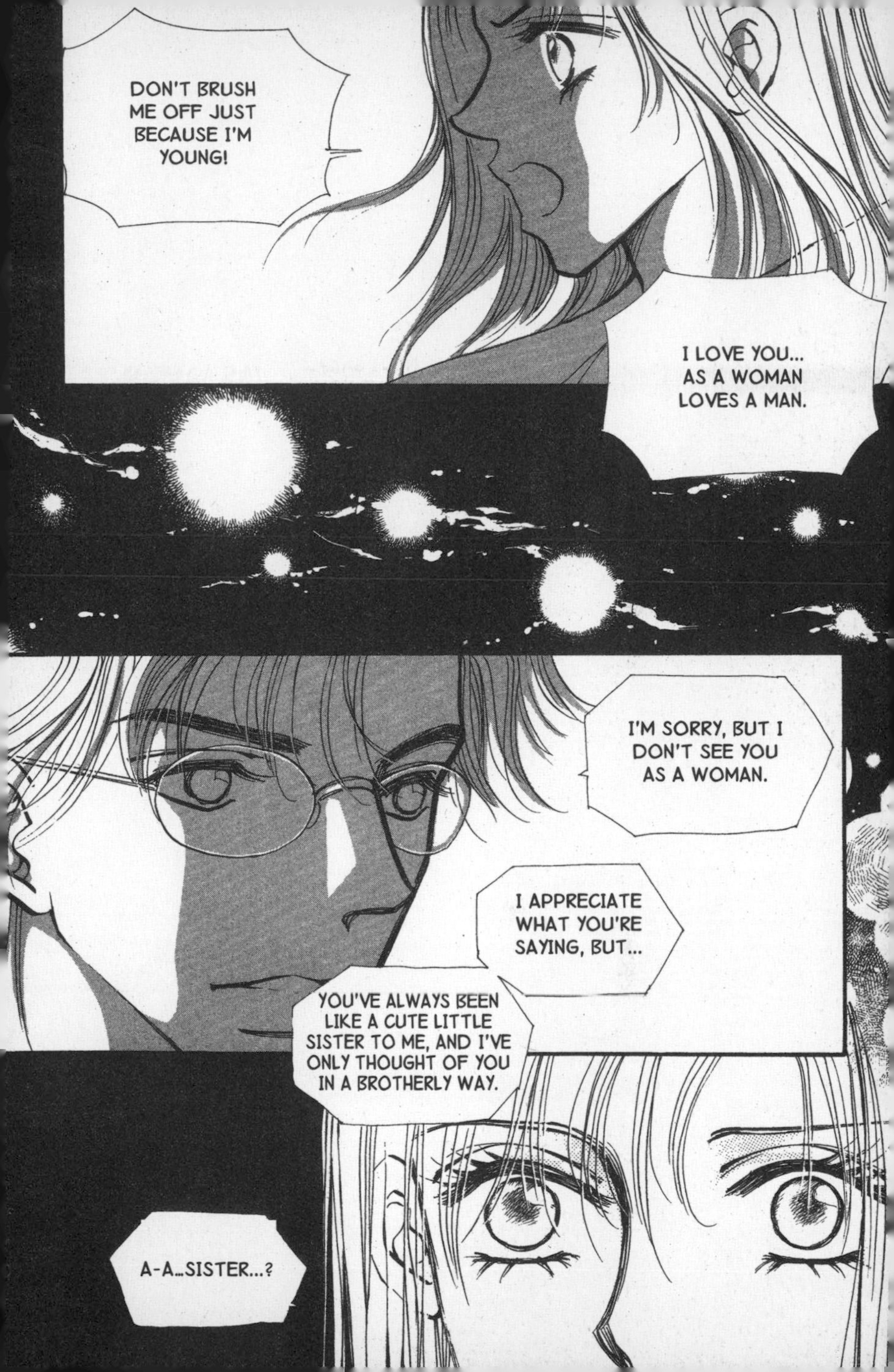
DON'T BRUSH ME OFF JUST BECAUSE I'M YOUNG!
I LOVE YOU... AS A WOMAN LOVES A MAN.
I'M SORRY, BUT I DON'T SEE YOU AS A WOMAN.
I APPRECIATE WHAT YOU'RE SAYING, BUT...
YOU'VE ALWAYS BEEN LIKE A CUTE LITTLE SISTER TO ME, AND I'VE ONLY THOUGHT OF YOU IN A BROTHERLY WAY.
A-A...SISTER...?

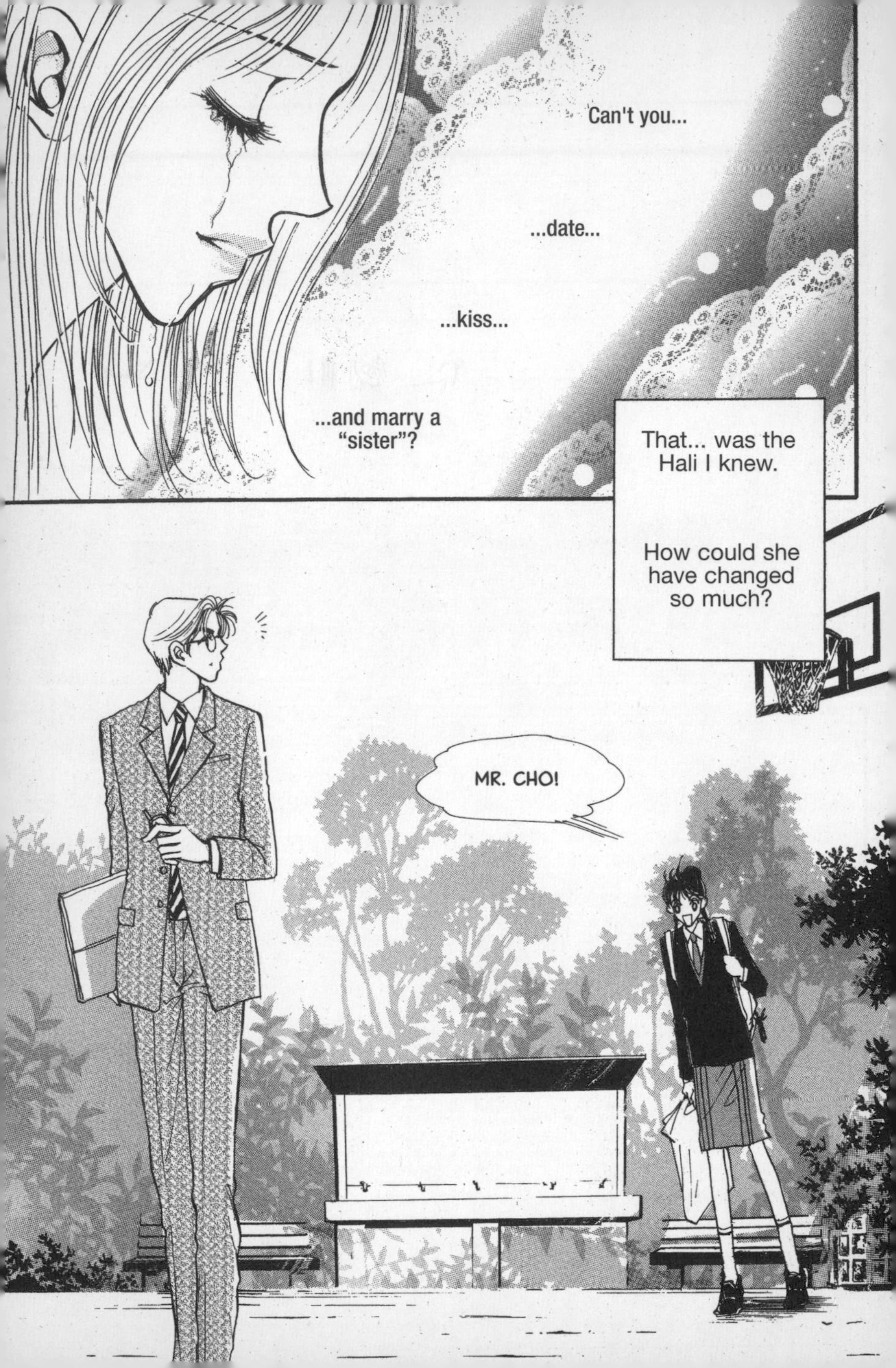
Can't you...
...date...
...kiss...
...and marry a "sister"?
That... was the Hali I knew.
How could she have changed so much?
MR. CHO!

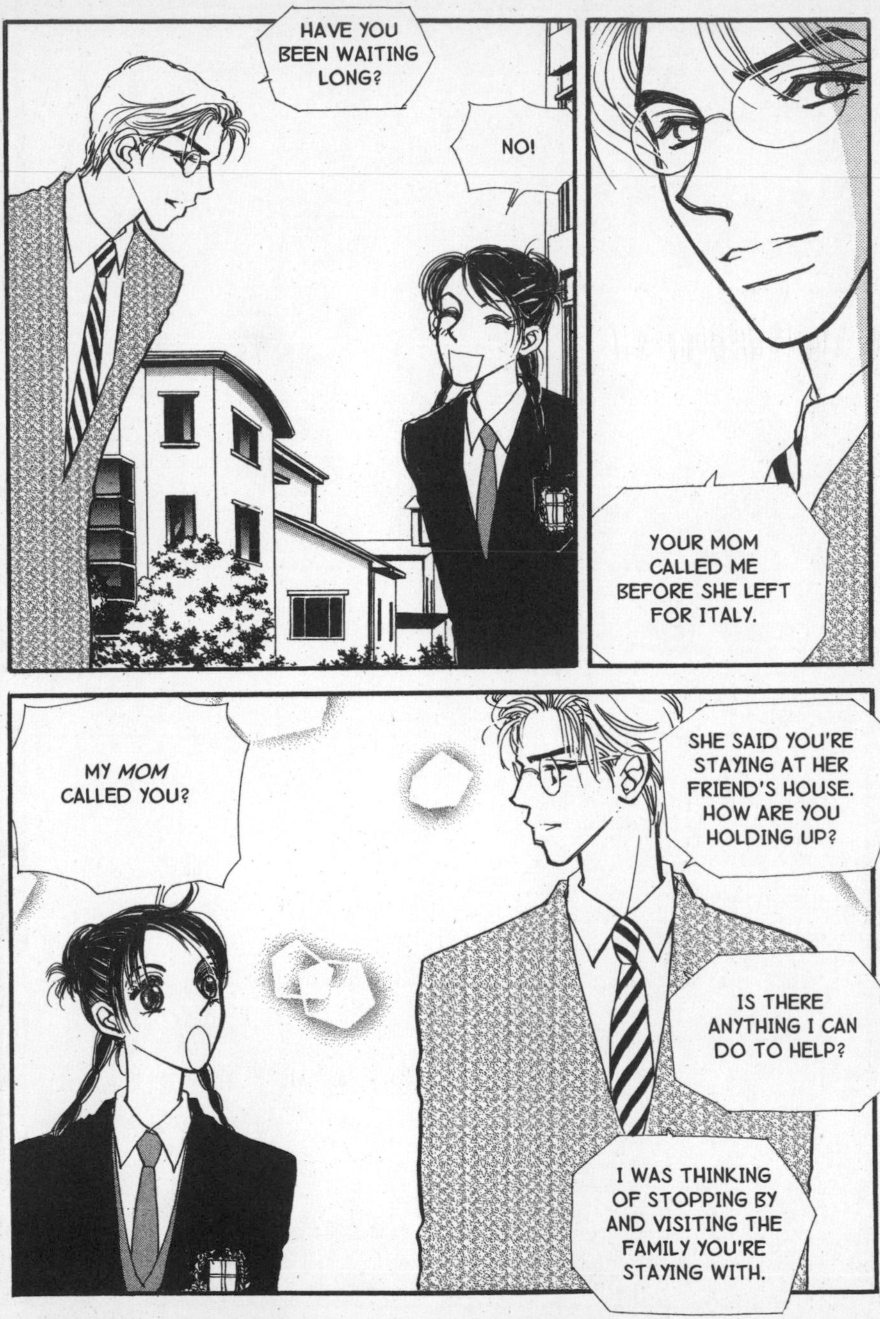
HAVE YOU BEEN WAITING LONG?
NO!
YOUR MOM CALLED ME BEFORE SHE LEFT FOR ITALY.
MY *MOM* CALLED YOU?
SHE SAID YOU'RE STAYING AT HER FRIEND'S HOUSE. HOW ARE YOU HOLDING UP?
IS THERE ANYTHING I CAN DO TO HELP?
I WAS THINKING OF STOPPING BY AND VISITING THE FAMILY YOU'RE STAYING WITH.

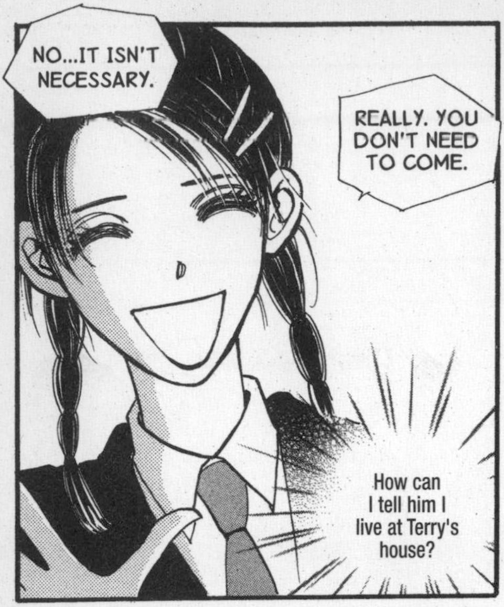
NO...IT ISN'T NECESSARY.
REALLY. YOU DON'T NEED TO COME.
How can I tell him I live at Terry's house?

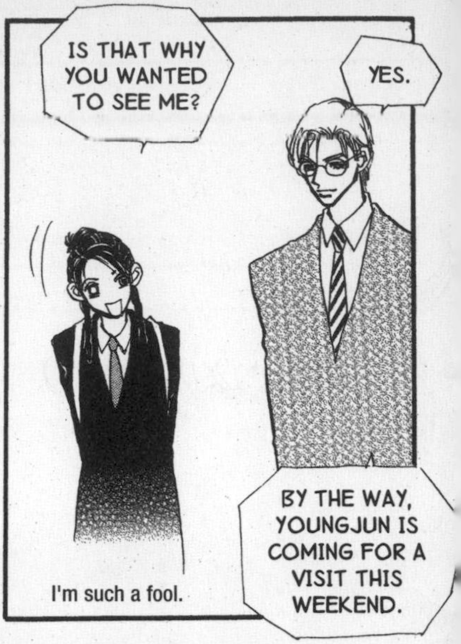
IS THAT WHY YOU WANTED TO SEE ME?
YES.
I'm such a fool.
BY THE WAY, YOUNGJUN IS COMING FOR A VISIT THIS WEEKEND.

I can't get my mind off Hajun and Terry. What's up with the name "Hali," anyway?

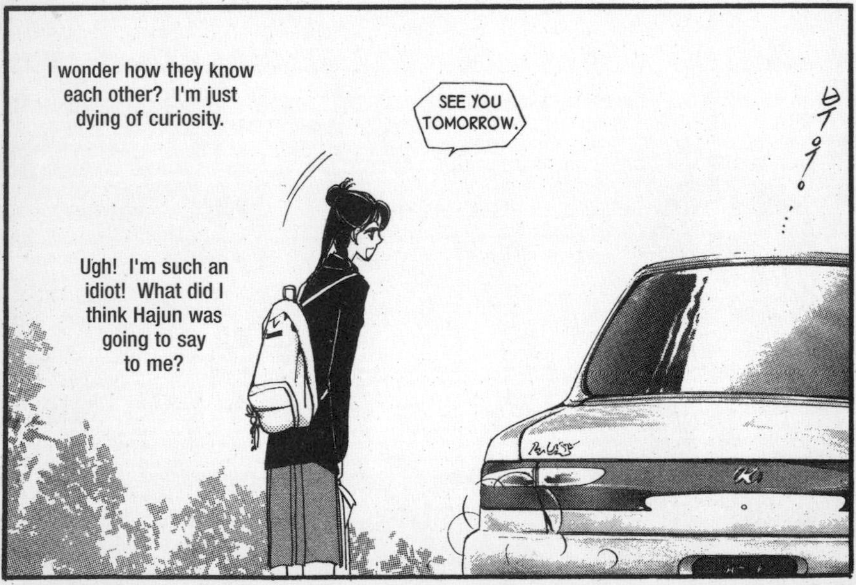
I wonder how they know each other? I'm just dying of curiosity.
SEE YOU TOMORROW.
Ugh! I'm such an idiot! What did I think Hajun was going to say to me?

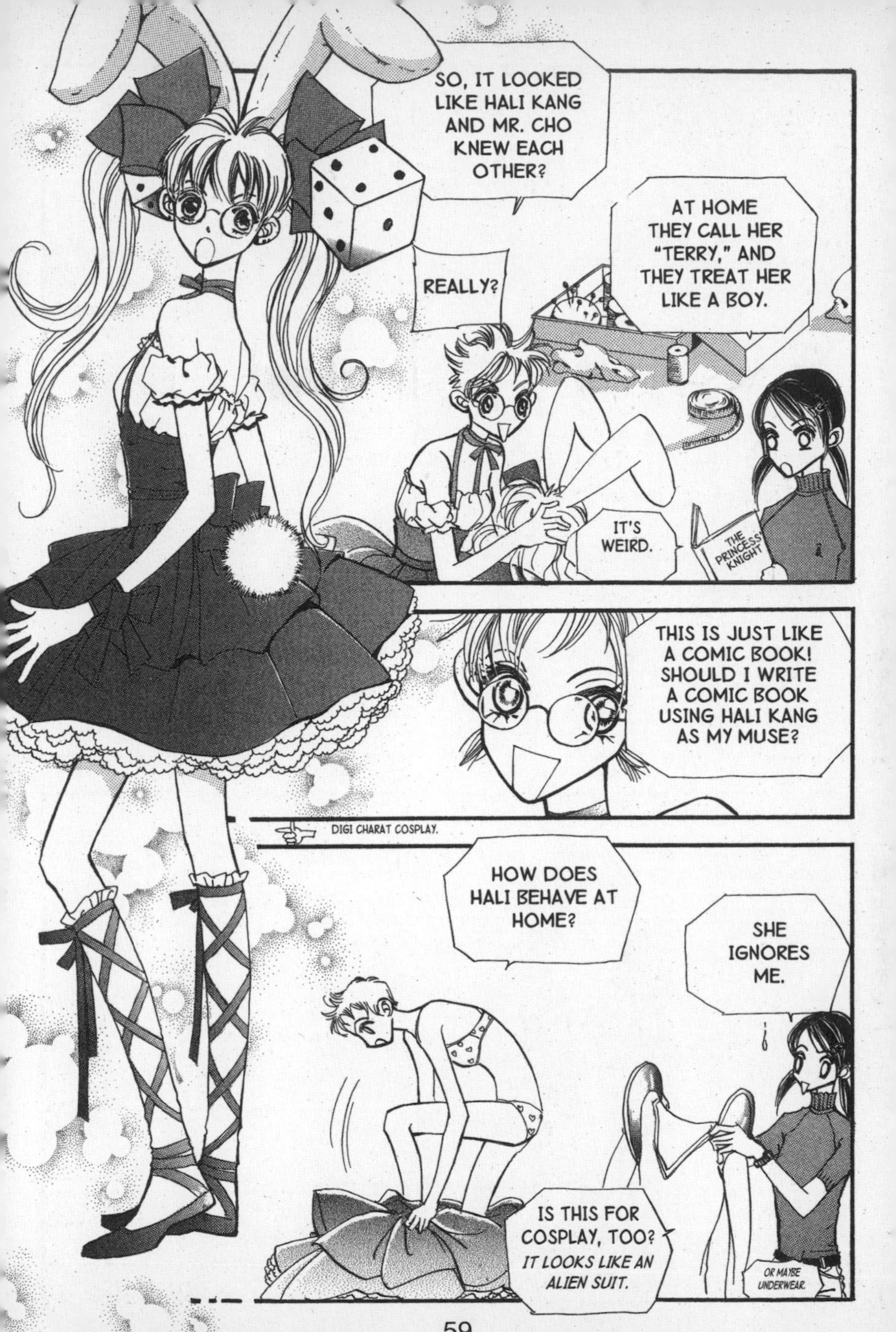
SO, IT LOOKED LIKE HALI KANG AND MR. CHO KNEW EACH OTHER?
REALLY?
AT HOME THEY CALL HER "TERRY," AND THEY TREAT HER LIKE A BOY.
IT'S WEIRD.
THE PRINCESS KNIGHT
THIS IS JUST LIKE A COMIC BOOK! SHOULD I WRITE A COMIC BOOK USING HALI KANG AS MY MUSE?
DIGI CHARAT COSPLAY.
HOW DOES HALI BEHAVE AT HOME?
SHE IGNORES ME.
IS THIS FOR COSPLAY, TOO?
IT LOOKS LIKE AN ALIEN SUIT.
OR MAYBE UNDERWEAR.

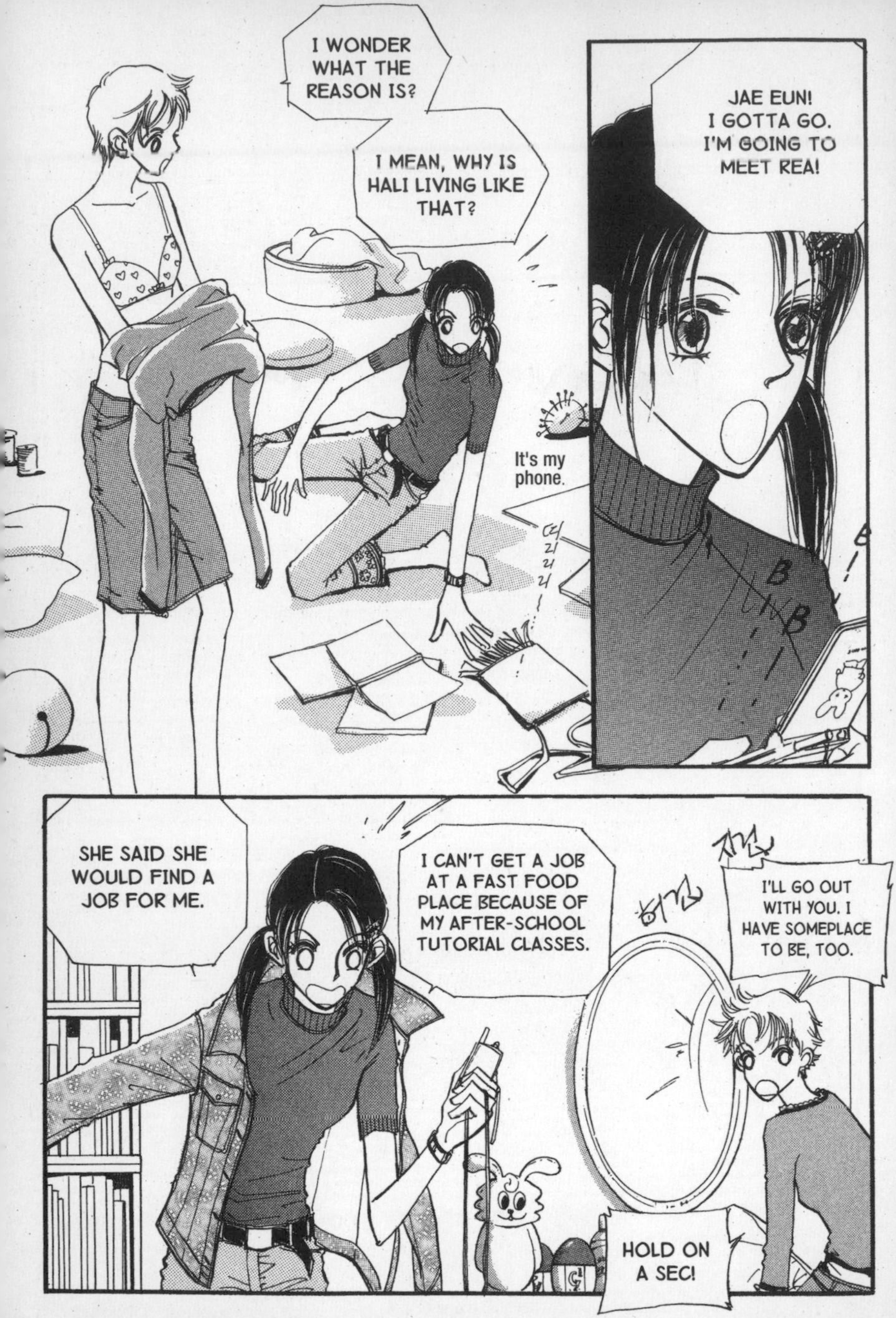

I WONDER WHAT THE REASON IS?
I MEAN, WHY IS HALI LIVING LIKE THAT?
It's my phone.
JAE EUN! I GOTTA GO. I'M GOING TO MEET REA!
B B B
SHE SAID SHE WOULD FIND A JOB FOR ME.
I CAN'T GET A JOB AT A FAST FOOD PLACE BECAUSE OF MY AFTER-SCHOOL TUTORIAL CLASSES.
I'LL GO OUT WITH YOU. I HAVE SOMEPLACE TO BE, TOO.
HOLD ON A SEC!

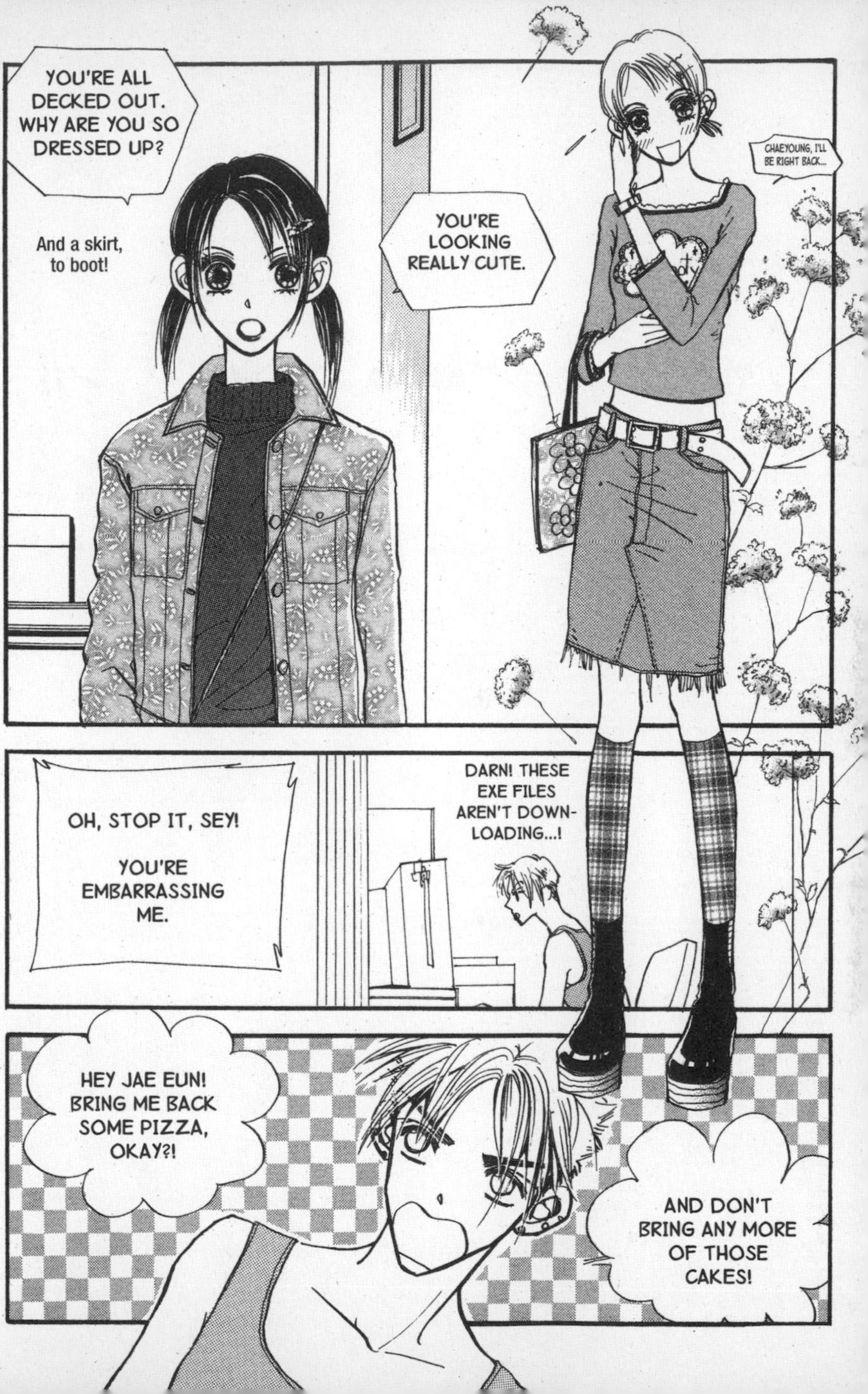
YOU'RE ALL DECKED OUT. WHY ARE YOU SO DRESSED UP?
And a skirt, to boot!
YOU'RE LOOKING REALLY CUTE.
CHAEYOUNG, I'LL BE RIGHT BACK...
OH, STOP IT, SEY!
YOU'RE EMBARRASSING ME.
DARN! THESE EXE FILES AREN'T DOWN-LOADING...!
HEY JAE EUN! BRING ME BACK SOME PIZZA, OKAY?!
AND DON'T BRING ANY MORE OF THOSE CAKES!

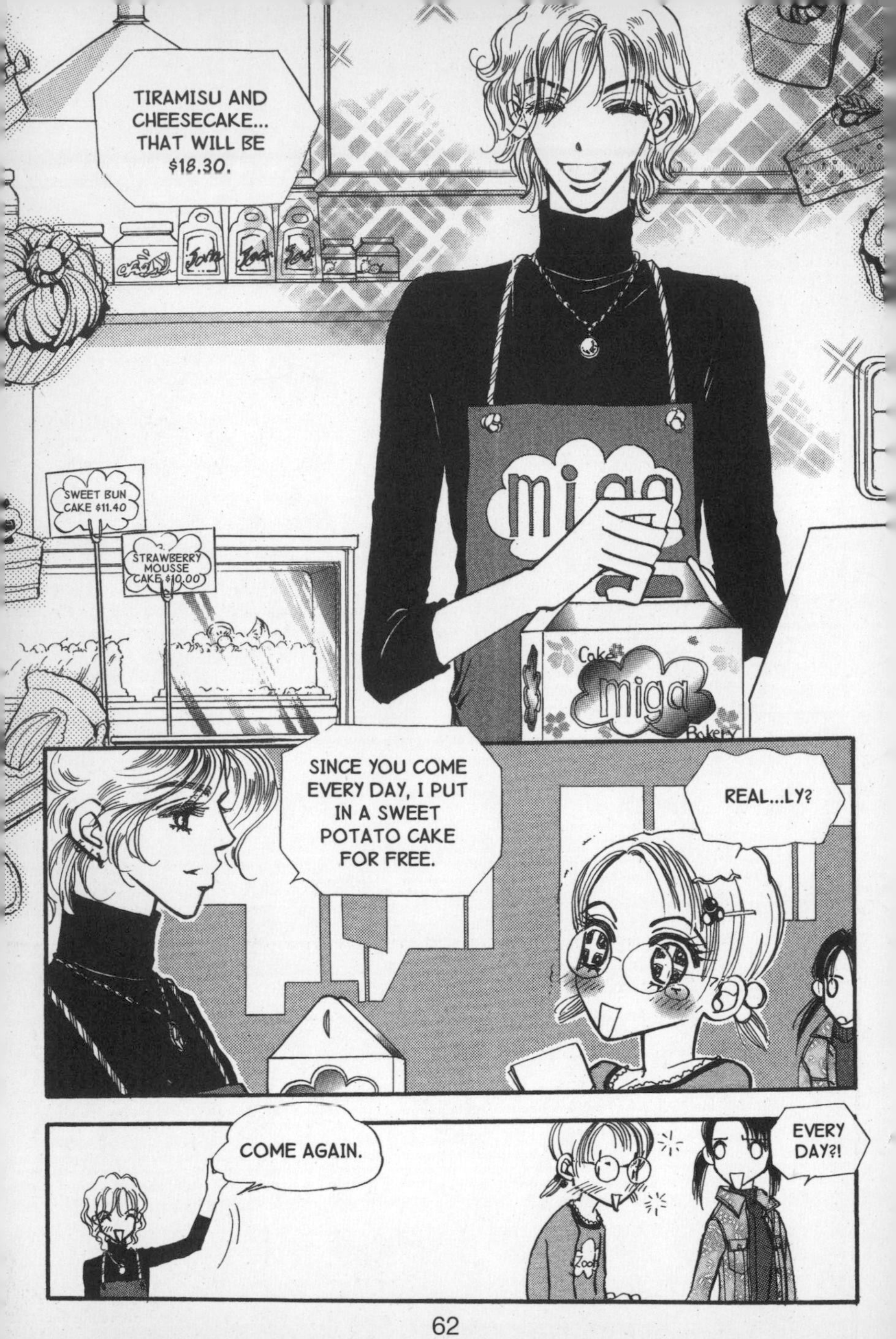
TIRAMISU AND CHEESECAKE... THAT WILL BE $18.30.
SWEET BUN CAKE $11.40
STRAWBERRY MOUSSE CAKE $10.00
miga
Cake
miga
Bakery
SINCE YOU COME EVERY DAY, I PUT IN A SWEET POTATO CAKE FOR FREE.
REAL...LY?
COME AGAIN.
EVERY DAY?!

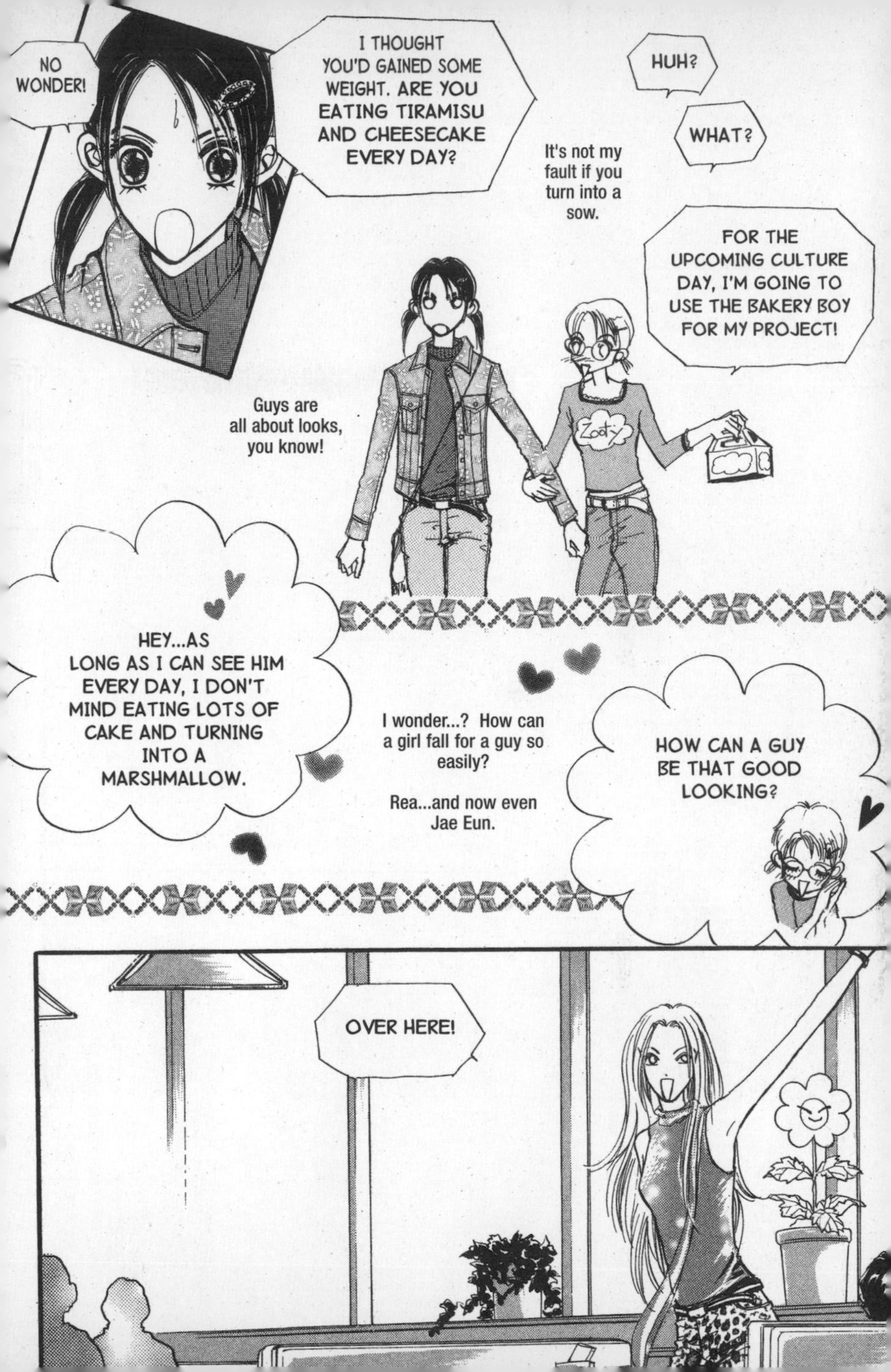
NO WONDER!
I THOUGHT YOU'D GAINED SOME WEIGHT. ARE YOU EATING TIRAMISU AND CHEESECAKE EVERY DAY?
HUH?
WHAT?
It's not my fault if you turn into a sow.
Guys are all about looks, you know!
FOR THE UPCOMING CULTURE DAY, I'M GOING TO USE THE BAKERY BOY FOR MY PROJECT!
Zooty
HEY...AS LONG AS I CAN SEE HIM EVERY DAY, I DON'T MIND EATING LOTS OF CAKE AND TURNING INTO A MARSHMALLOW.
I wonder...? How can a girl fall for a guy so easily?
Rea...and now even Jae Eun.
HOW CAN A GUY BE THAT GOOD LOOKING?
OVER HERE!

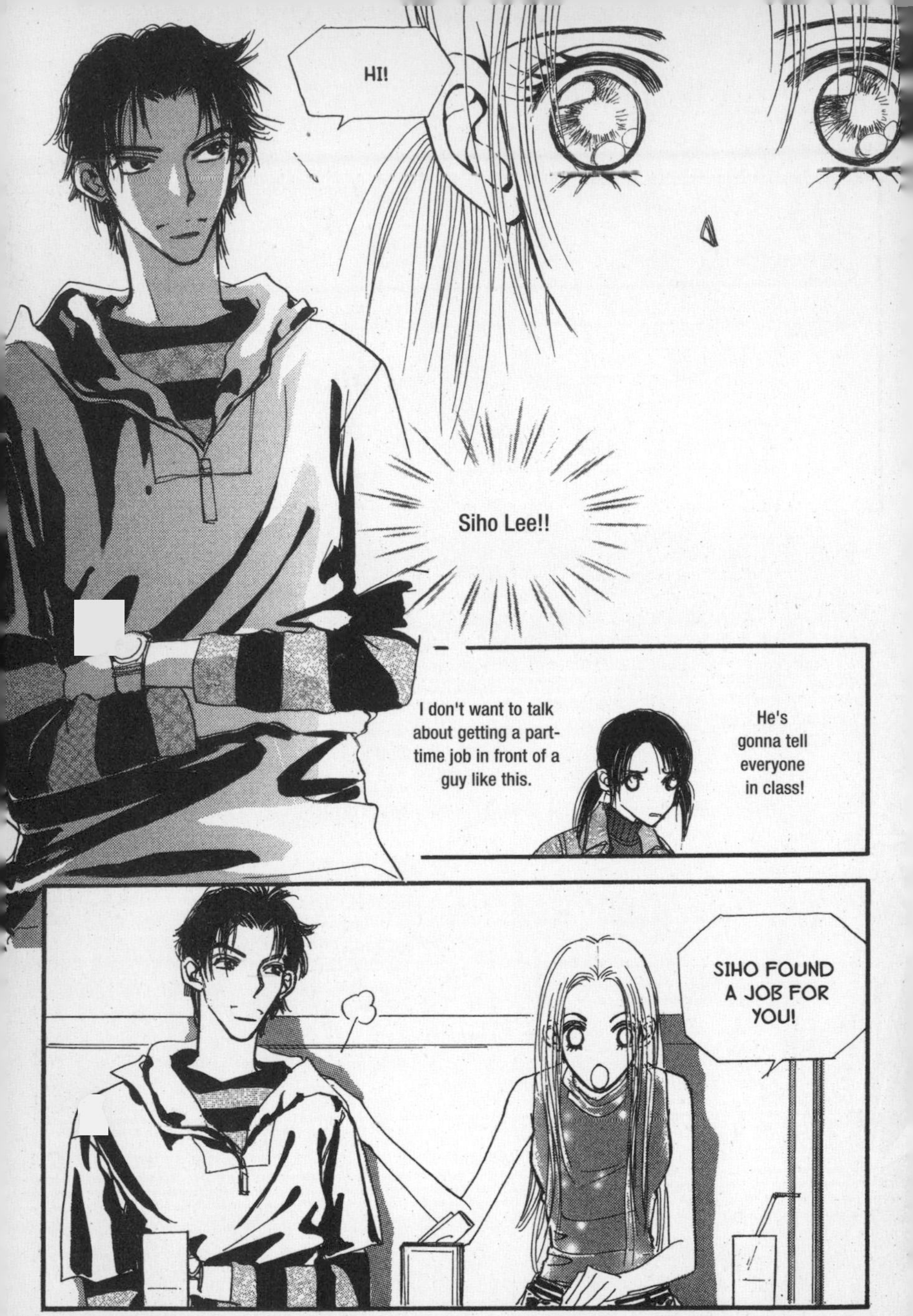
HI!
Siho Lee!!
I don't want to talk about getting a part-time job in front of a guy like this.
He's gonna tell everyone in class!
SIHO FOUND A JOB FOR YOU!

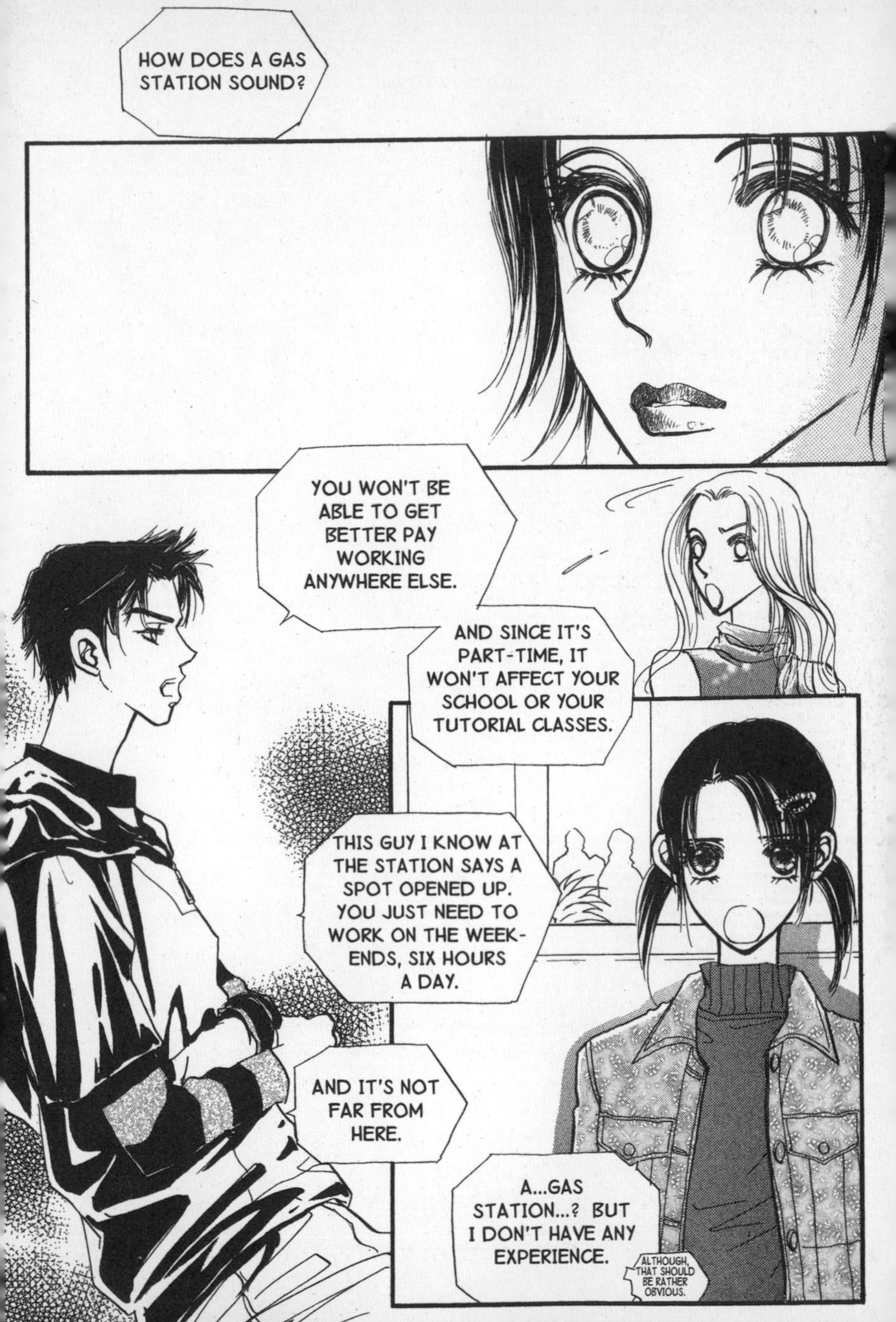
HOW DOES A GAS STATION SOUND?
YOU WON'T BE ABLE TO GET BETTER PAY WORKING ANYWHERE ELSE.
AND SINCE IT'S PART-TIME, IT WON'T AFFECT YOUR SCHOOL OR YOUR TUTORIAL CLASSES.
THIS GUY I KNOW AT THE STATION SAYS A SPOT OPENED UP. YOU JUST NEED TO WORK ON THE WEEK-ENDS, SIX HOURS A DAY.
AND IT'S NOT FAR FROM HERE.
A...GAS STATION...? BUT I DON'T HAVE ANY EXPERIENCE.
ALTHOUGH, THAT SHOULD BE RATHER OBVIOUS.

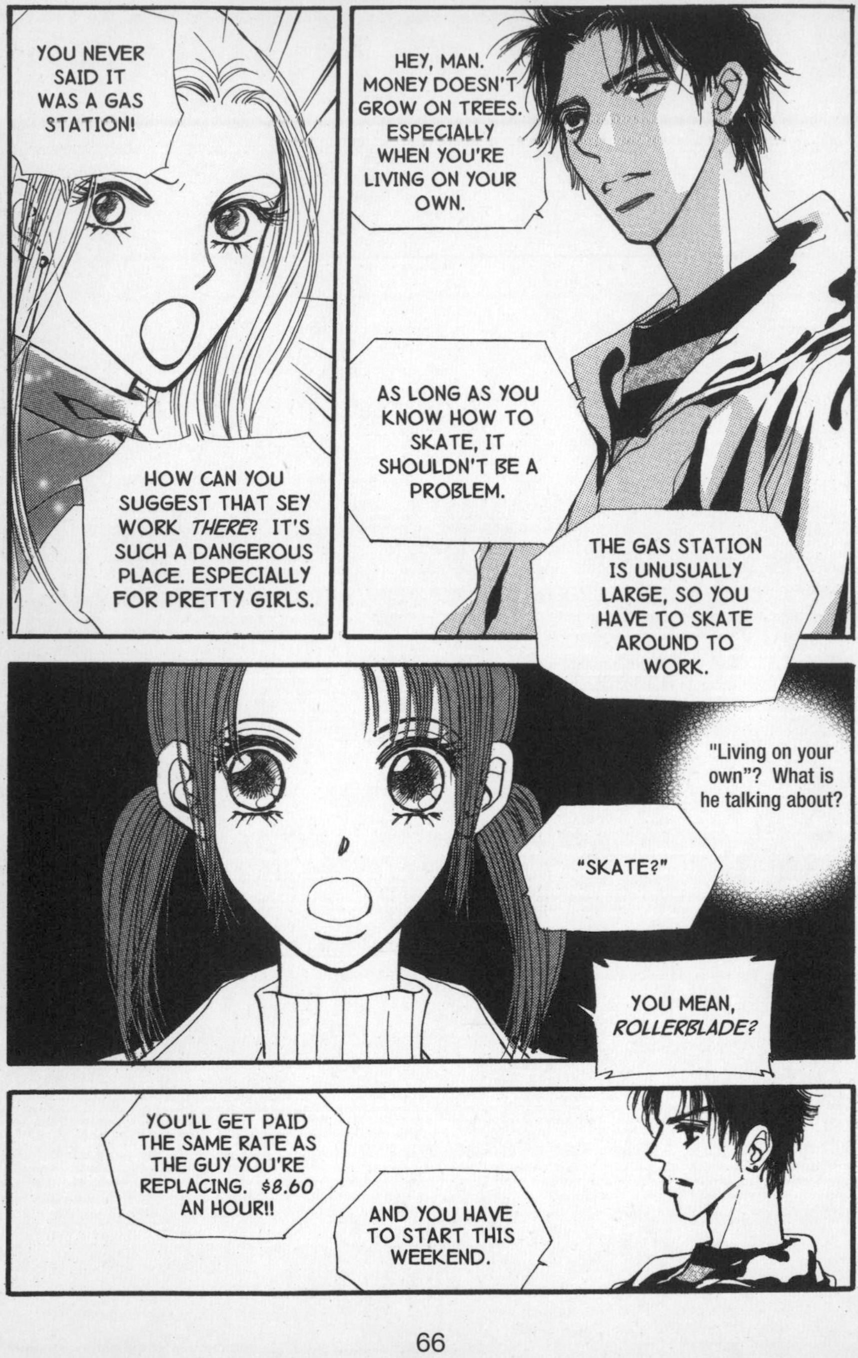
YOU NEVER SAID IT WAS A GAS STATION!
HOW CAN YOU SUGGEST THAT SEY WORK *THERE*? IT'S SUCH A DANGEROUS PLACE. ESPECIALLY FOR PRETTY GIRLS.
HEY, MAN. MONEY DOESN'T GROW ON TREES. ESPECIALLY WHEN YOU'RE LIVING ON YOUR OWN.
AS LONG AS YOU KNOW HOW TO SKATE, IT SHOULDN'T BE A PROBLEM.
THE GAS STATION IS UNUSUALLY LARGE, SO YOU HAVE TO SKATE AROUND TO WORK.
"Living on your own"? What is he talking about?
"SKATE?"
YOU MEAN, *ROLLERBLADE?*
YOU'LL GET PAID THE SAME RATE AS THE GUY YOU'RE REPLACING. *$8.60* AN HOUR!!
AND YOU HAVE TO START THIS WEEKEND.

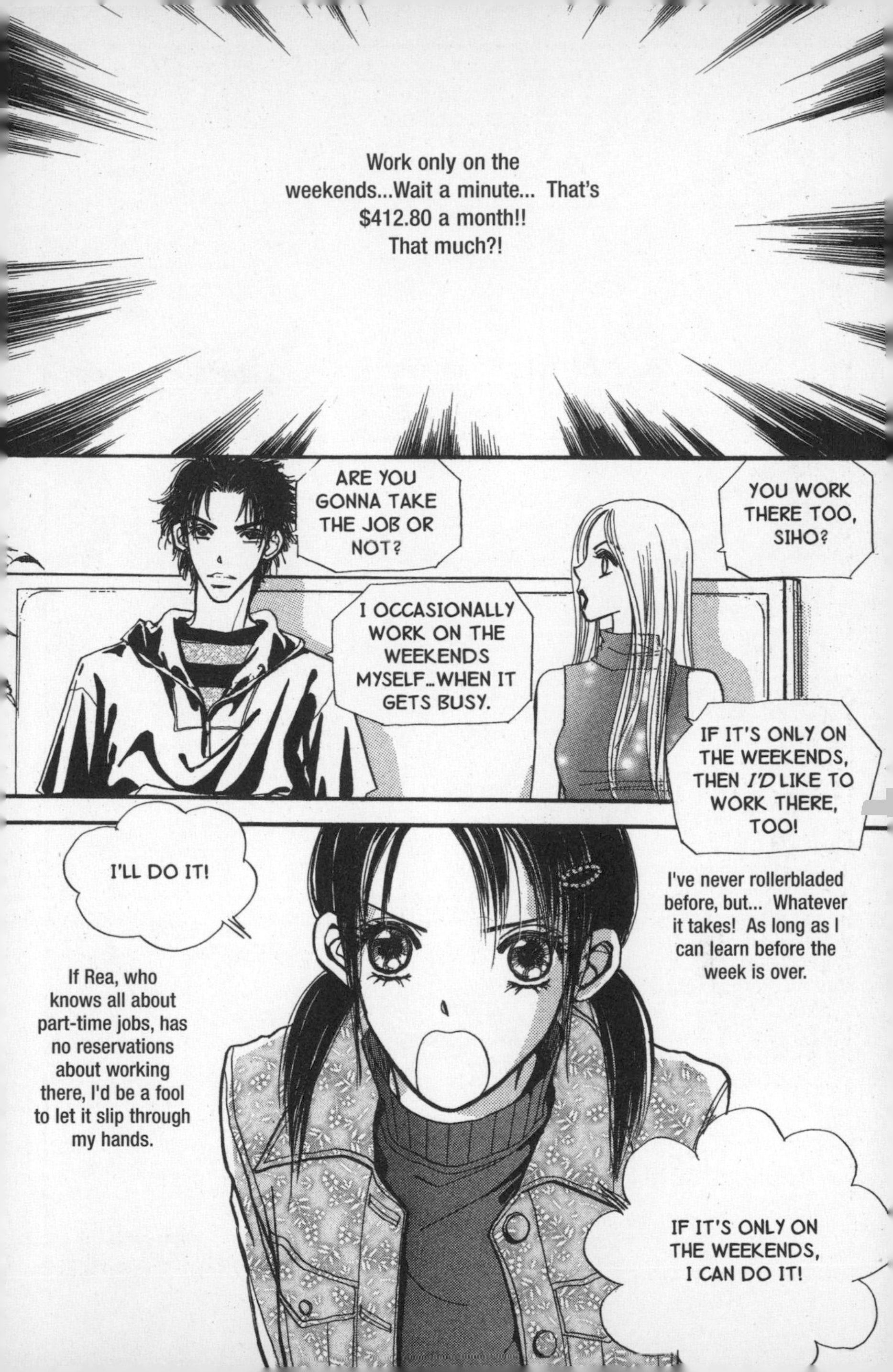
Work only on the weekends...Wait a minute... That's $412.80 a month!! That much?!
ARE YOU GONNA TAKE THE JOB OR NOT?
I OCCASIONALLY WORK ON THE WEEKENDS MYSELF...WHEN IT GETS BUSY.
YOU WORK THERE TOO, SIHO?
IF IT'S ONLY ON THE WEEKENDS, THEN I'D LIKE TO WORK THERE, TOO!
I'LL DO IT!
If Rea, who knows all about part-time jobs, has no reservations about working there, I'd be a fool to let it slip through my hands.
I've never rollerbladed before, but... Whatever it takes! As long as I can learn before the week is over.
IF IT'S ONLY ON THE WEEKENDS, I CAN DO IT!

GOOD!

All these events were kicked into motion because I was too simple-minded, stupid and self-absorbed!

She must be having a hard time, too. I heard she doesn't have a mother, and she's living at someone's house.

SALE 30%.

I THINK HE MISUNDERSTOOD WHAT I TOLD HIM ABOUT SEY. SIHO, YOU'RE IMPOSSIBLE...

EEK! $161.00.

They're this expensive?

$856.00!

HERE'S ONE FOR $128.00.

WOW, IT'S SO HEAVY.

IT'S AN INVESTMENT. I HAVE TO THINK OF IT AS AN INVESTMENT.

HOW AM I GONNA LEARN HOW TO SKATE BY THIS WEEKEND?

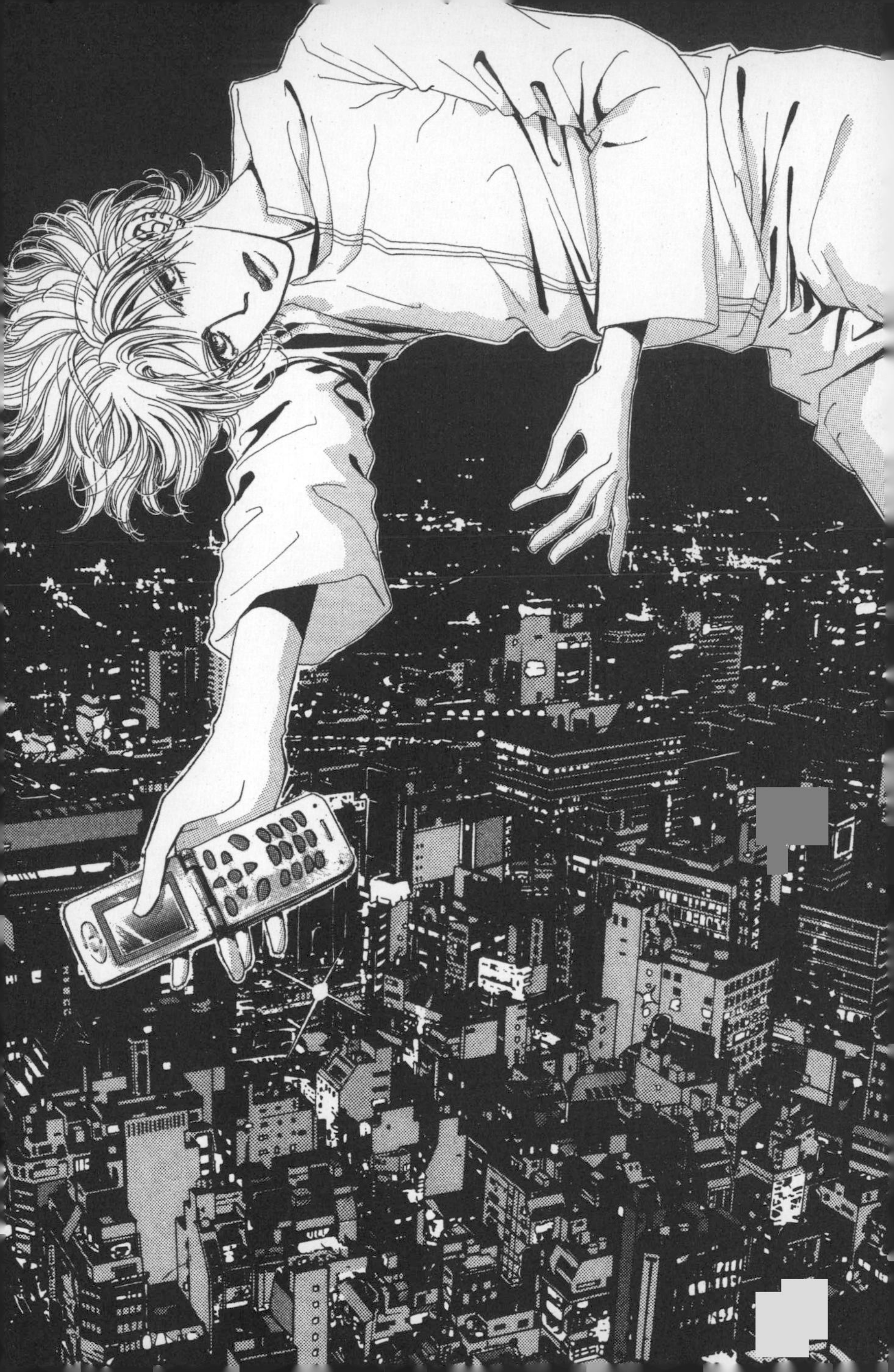

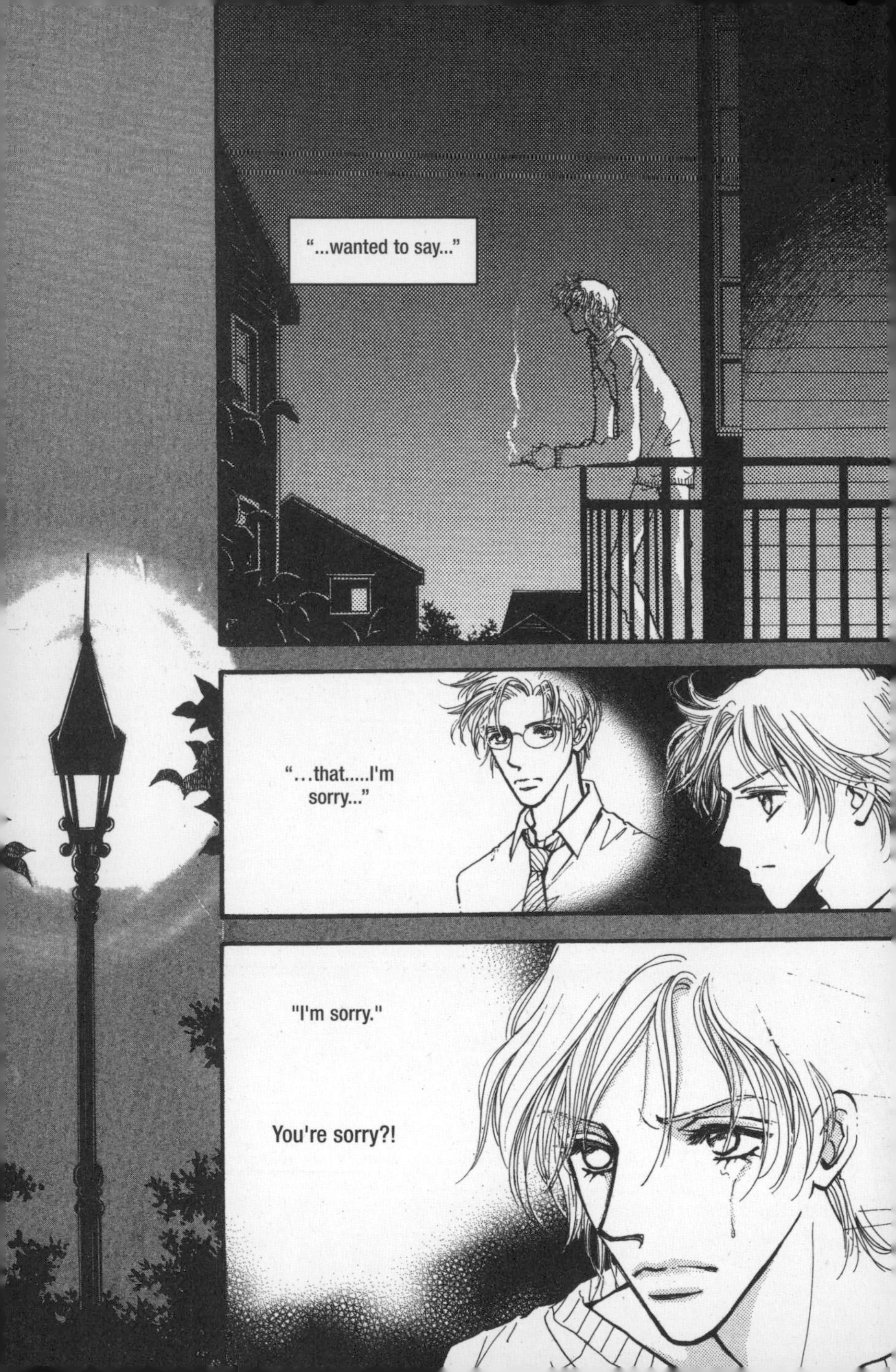
"...wanted to say..."
"...that.....I'm sorry..."
"I'm sorry."
You're sorry?!

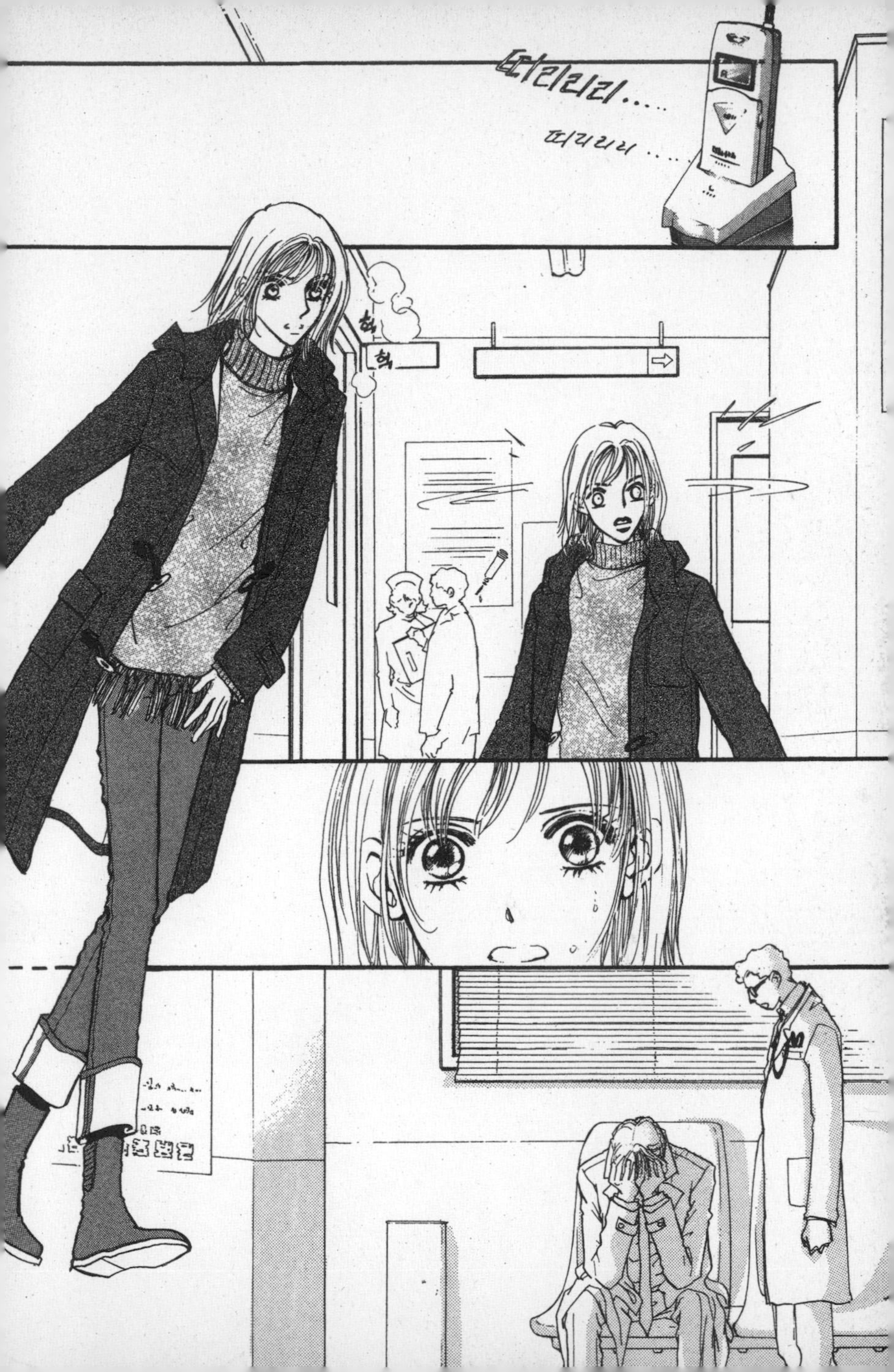
따리리리......
띠리리리......
헉
헉

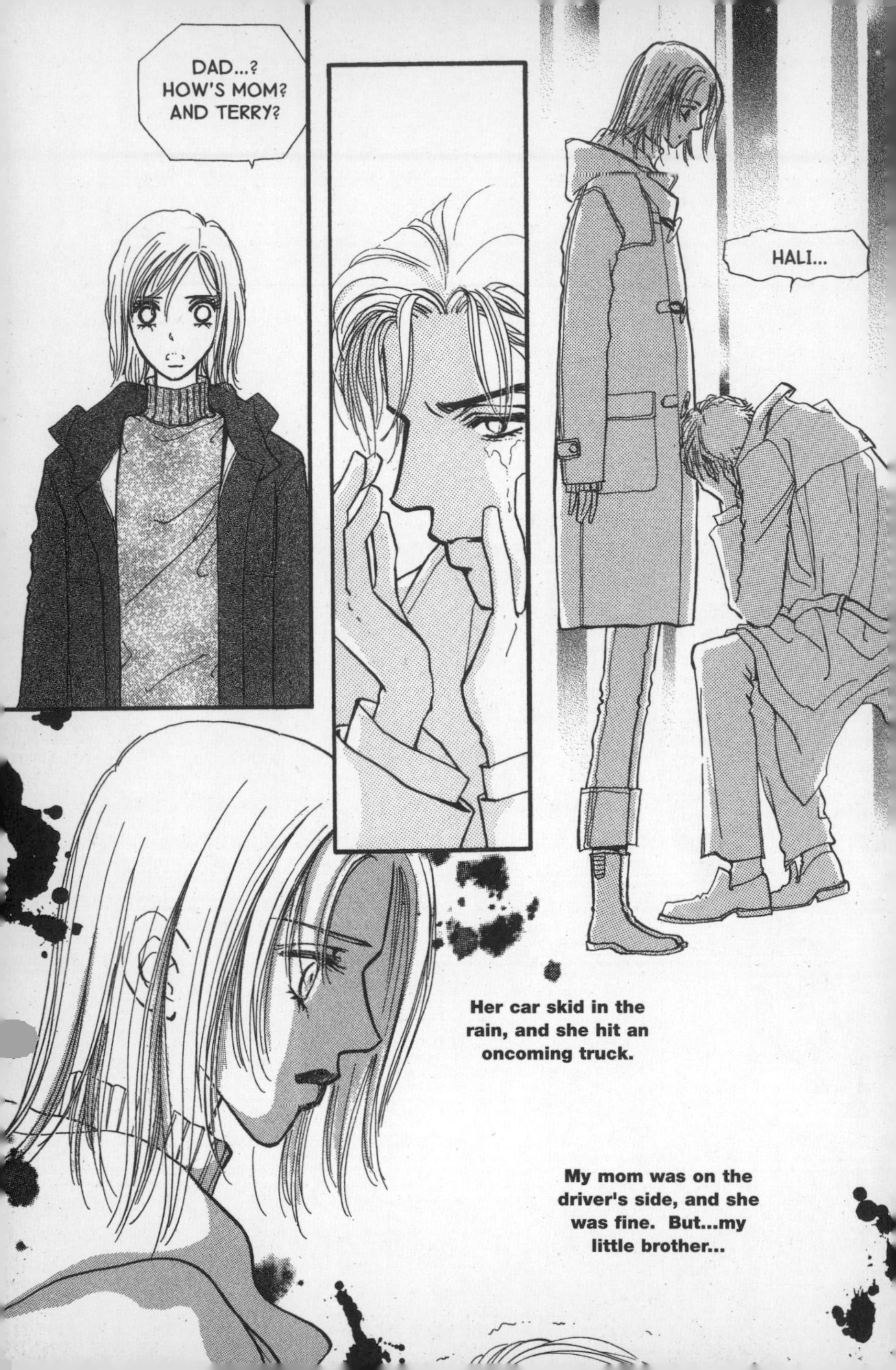
DAD...? HOW'S MOM? AND TERRY?
HALI...
Her car skid in the rain, and she hit an oncoming truck.
My mom was on the driver's side, and she was fine. But...my little brother...

A cold winter
became colder.
He was only 14.

My rival.
My sibling.

Dad and I fought with
him constantly. He
was only a year
younger than me, and
he had received all of
mom's love.

My mom could never
have imagined such
a tragedy.

One moment, he was
riding in the car with
her. And then...he
was gone.

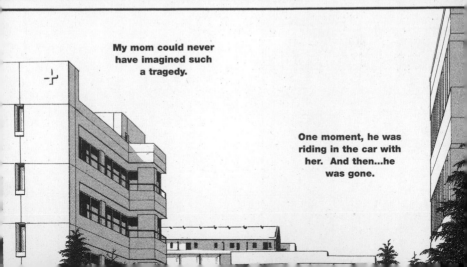

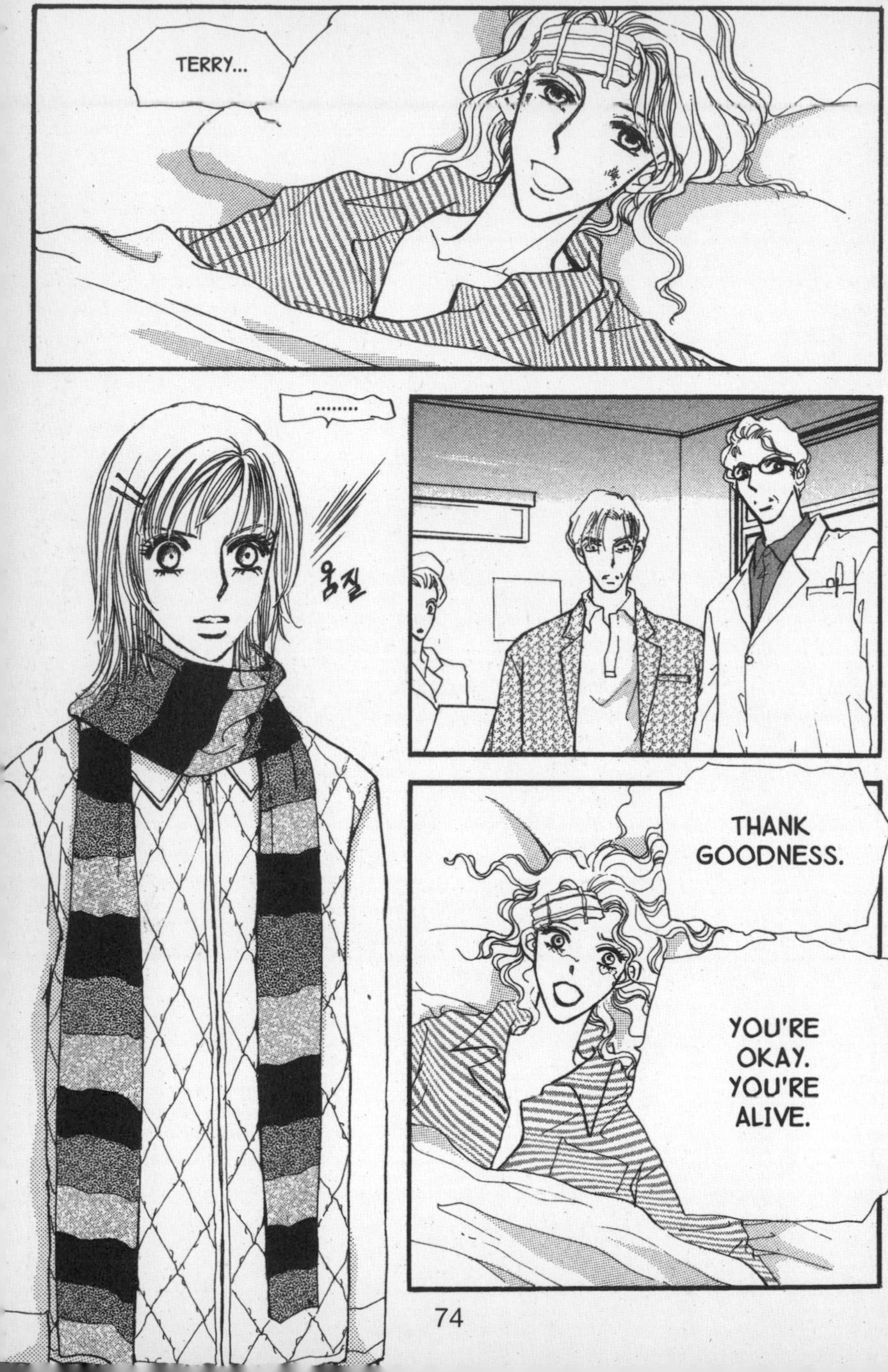

TERRY...
....
움찔
THANK GOODNESS.
YOU'RE OKAY. YOU'RE ALIVE.

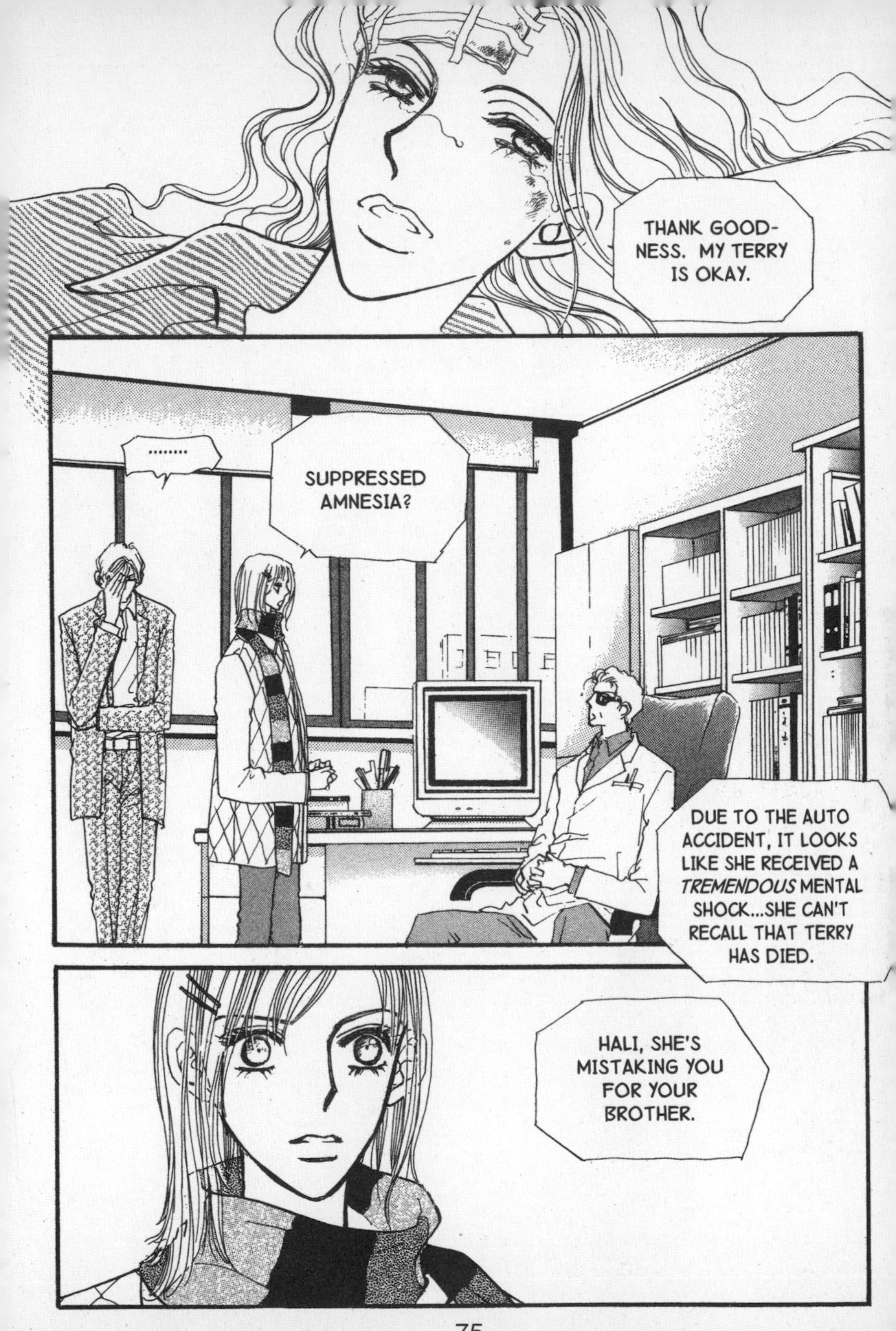
THANK GOOD-NESS. MY TERRY IS OKAY.
....
SUPPRESSED AMNESIA?
DUE TO THE AUTO ACCIDENT, IT LOOKS LIKE SHE RECEIVED A *TREMENDOUS* MENTAL SHOCK...SHE CAN'T RECALL THAT TERRY HAS DIED.
HALI, SHE'S MISTAKING YOU FOR YOUR BROTHER.

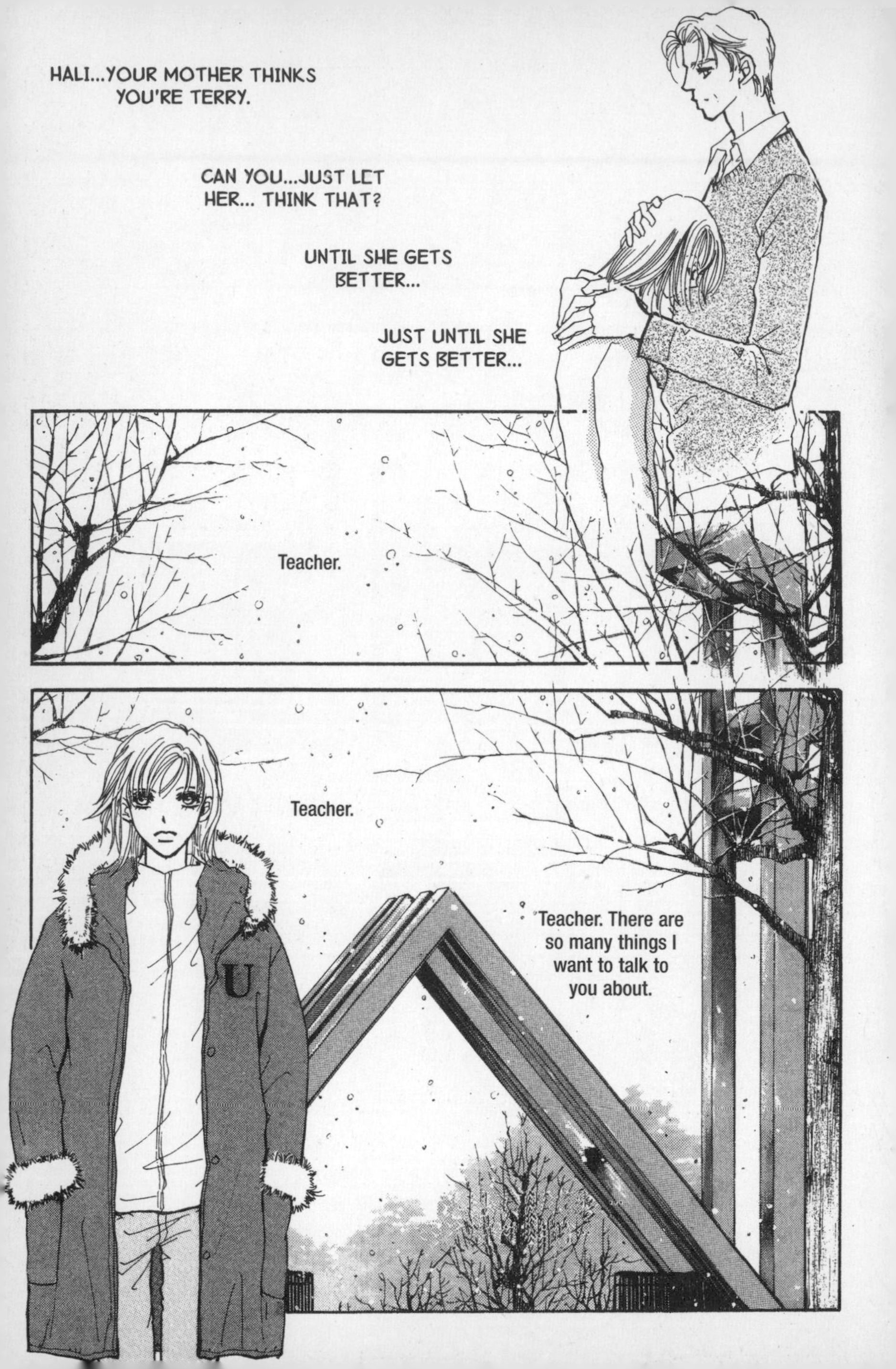
HALI...YOUR MOTHER THINKS YOU'RE TERRY.
CAN YOU...JUST LET HER... THINK THAT?
UNTIL SHE GETS BETTER...
JUST UNTIL SHE GETS BETTER...
Teacher.
Teacher.
Teacher. There are so many things I want to talk to you about.
U

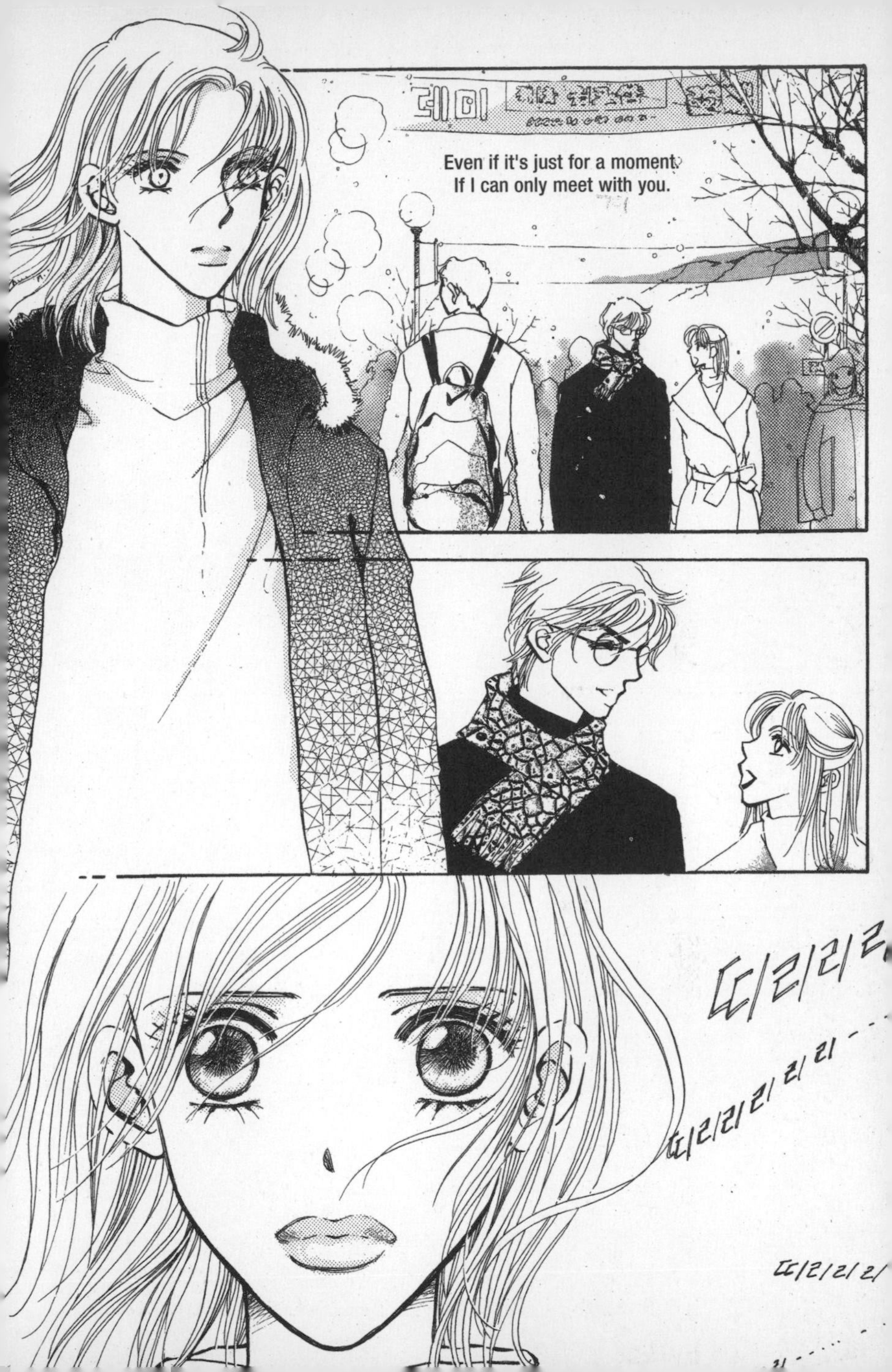
Even if it's just for a moment.
If I can only meet with you.
띠리리리
띠리리리리리리
띠리리리

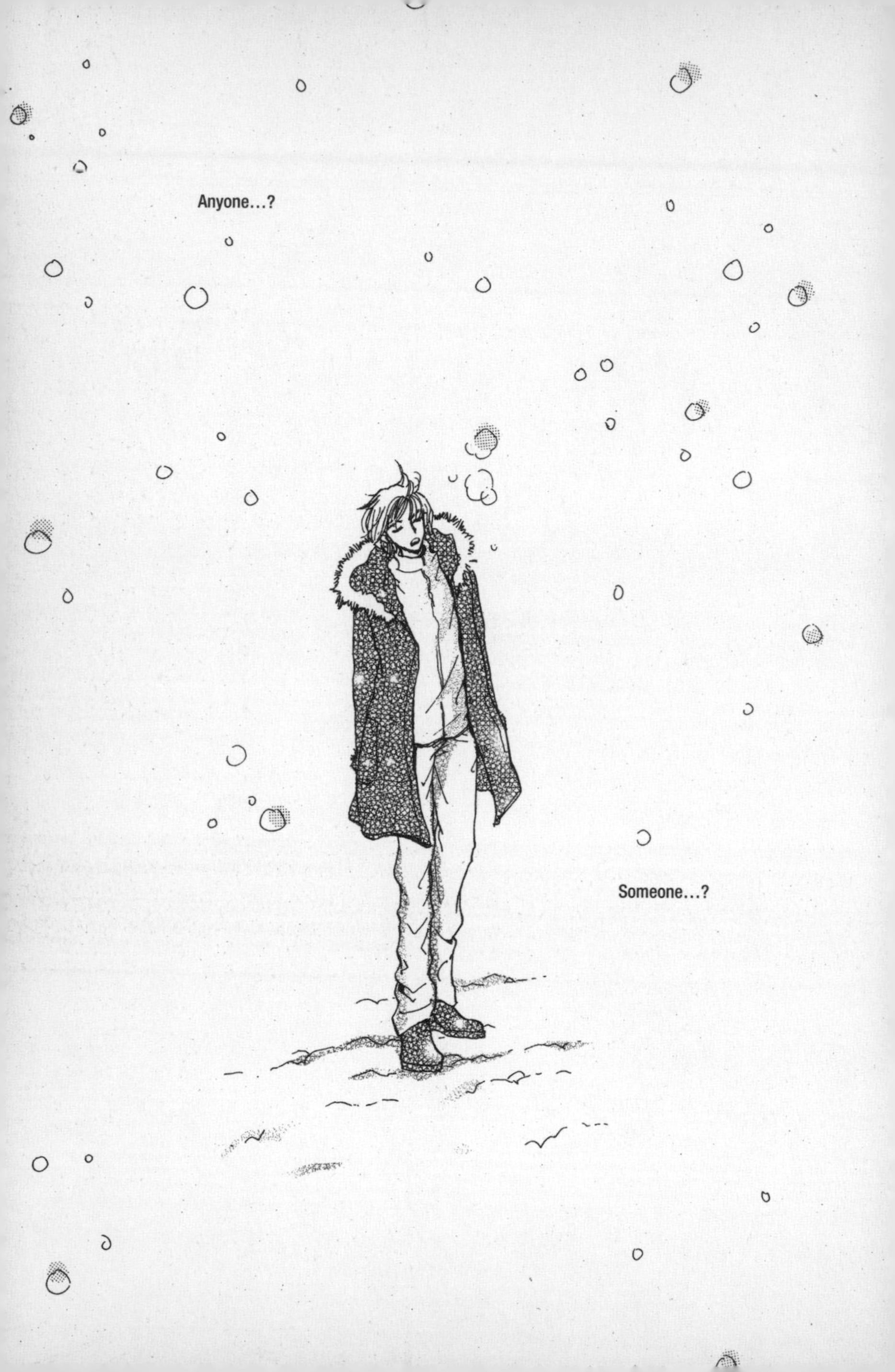
Anyone...?
Someone...?

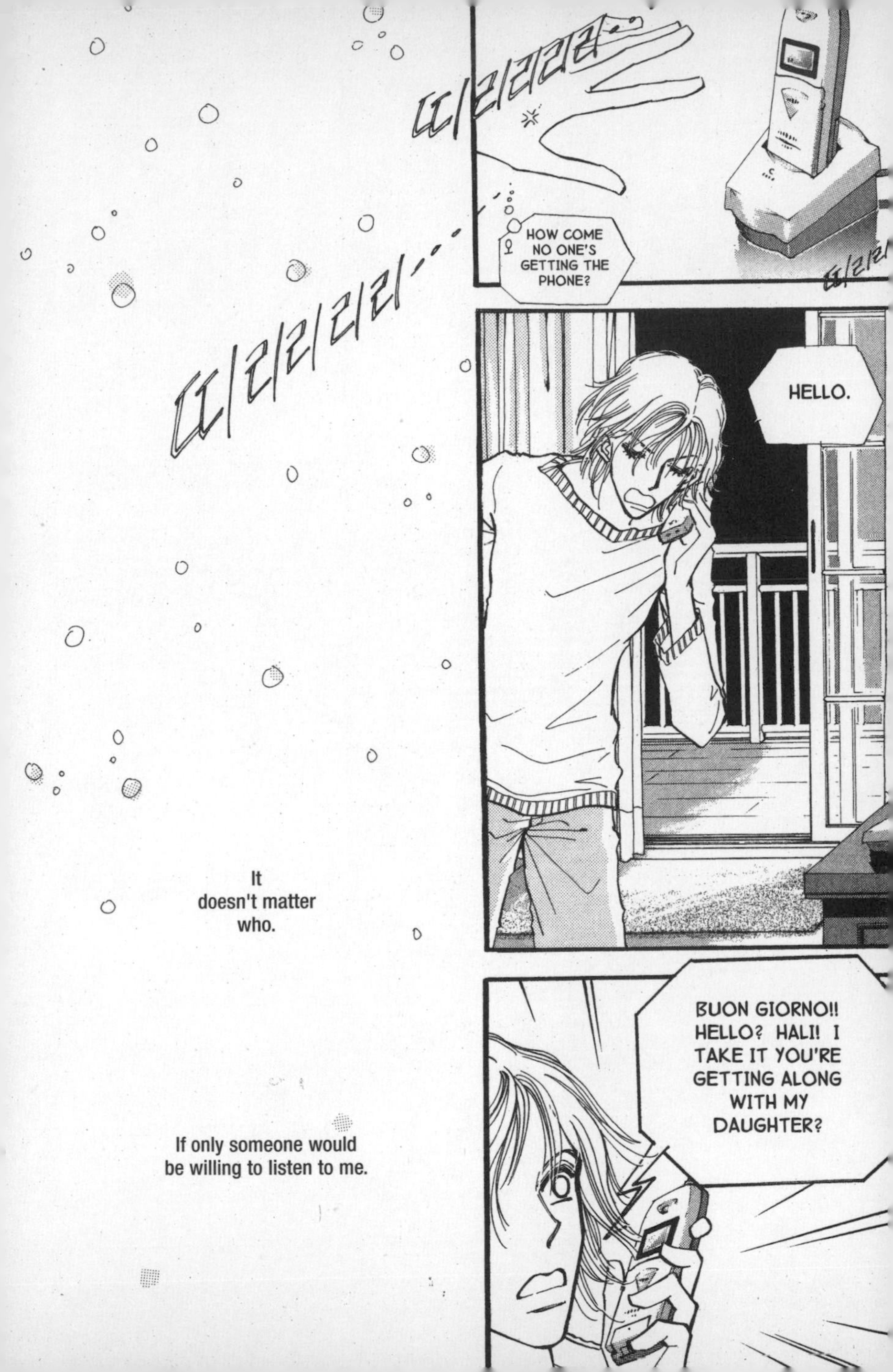

It doesn't matter who.
If only someone would be willing to listen to me.
HOW COME NO ONE'S GETTING THE PHONE?
HELLO.
BUON GIORNO!! HELLO? HALI! I TAKE IT YOU'RE GETTING ALONG WITH MY DAUGHTER?

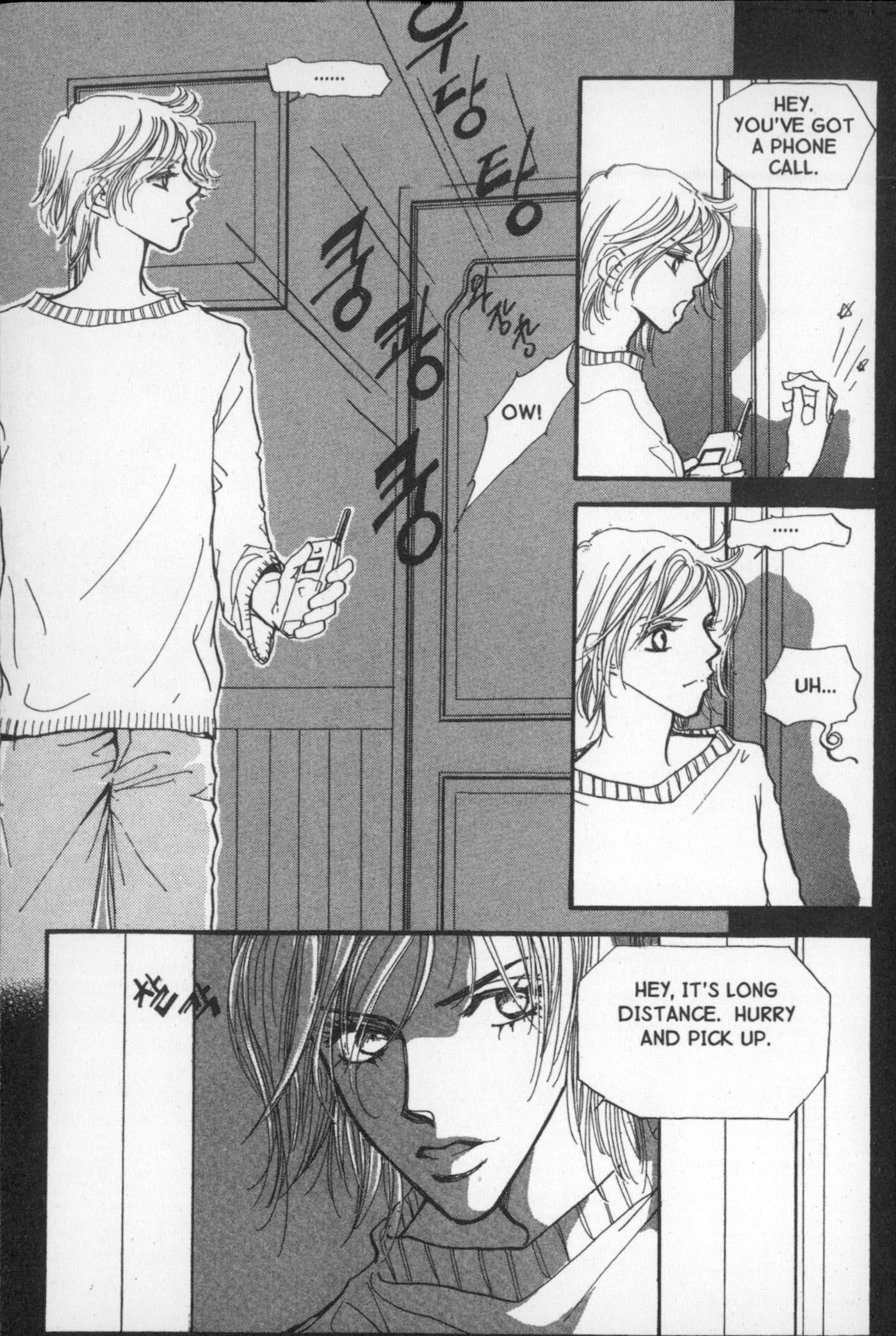

......
우당탕
쿵쾅쿵
와장창
OW!
HEY. YOU'VE GOT A PHONE CALL.
.....
UH...
HEY, IT'S LONG DISTANCE. HURRY AND PICK UP.

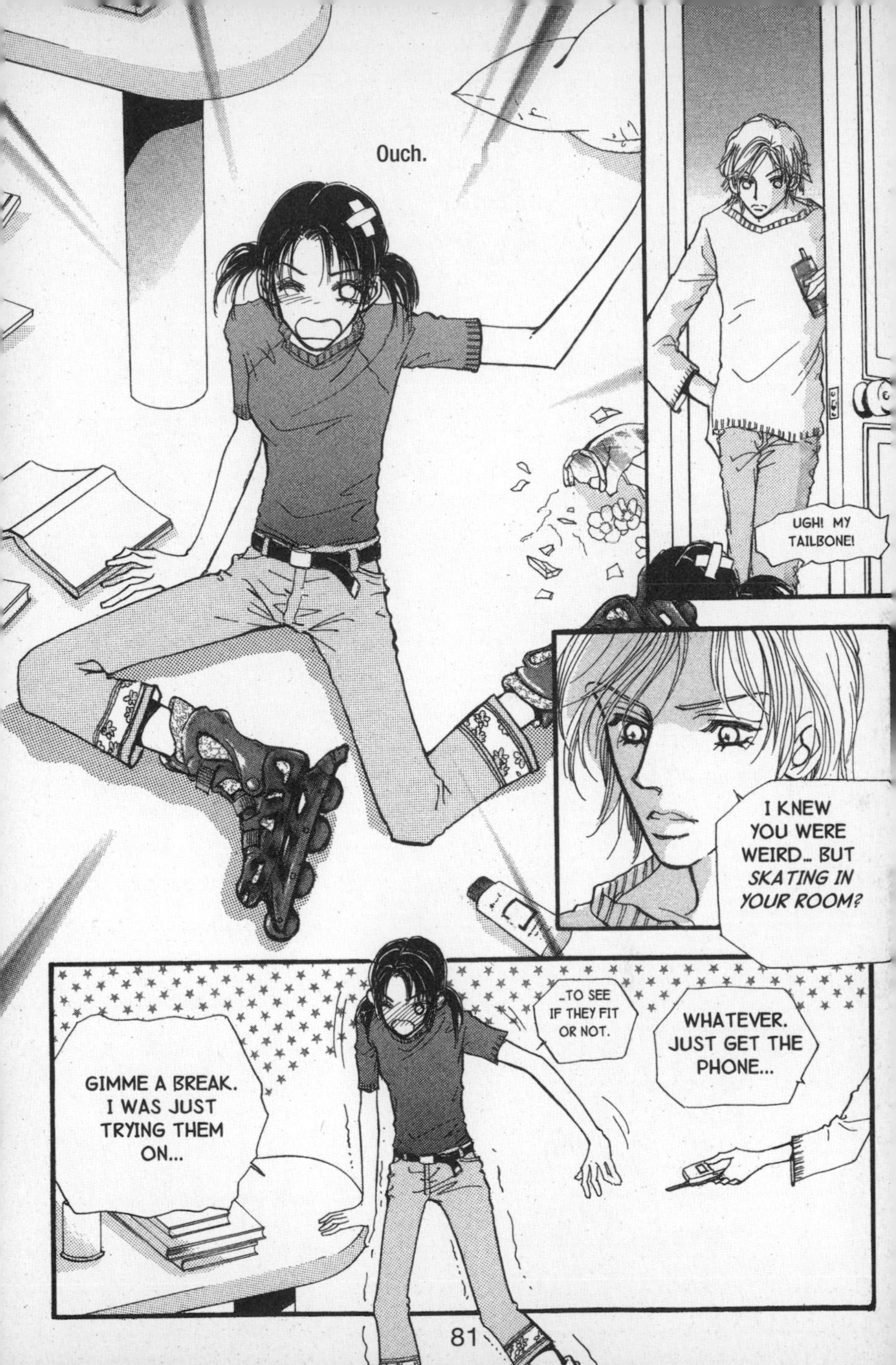
Ouch.
UGH! MY TAILBONE!
I KNEW YOU WERE WEIRD... BUT SKATING IN YOUR ROOM?
GIMME A BREAK. I WAS JUST TRYING THEM ON...
...TO SEE IF THEY FIT OR NOT.
WHATEVER. JUST GET THE PHONE...

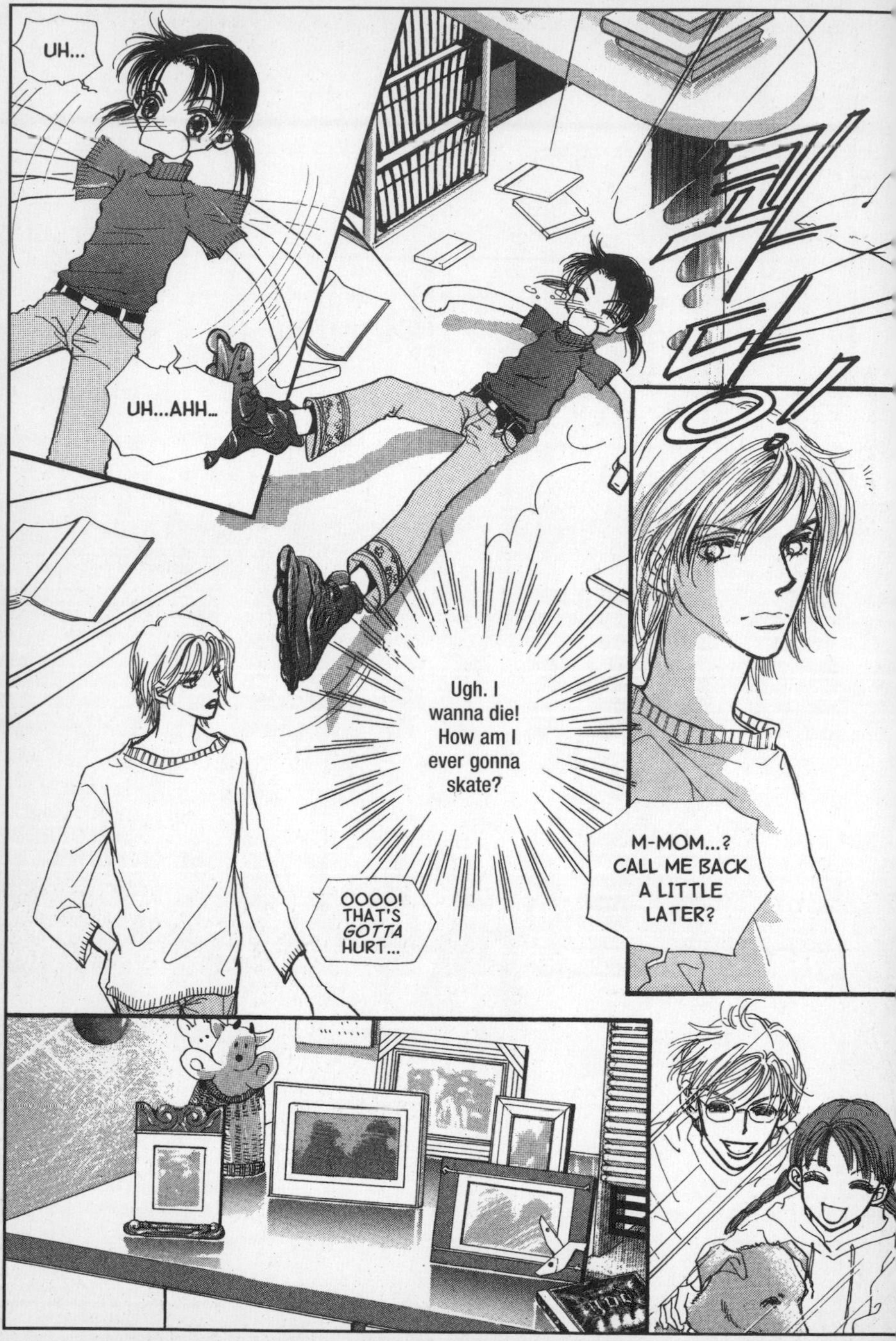
UH...
UH...AHH...
Ugh. I wanna die! How am I ever gonna skate?
OOOO! THAT'S *GOTTA* HURT...
M-MOM...? CALL ME BACK A LITTLE LATER?

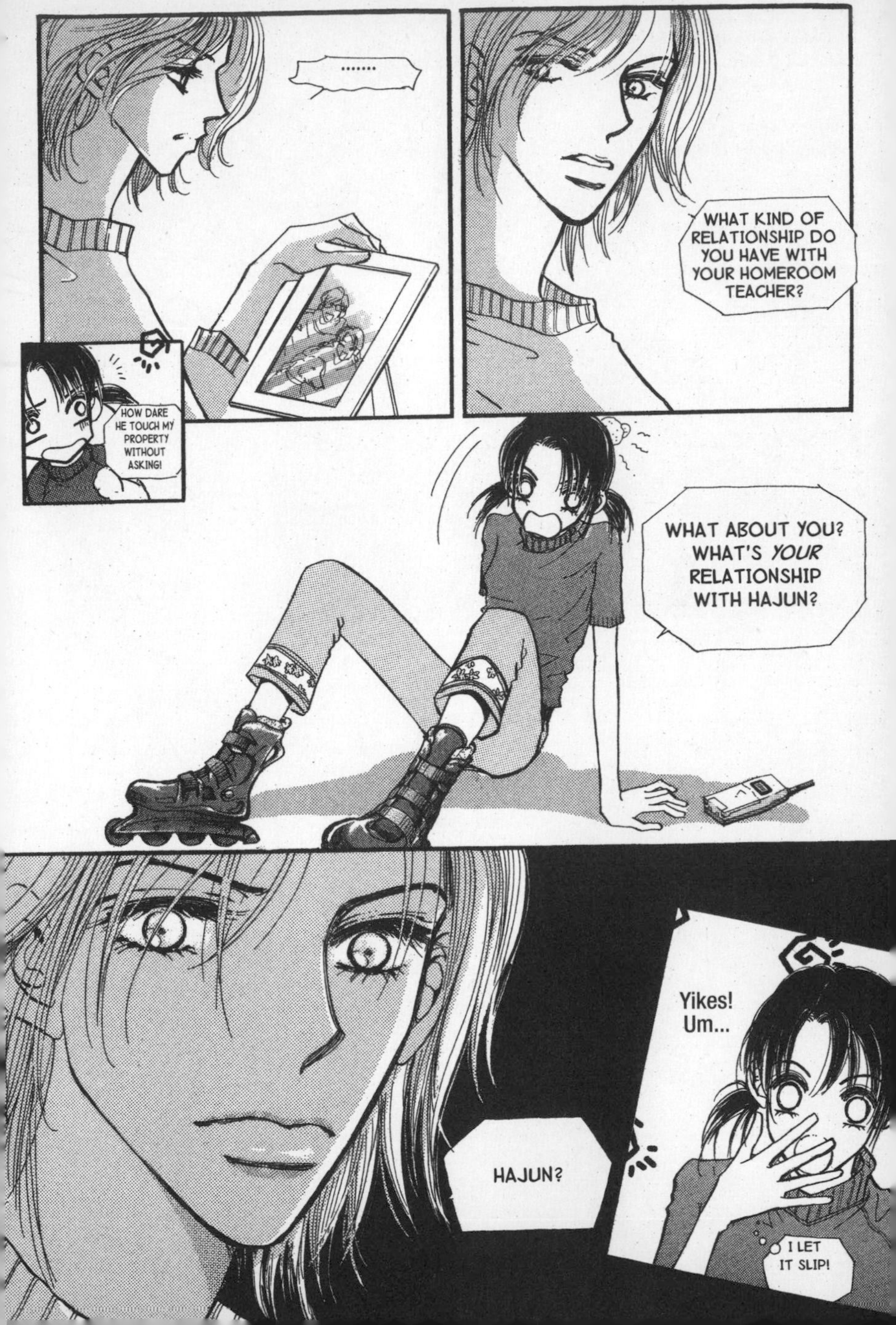
....
WHAT KIND OF RELATIONSHIP DO YOU HAVE WITH YOUR HOMEROOM TEACHER?
HOW DARE HE TOUCH MY PROPERTY WITHOUT ASKING!
WHAT ABOUT YOU? WHAT'S *YOUR* RELATIONSHIP WITH HAJUN?
HAJUN?
Yikes! Um...
I LET IT SLIP!

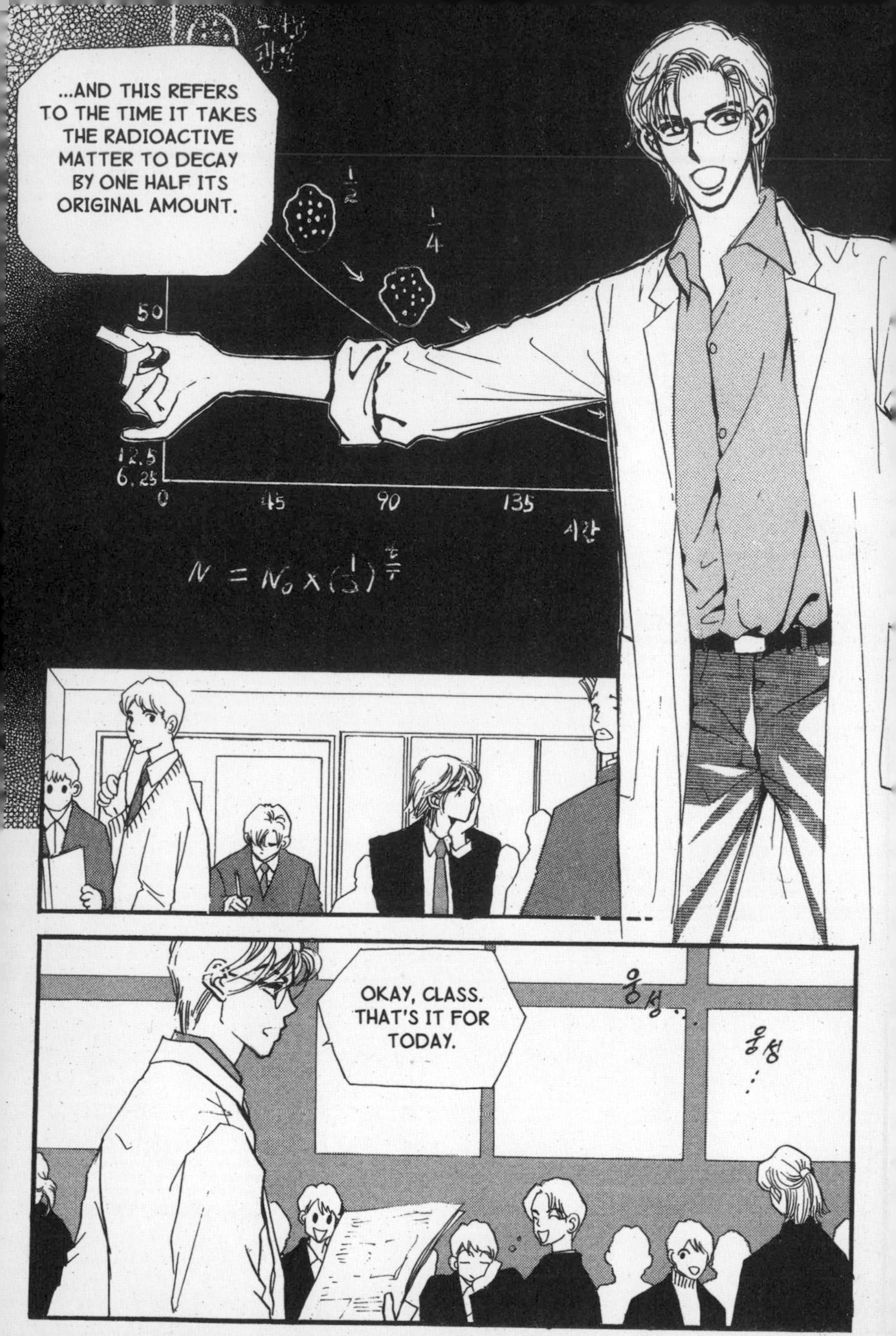
...AND THIS REFERS TO THE TIME IT TAKES THE RADIOACTIVE MATTER TO DECAY BY ONE HALF ITS ORIGINAL AMOUNT.
1/2
1/4
50
12.5
6.25
0
45
90
135
시간
OKAY, CLASS. THAT'S IT FOR TODAY.
웅성...
웅성...

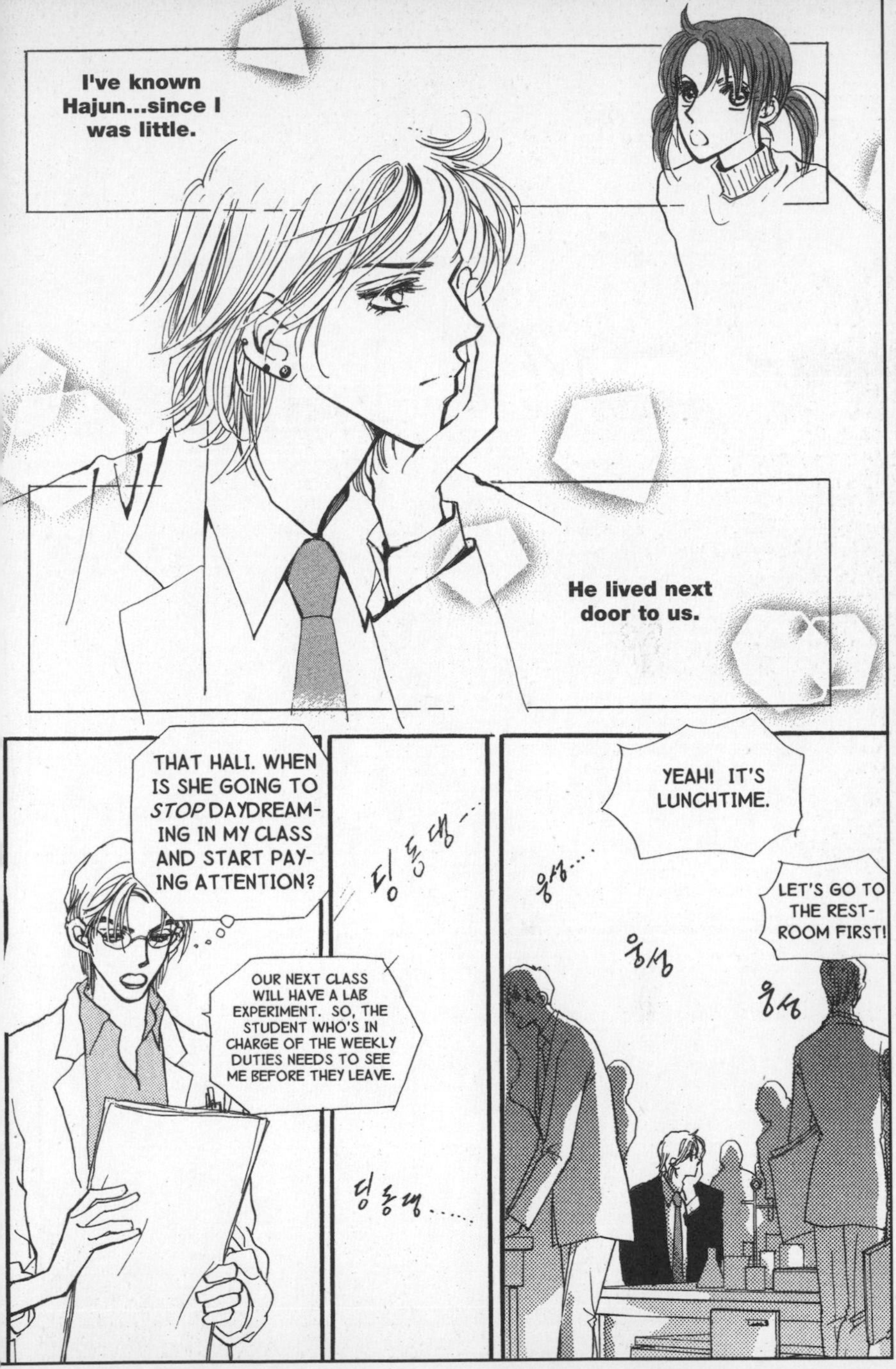
I've known Hajun...since I was little.
He lived next door to us.
THAT HALI. WHEN IS SHE GOING TO *STOP* DAYDREAMING IN MY CLASS AND START PAYING ATTENTION?
OUR NEXT CLASS WILL HAVE A LAB EXPERIMENT. SO, THE STUDENT WHO'S IN CHARGE OF THE WEEKLY DUTIES NEEDS TO SEE ME BEFORE THEY LEAVE.
딩동댕~
딩동댕......
YEAH! IT'S LUNCHTIME.
웅성....
LET'S GO TO THE RESTROOM FIRST!
웅성
웅성

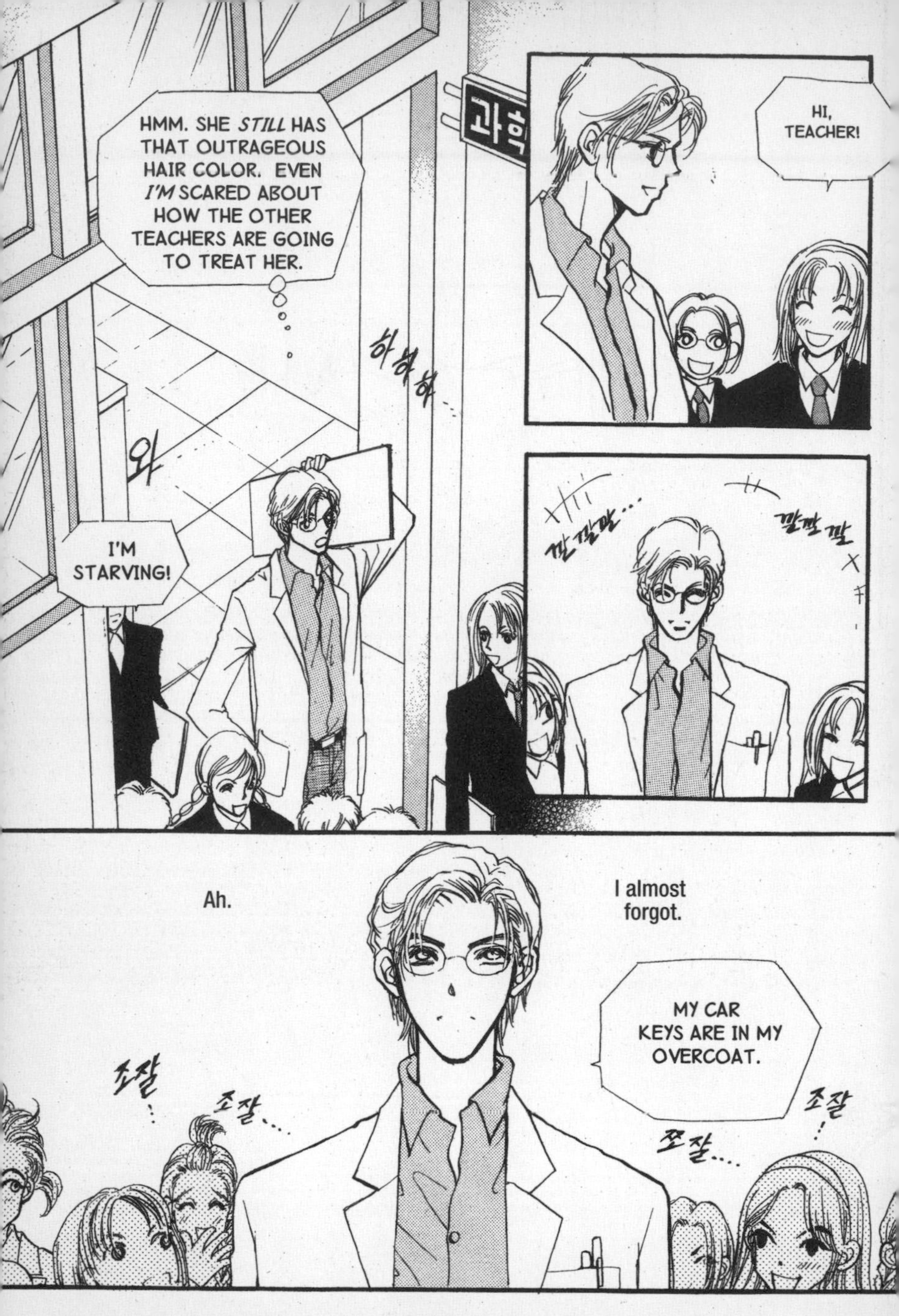
HMM. SHE *STILL* HAS THAT OUTRAGEOUS HAIR COLOR. EVEN *I'M* SCARED ABOUT HOW THE OTHER TEACHERS ARE GOING TO TREAT HER.
하하하
와
I'M STARVING!
HI, TEACHER!
깔깔깔...
깔깔 깔
Ah.
I almost forgot.
MY CAR KEYS ARE IN MY OVERCOAT.
조잘
조잘...
쪼잘...
조잘

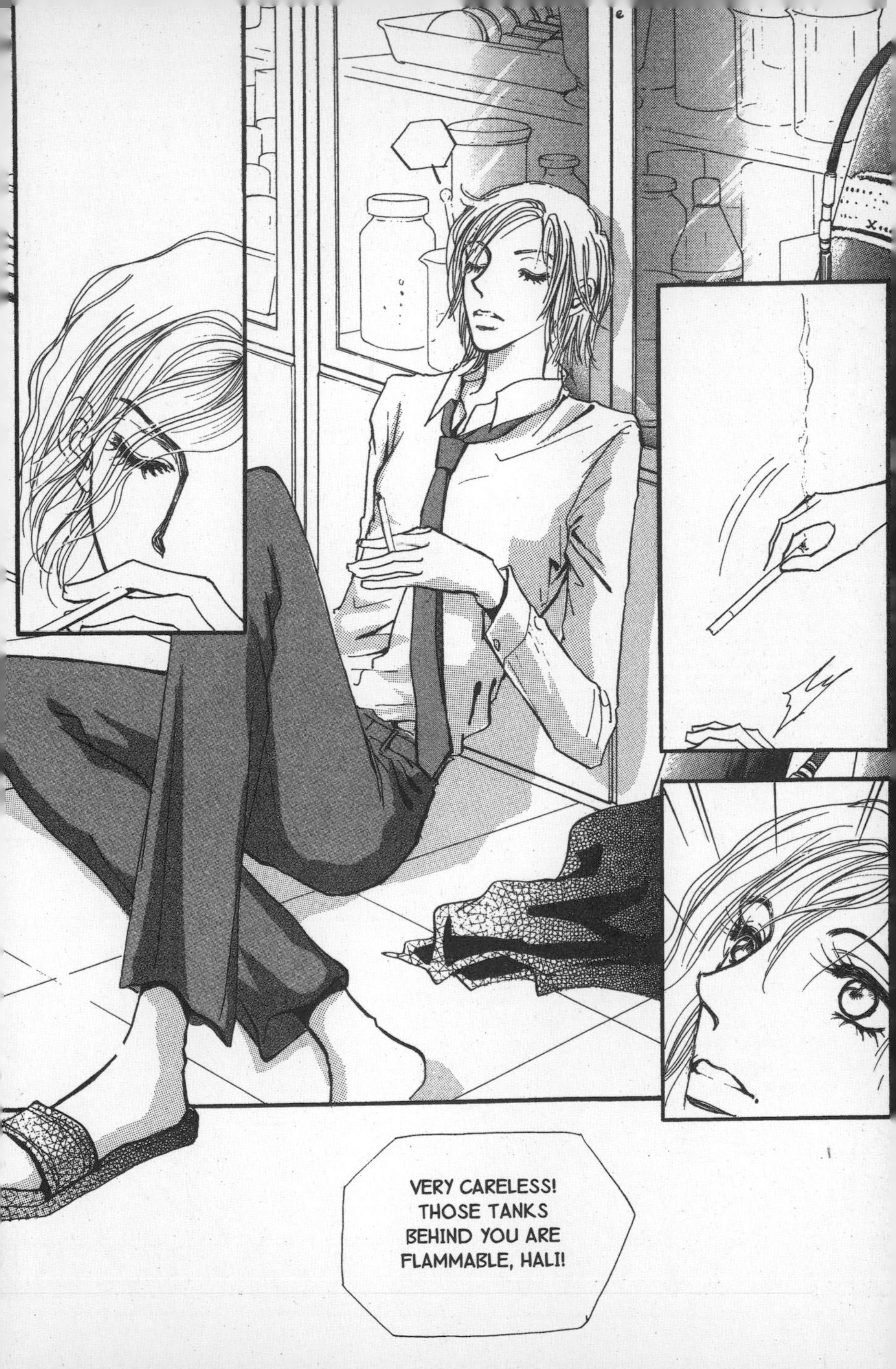
VERY CARELESS! THOSE TANKS BEHIND YOU ARE FLAMMABLE, HALI!

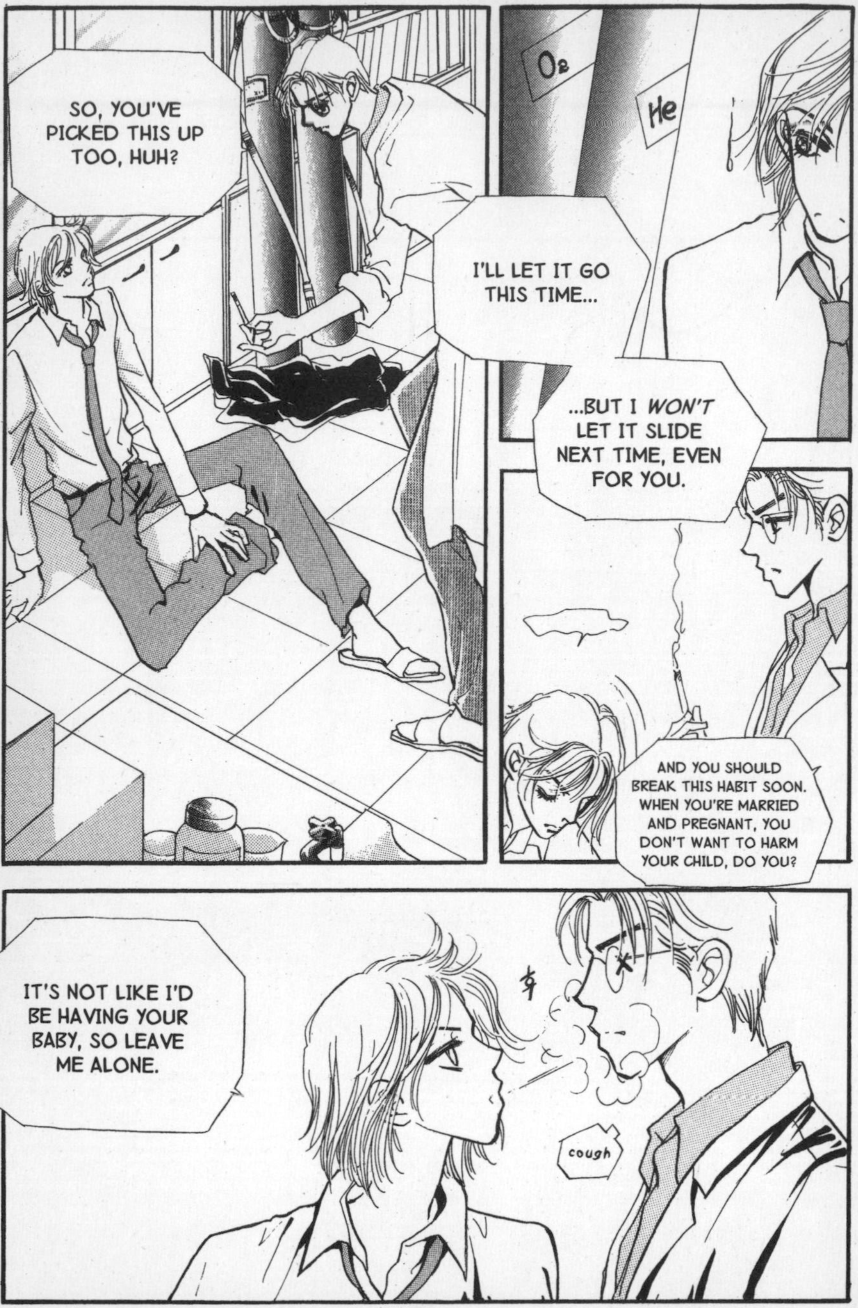
SO, YOU'VE PICKED THIS UP TOO, HUH?
I'LL LET IT GO THIS TIME...
O_2
He
...BUT I *WON'T* LET IT SLIDE NEXT TIME, EVEN FOR YOU.
AND YOU SHOULD BREAK THIS HABIT SOON. WHEN YOU'RE MARRIED AND PREGNANT, YOU DON'T WANT TO HARM YOUR CHILD, DO YOU?
IT'S NOT LIKE I'D BE HAVING YOUR BABY, SO LEAVE ME ALONE.
cough

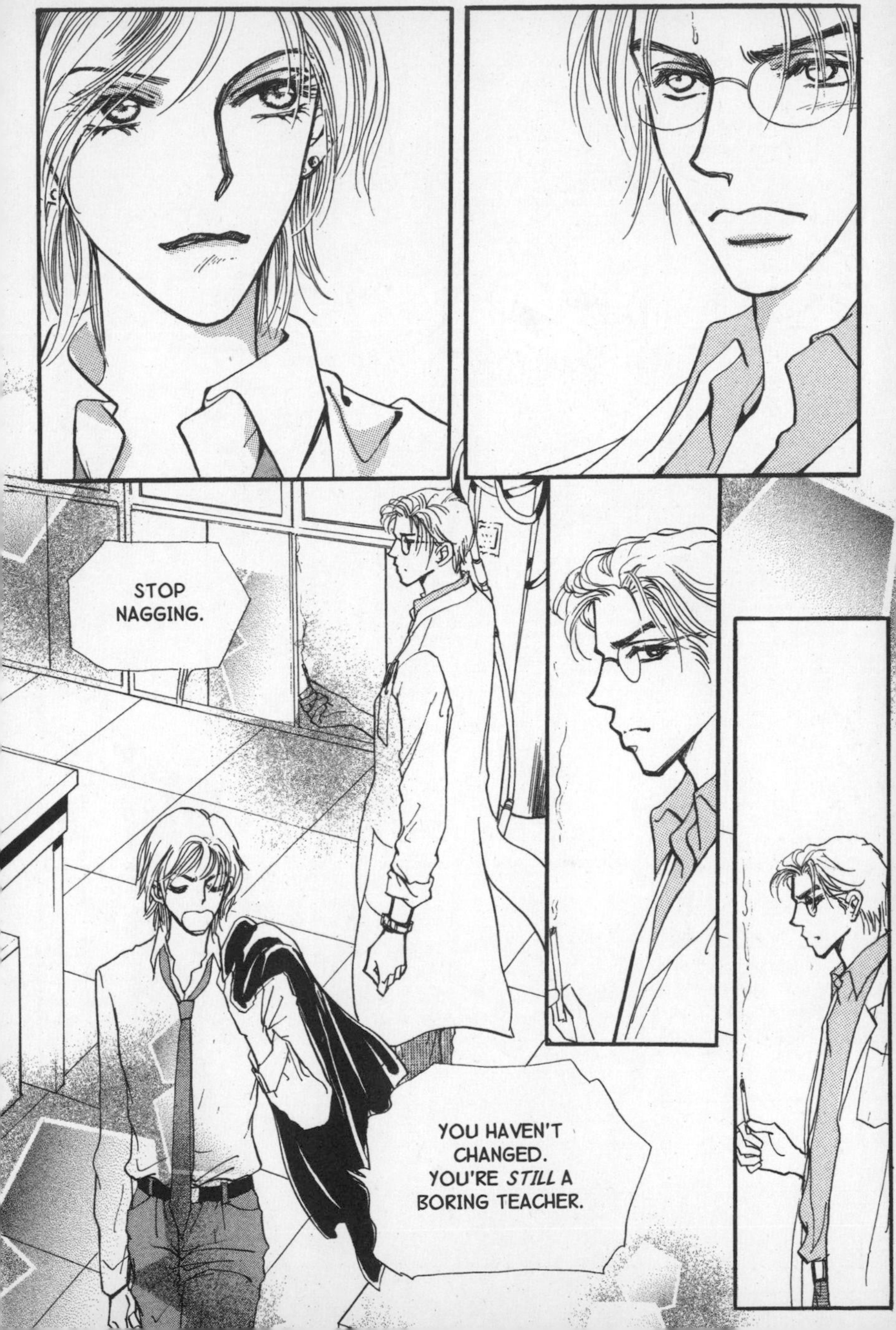
STOP NAGGING.
YOU HAVEN'T CHANGED. YOU'RE *STILL* A BORING TEACHER.

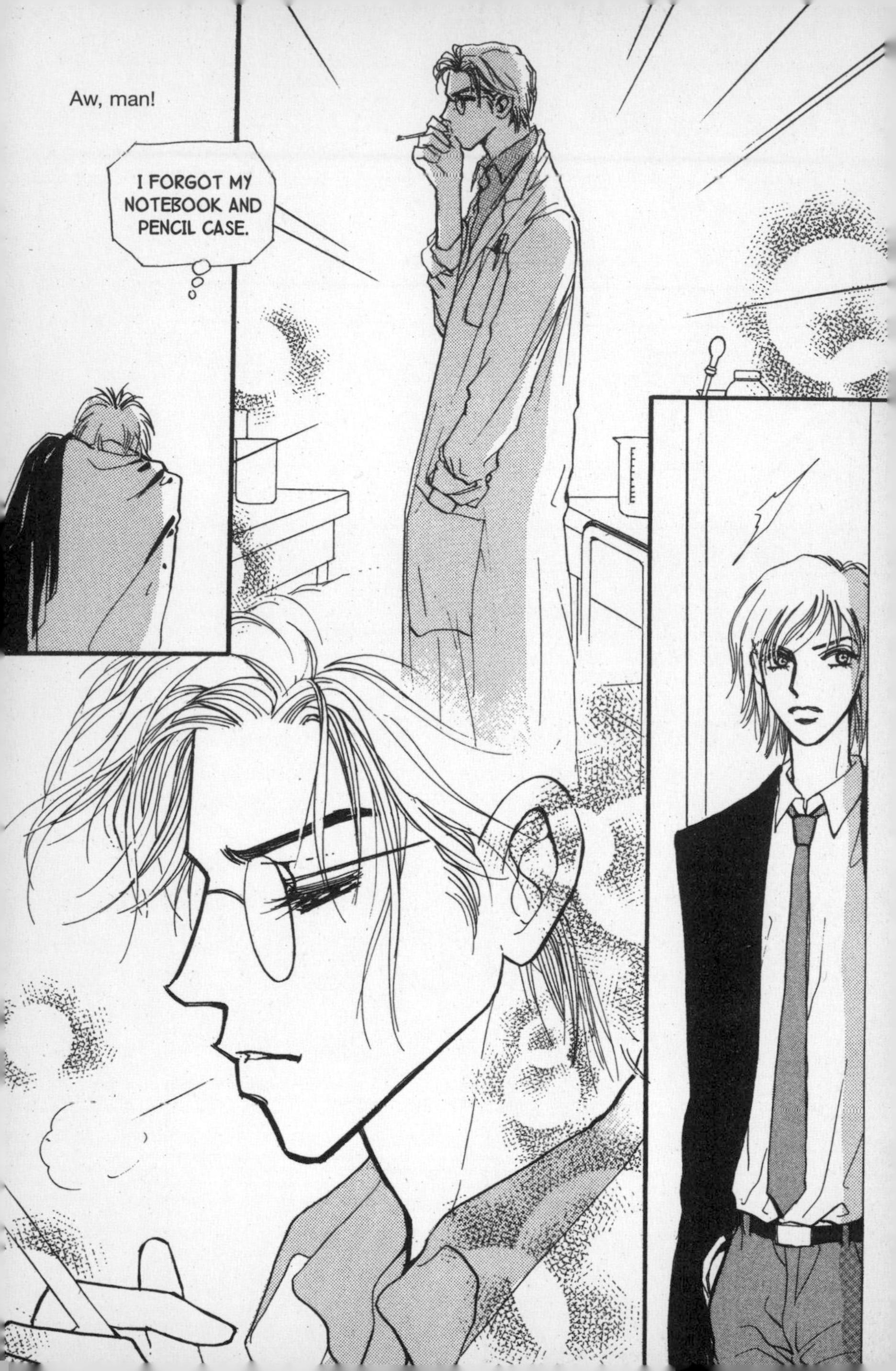
Aw, man!
I FORGOT MY NOTEBOOK AND PENCIL CASE.

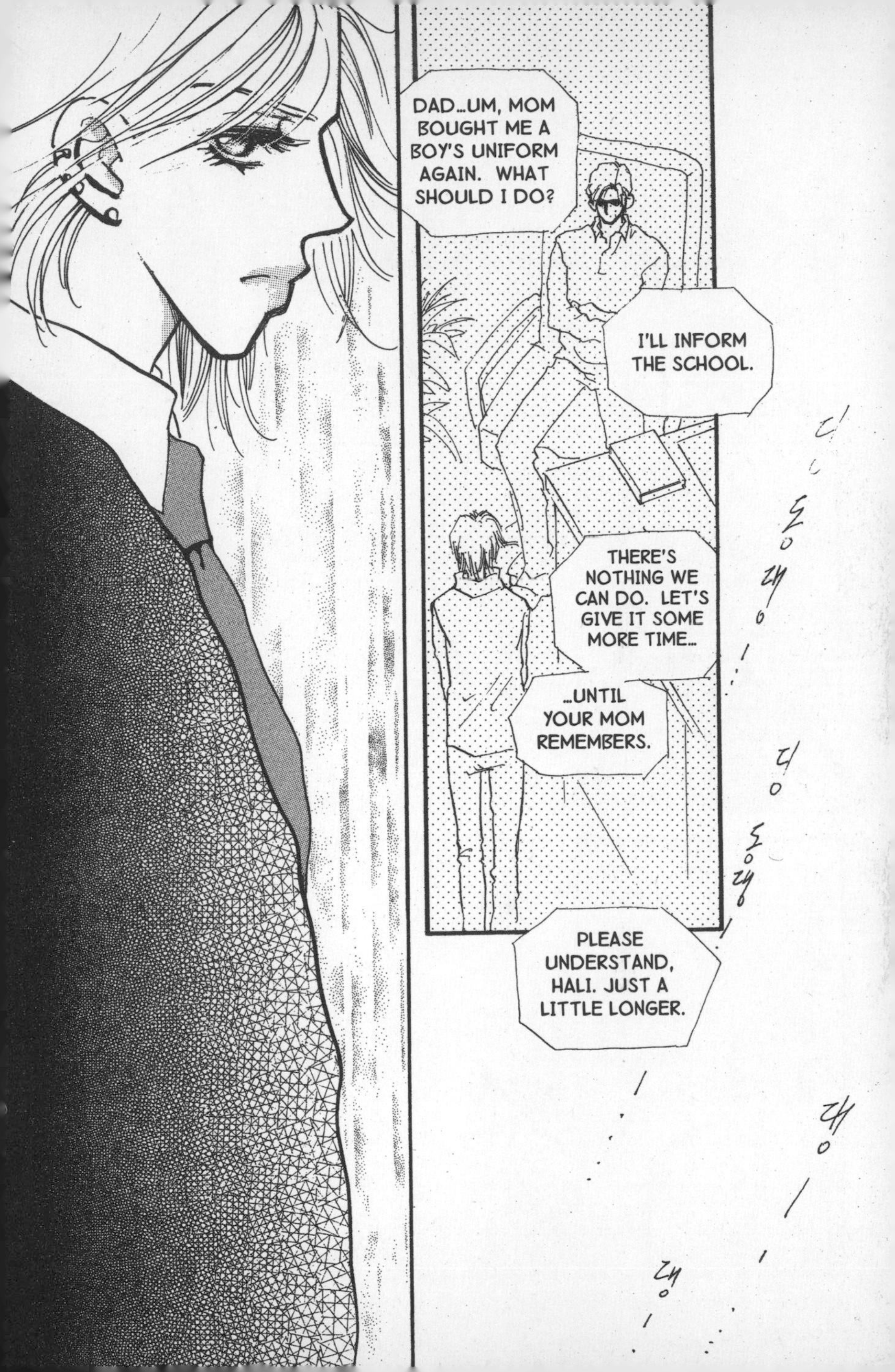
DAD...UM, MOM BOUGHT ME A BOY'S UNIFORM AGAIN. WHAT SHOULD I DO?
I'LL INFORM THE SCHOOL.
THERE'S NOTHING WE CAN DO. LET'S GIVE IT SOME MORE TIME...
...UNTIL YOUR MOM REMEMBERS.
PLEASE UNDERSTAND, HALI. JUST A LITTLE LONGER.

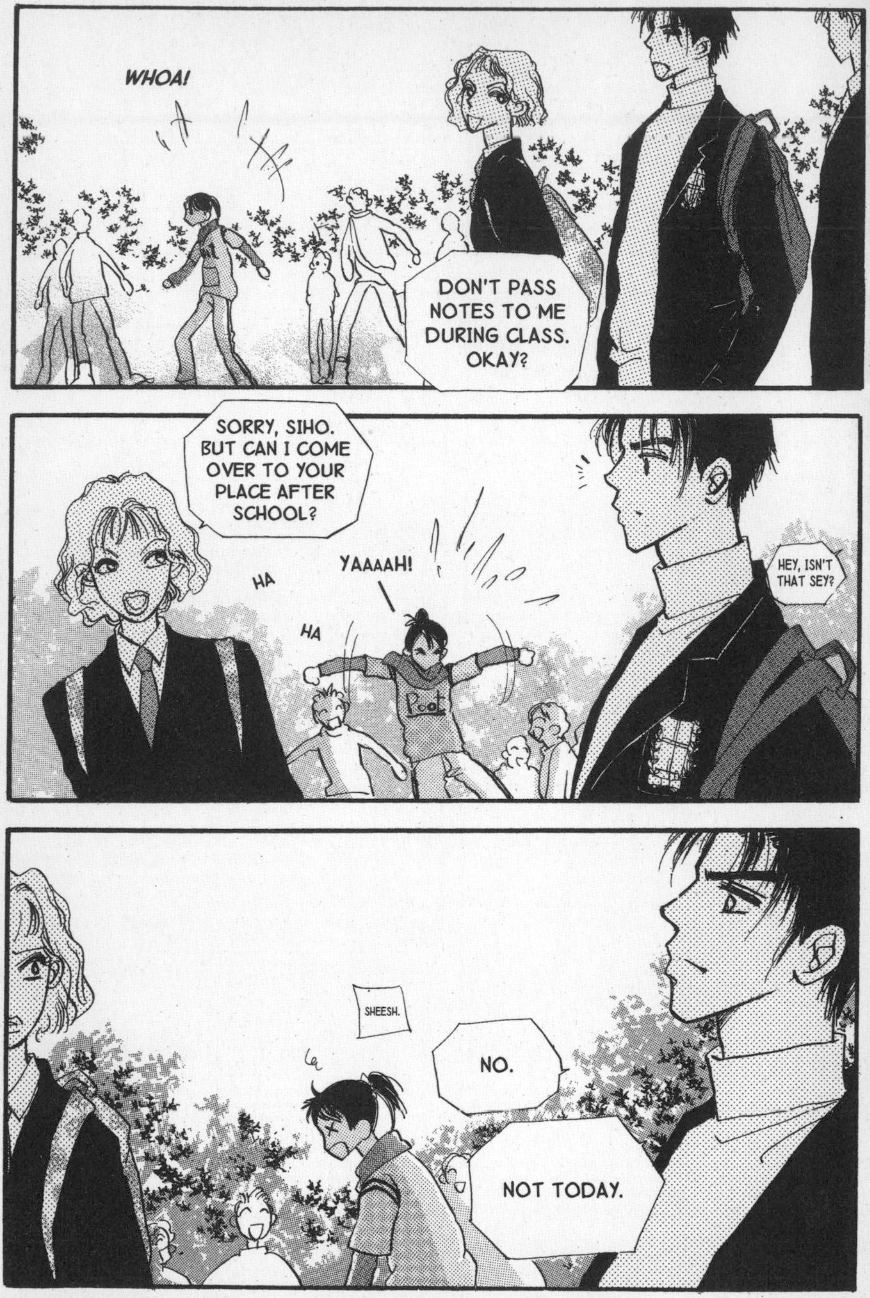
WHOA!
DON'T PASS NOTES TO ME DURING CLASS. OKAY?
SORRY, SIHO. BUT CAN I COME OVER TO YOUR PLACE AFTER SCHOOL?
HA
HA
YAAAAH!
HEY, ISN'T THAT SEY?
SHEESH.
NO.
NOT TODAY.

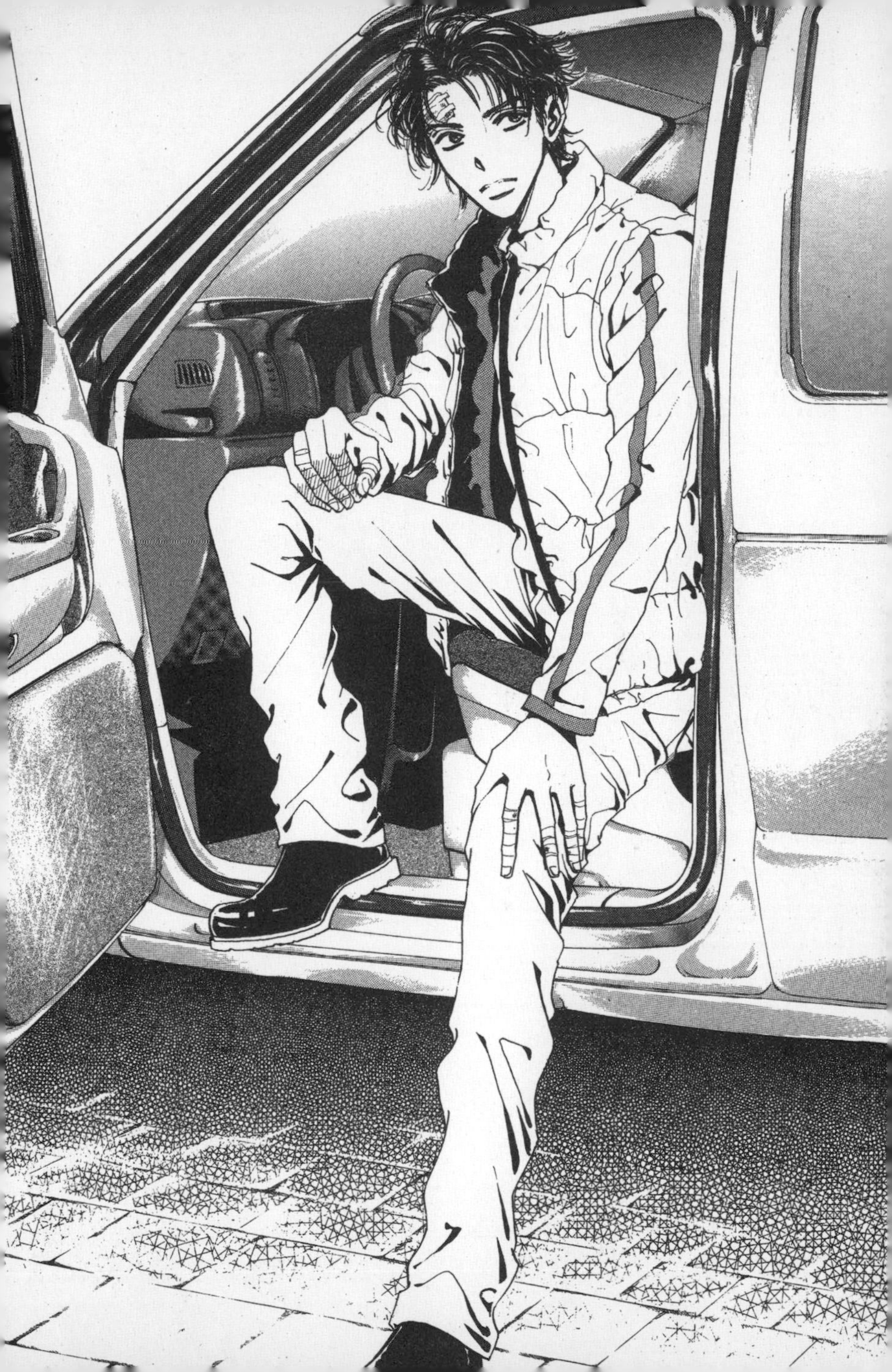

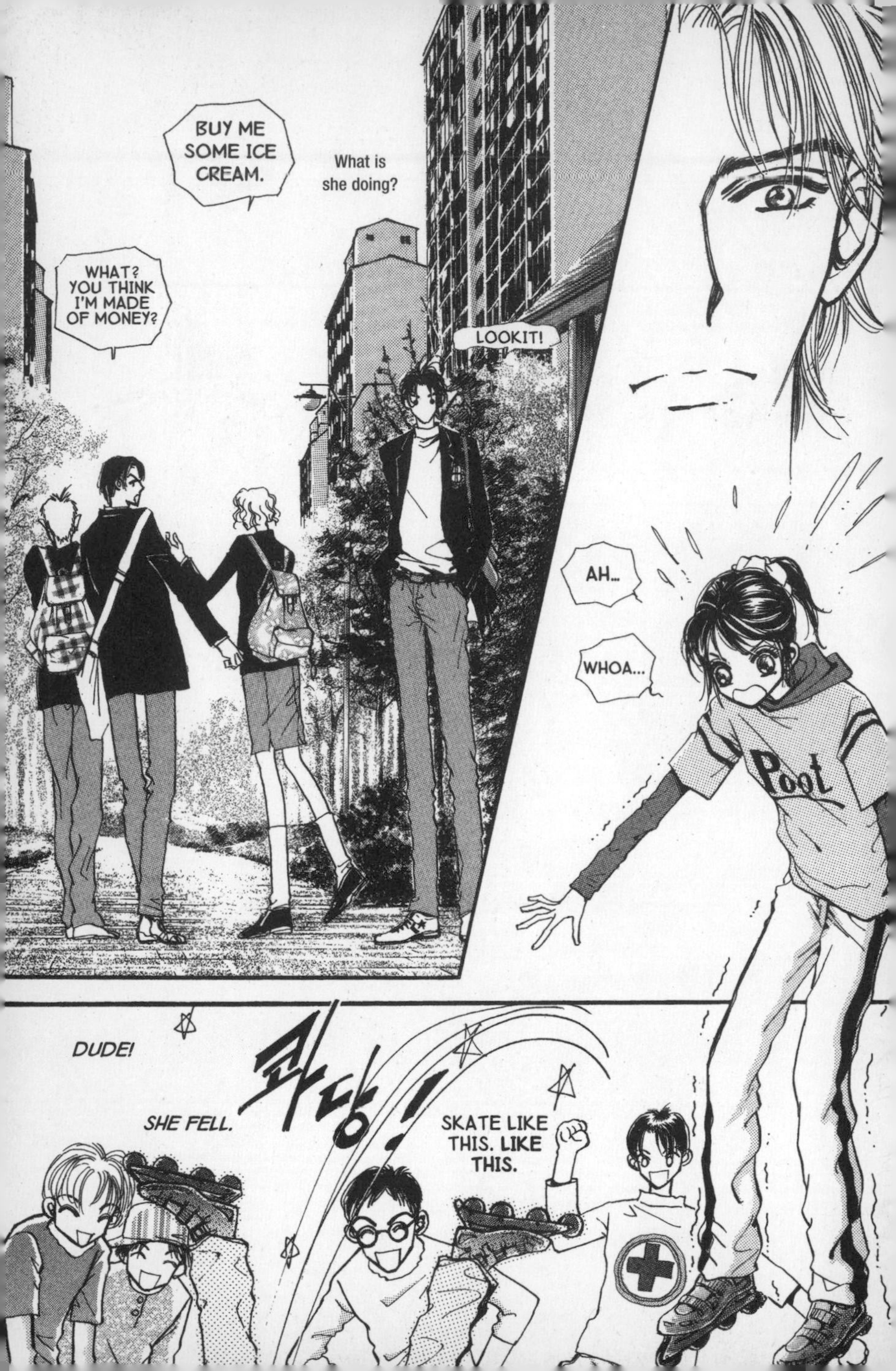
BUY ME SOME ICE CREAM.
What is she doing?
WHAT? YOU THINK I'M MADE OF MONEY?
LOOKIT!
AH...
WHOA...
DUDE!
콰당!
SHE FELL.
SKATE LIKE THIS. LIKE THIS.

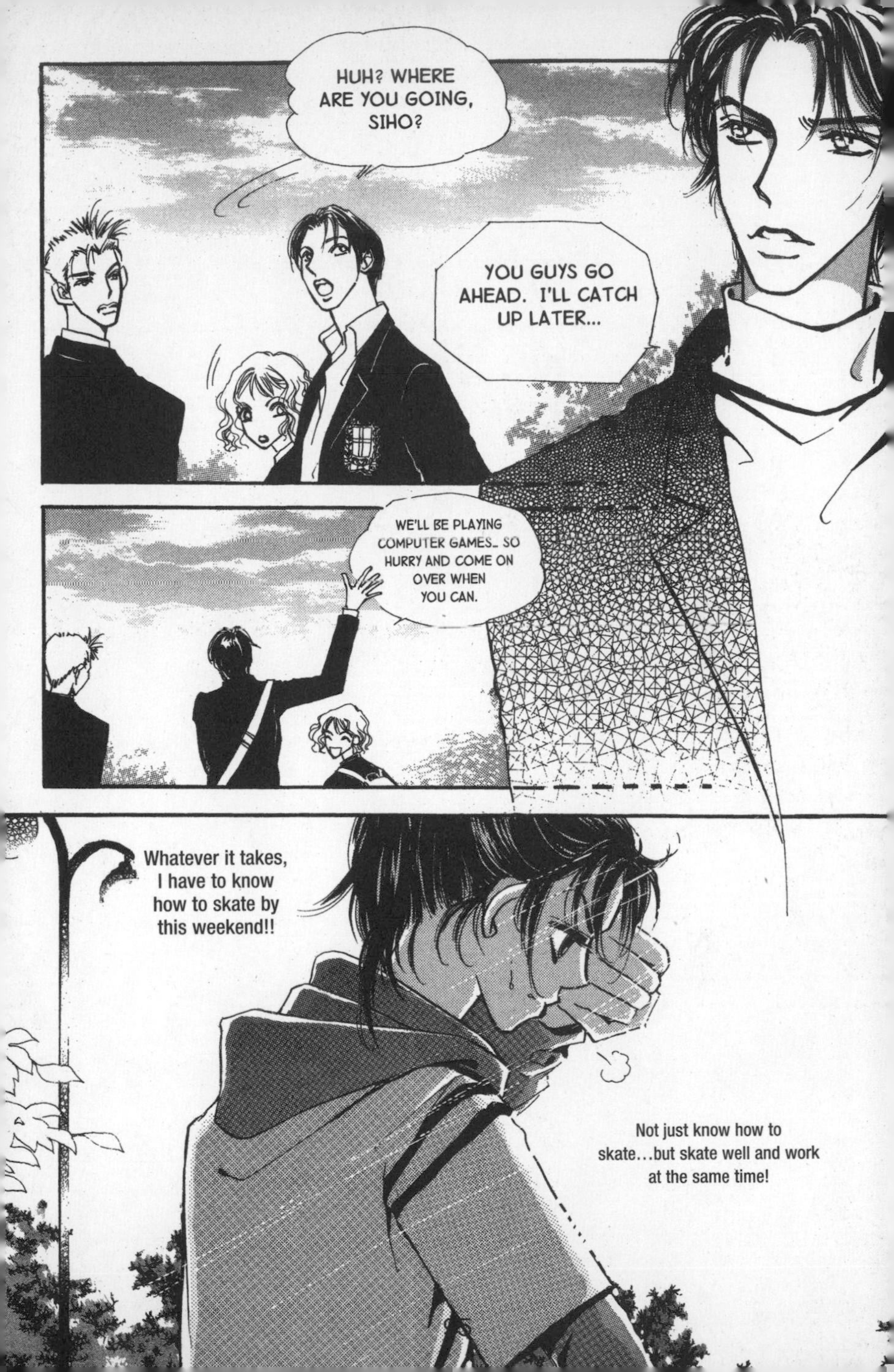
HUH? WHERE ARE YOU GOING, SIHO?
YOU GUYS GO AHEAD. I'LL CATCH UP LATER...
WE'LL BE PLAYING COMPUTER GAMES... SO HURRY AND COME ON OVER WHEN YOU CAN.
Whatever it takes, I have to know how to skate by this weekend!!
Not just know how to skate...but skate well and work at the same time!

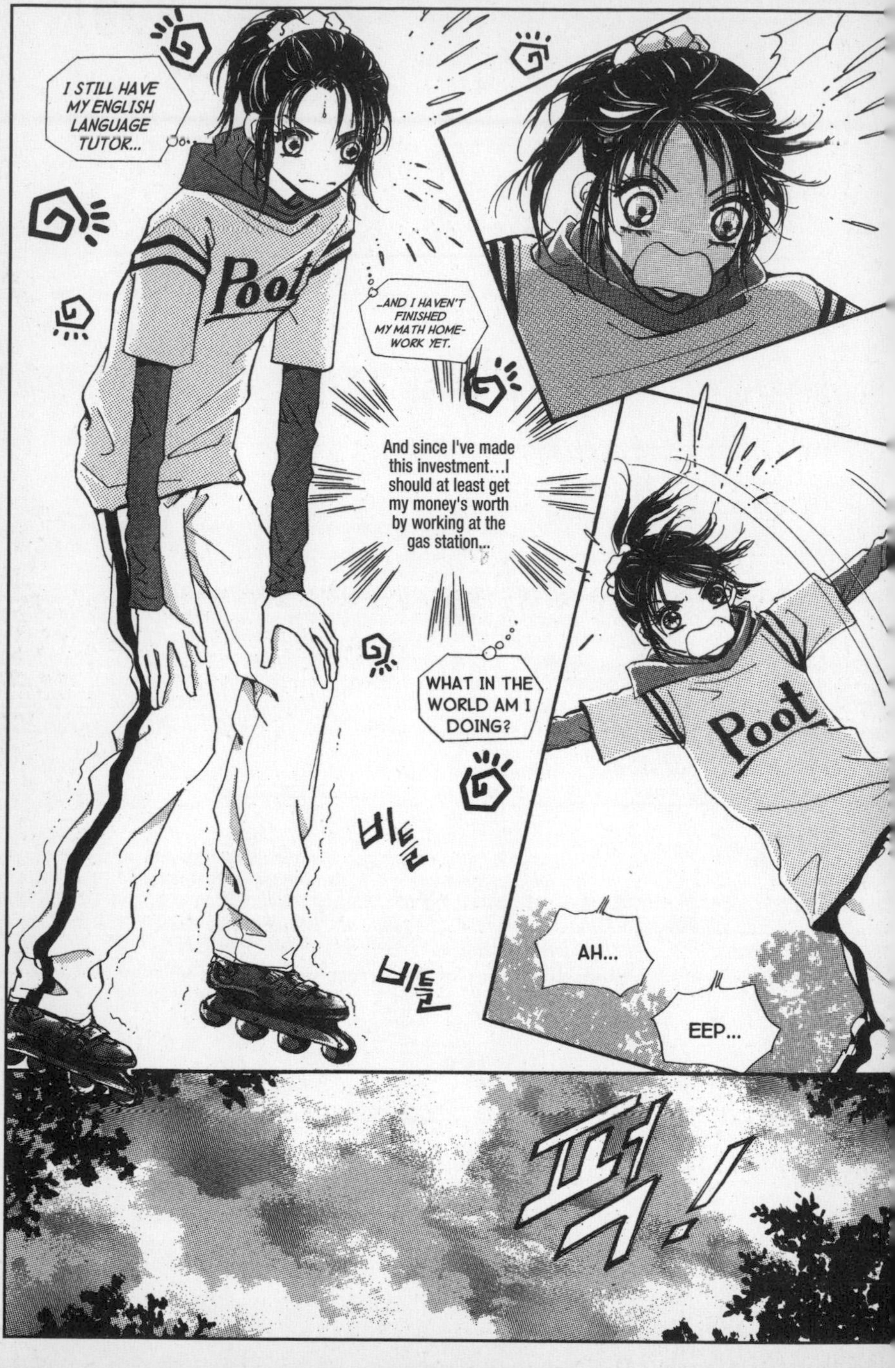
I STILL HAVE MY ENGLISH LANGUAGE TUTOR...
...AND I HAVEN'T FINISHED MY MATH HOME-WORK YET.
And since I've made this investment…I should at least get my money's worth by working at the gas station...
WHAT IN THE WORLD AM I DOING?
비틀
비틀
AH...
EEP...
퍽!

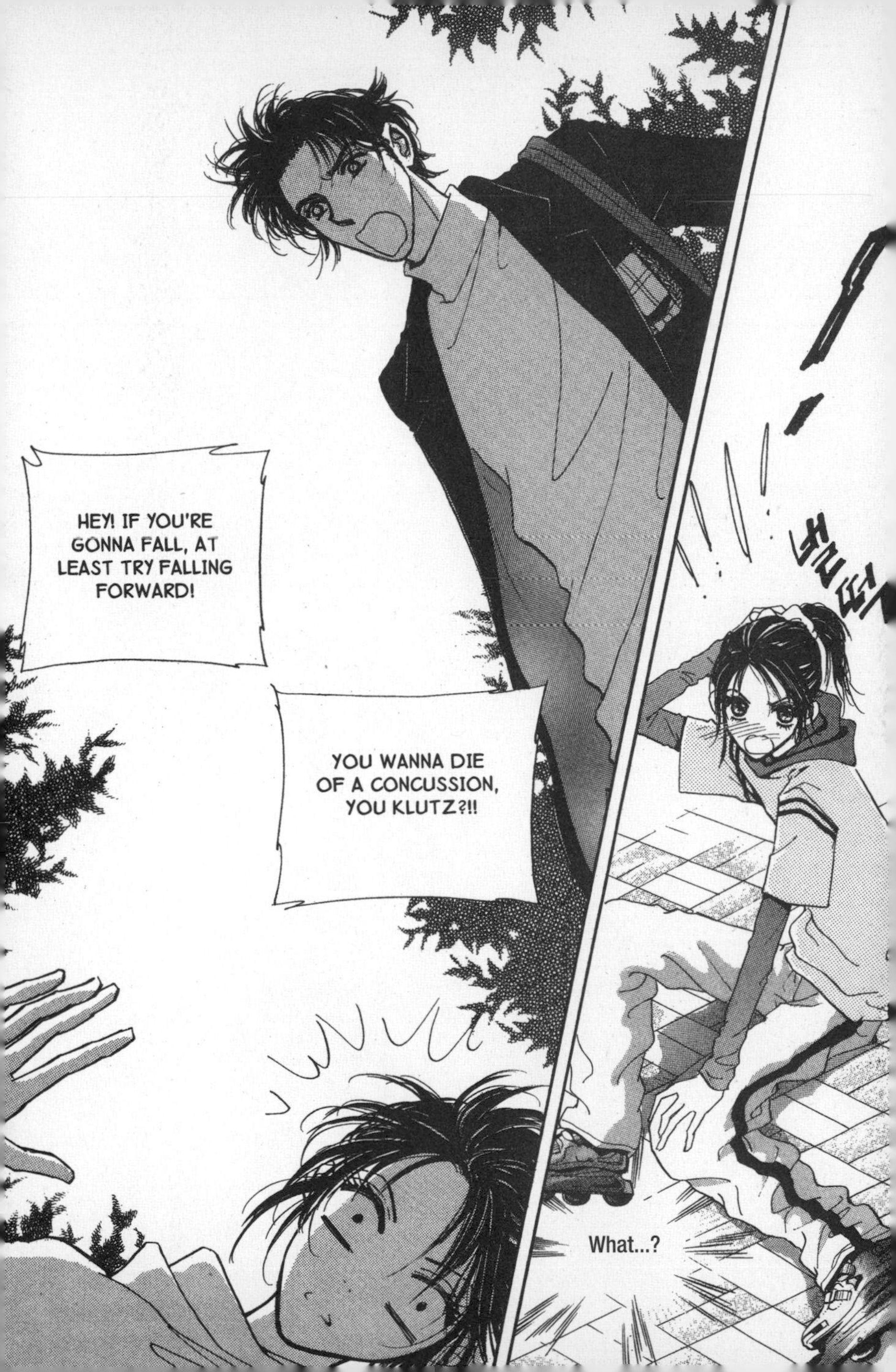
HEY! IF YOU'RE GONNA FALL, AT LEAST TRY FALLING FORWARD!
YOU WANNA DIE OF A CONCUSSION, YOU KLUTZ?!!
벌떡
What...?

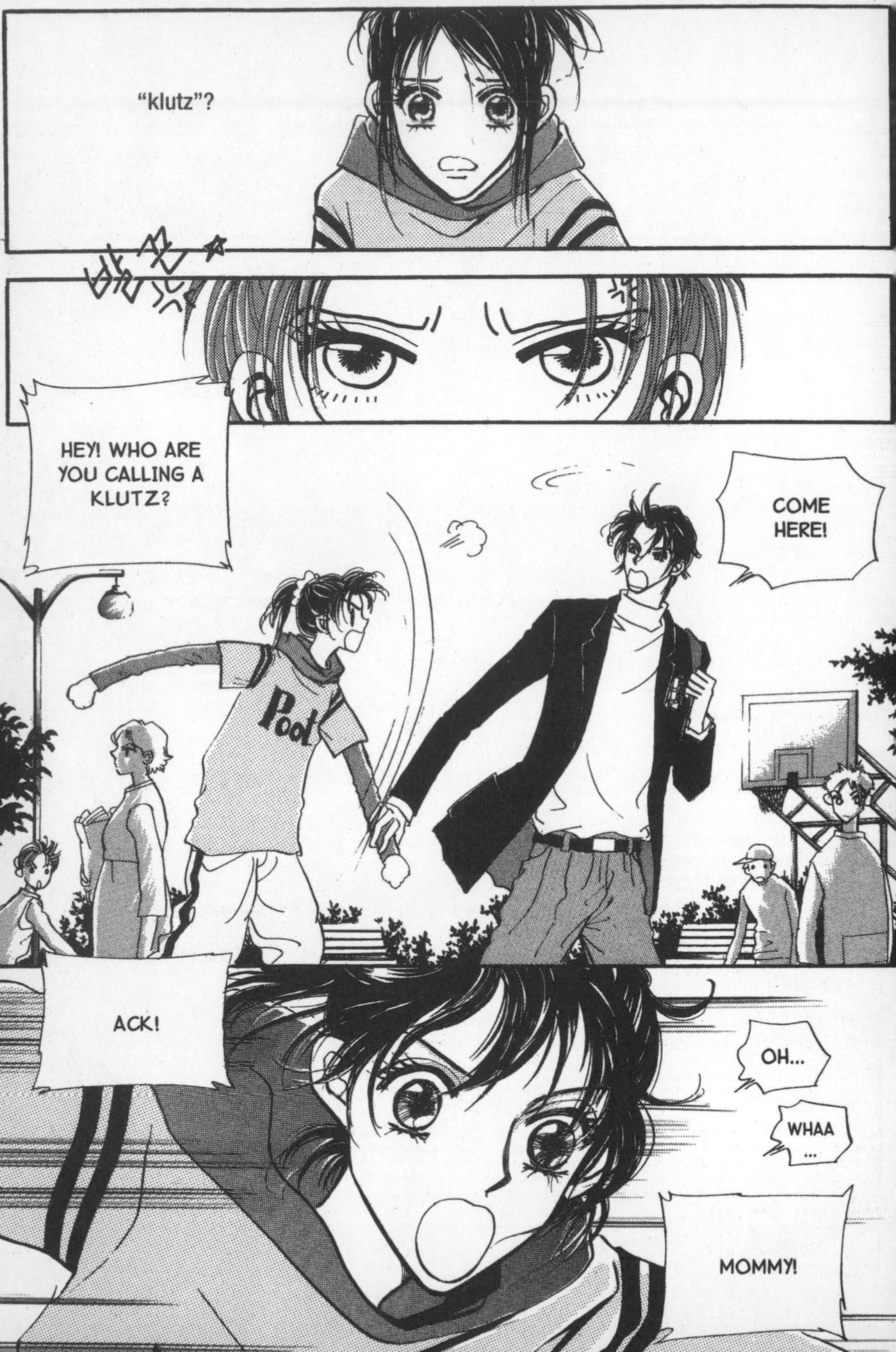
"klutz"?
HEY! WHO ARE YOU CALLING A KLUTZ?
COME HERE!
ACK!
OH...
WHAA ...
MOMMY!

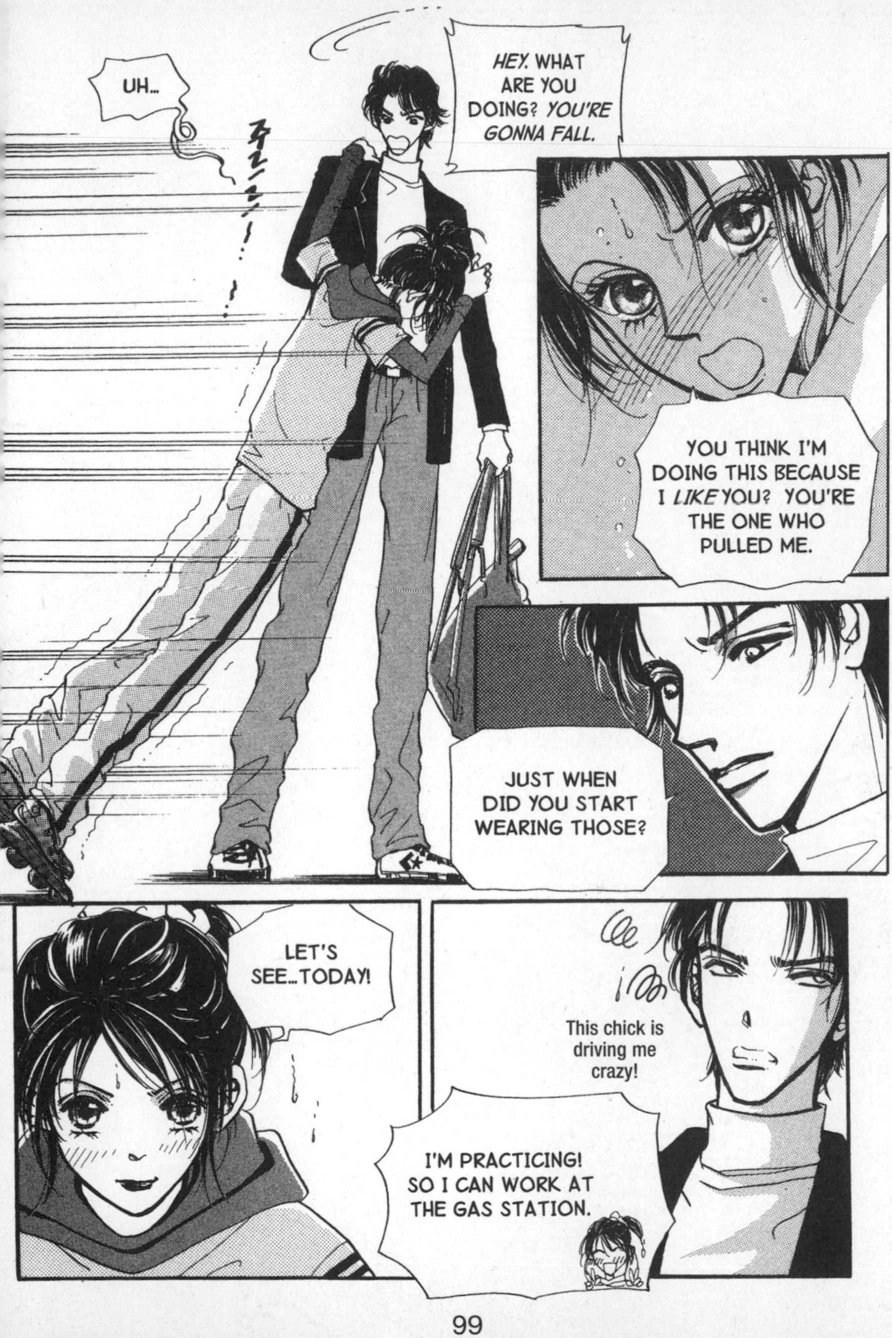
UH...
HEY. WHAT ARE YOU DOING? YOU'RE GONNA FALL.
YOU THINK I'M DOING THIS BECAUSE I LIKE YOU? YOU'RE THE ONE WHO PULLED ME.
JUST WHEN DID YOU START WEARING THOSE?
LET'S SEE...TODAY!
This chick is driving me crazy!
I'M PRACTICING! SO I CAN WORK AT THE GAS STATION.

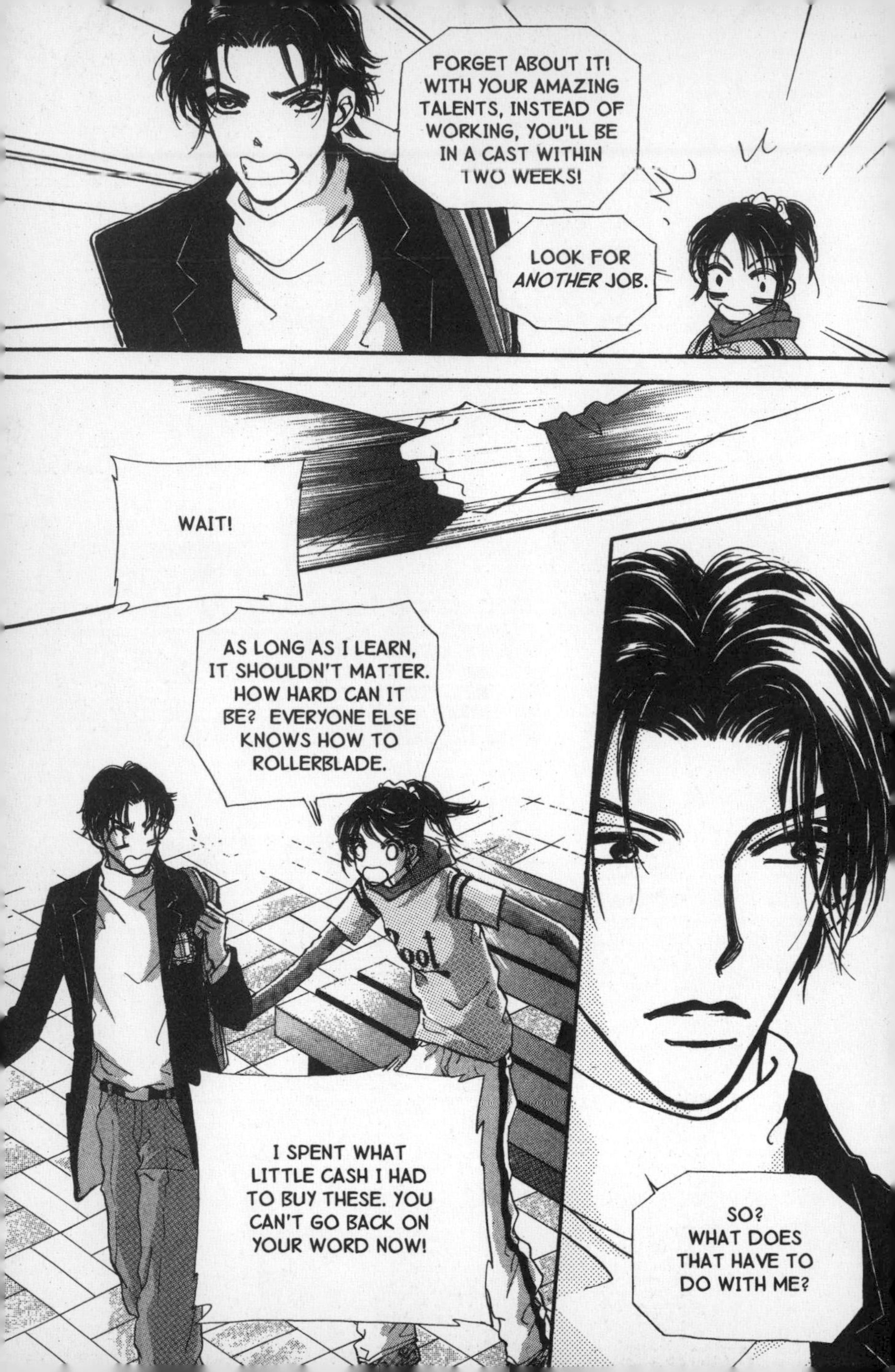
FORGET ABOUT IT! WITH YOUR AMAZING TALENTS, INSTEAD OF WORKING, YOU'LL BE IN A CAST WITHIN TWO WEEKS!
LOOK FOR *ANOTHER* JOB.
WAIT!
AS LONG AS I LEARN, IT SHOULDN'T MATTER. HOW HARD CAN IT BE? EVERYONE ELSE KNOWS HOW TO ROLLERBLADE.
I SPENT WHAT LITTLE CASH I HAD TO BUY THESE. YOU CAN'T GO BACK ON YOUR WORD NOW!
SO? WHAT DOES THAT HAVE TO DO WITH ME?

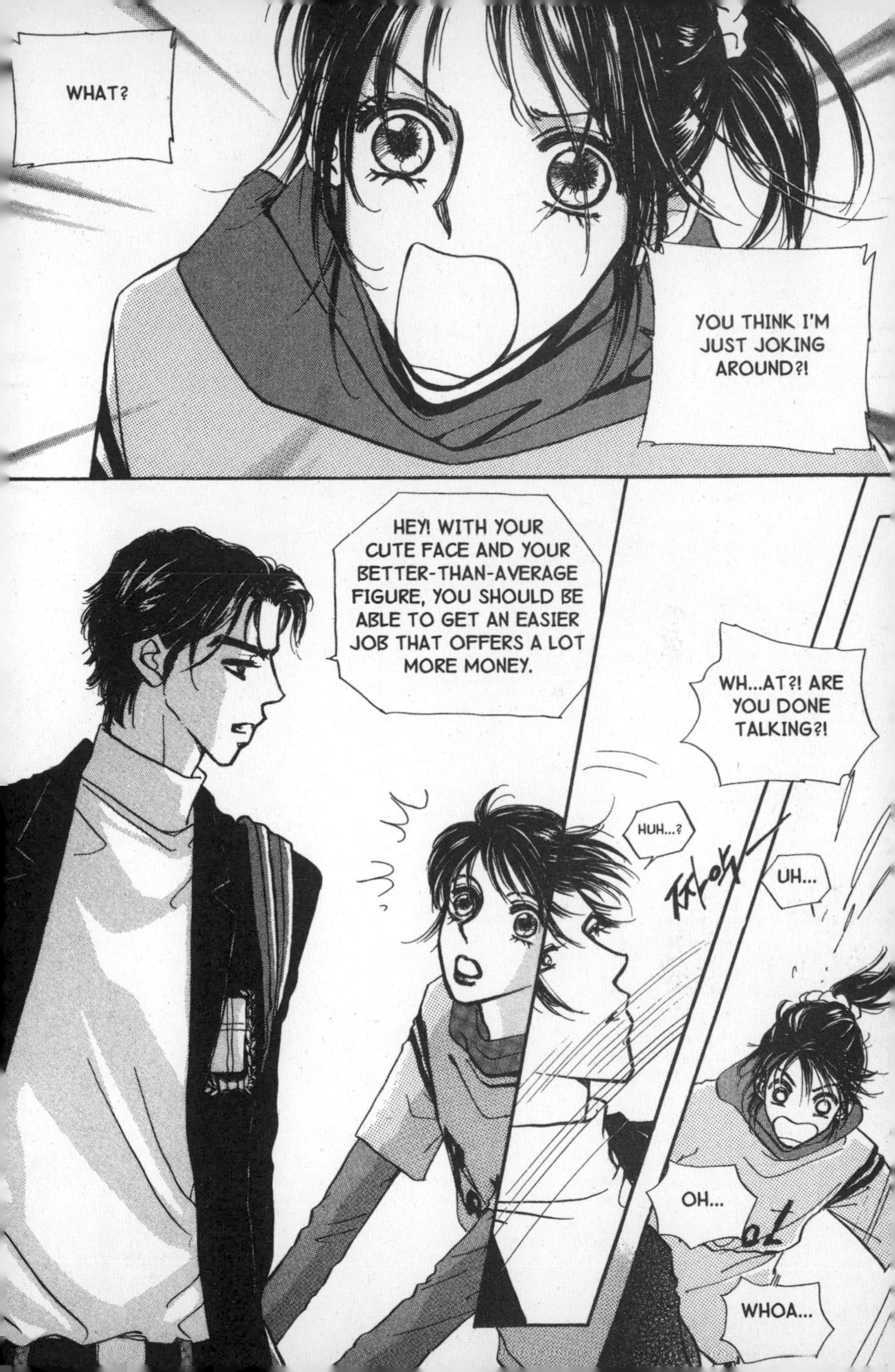
WHAT?
YOU THINK I'M JUST JOKING AROUND?!
HEY! WITH YOUR CUTE FACE AND YOUR BETTER-THAN-AVERAGE FIGURE, YOU SHOULD BE ABLE TO GET AN EASIER JOB THAT OFFERS A LOT MORE MONEY.
HUH...?
WH...AT?! ARE YOU DONE TALKING?!
UH...
OH...
WHOA...

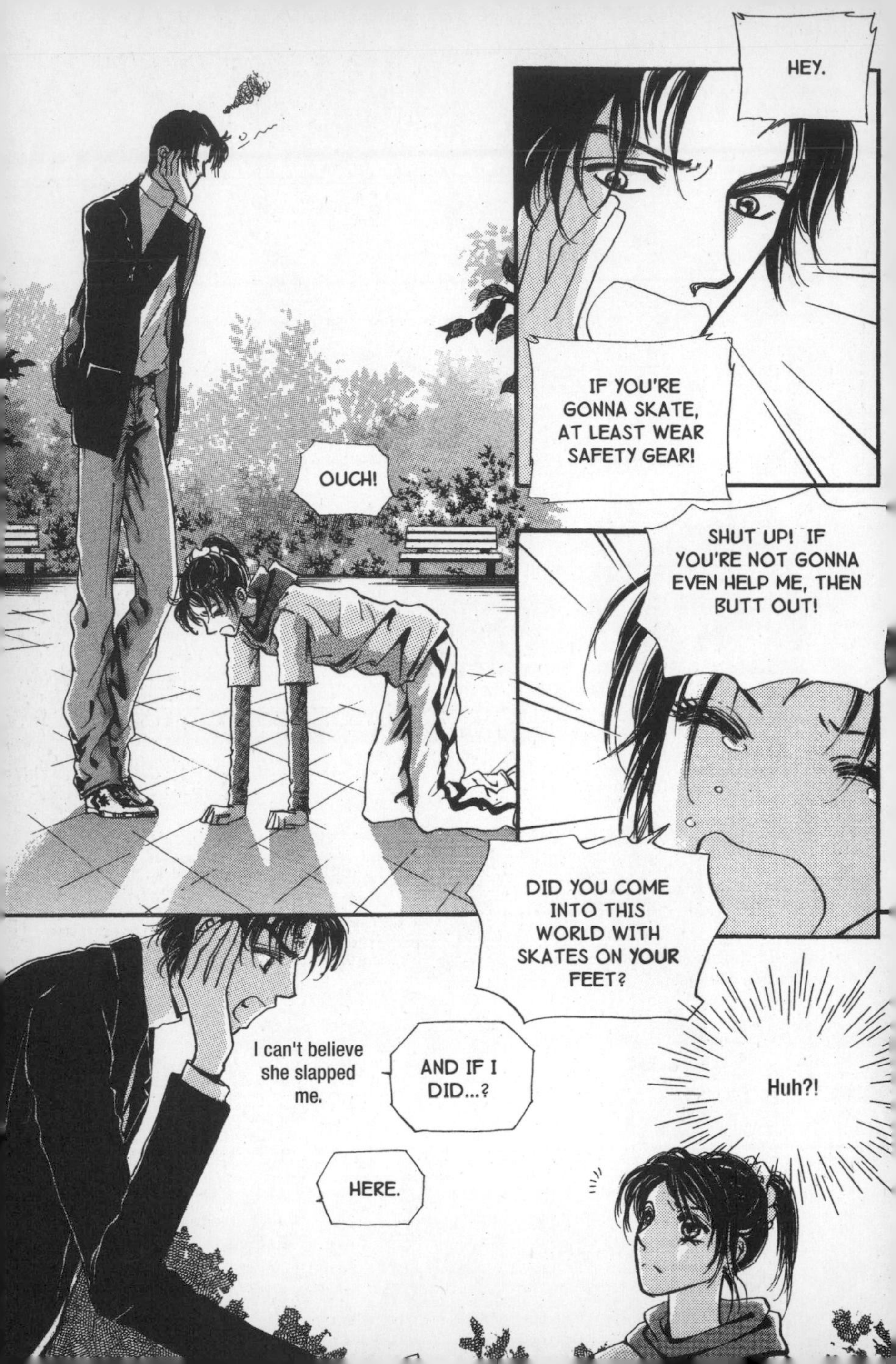
OUCH!
HEY.
IF YOU'RE GONNA SKATE, AT LEAST WEAR SAFETY GEAR!
SHUT UP! IF YOU'RE NOT GONNA EVEN HELP ME, THEN BUTT OUT!
DID YOU COME INTO THIS WORLD WITH SKATES ON YOUR FEET?
I can't believe she slapped me.
AND IF I DID...?
Huh?!
HERE.

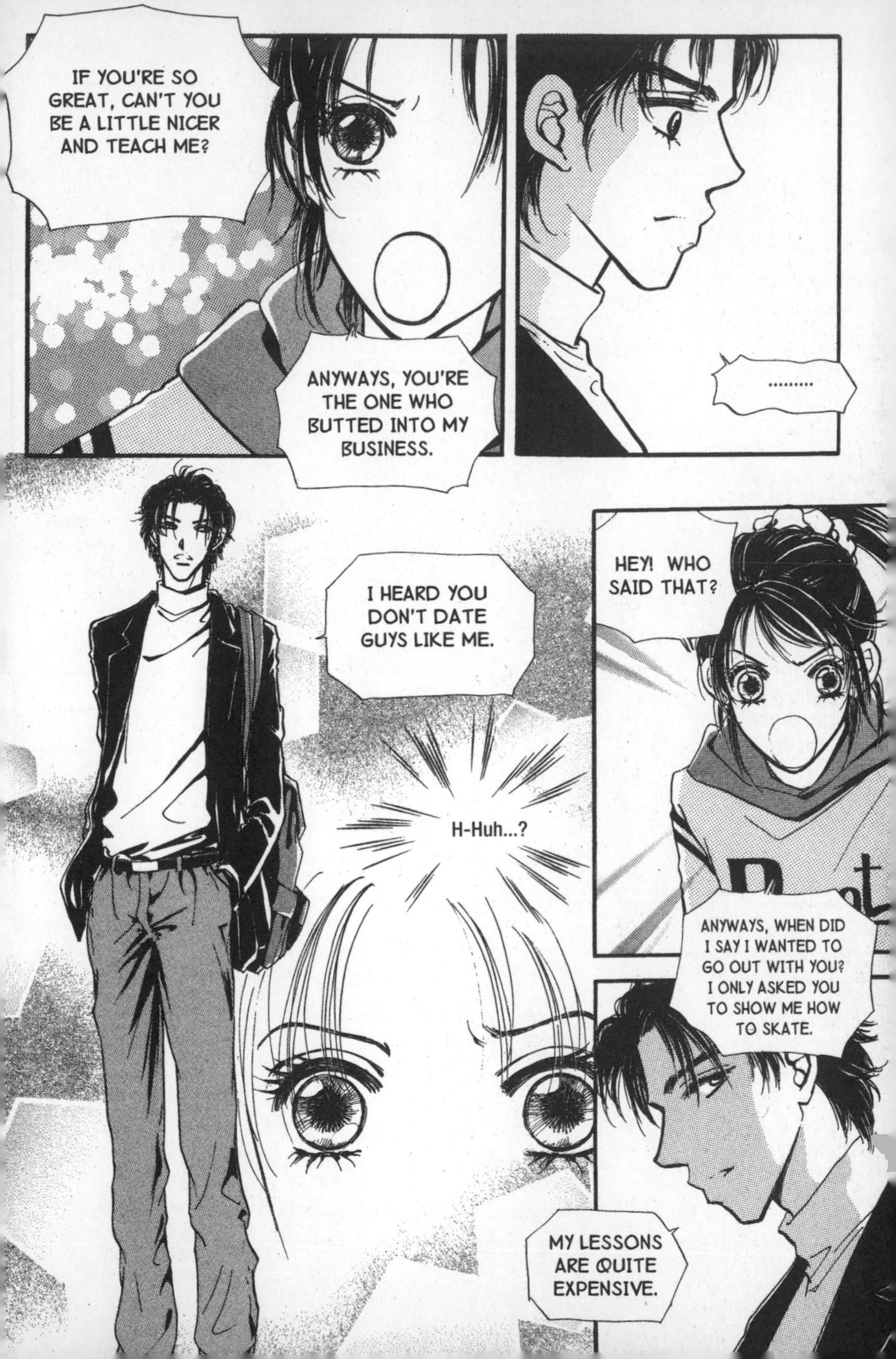
IF YOU'RE SO GREAT, CAN'T YOU BE A LITTLE NICER AND TEACH ME?
ANYWAYS, YOU'RE THE ONE WHO BUTTED INTO MY BUSINESS.
....
I HEARD YOU DON'T DATE GUYS LIKE ME.
H-Huh...?
HEY! WHO SAID THAT?
ANYWAYS, WHEN DID I SAY I WANTED TO GO OUT WITH YOU? I ONLY ASKED YOU TO SHOW ME HOW TO SKATE.
MY LESSONS ARE QUITE EXPENSIVE.

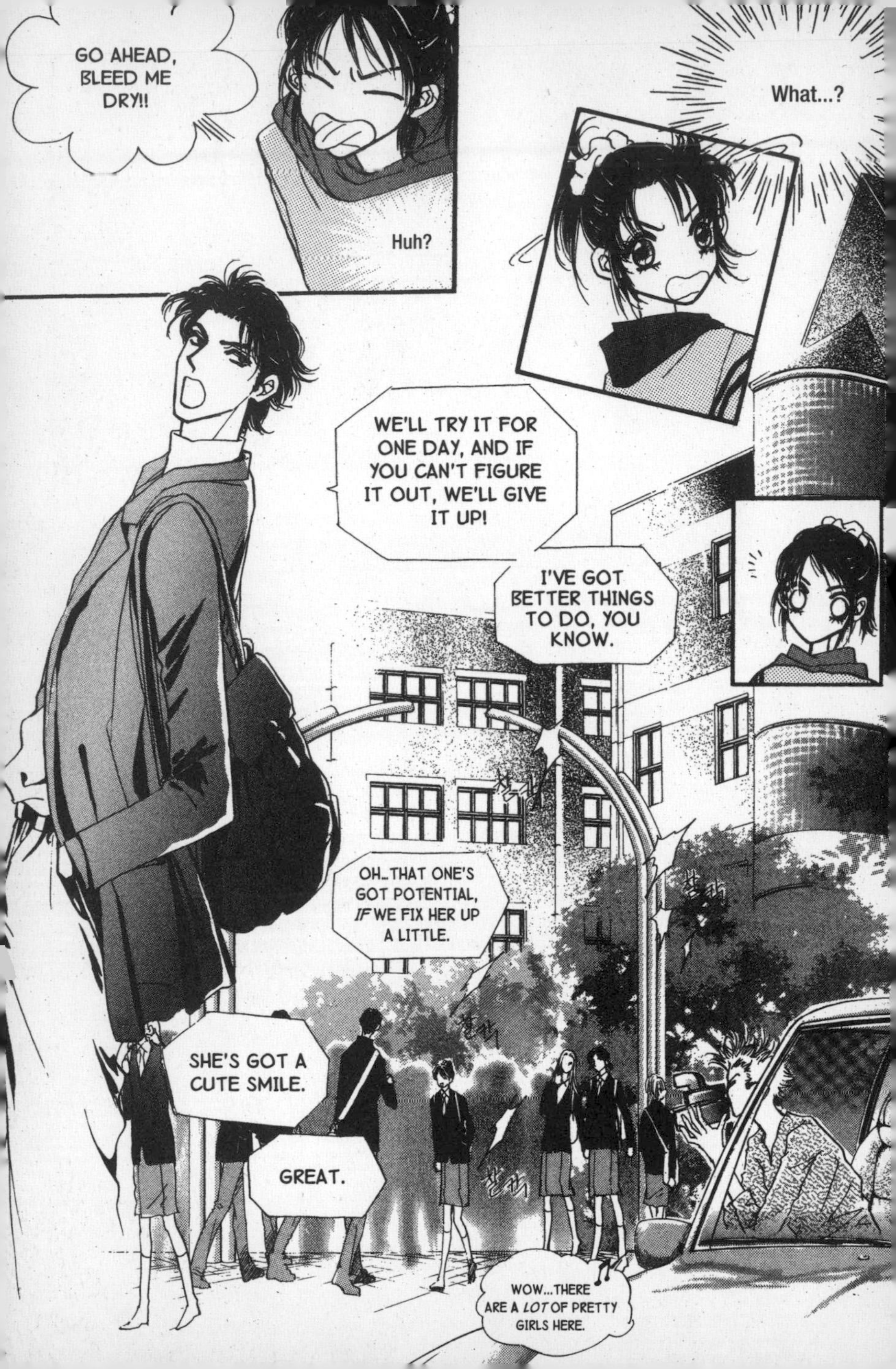
GO AHEAD, BLEED ME DRY!!
Huh?
What...?
WE'LL TRY IT FOR ONE DAY, AND IF YOU CAN'T FIGURE IT OUT, WE'LL GIVE IT UP!
I'VE GOT BETTER THINGS TO DO, YOU KNOW.
OH...THAT ONE'S GOT POTENTIAL, *IF* WE FIX HER UP A LITTLE.
SHE'S GOT A CUTE SMILE.
GREAT.
WOW...THERE ARE A *LOT* OF PRETTY GIRLS HERE.

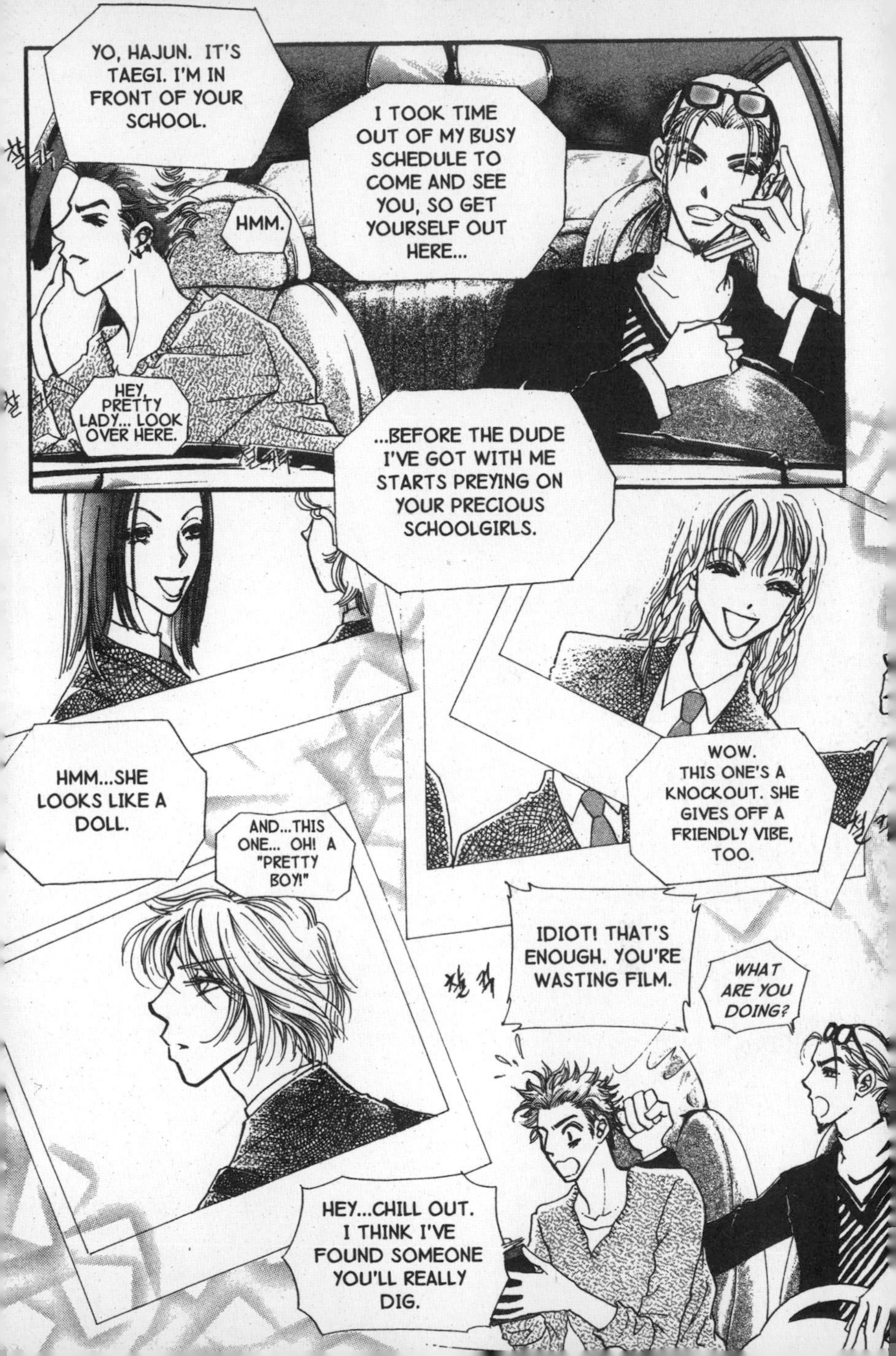
YO, HAJUN. IT'S TAEGI. I'M IN FRONT OF YOUR SCHOOL.
HMM.
I TOOK TIME OUT OF MY BUSY SCHEDULE TO COME AND SEE YOU, SO GET YOURSELF OUT HERE...
HEY, PRETTY LADY... LOOK OVER HERE.
...BEFORE THE DUDE I'VE GOT WITH ME STARTS PREYING ON YOUR PRECIOUS SCHOOLGIRLS.
HMM...SHE LOOKS LIKE A DOLL.
AND...THIS ONE... OH! A "PRETTY BOY!"
WOW. THIS ONE'S A KNOCKOUT. SHE GIVES OFF A FRIENDLY VIBE, TOO.
IDIOT! THAT'S ENOUGH. YOU'RE WASTING FILM.
WHAT ARE YOU DOING?
HEY...CHILL OUT. I THINK I'VE FOUND SOMEONE YOU'LL REALLY DIG.

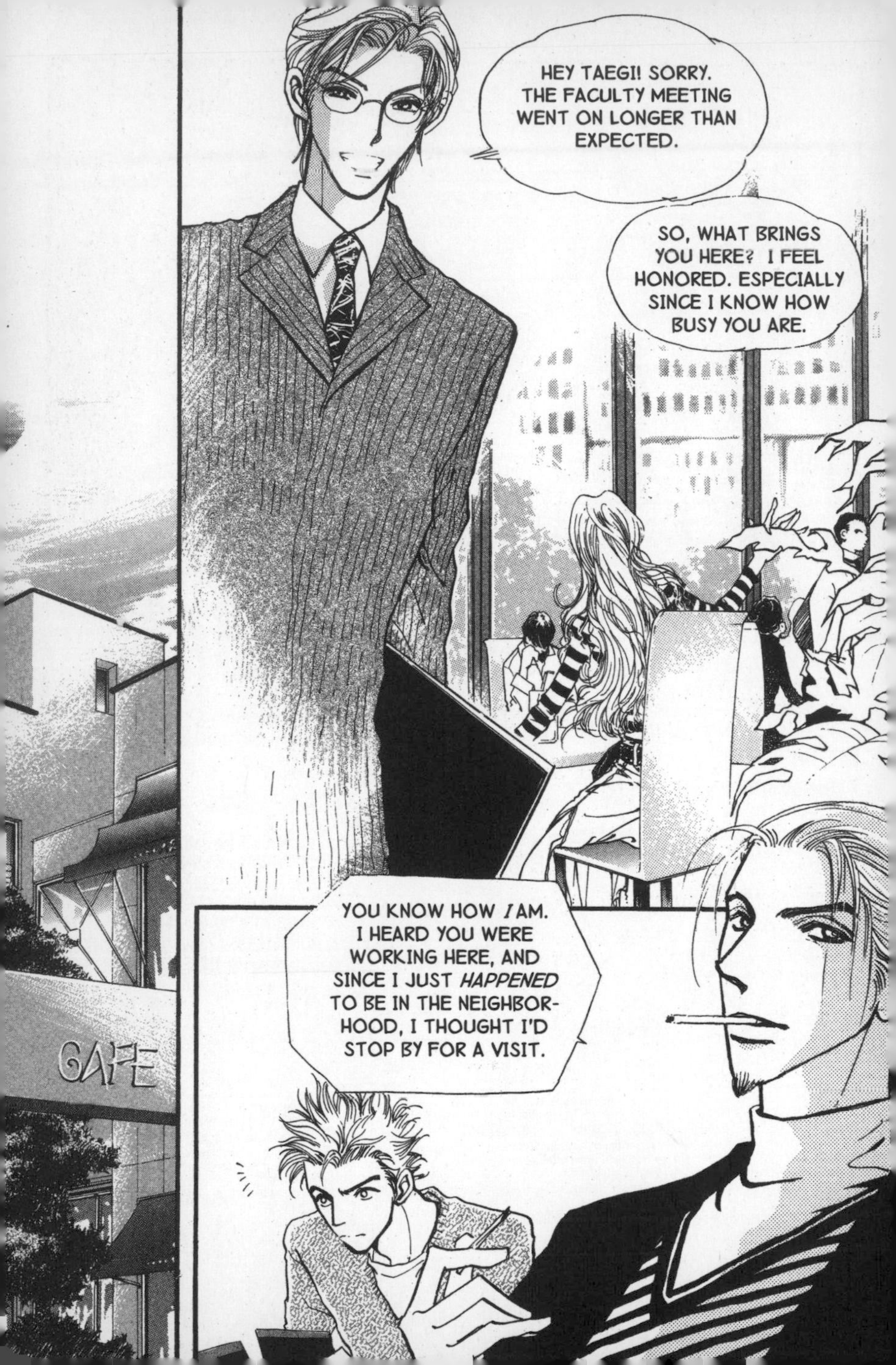
HEY TAEGI! SORRY. THE FACULTY MEETING WENT ON LONGER THAN EXPECTED.
SO, WHAT BRINGS YOU HERE? I FEEL HONORED. ESPECIALLY SINCE I KNOW HOW BUSY YOU ARE.
CAFE
YOU KNOW HOW *I* AM. I HEARD YOU WERE WORKING HERE, AND SINCE I JUST *HAPPENED* TO BE IN THE NEIGHBOR-HOOD, I THOUGHT I'D STOP BY FOR A VISIT.

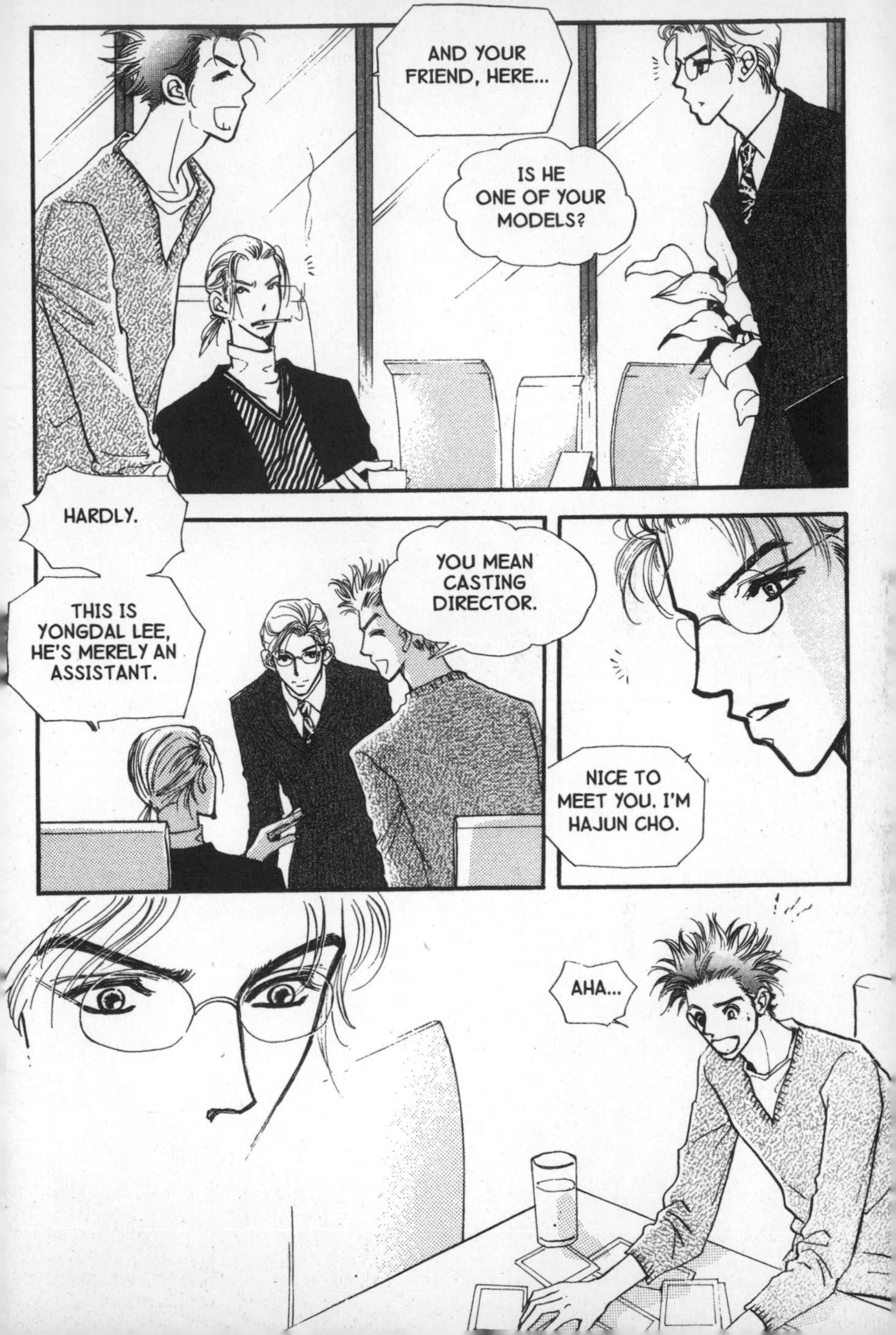
AND YOUR FRIEND, HERE...
IS HE ONE OF YOUR MODELS?
HARDLY.
THIS IS YONGDAL LEE, HE'S MERELY AN ASSISTANT.
YOU MEAN CASTING DIRECTOR.
NICE TO MEET YOU. I'M HAJUN CHO.
AHA...

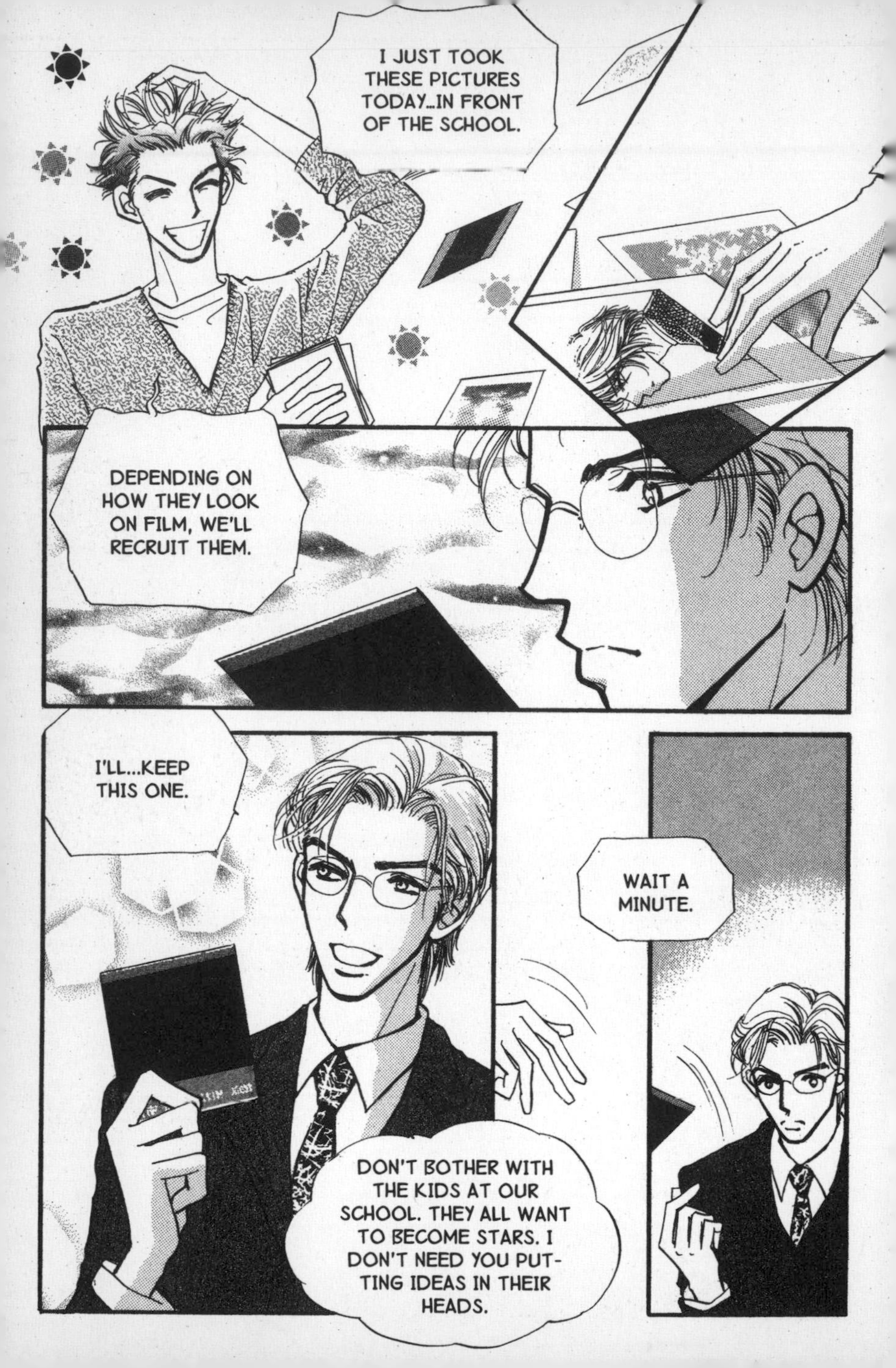
I JUST TOOK THESE PICTURES TODAY...IN FRONT OF THE SCHOOL.
DEPENDING ON HOW THEY LOOK ON FILM, WE'LL RECRUIT THEM.
I'LL...KEEP THIS ONE.
DON'T BOTHER WITH THE KIDS AT OUR SCHOOL. THEY ALL WANT TO BECOME STARS. I DON'T NEED YOU PUT-TING IDEAS IN THEIR HEADS.
WAIT A MINUTE.

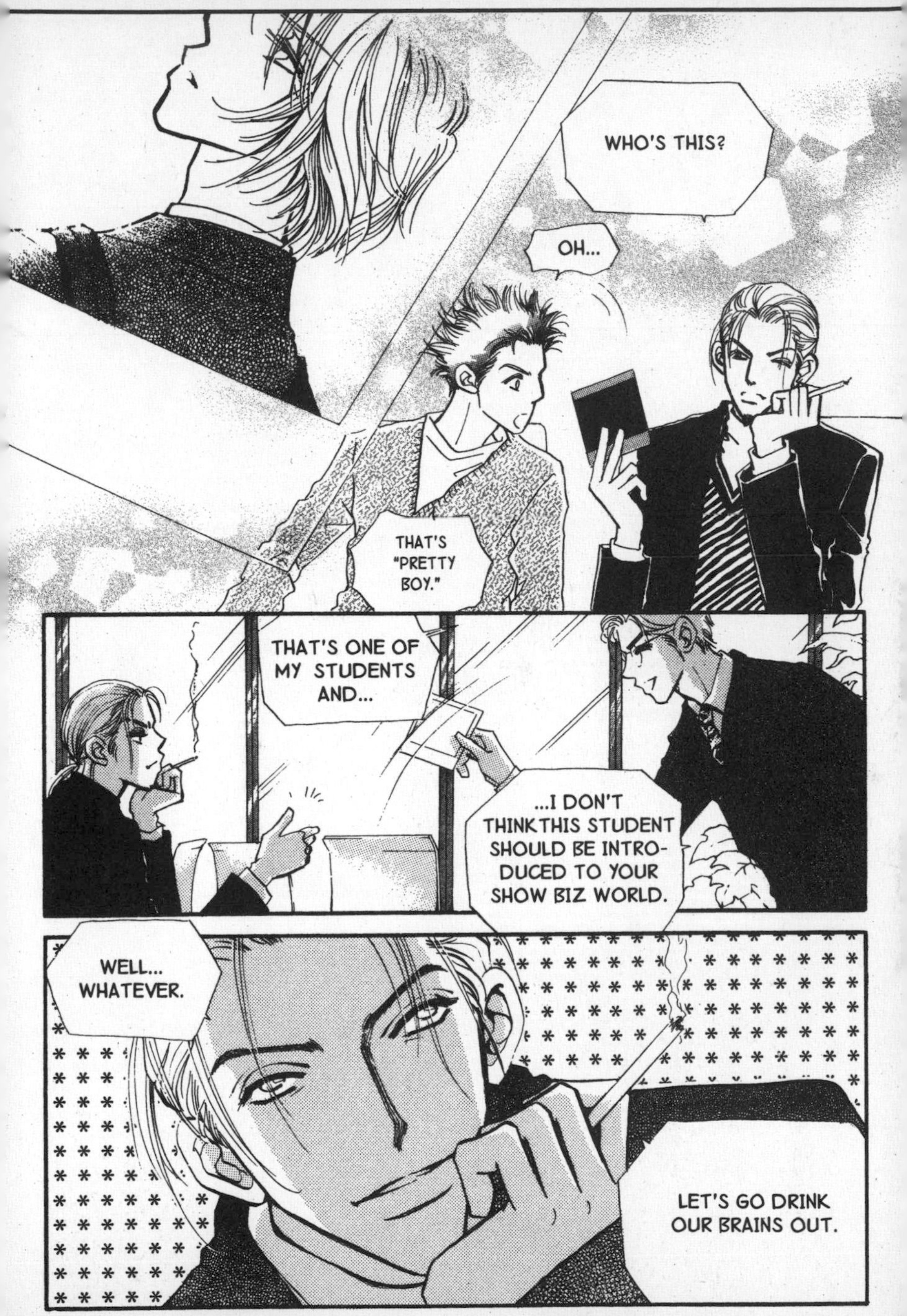
WHO'S THIS?
OH...
THAT'S "PRETTY BOY."
THAT'S ONE OF MY STUDENTS AND...
...I DON'T THINK THIS STUDENT SHOULD BE INTRO- DUCED TO YOUR SHOW BIZ WORLD.
WELL... WHATEVER.
LET'S GO DRINK OUR BRAINS OUT.

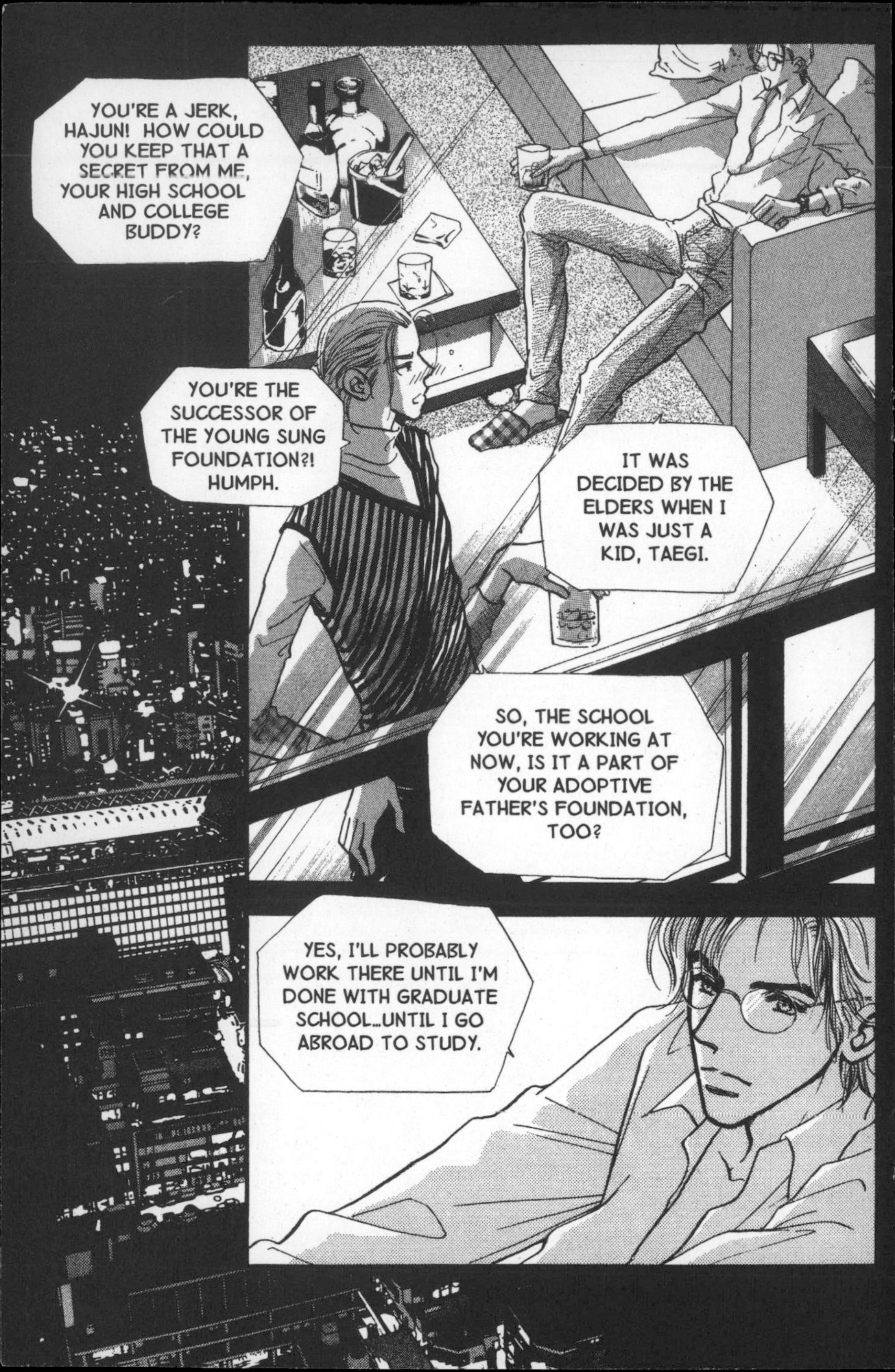
YOU'RE A JERK, HAJUN! HOW COULD YOU KEEP THAT A SECRET FROM ME, YOUR HIGH SCHOOL AND COLLEGE BUDDY?
YOU'RE THE SUCCESSOR OF THE YOUNG SUNG FOUNDATION?! HUMPH.
IT WAS DECIDED BY THE ELDERS WHEN I WAS JUST A KID, TAEGI.
SO, THE SCHOOL YOU'RE WORKING AT NOW, IS IT A PART OF YOUR ADOPTIVE FATHER'S FOUNDATION, TOO?
YES, I'LL PROBABLY WORK THERE UNTIL I'M DONE WITH GRADUATE SCHOOL...UNTIL I GO ABROAD TO STUDY.

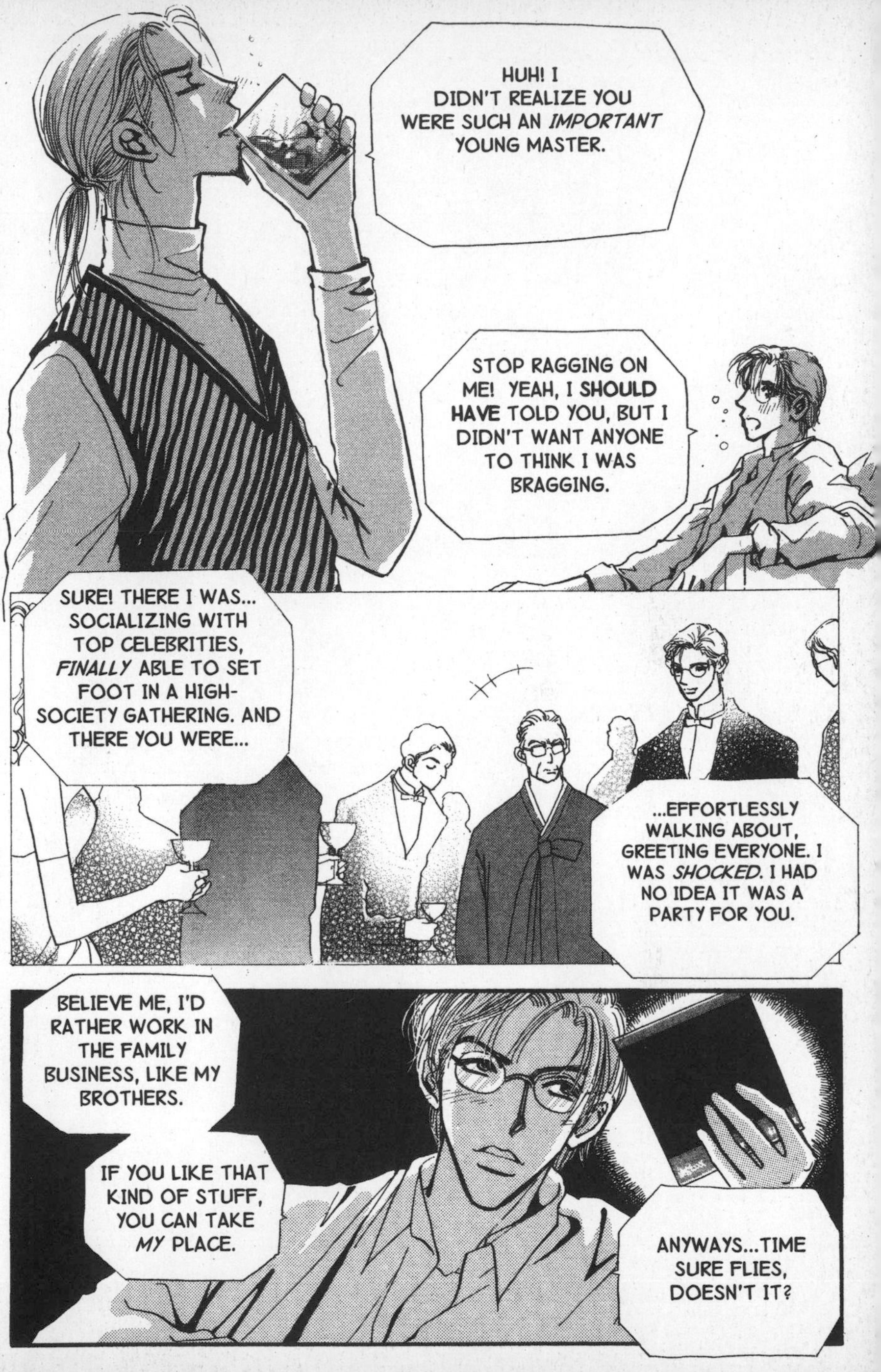
HUH! I DIDN'T REALIZE YOU WERE SUCH AN *IMPORTANT* YOUNG MASTER.
STOP RAGGING ON ME! YEAH, I **SHOULD HAVE** TOLD YOU, BUT I DIDN'T WANT ANYONE TO THINK I WAS BRAGGING.
SURE! THERE I WAS... SOCIALIZING WITH TOP CELEBRITIES, *FINALLY* ABLE TO SET FOOT IN A HIGH-SOCIETY GATHERING. AND THERE YOU WERE...
...EFFORTLESSLY WALKING ABOUT, GREETING EVERYONE. I WAS *SHOCKED*. I HAD NO IDEA IT WAS A PARTY FOR YOU.
BELIEVE ME, I'D RATHER WORK IN THE FAMILY BUSINESS, LIKE MY BROTHERS.
IF YOU LIKE THAT KIND OF STUFF, YOU CAN TAKE *MY* PLACE.
ANYWAYS...TIME SURE FLIES, DOESN'T IT?

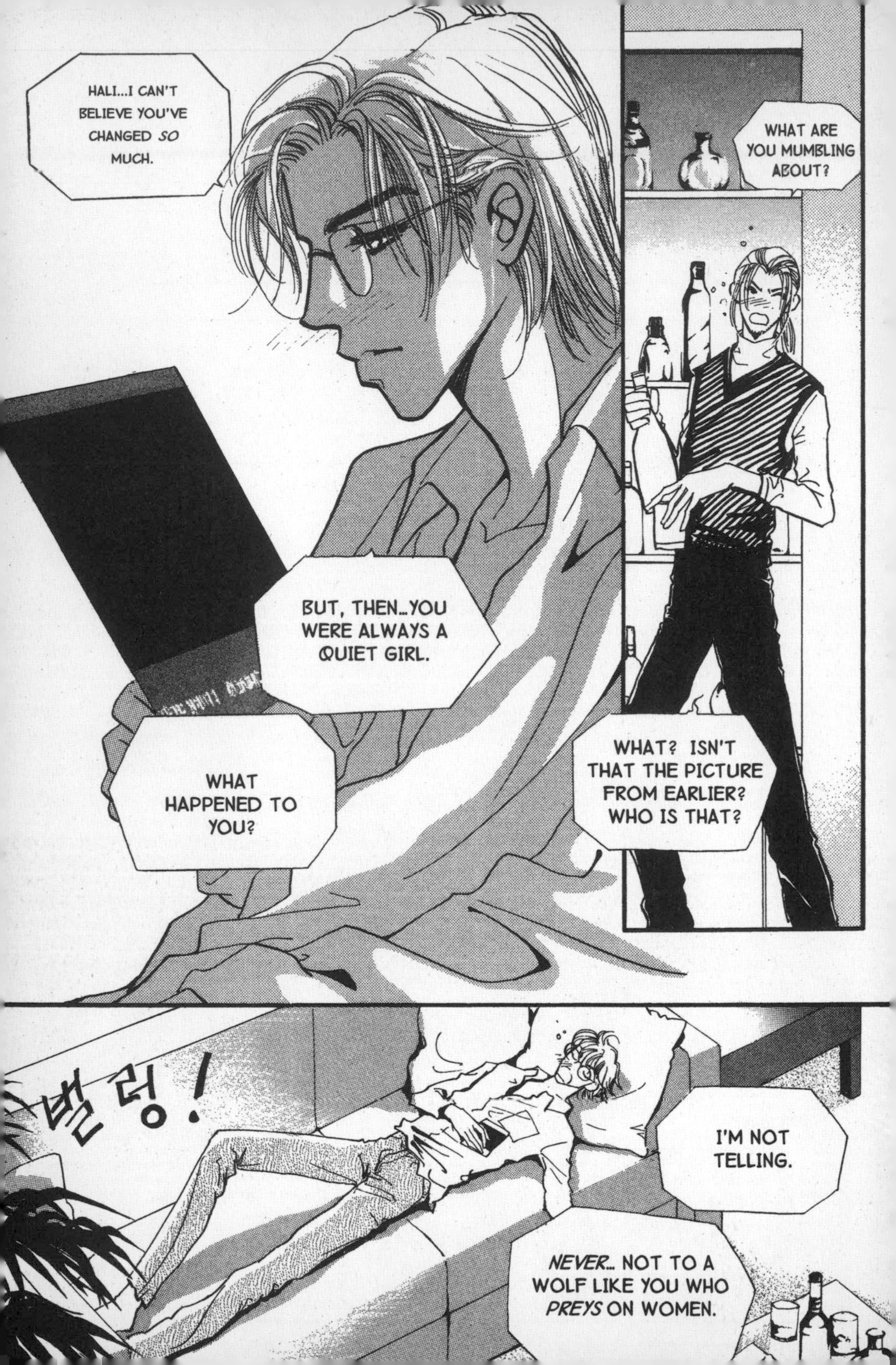
HALI...I CAN'T BELIEVE YOU'VE CHANGED *SO* MUCH.
BUT, THEN...YOU WERE ALWAYS A QUIET GIRL.
WHAT HAPPENED TO YOU?
WHAT ARE YOU MUMBLING ABOUT?
WHAT? ISN'T THAT THE PICTURE FROM EARLIER? WHO IS THAT?
벌렁!
I'M NOT TELLING.
NEVER... NOT TO A WOLF LIKE YOU WHO *PREYS* ON WOMEN.

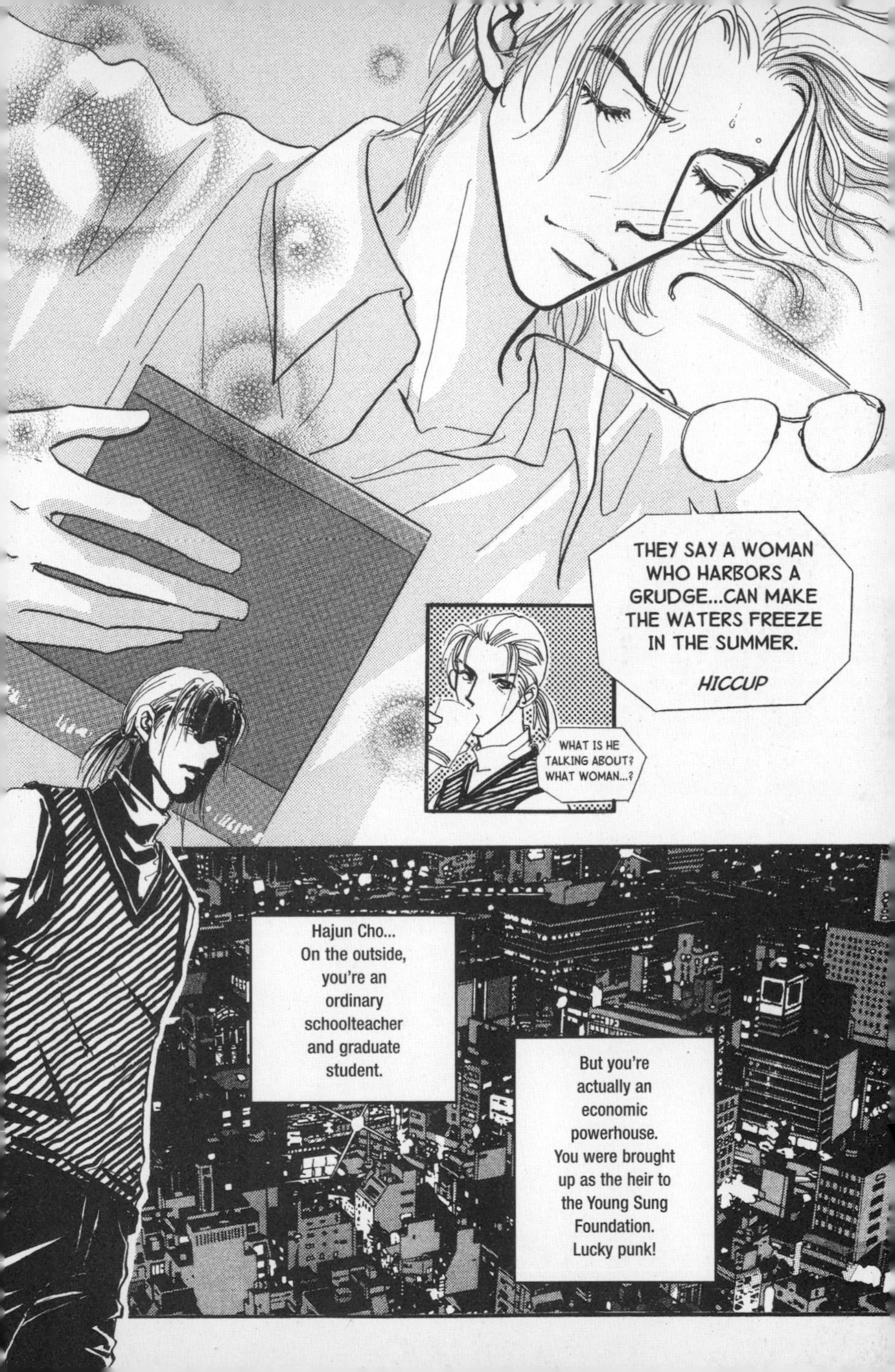
THEY SAY A WOMAN WHO HARBORS A GRUDGE...CAN MAKE THE WATERS FREEZE IN THE SUMMER.
HICCUP
WHAT IS HE TALKING ABOUT? WHAT WOMAN...?
Hajun Cho... On the outside, you're an ordinary schoolteacher and graduate student.
But you're actually an economic powerhouse. You were brought up as the heir to the Young Sung Foundation. Lucky punk!

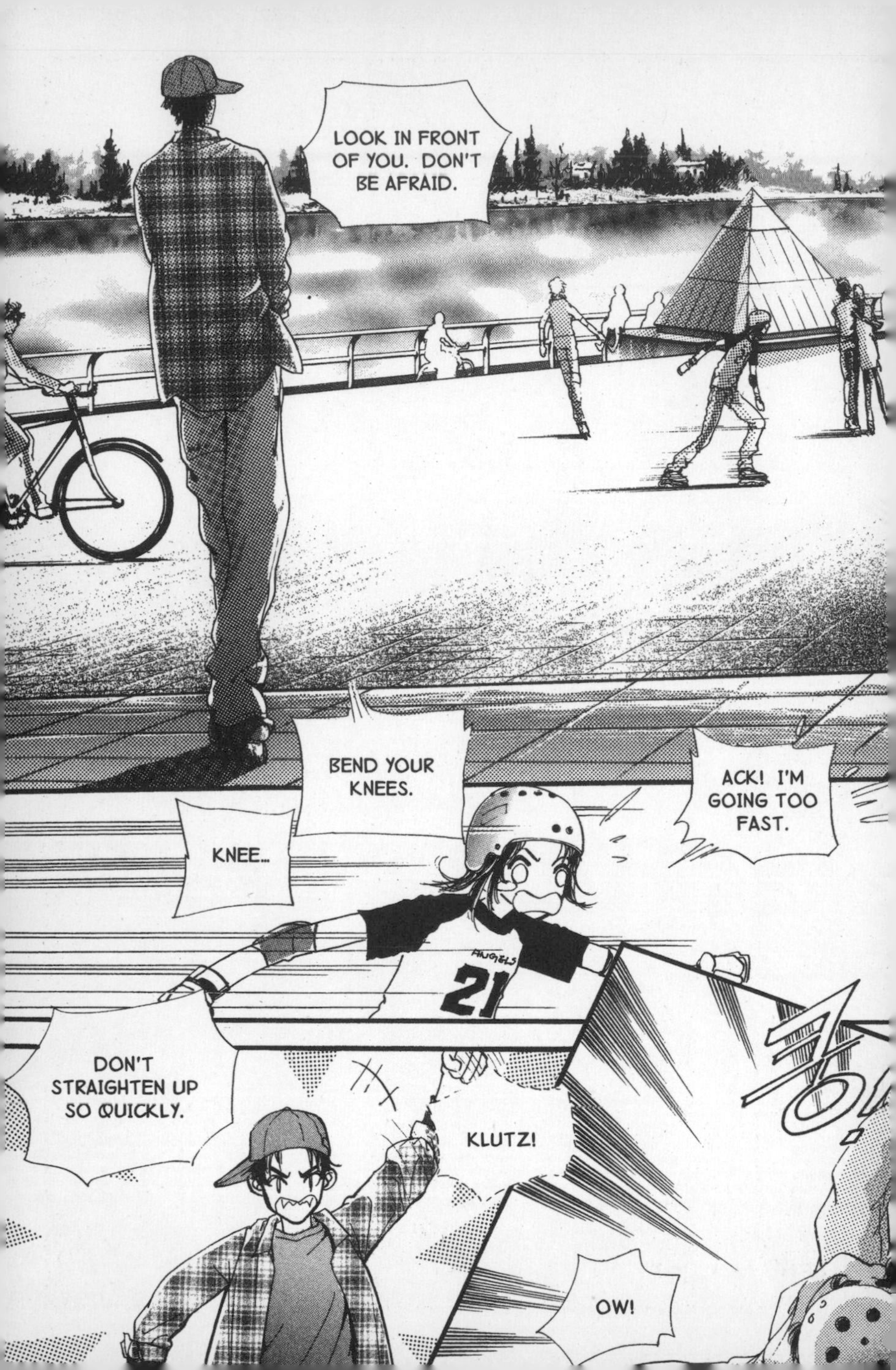

LOOK IN FRONT OF YOU. DON'T BE AFRAID.
KNEE...
BEND YOUR KNEES.
ACK! I'M GOING TOO FAST.
ANGELS 21
DON'T STRAIGHTEN UP SO QUICKLY.
KLUTZ!
OW!

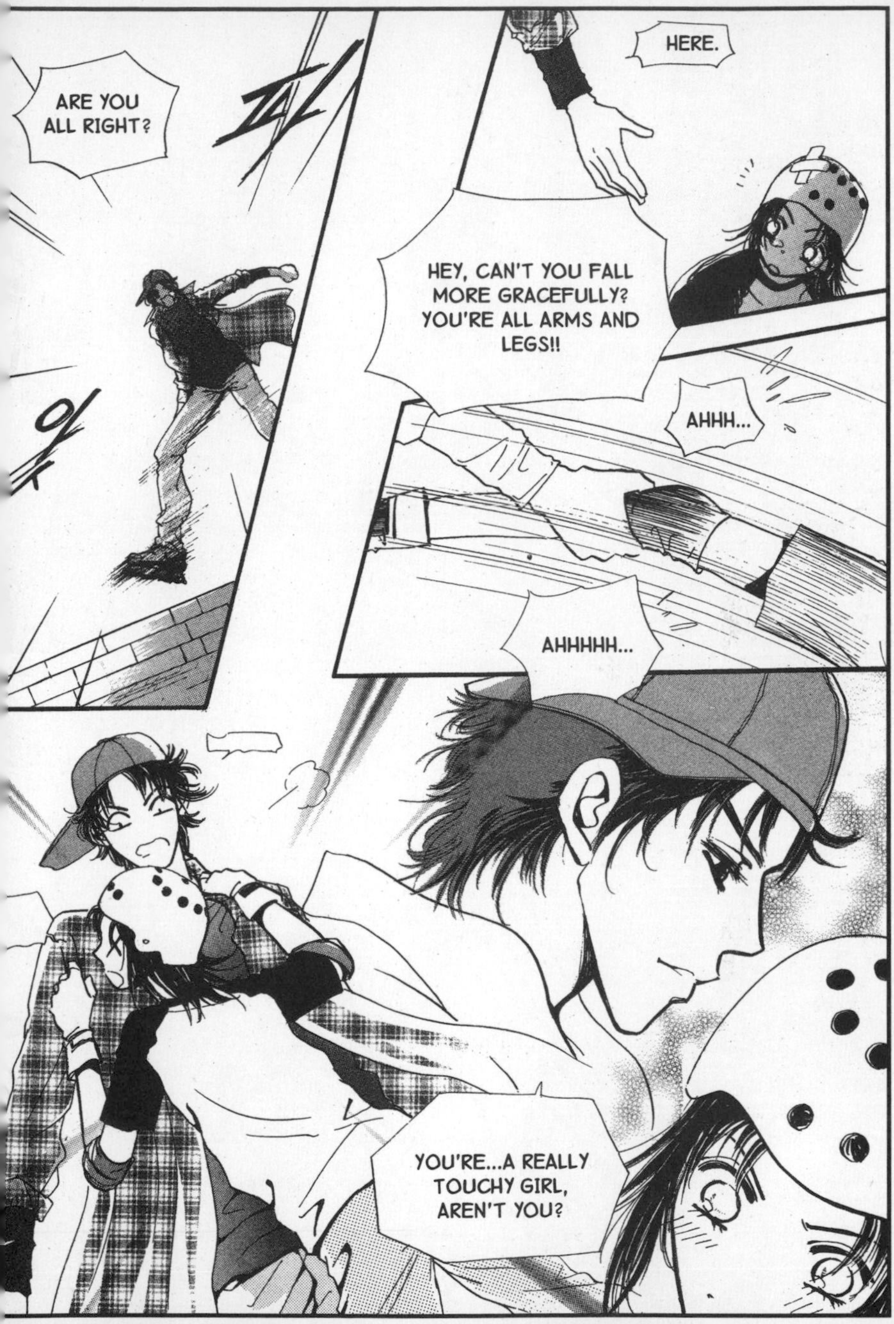
ARE YOU ALL RIGHT?
HERE.
HEY, CAN'T YOU FALL MORE GRACEFULLY? YOU'RE ALL ARMS AND LEGS!!
AHHH...
AHHHHH...
YOU'RE...A REALLY TOUCHY GIRL, AREN'T YOU?

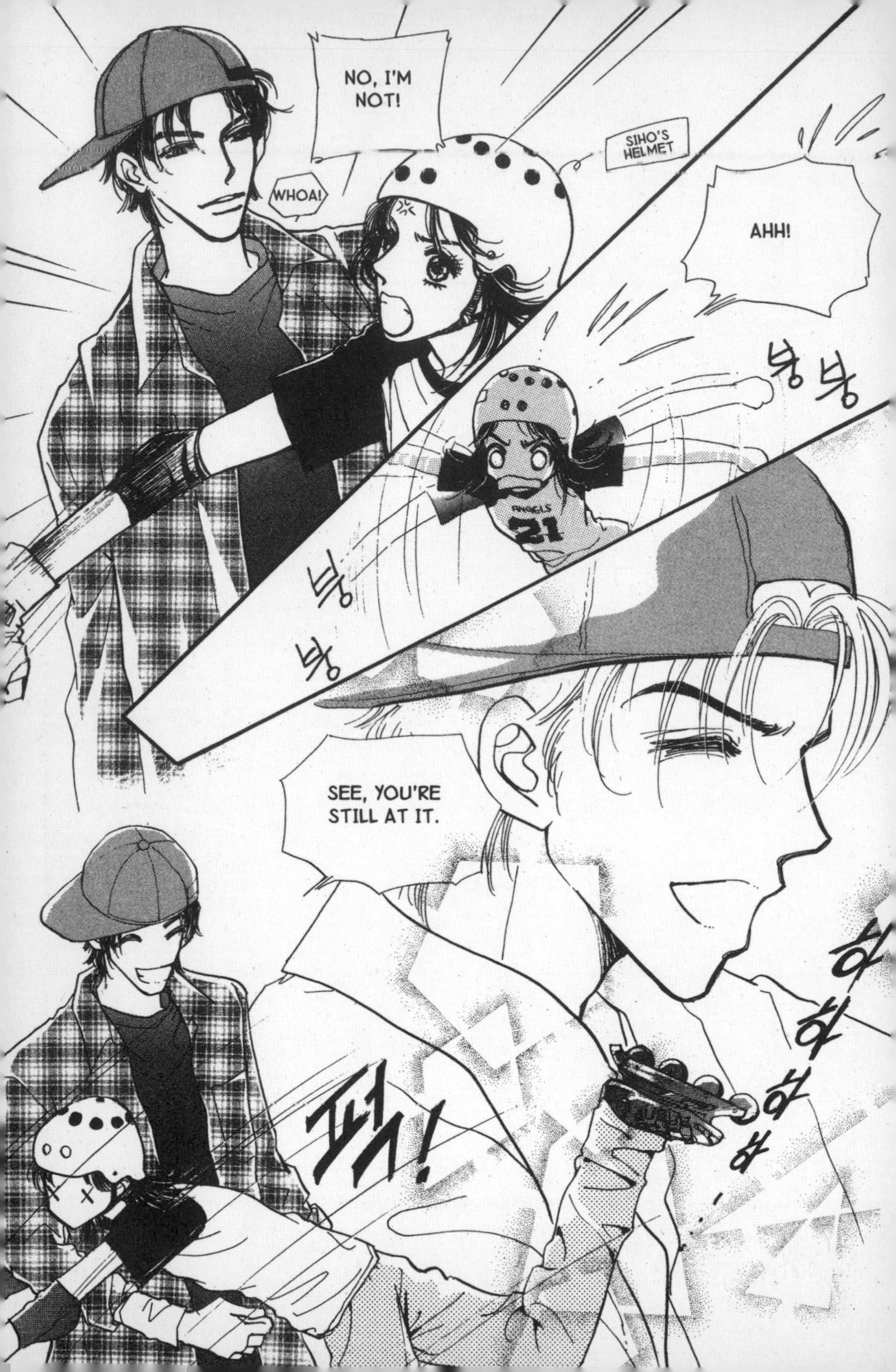
NO, I'M NOT!
WHOA!
SIHO'S HELMET
AHH!
붕붕
붕
붕
SEE, YOU'RE STILL AT IT.
퍽!
하하하하

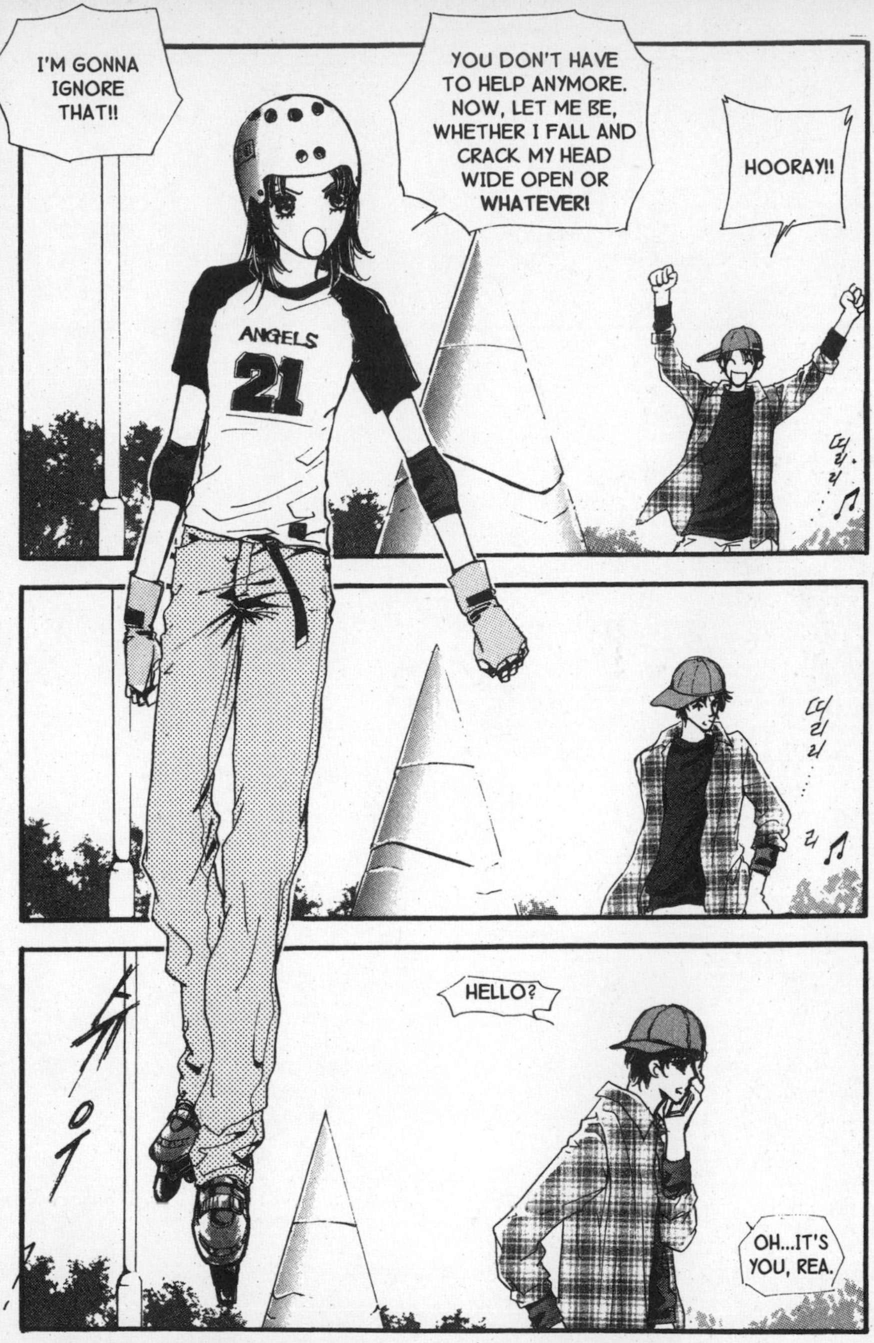
I'M GONNA IGNORE THAT!!
YOU DON'T HAVE TO HELP ANYMORE. NOW, LET ME BE, WHETHER I FALL AND CRACK MY HEAD WIDE OPEN OR WHATEVER!
HOORAY!!
ANGELS 21
HELLO?
OH...IT'S YOU, REA.

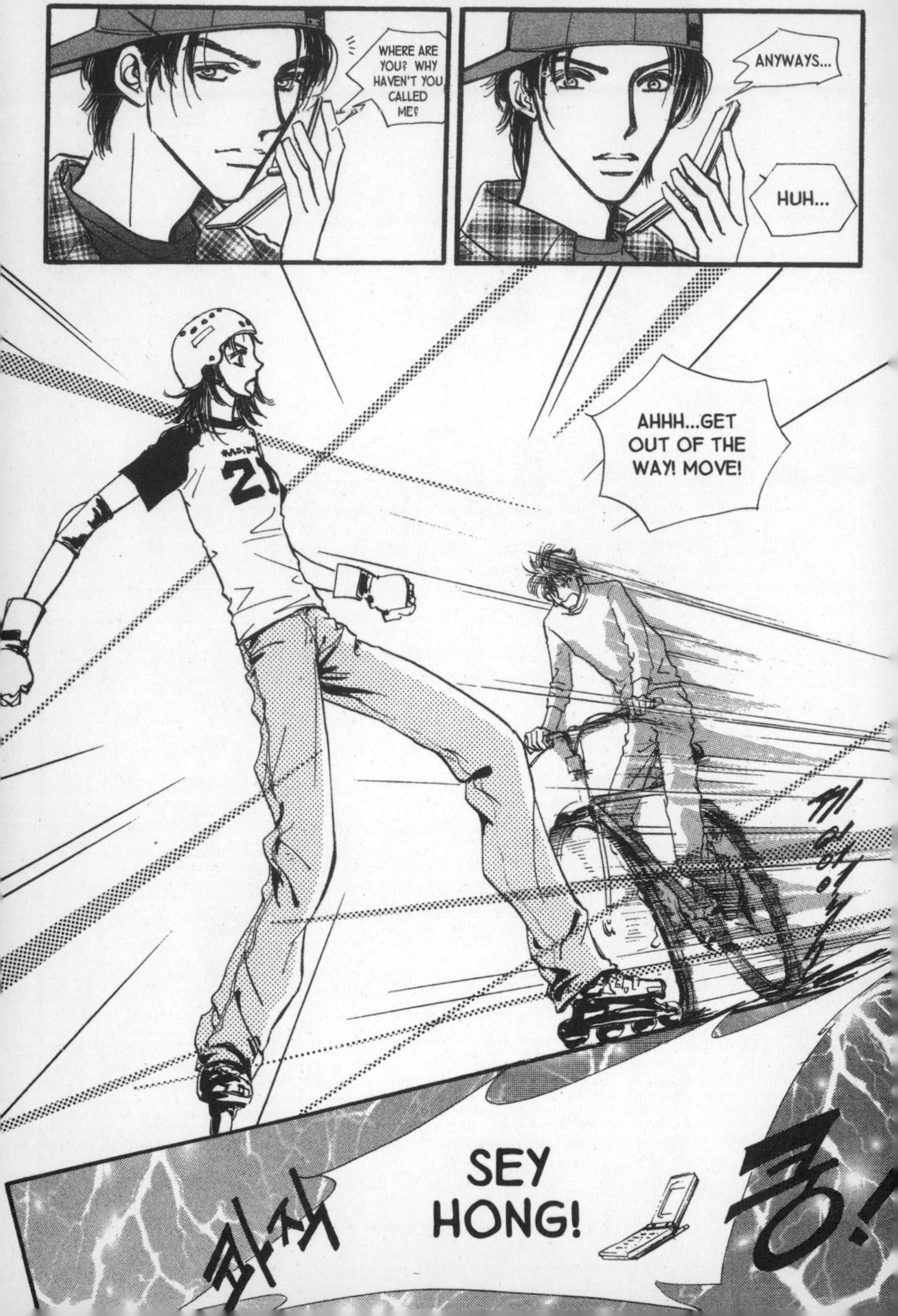
WHERE ARE YOU? WHY HAVEN'T YOU CALLED ME?
ANYWAYS...
HUH...
AHHH...GET OUT OF THE WAY! MOVE!
SEY HONG!
쿵!

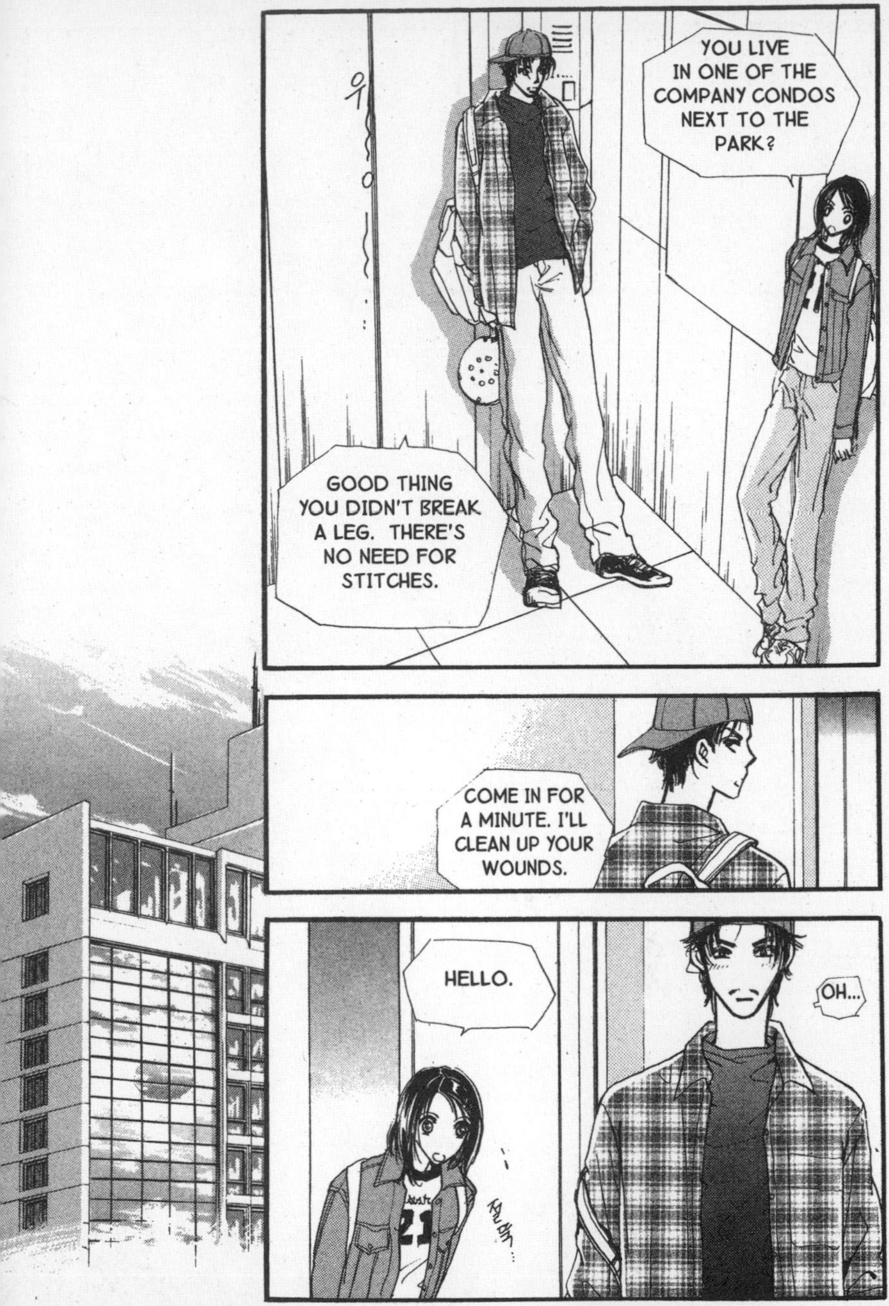
YOU LIVE IN ONE OF THE COMPANY CONDOS NEXT TO THE PARK?
GOOD THING YOU DIDN'T BREAK A LEG. THERE'S NO NEED FOR STITCHES.
COME IN FOR A MINUTE. I'LL CLEAN UP YOUR WOUNDS.
HELLO.
OH...

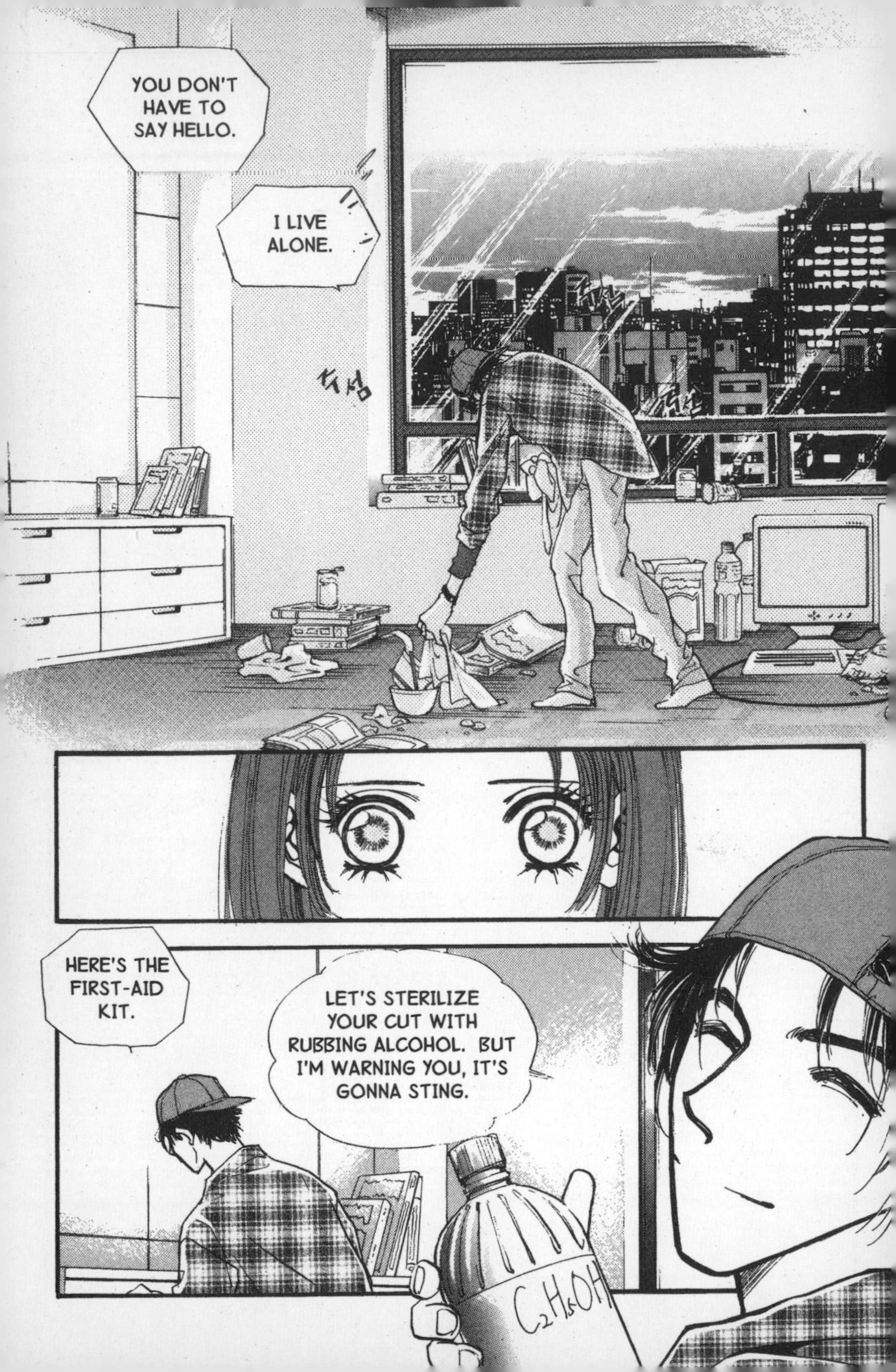
YOU DON'T HAVE TO SAY HELLO.
I LIVE ALONE.
HERE'S THE FIRST-AID KIT.
LET'S STERILIZE YOUR CUT WITH RUBBING ALCOHOL. BUT I'M WARNING YOU, IT'S GONNA STING.
C2H5OH

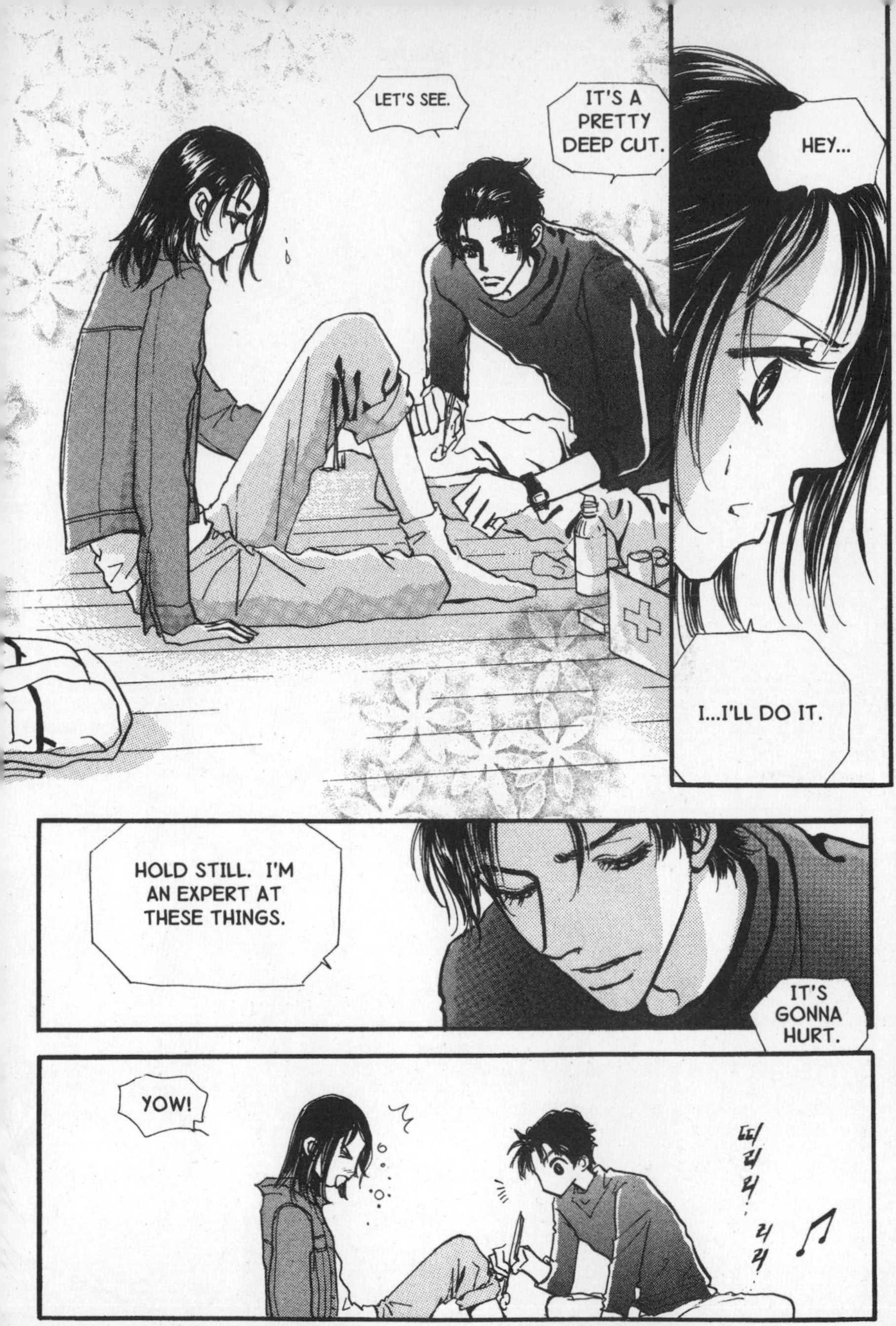
LET'S SEE.
IT'S A PRETTY DEEP CUT.
HEY...
I...I'LL DO IT.
HOLD STILL. I'M AN EXPERT AT THESE THINGS.
IT'S GONNA HURT.
YOW!
띠리리· 리리·

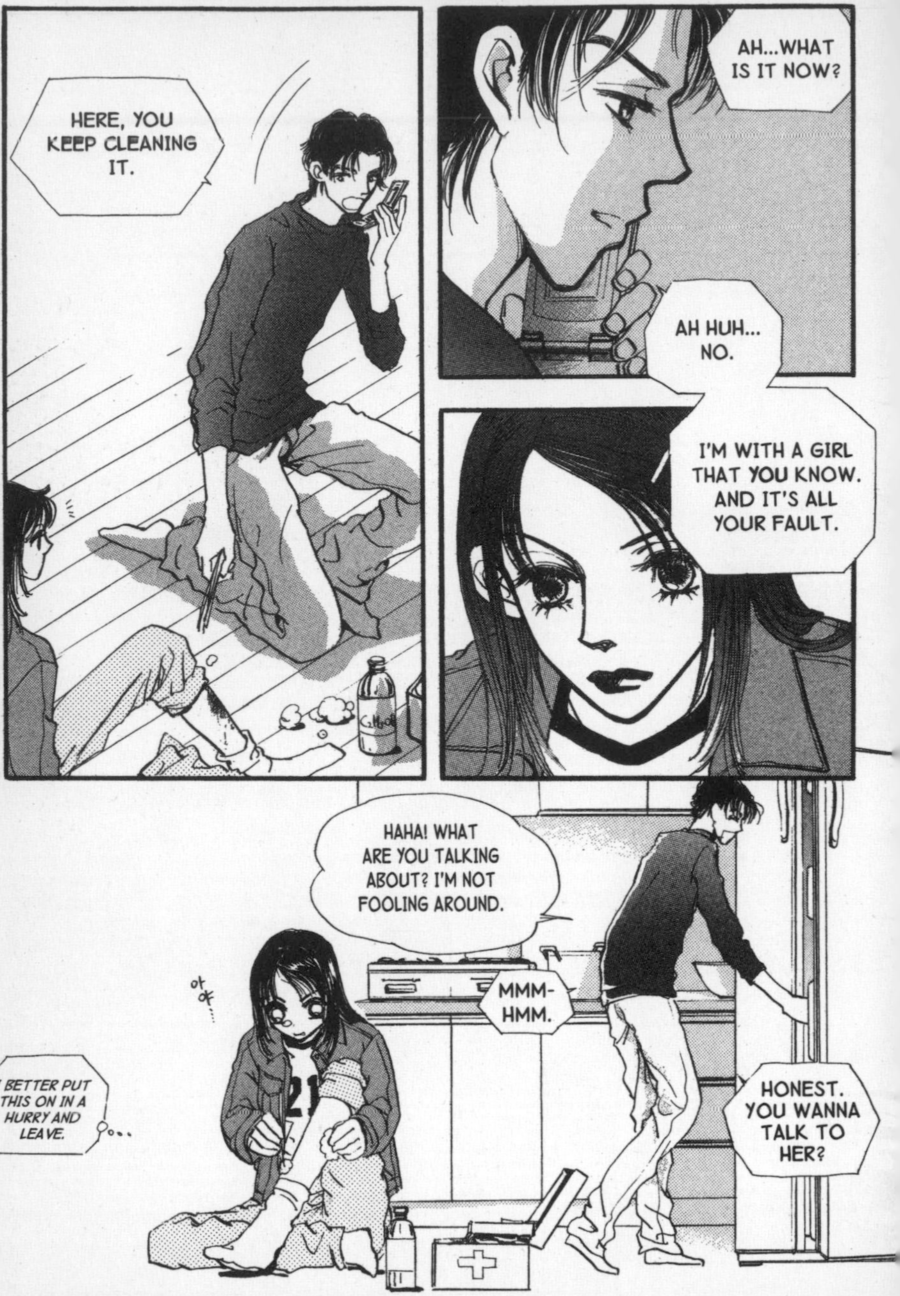
HERE, YOU KEEP CLEANING IT.
AH...WHAT IS IT NOW?
AH HUH... NO.
I'M WITH A GIRL THAT YOU KNOW. AND IT'S ALL YOUR FAULT.
HAHA! WHAT ARE YOU TALKING ABOUT? I'M NOT FOOLING AROUND.
MMM-HMM.
I BETTER PUT THIS ON IN A HURRY AND LEAVE.
HONEST. YOU WANNA TALK TO HER?

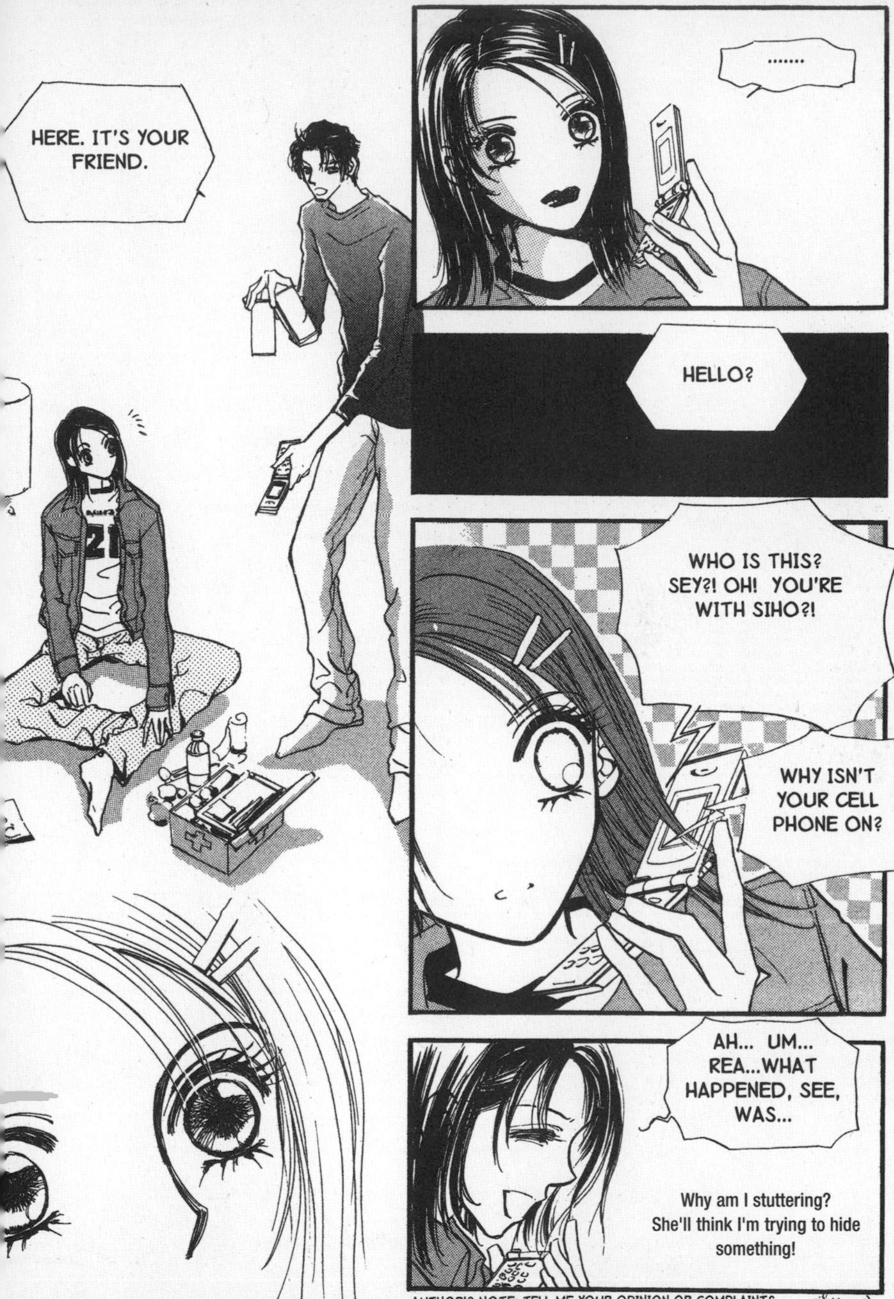
HERE. IT'S YOUR FRIEND.
....
HELLO?
WHO IS THIS? SEY?! OH! YOU'RE WITH SIHO?!
WHY ISN'T YOUR CELL PHONE ON?
AH... UM... REA...WHAT HAPPENED, SEE, WAS...
Why am I stuttering? She'll think I'm trying to hide something!

AUTHOR'S NOTE: TELL ME YOUR OPINION OR COMPLAINTS ABOUT I.N.V.U. AT THE FOLLOWING WEBSITE: HTTP://MYHOME.NETSGO.COM/PHANTASMA. IT'S MY HOME PAGE.

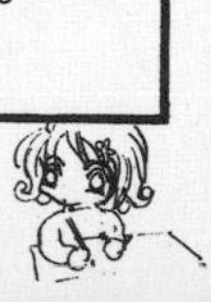

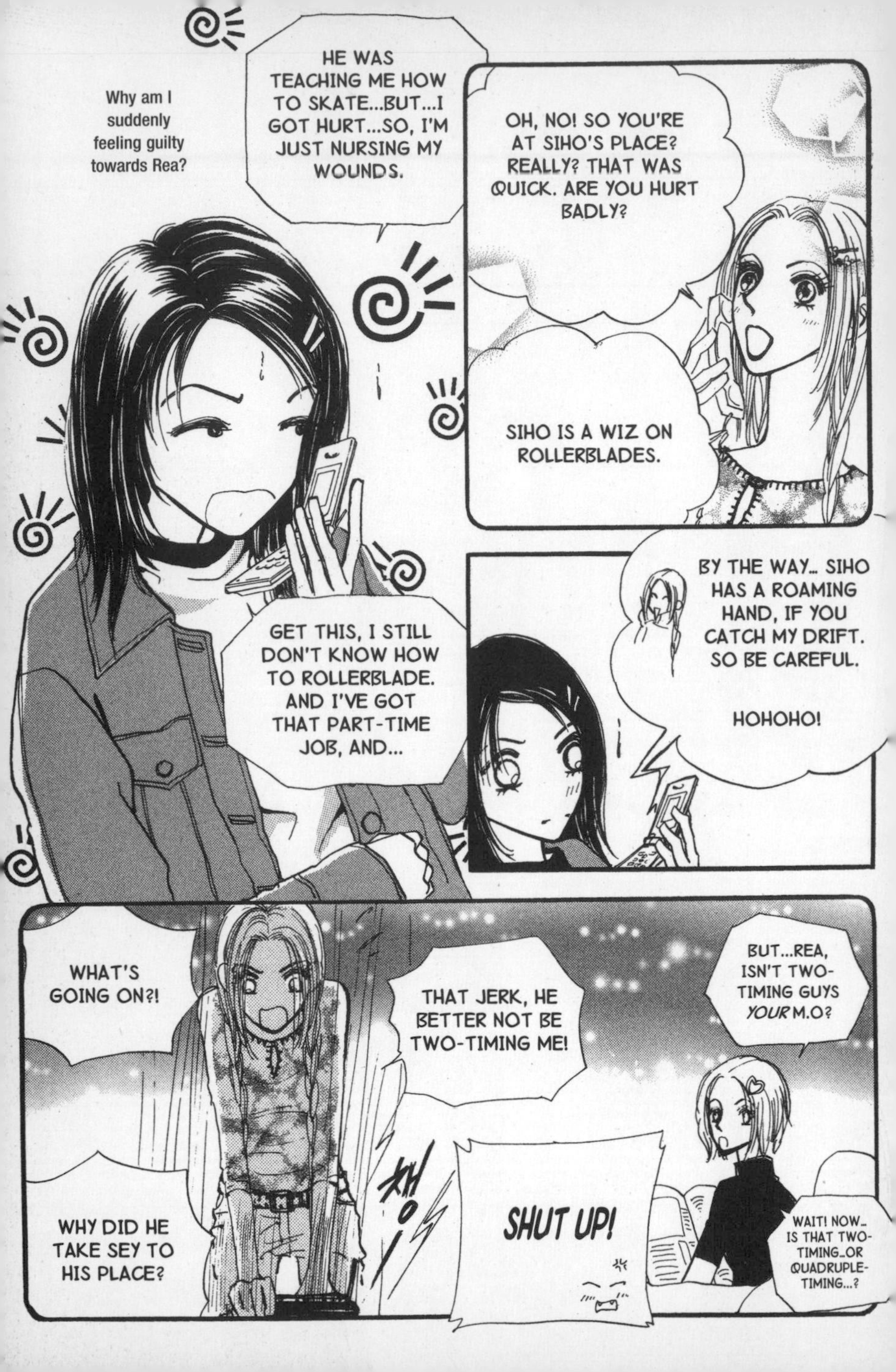
Why am I suddenly feeling guilty towards Rea?
HE WAS TEACHING ME HOW TO SKATE...BUT...I GOT HURT...SO, I'M JUST NURSING MY WOUNDS.
GET THIS, I STILL DON'T KNOW HOW TO ROLLERBLADE. AND I'VE GOT THAT PART-TIME JOB, AND...
OH, NO! SO YOU'RE AT SIHO'S PLACE? REALLY? THAT WAS QUICK. ARE YOU HURT BADLY?
SIHO IS A WIZ ON ROLLERBLADES.
BY THE WAY... SIHO HAS A ROAMING HAND, IF YOU CATCH MY DRIFT. SO BE CAREFUL.
HOHOHO!
WHAT'S GOING ON?!
THAT JERK, HE BETTER NOT BE TWO-TIMING ME!
BUT...REA, ISN'T TWO-TIMING GUYS *YOUR* M.O?
WHY DID HE TAKE SEY TO HIS PLACE?
SHUT UP!
WAIT! NOW... IS THAT TWO-TIMING...OR QUADRUPLE-TIMING...?

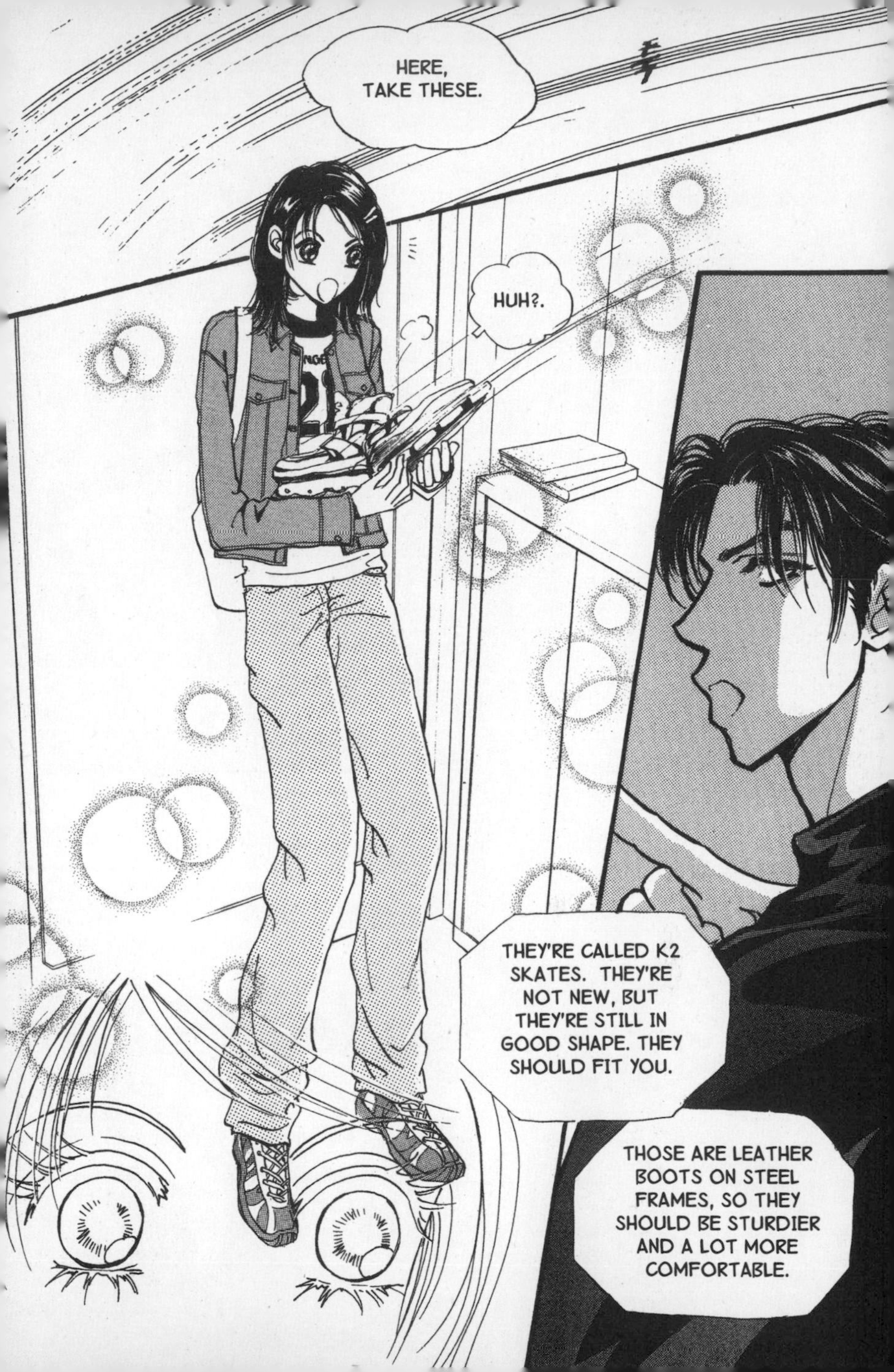
HERE, TAKE THESE.
HUH?.
THEY'RE CALLED K2 SKATES. THEY'RE NOT NEW, BUT THEY'RE STILL IN GOOD SHAPE. THEY SHOULD FIT YOU.
THOSE ARE LEATHER BOOTS ON STEEL FRAMES, SO THEY SHOULD BE STURDIER AND A LOT MORE COMFORTABLE.

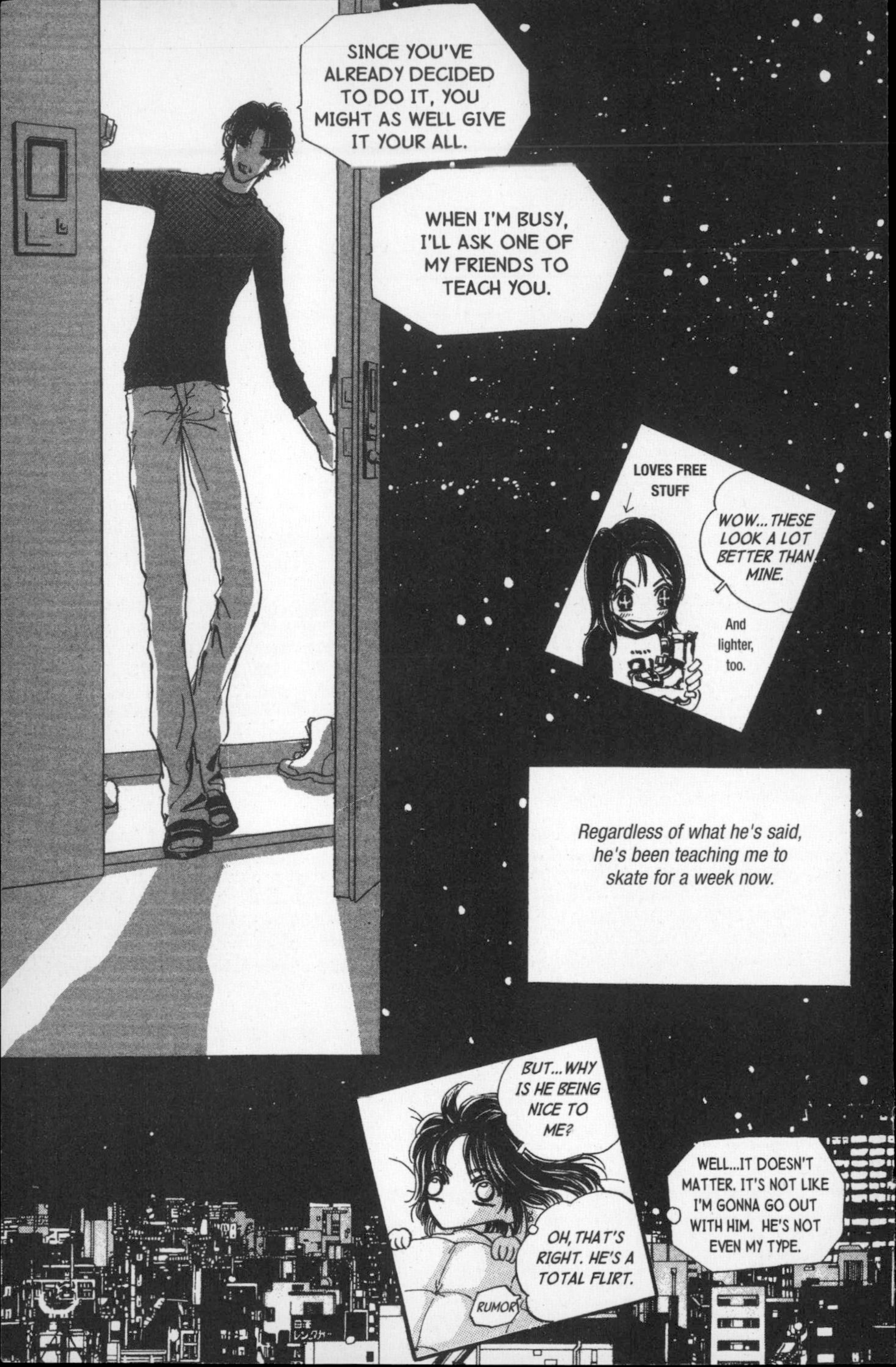

SINCE YOU'VE ALREADY DECIDED TO DO IT, YOU MIGHT AS WELL GIVE IT YOUR ALL.
WHEN I'M BUSY, I'LL ASK ONE OF MY FRIENDS TO TEACH YOU.
LOVES FREE STUFF
WOW...THESE LOOK A LOT BETTER THAN MINE.
And lighter, too.
Regardless of what he's said, he's been teaching me to skate for a week now.
BUT...WHY IS HE BEING NICE TO ME?
OH, THAT'S RIGHT. HE'S A TOTAL FLIRT.
RUMOR
WELL...IT DOESN'T MATTER. IT'S NOT LIKE I'M GONNA GO OUT WITH HIM. HE'S NOT EVEN MY TYPE.

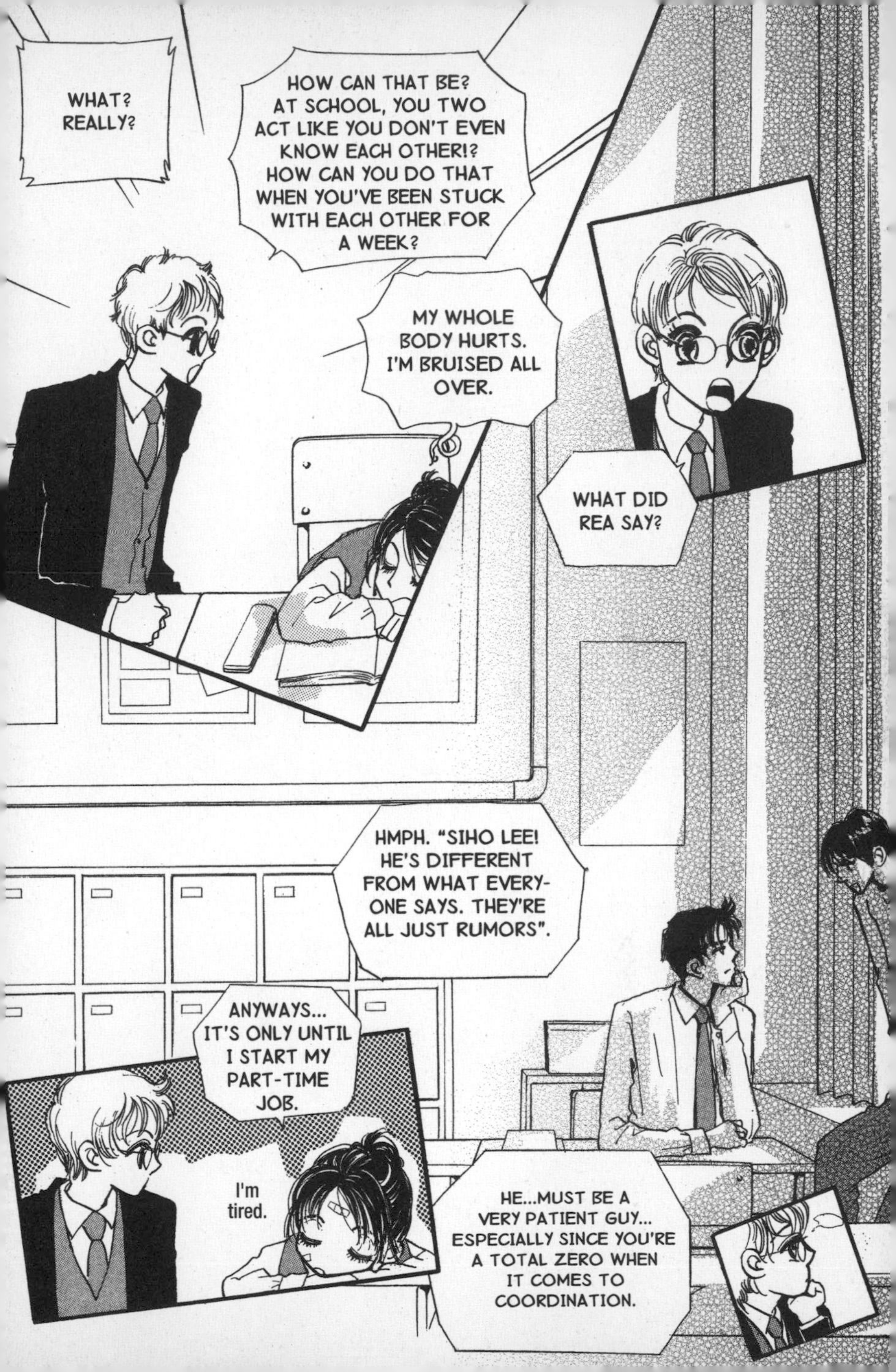
WHAT? REALLY?
HOW CAN THAT BE? AT SCHOOL, YOU TWO ACT LIKE YOU DON'T EVEN KNOW EACH OTHER!? HOW CAN YOU DO THAT WHEN YOU'VE BEEN STUCK WITH EACH OTHER FOR A WEEK?
MY WHOLE BODY HURTS. I'M BRUISED ALL OVER.
WHAT DID REA SAY?
HMPH. "SIHO LEE! HE'S DIFFERENT FROM WHAT EVERY-ONE SAYS. THEY'RE ALL JUST RUMORS".
ANYWAYS... IT'S ONLY UNTIL I START MY PART-TIME JOB.
I'm tired.
HE...MUST BE A VERY PATIENT GUY... ESPECIALLY SINCE YOU'RE A TOTAL ZERO WHEN IT COMES TO COORDINATION.

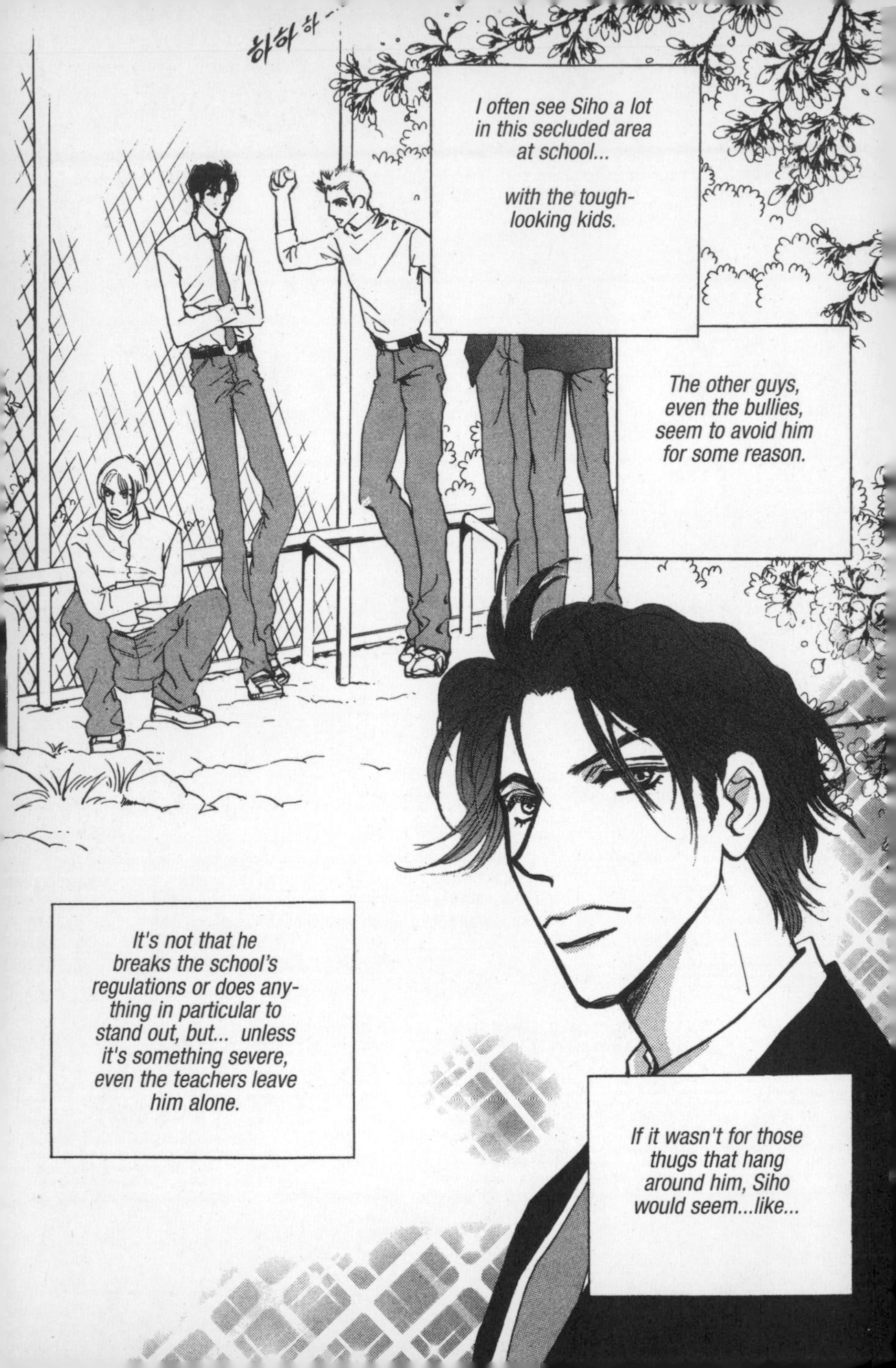

하하 하
I often see Siho a lot in this secluded area at school...
with the tough-looking kids.
The other guys, even the bullies, seem to avoid him for some reason.
It's not that he breaks the school's regulations or does anything in particular to stand out, but... unless it's something severe, even the teachers leave him alone.
If it wasn't for those thugs that hang around him, Siho would seem...like...

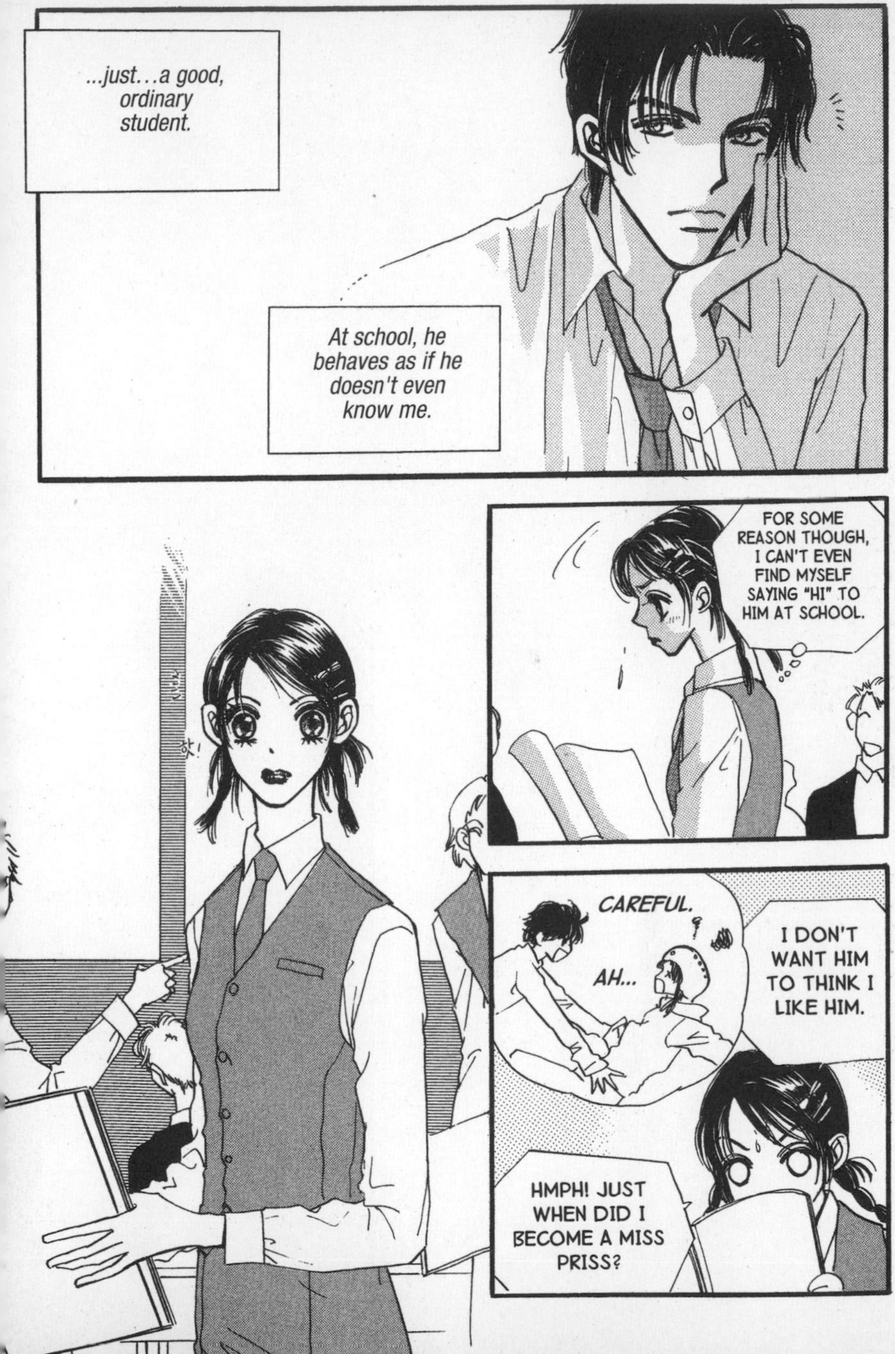
...just...a good, ordinary student.
At school, he behaves as if he doesn't even know me.
FOR SOME REASON THOUGH, I CAN'T EVEN FIND MYSELF SAYING "HI" TO HIM AT SCHOOL.
CAREFUL.
AH...
I DON'T WANT HIM TO THINK I LIKE HIM.
HMPH! JUST WHEN DID I BECOME A MISS PRISS?

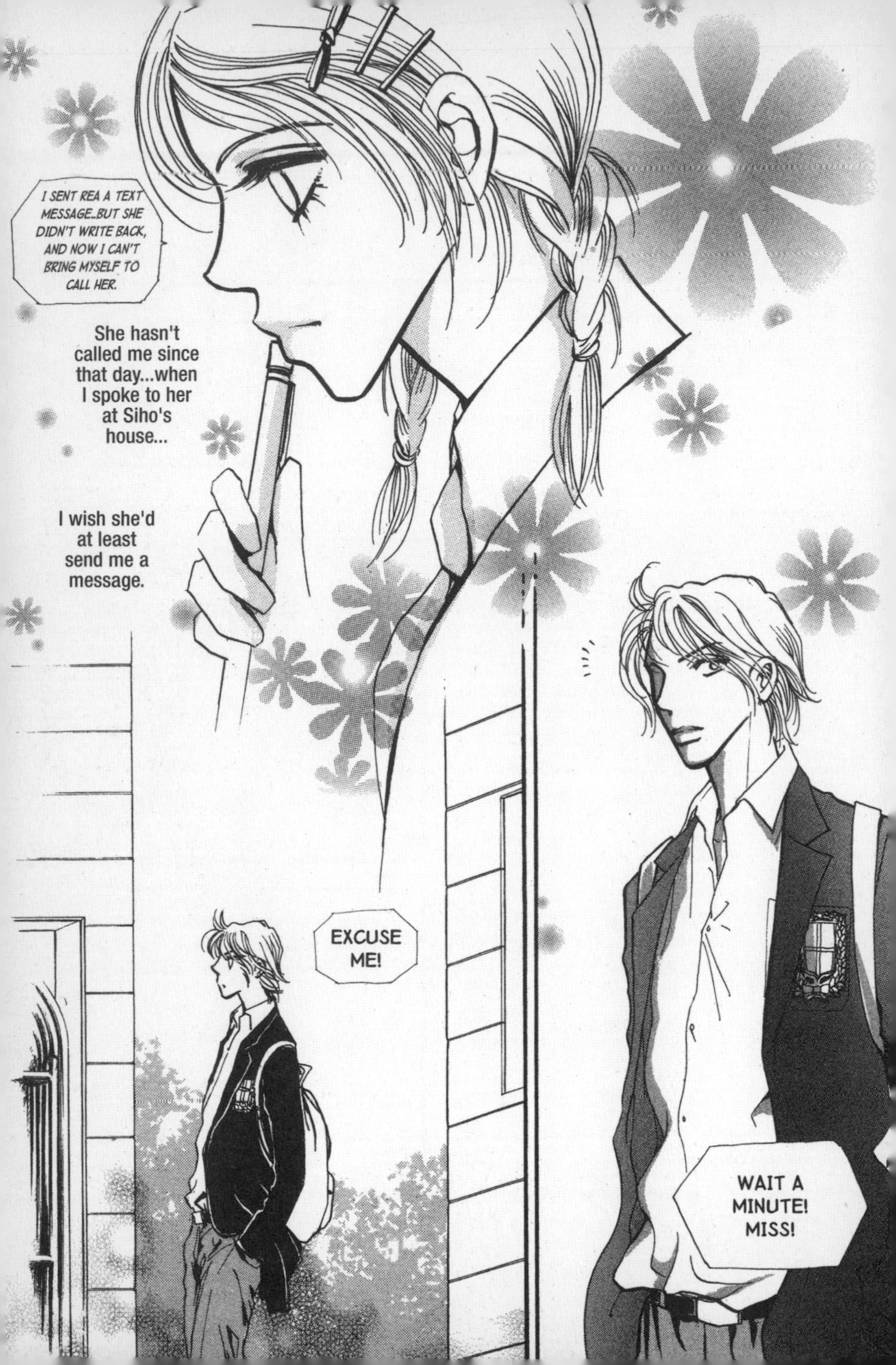
I SENT REA A TEXT MESSAGE...BUT SHE DIDN'T WRITE BACK, AND NOW I CAN'T BRING MYSELF TO CALL HER.
She hasn't called me since that day...when I spoke to her at Siho's house...
I wish she'd at least send me a message.
EXCUSE ME!
WAIT A MINUTE! MISS!

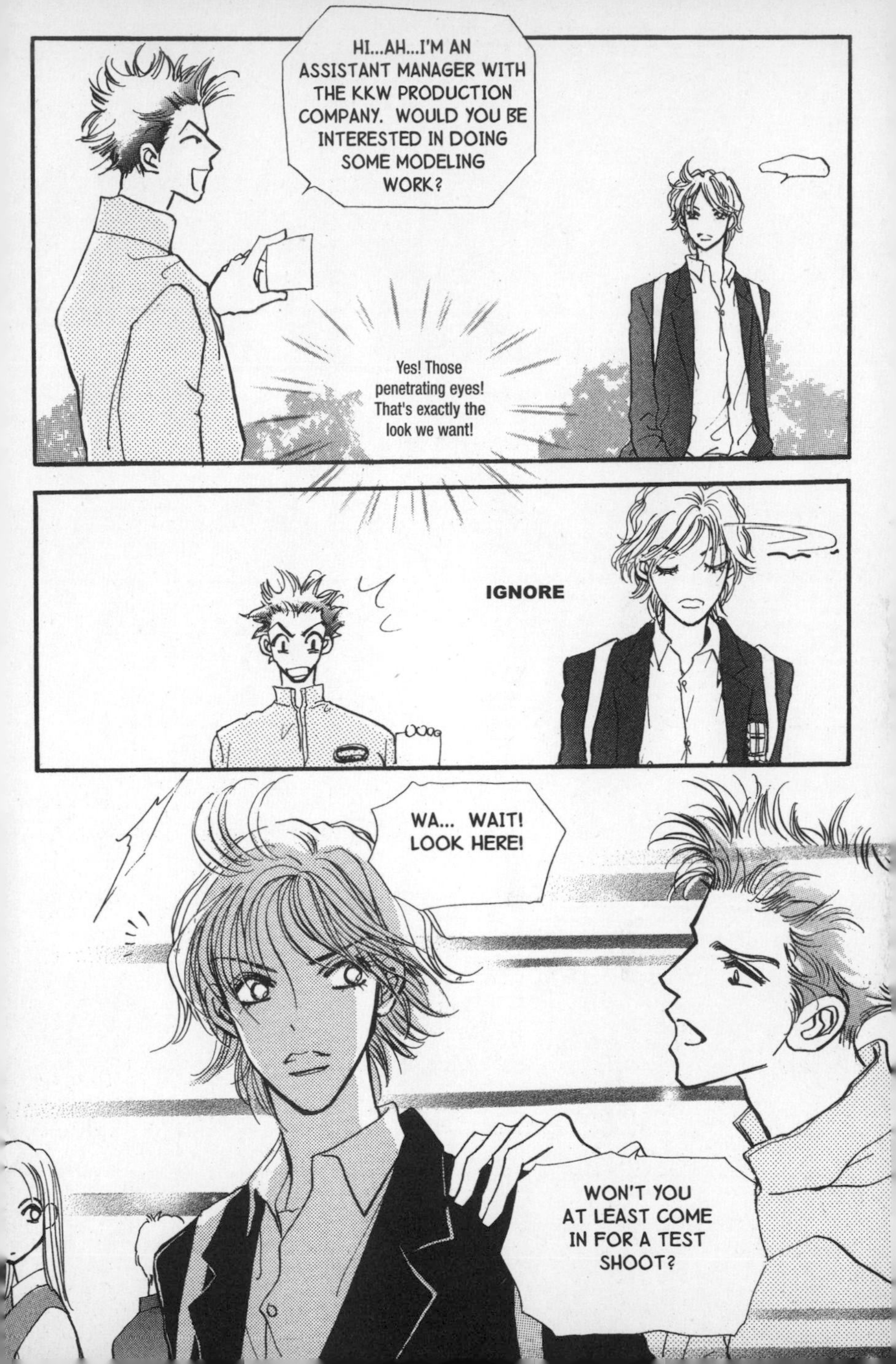
HI...AH...I'M AN ASSISTANT MANAGER WITH THE KKW PRODUCTION COMPANY. WOULD YOU BE INTERESTED IN DOING SOME MODELING WORK?
Yes! Those penetrating eyes! That's exactly the look we want!
IGNORE
WA... WAIT! LOOK HERE!
WON'T YOU AT LEAST COME IN FOR A TEST SHOOT?

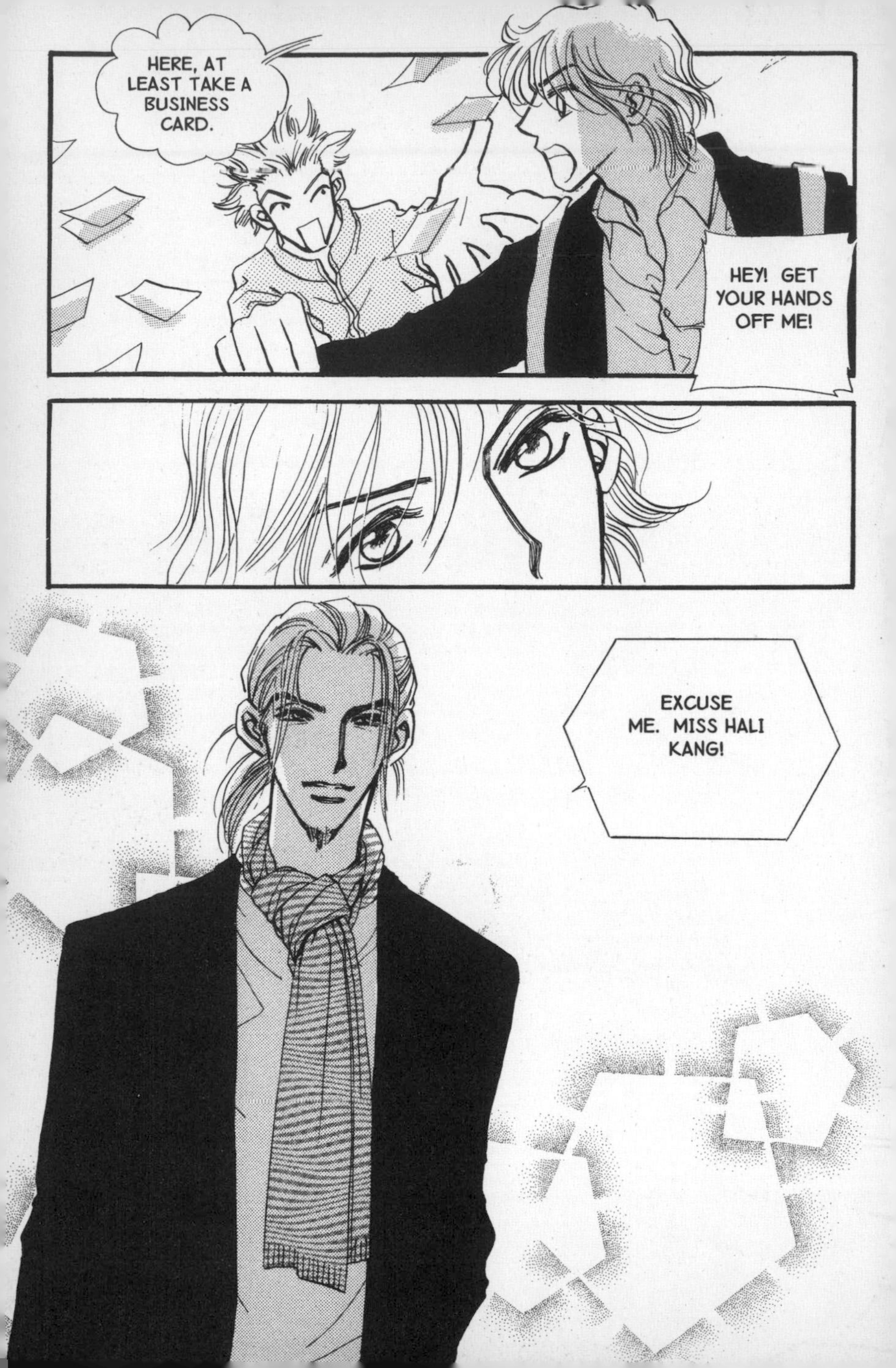
HERE, AT LEAST TAKE A BUSINESS CARD.
HEY! GET YOUR HANDS OFF ME!
EXCUSE ME. MISS HALI KANG!

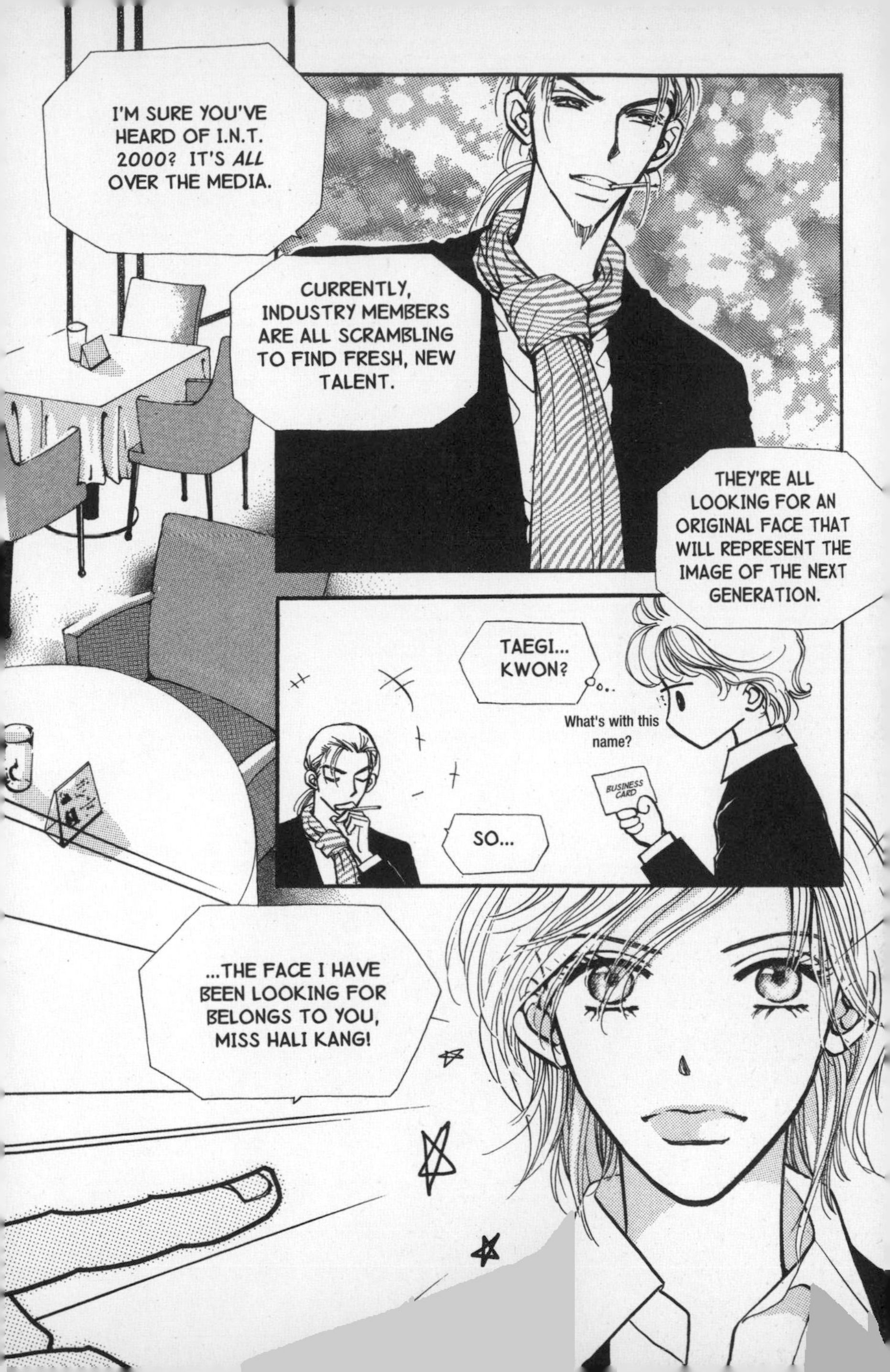
I'M SURE YOU'VE HEARD OF I.N.T. 2000? IT'S *ALL* OVER THE MEDIA.
CURRENTLY, INDUSTRY MEMBERS ARE ALL SCRAMBLING TO FIND FRESH, NEW TALENT.
THEY'RE ALL LOOKING FOR AN ORIGINAL FACE THAT WILL REPRESENT THE IMAGE OF THE NEXT GENERATION.
TAEGI... KWON?
What's with this name?
BUSINESS CARD
SO...
...THE FACE I HAVE BEEN LOOKING FOR BELONGS TO YOU, MISS HALI KANG!

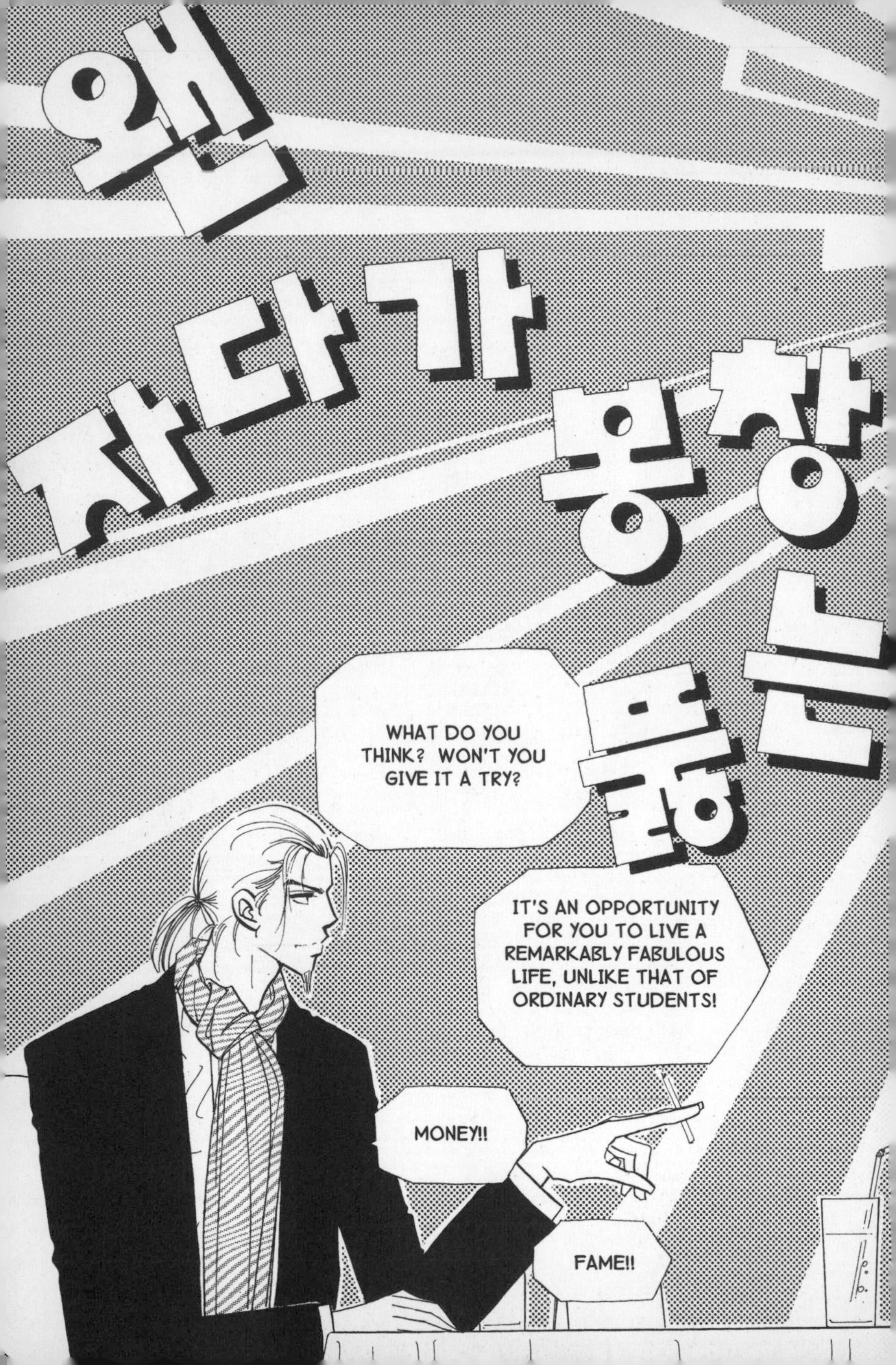
WHAT DO YOU THINK? WON'T YOU GIVE IT A TRY?
IT'S AN OPPORTUNITY FOR YOU TO LIVE A REMARKABLY FABULOUS LIFE, UNLIKE THAT OF ORDINARY STUDENTS!
MONEY!!
FAME!!

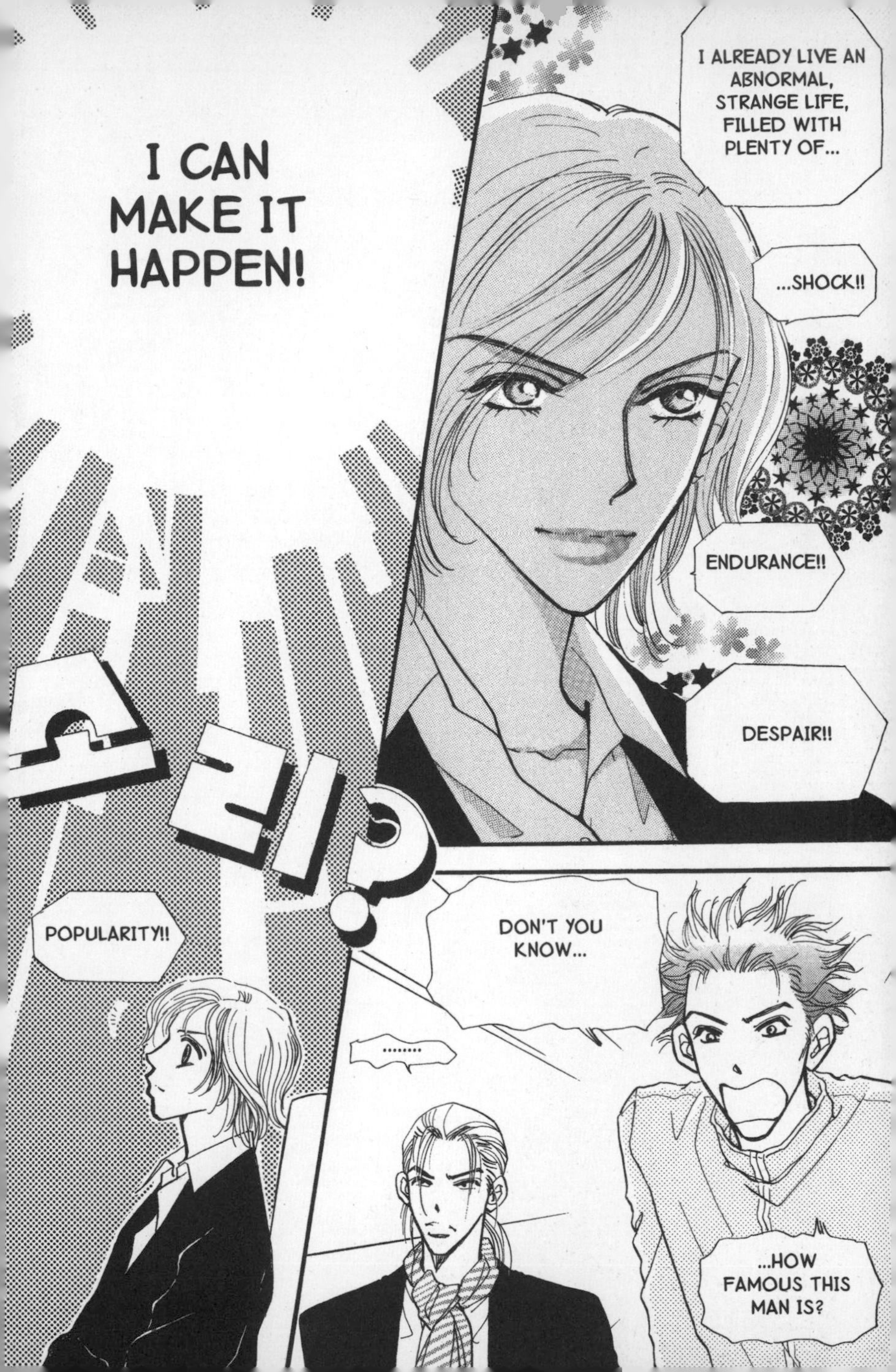
I CAN MAKE IT HAPPEN!
POPULARITY!!
I ALREADY LIVE AN ABNORMAL, STRANGE LIFE, FILLED WITH PLENTY OF...
...SHOCK!!
ENDURANCE!!
DESPAIR!!
DON'T YOU KNOW...
....
...HOW FAMOUS THIS MAN IS?

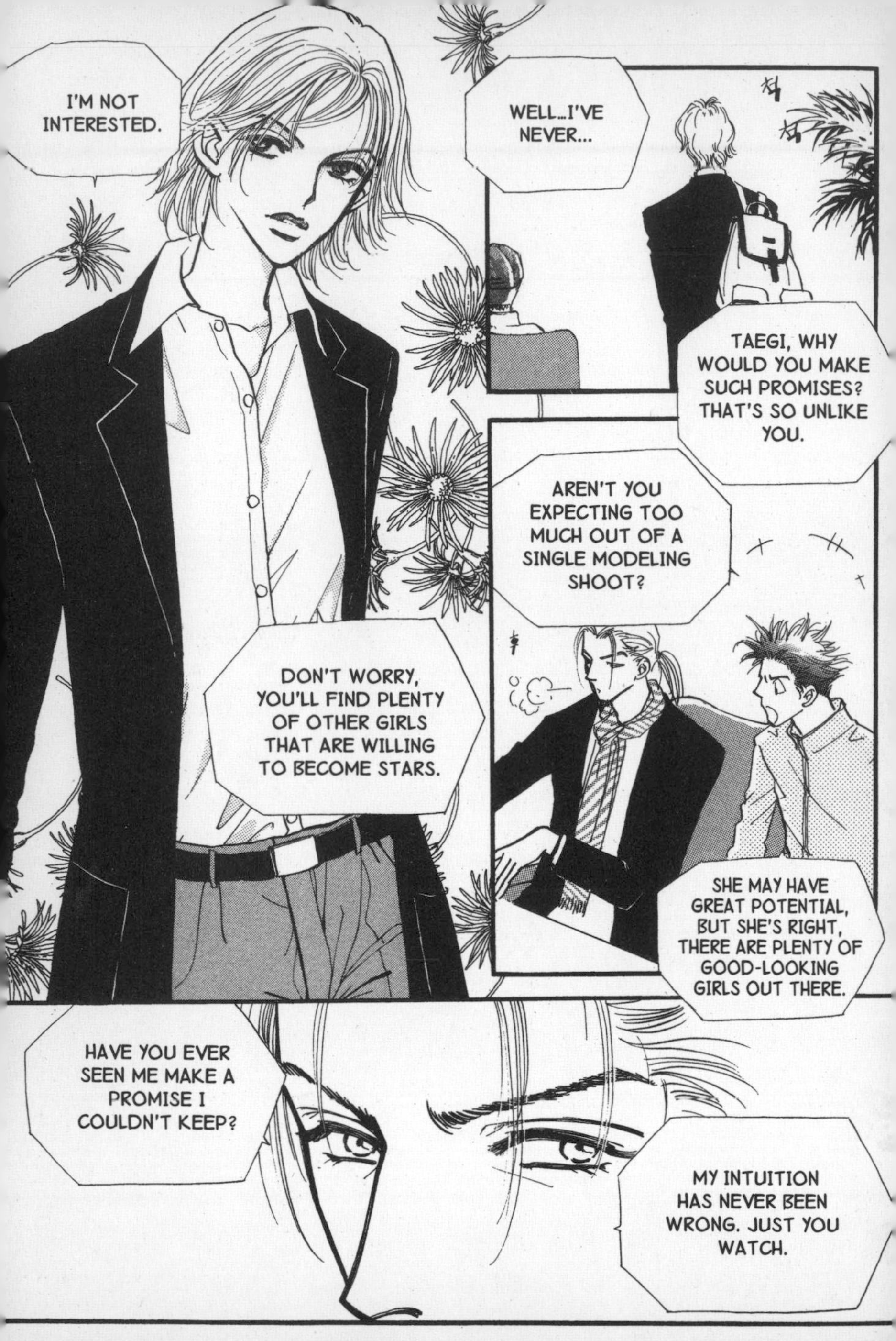
I'M NOT INTERESTED.
DON'T WORRY, YOU'LL FIND PLENTY OF OTHER GIRLS THAT ARE WILLING TO BECOME STARS.
WELL...I'VE NEVER...
TAEGI, WHY WOULD YOU MAKE SUCH PROMISES? THAT'S SO UNLIKE YOU.
AREN'T YOU EXPECTING TOO MUCH OUT OF A SINGLE MODELING SHOOT?
SHE MAY HAVE GREAT POTENTIAL, BUT SHE'S RIGHT, THERE ARE PLENTY OF GOOD-LOOKING GIRLS OUT THERE.
HAVE YOU EVER SEEN ME MAKE A PROMISE I COULDN'T KEEP?
MY INTUITION HAS NEVER BEEN WRONG. JUST YOU WATCH.

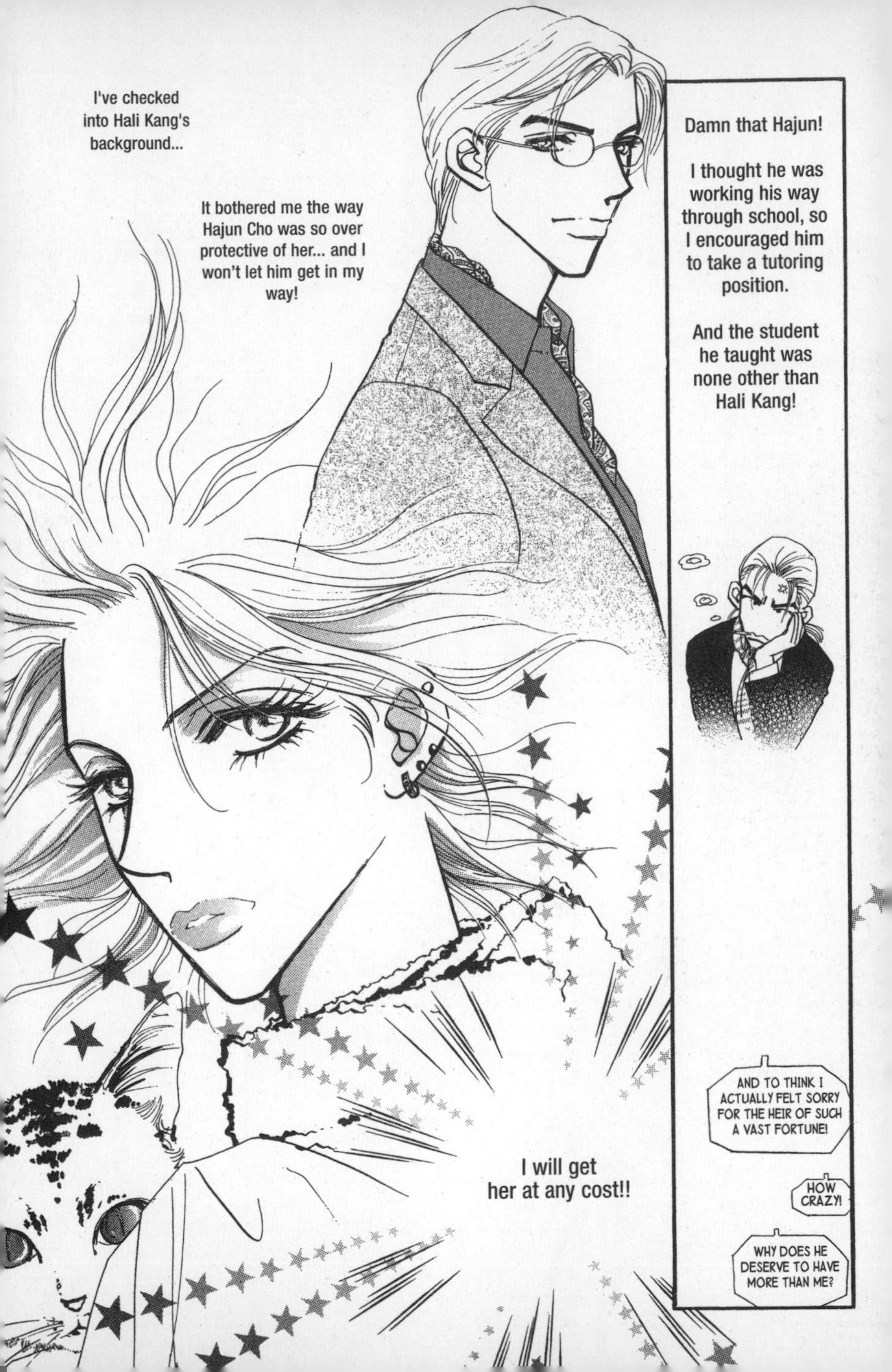
I've checked into Hali Kang's background...
It bothered me the way Hajun Cho was so over protective of her... and I won't let him get in my way!
I will get her at any cost!!
Damn that Hajun!
I thought he was working his way through school, so I encouraged him to take a tutoring position.
And the student he taught was none other than Hali Kang!
AND TO THINK I ACTUALLY FELT SORRY FOR THE HEIR OF SUCH A VAST FORTUNE!
HOW CRAZY!
WHY DOES HE DESERVE TO HAVE MORE THAN ME?

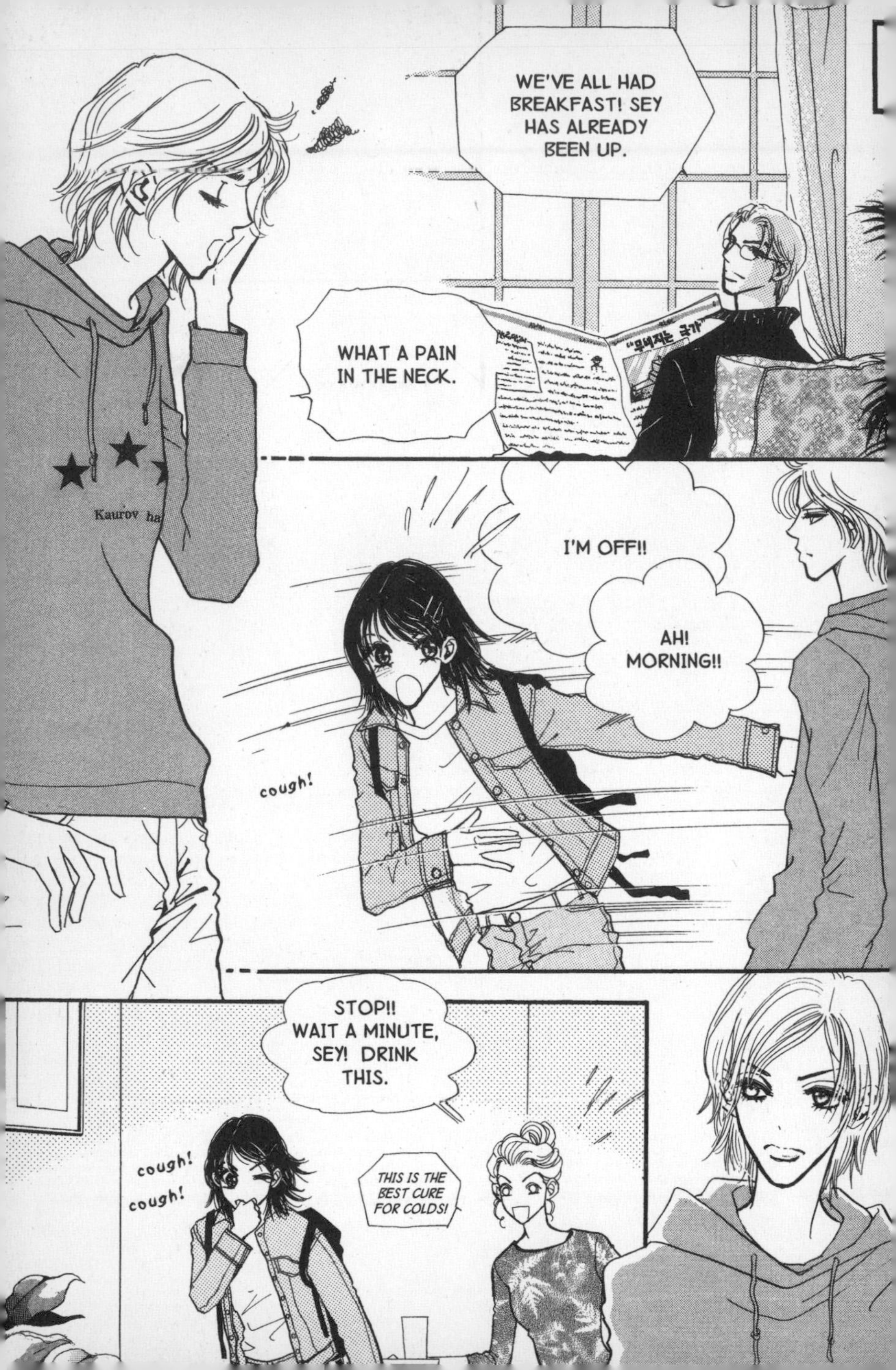
WE'VE ALL HAD BREAKFAST! SEY HAS ALREADY BEEN UP.
WHAT A PAIN IN THE NECK.
I'M OFF!!
AH! MORNING!!
cough!
STOP!! WAIT A MINUTE, SEY! DRINK THIS.
cough!
cough!
THIS IS THE BEST CURE FOR COLDS!

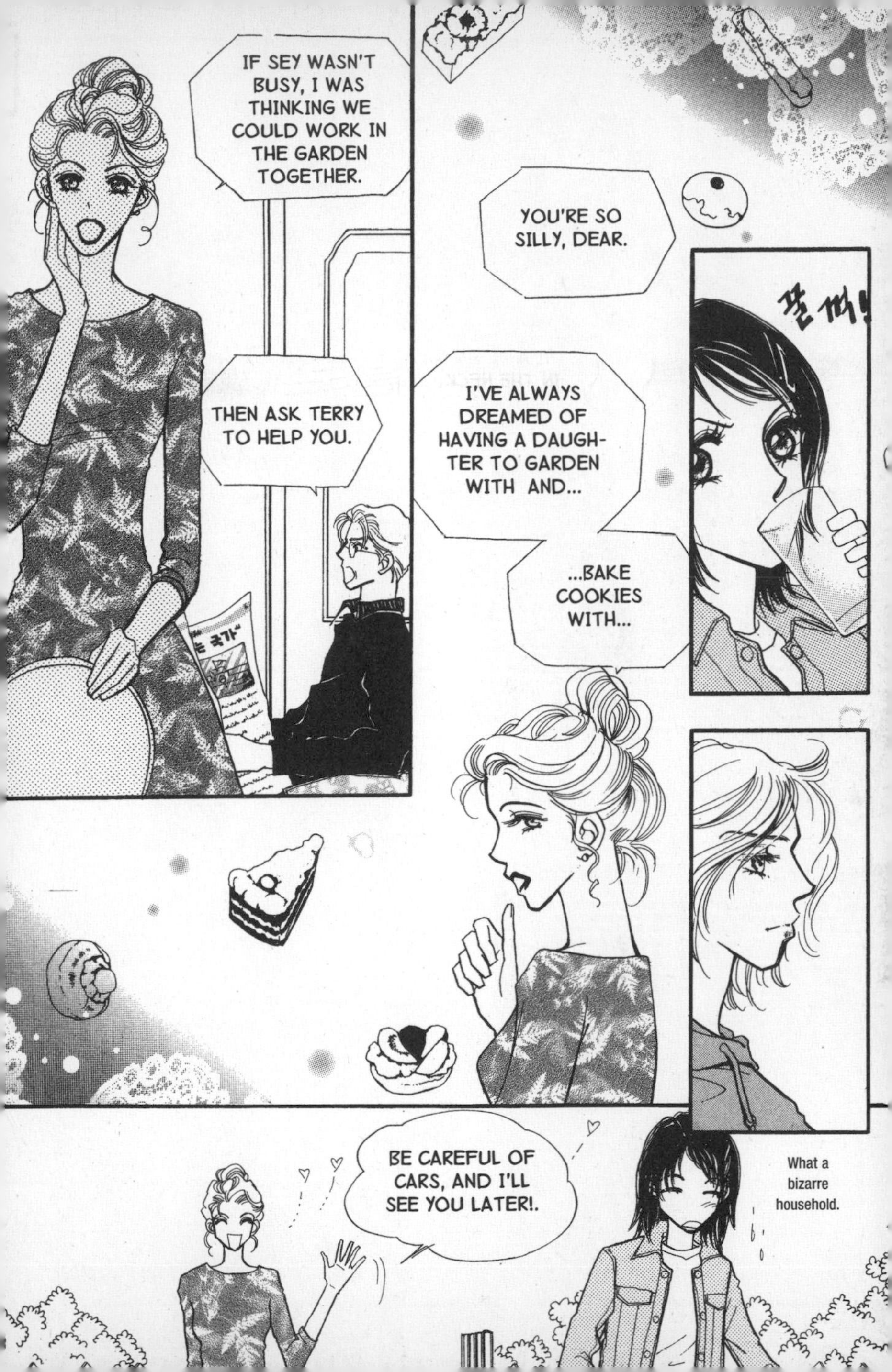
IF SEY WASN'T BUSY, I WAS THINKING WE COULD WORK IN THE GARDEN TOGETHER.
THEN ASK TERRY TO HELP YOU.
YOU'RE SO SILLY, DEAR.
I'VE ALWAYS DREAMED OF HAVING A DAUGHTER TO GARDEN WITH AND...
...BAKE COOKIES WITH...
꿀꺽!
BE CAREFUL OF CARS, AND I'LL SEE YOU LATER!.
What a bizarre household.

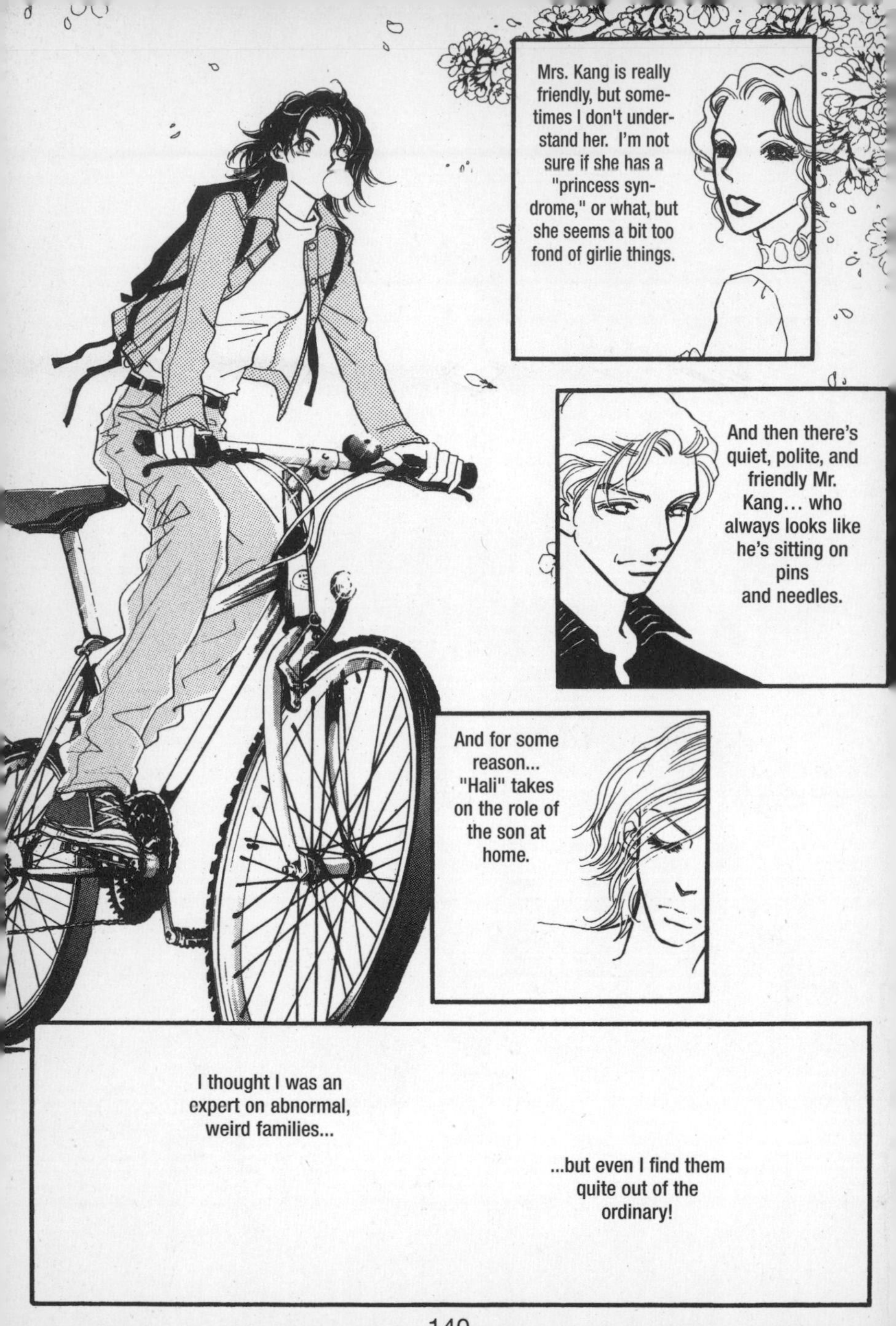
Mrs. Kang is really friendly, but sometimes I don't understand her. I'm not sure if she has a "princess syndrome," or what, but she seems a bit too fond of girlie things.
And then there's quiet, polite, and friendly Mr. Kang… who always looks like he's sitting on pins and needles.
And for some reason... "Hali" takes on the role of the son at home.
I thought I was an expert on abnormal, weird families...
...but even I find them quite out of the ordinary!

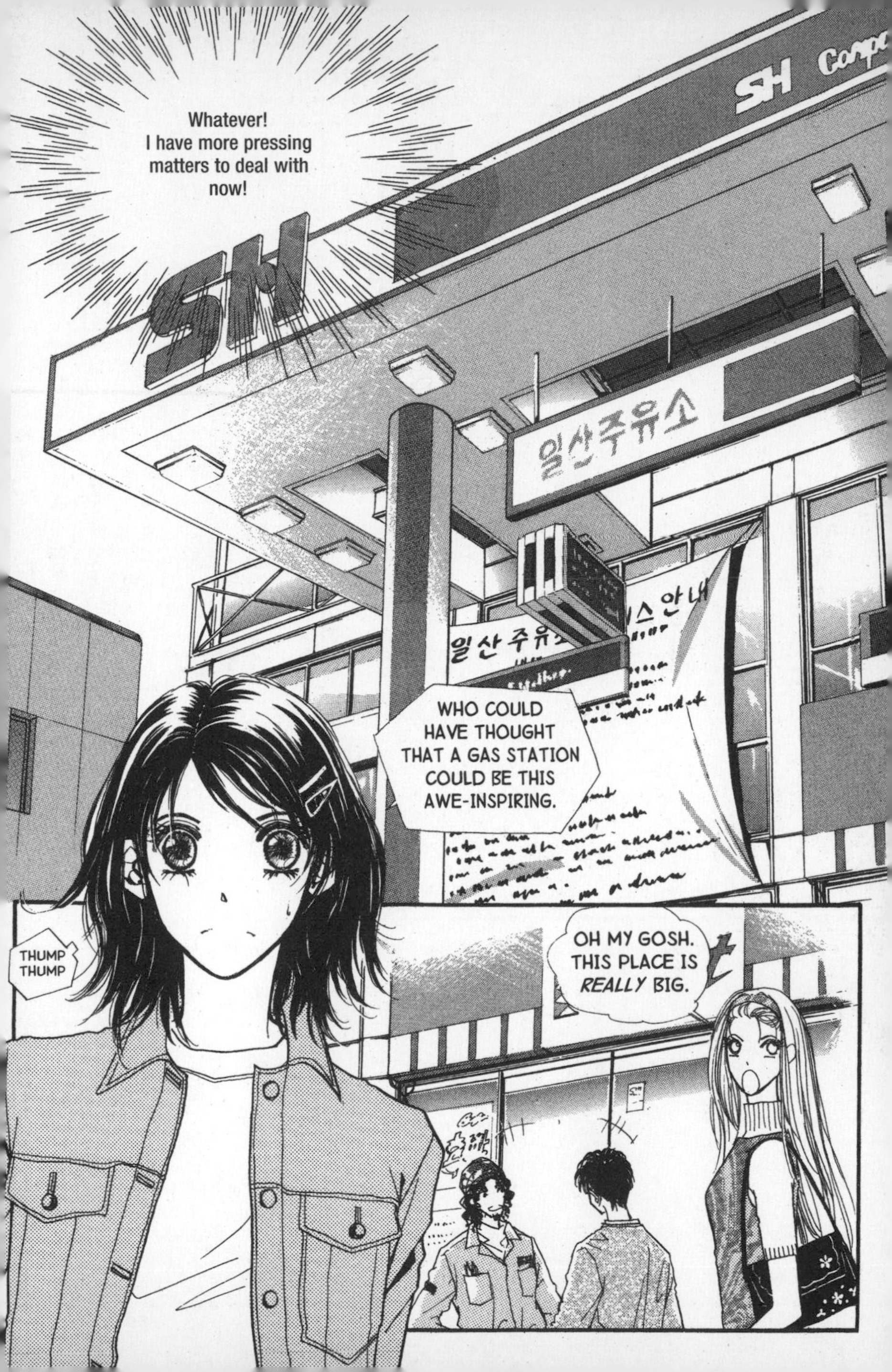
Whatever! I have more pressing matters to deal with now!
일산주유소
WHO COULD HAVE THOUGHT THAT A GAS STATION COULD BE THIS AWE-INSPIRING.
THUMP THUMP
OH MY GOSH. THIS PLACE IS *REALLY* BIG.

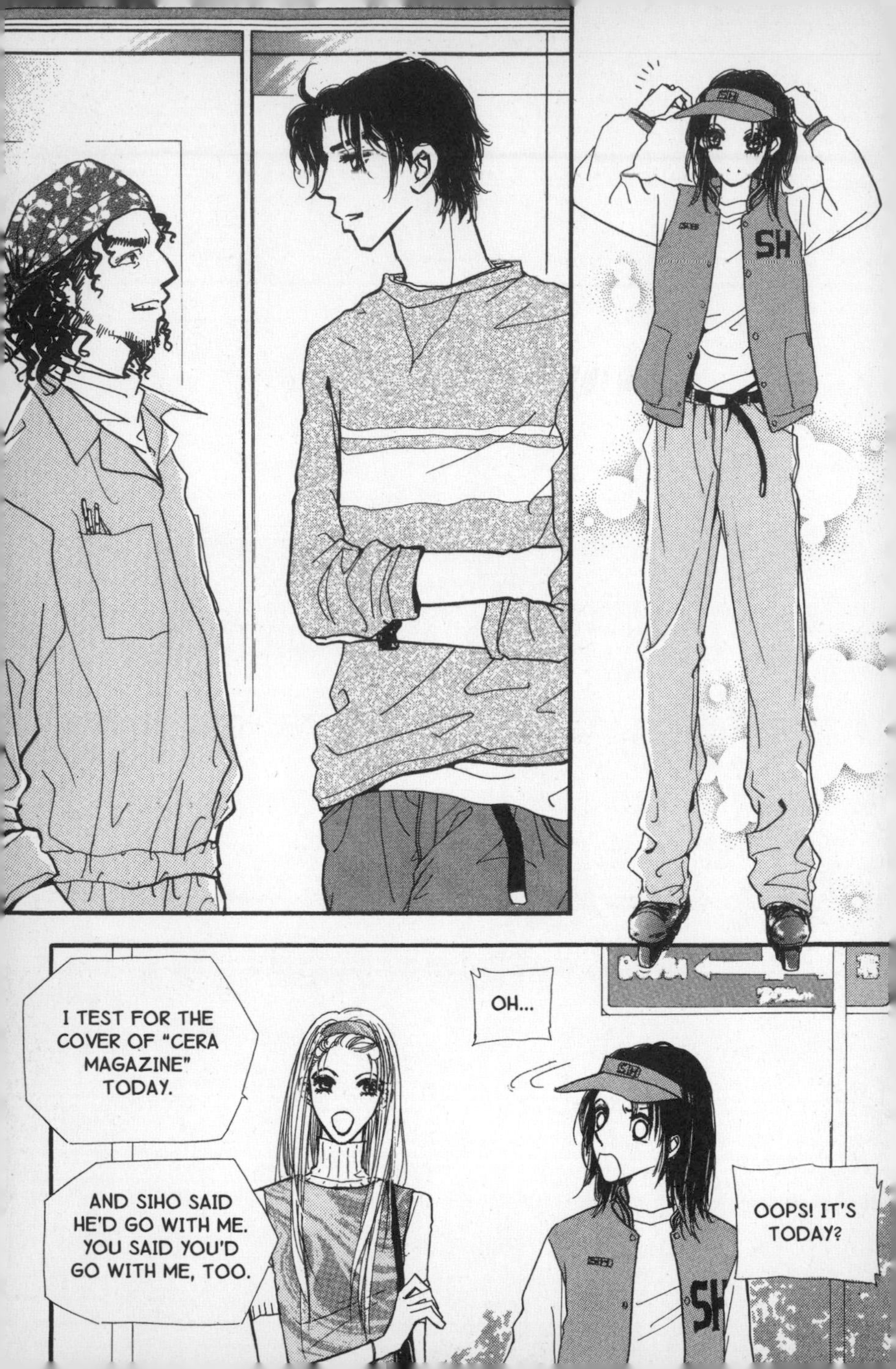
I TEST FOR THE COVER OF "CERA MAGAZINE" TODAY.
AND SIHO SAID HE'D GO WITH ME. YOU SAID YOU'D GO WITH ME, TOO.
OH...
OOPS! IT'S TODAY?

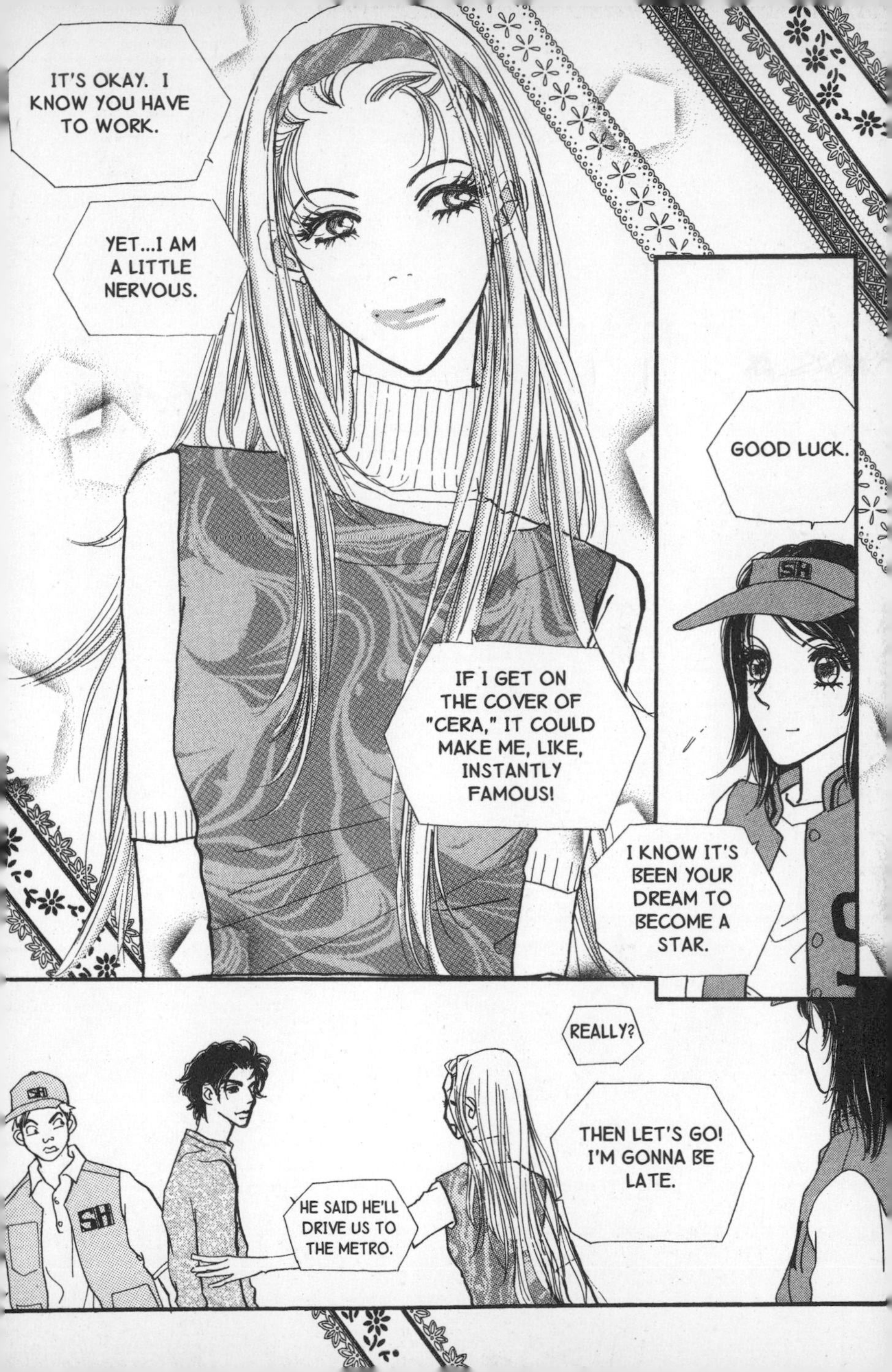
IT'S OKAY. I KNOW YOU HAVE TO WORK.
YET...I AM A LITTLE NERVOUS.
IF I GET ON THE COVER OF "CERA," IT COULD MAKE ME, LIKE, INSTANTLY FAMOUS!
GOOD LUCK.
I KNOW IT'S BEEN YOUR DREAM TO BECOME A STAR.
HE SAID HE'LL DRIVE US TO THE METRO.
REALLY?
THEN LET'S GO! I'M GONNA BE LATE.

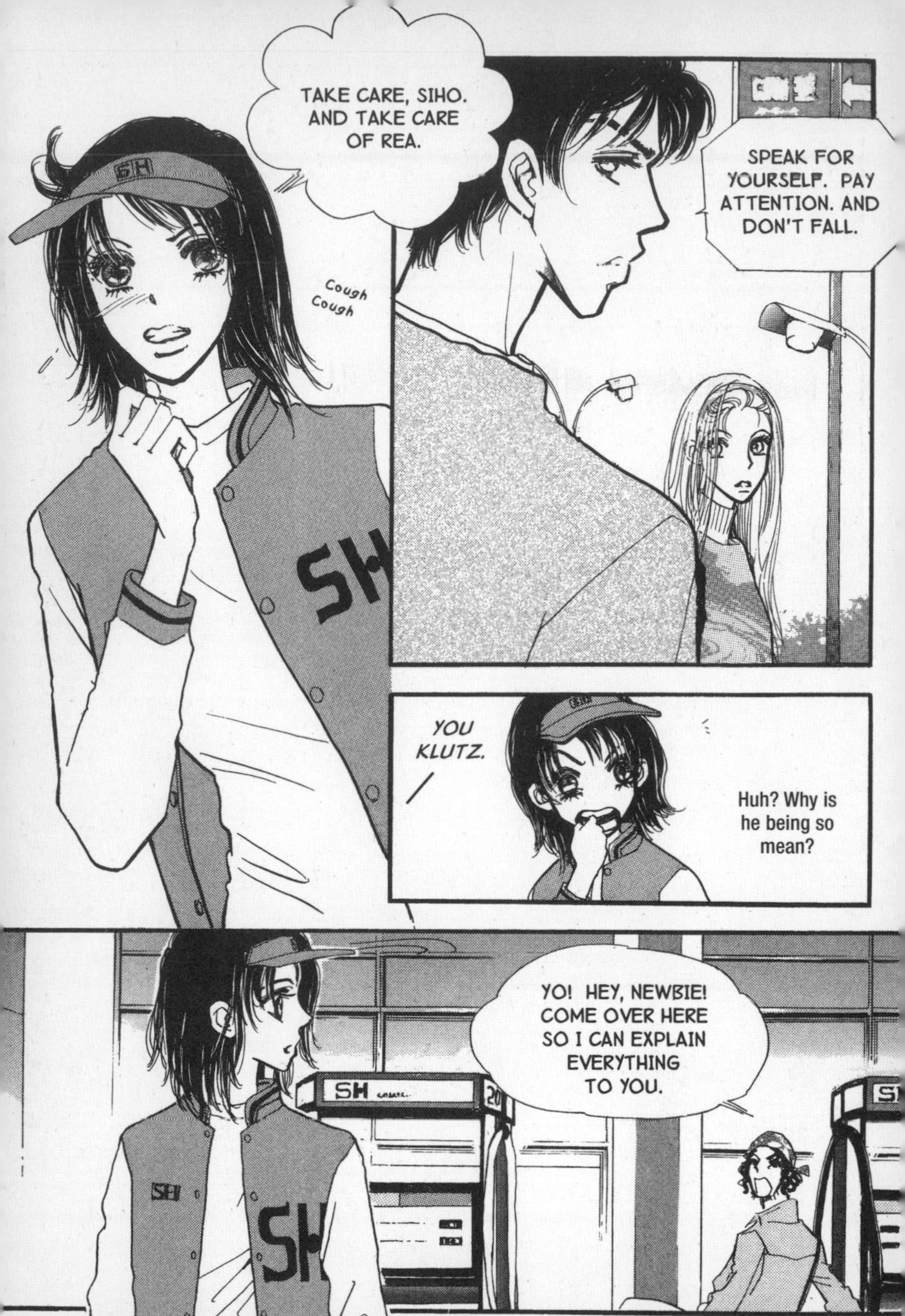
TAKE CARE, SIHO. AND TAKE CARE OF REA.
Cough Cough
SPEAK FOR YOURSELF. PAY ATTENTION. AND DON'T FALL.
YOU KLUTZ.
Huh? Why is he being so mean?
YO! HEY, NEWBIE! COME OVER HERE SO I CAN EXPLAIN EVERYTHING TO YOU.

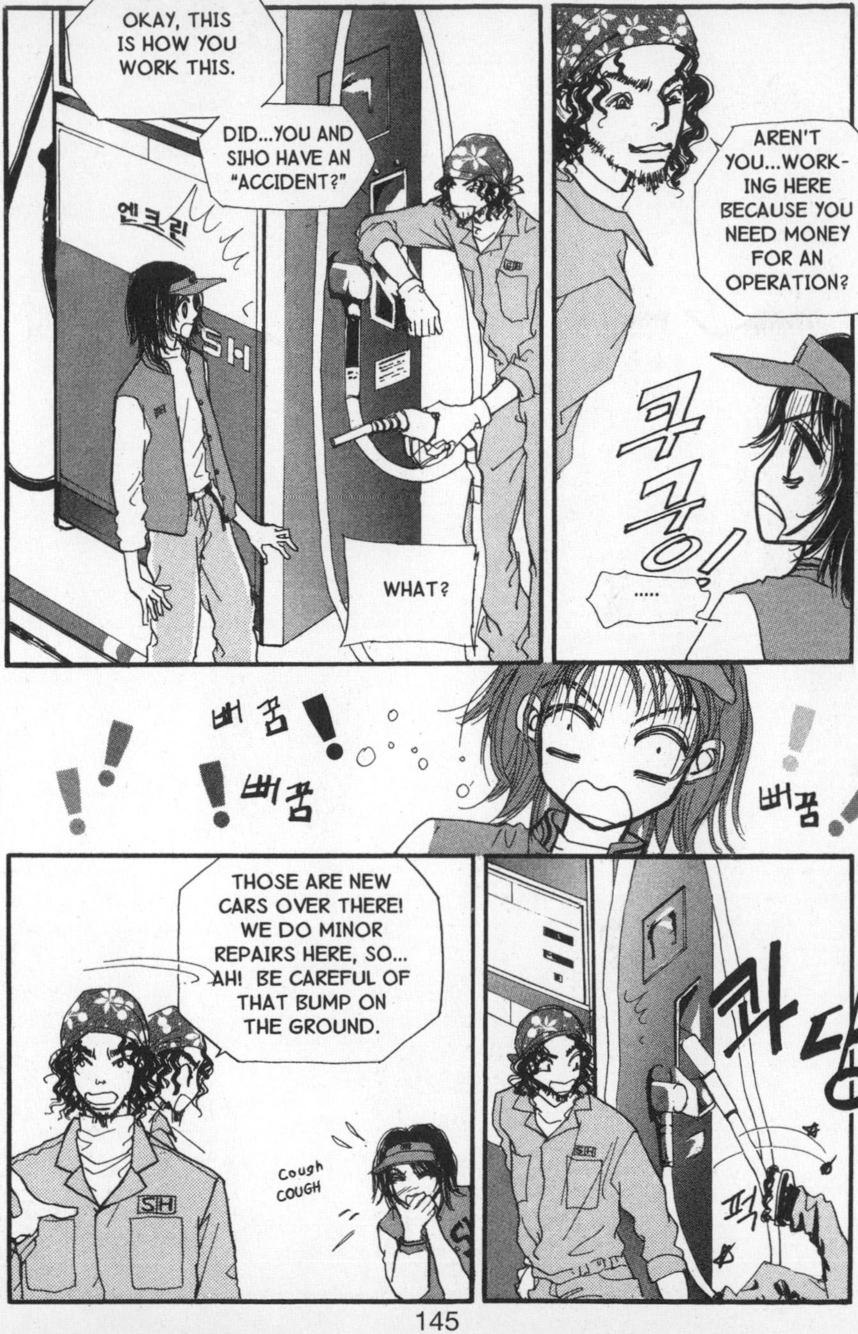
OKAY, THIS IS HOW YOU WORK THIS.
DID...YOU AND SIHO HAVE AN "ACCIDENT?"
엔크린
SH
WHAT?
AREN'T YOU...WORKING HERE BECAUSE YOU NEED MONEY FOR AN OPERATION?
쿠궁!
.....
삐끔
삐끔
삐끔
THOSE ARE NEW CARS OVER THERE! WE DO MINOR REPAIRS HERE, SO... AH! BE CAREFUL OF THAT BUMP ON THE GROUND.
SH
Cough COUGH
콰당
퍽

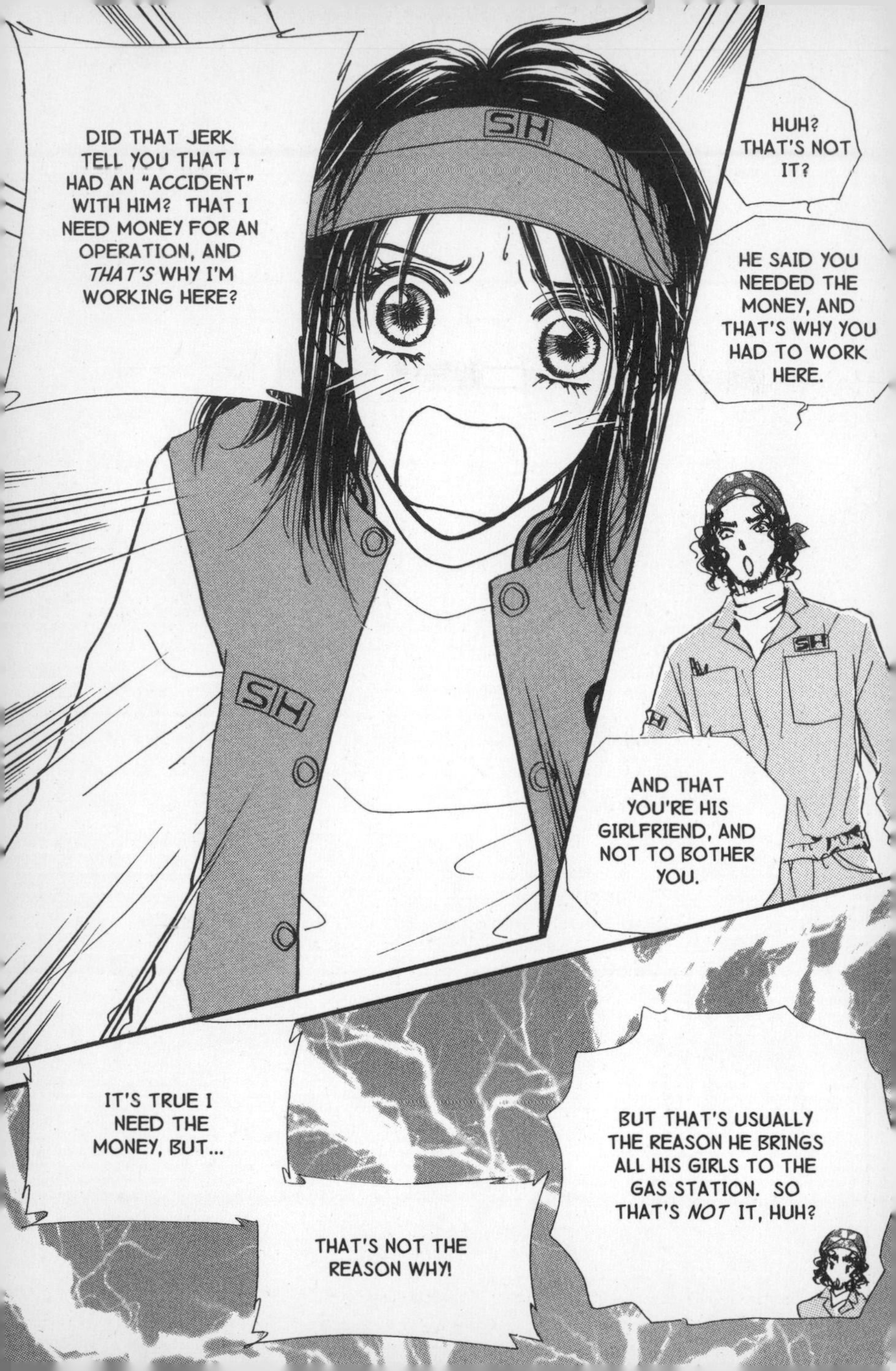
DID THAT JERK TELL YOU THAT I HAD AN "ACCIDENT" WITH HIM? THAT I NEED MONEY FOR AN OPERATION, AND *THAT'S* WHY I'M WORKING HERE?
HUH? THAT'S NOT IT?
HE SAID YOU NEEDED THE MONEY, AND THAT'S WHY YOU HAD TO WORK HERE.
AND THAT YOU'RE HIS GIRLFRIEND, AND NOT TO BOTHER YOU.
IT'S TRUE I NEED THE MONEY, BUT...
THAT'S NOT THE REASON WHY!
BUT THAT'S USUALLY THE REASON HE BRINGS ALL HIS GIRLS TO THE GAS STATION. SO THAT'S *NOT* IT, HUH?

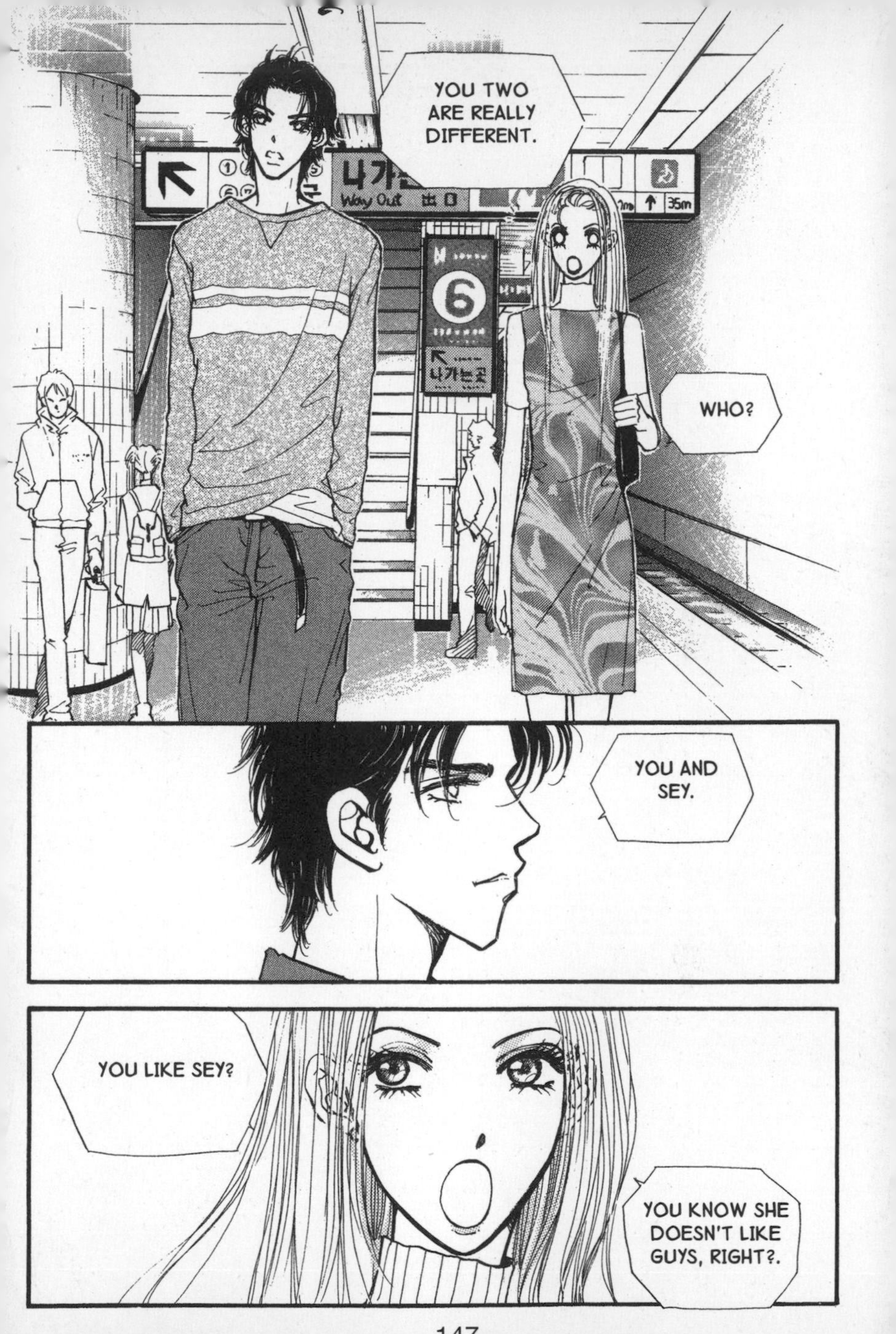
YOU TWO ARE REALLY DIFFERENT.
Way Out 出口
WHO?
YOU AND SEY.
YOU LIKE SEY?
YOU KNOW SHE DOESN'T LIKE GUYS, RIGHT?.

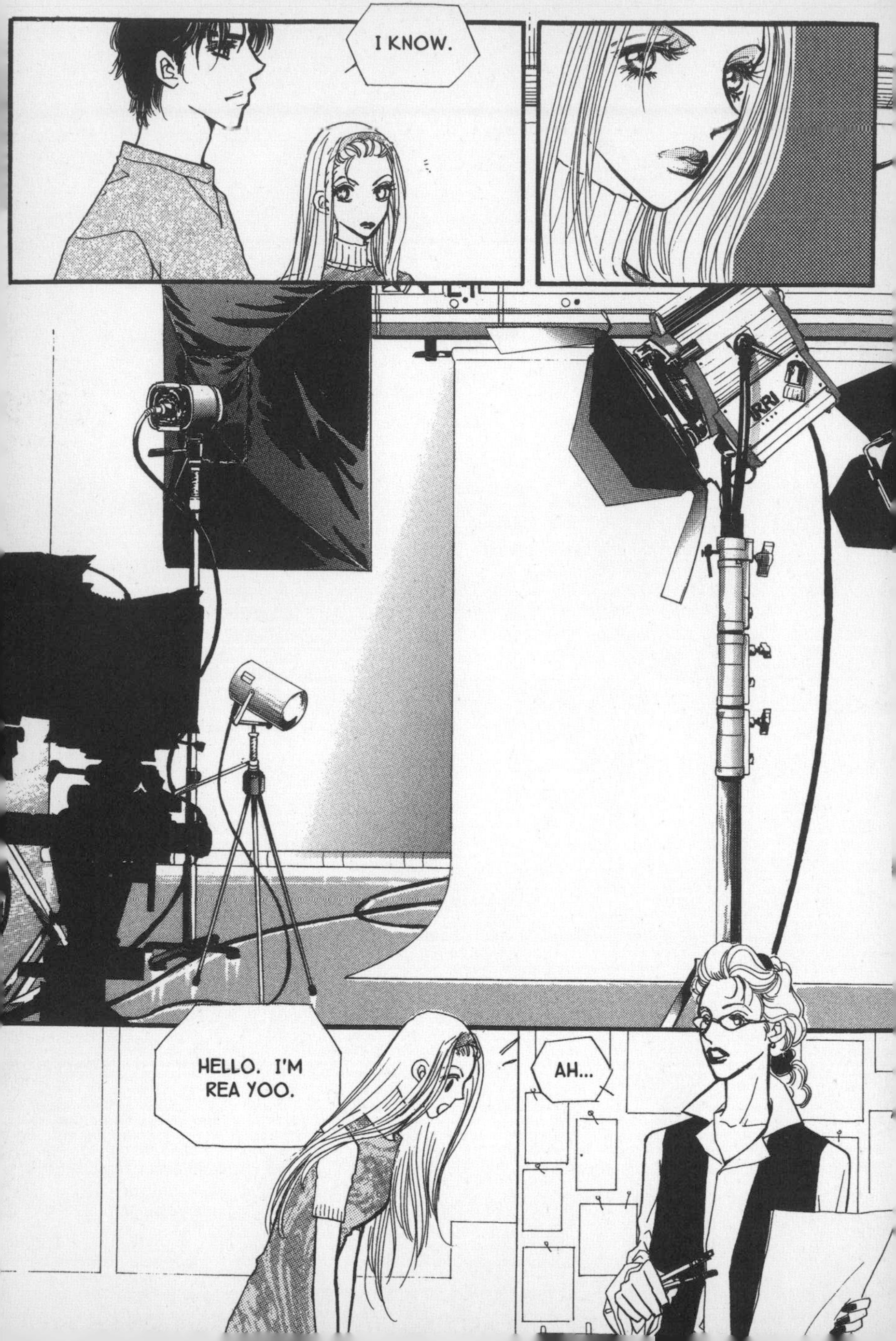
I KNOW.
HELLO. I'M REA YOO.
AH...

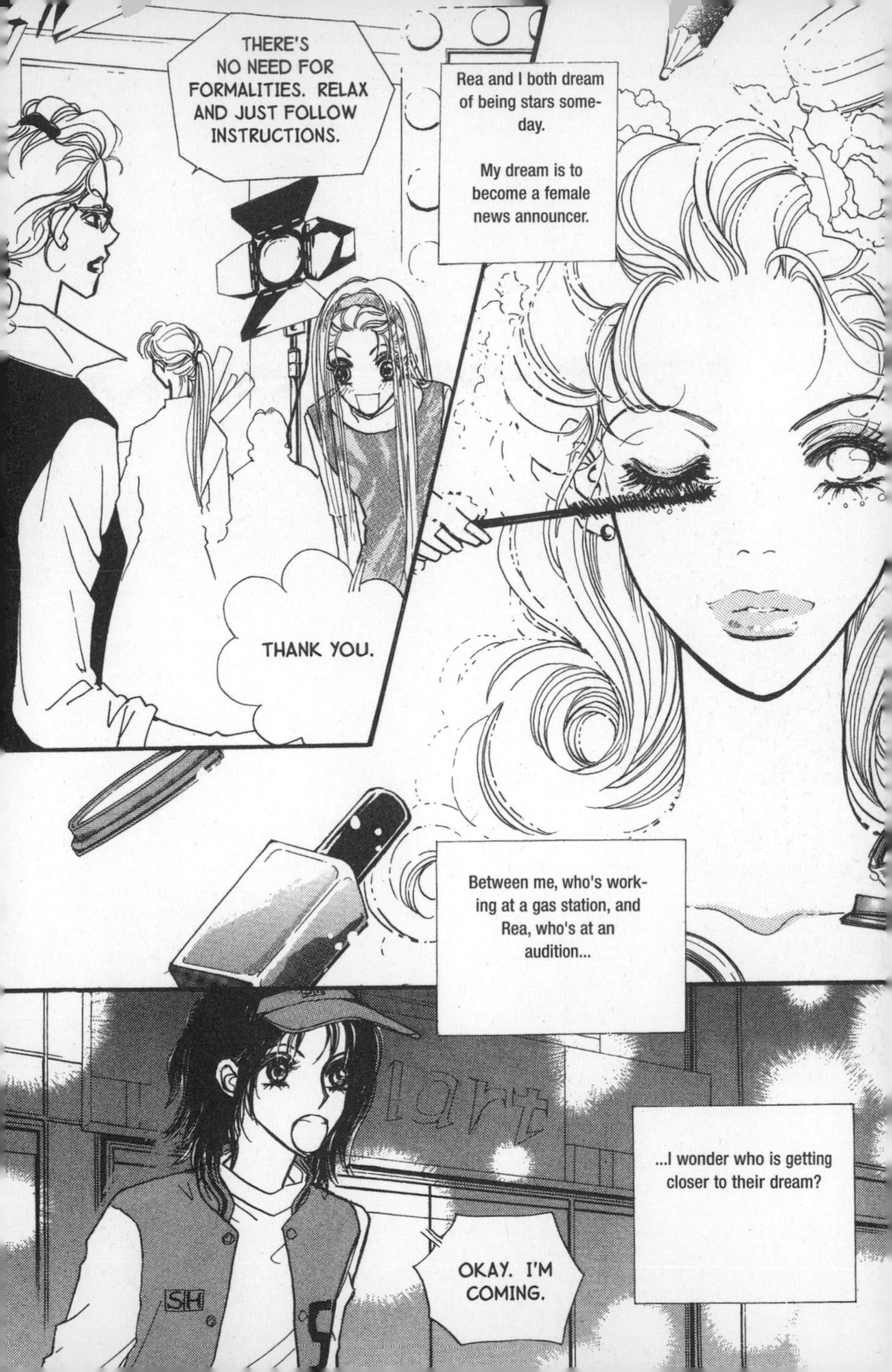
THERE'S NO NEED FOR FORMALITIES. RELAX AND JUST FOLLOW INSTRUCTIONS.
THANK YOU.
Rea and I both dream of being stars some-day.
My dream is to become a female news announcer.
Between me, who's work-ing at a gas station, and Rea, who's at an audition...
...I wonder who is getting closer to their dream?
OKAY. I'M COMING.

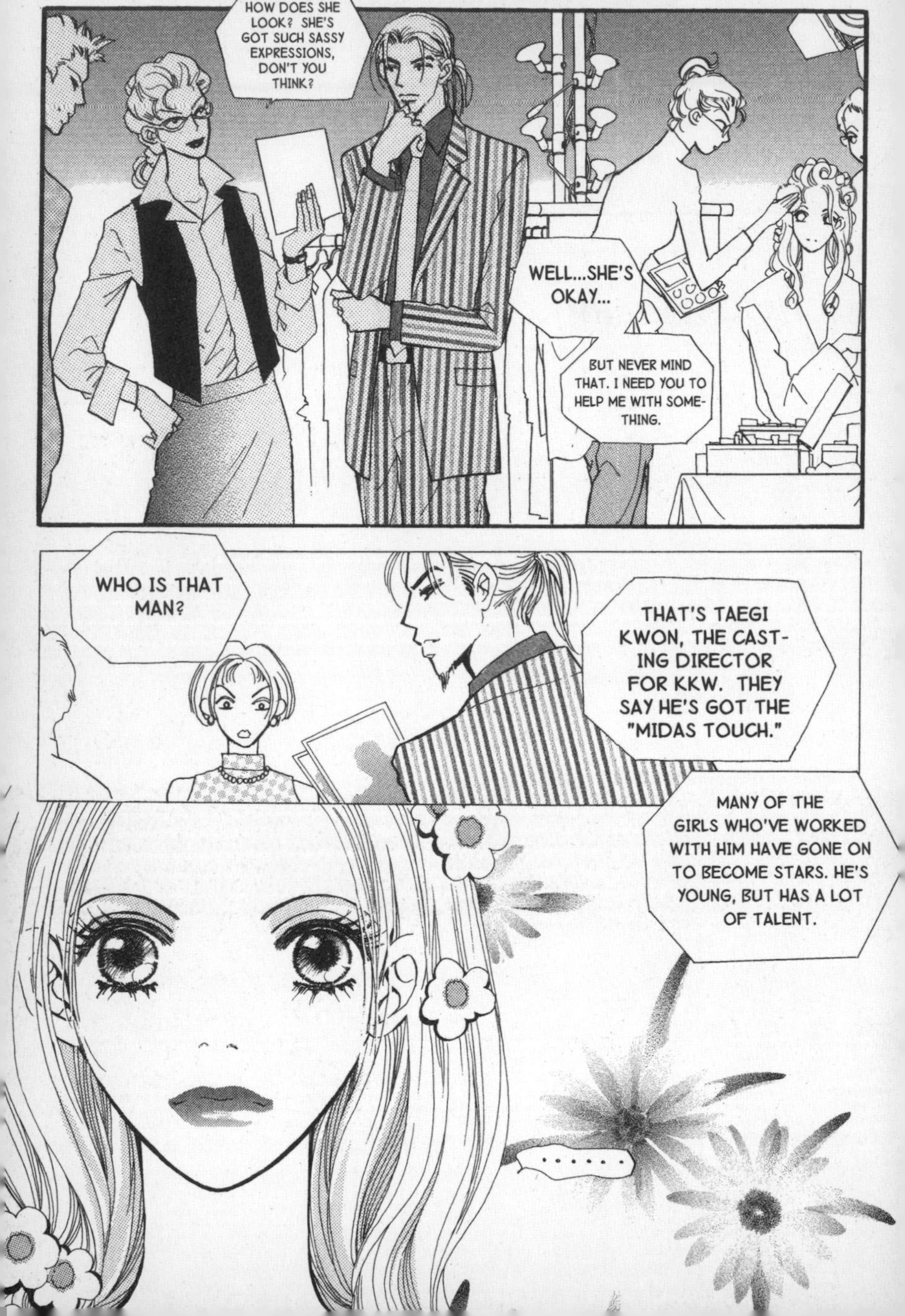
HOW DOES SHE LOOK? SHE'S GOT SUCH SASSY EXPRESSIONS, DON'T YOU THINK?
WELL...SHE'S OKAY...
BUT NEVER MIND THAT. I NEED YOU TO HELP ME WITH SOME-THING.
WHO IS THAT MAN?
THAT'S TAEGI KWON, THE CAST-ING DIRECTOR FOR KKW. THEY SAY HE'S GOT THE "MIDAS TOUCH."
MANY OF THE GIRLS WHO'VE WORKED WITH HIM HAVE GONE ON TO BECOME STARS. HE'S YOUNG, BUT HAS A LOT OF TALENT.
......

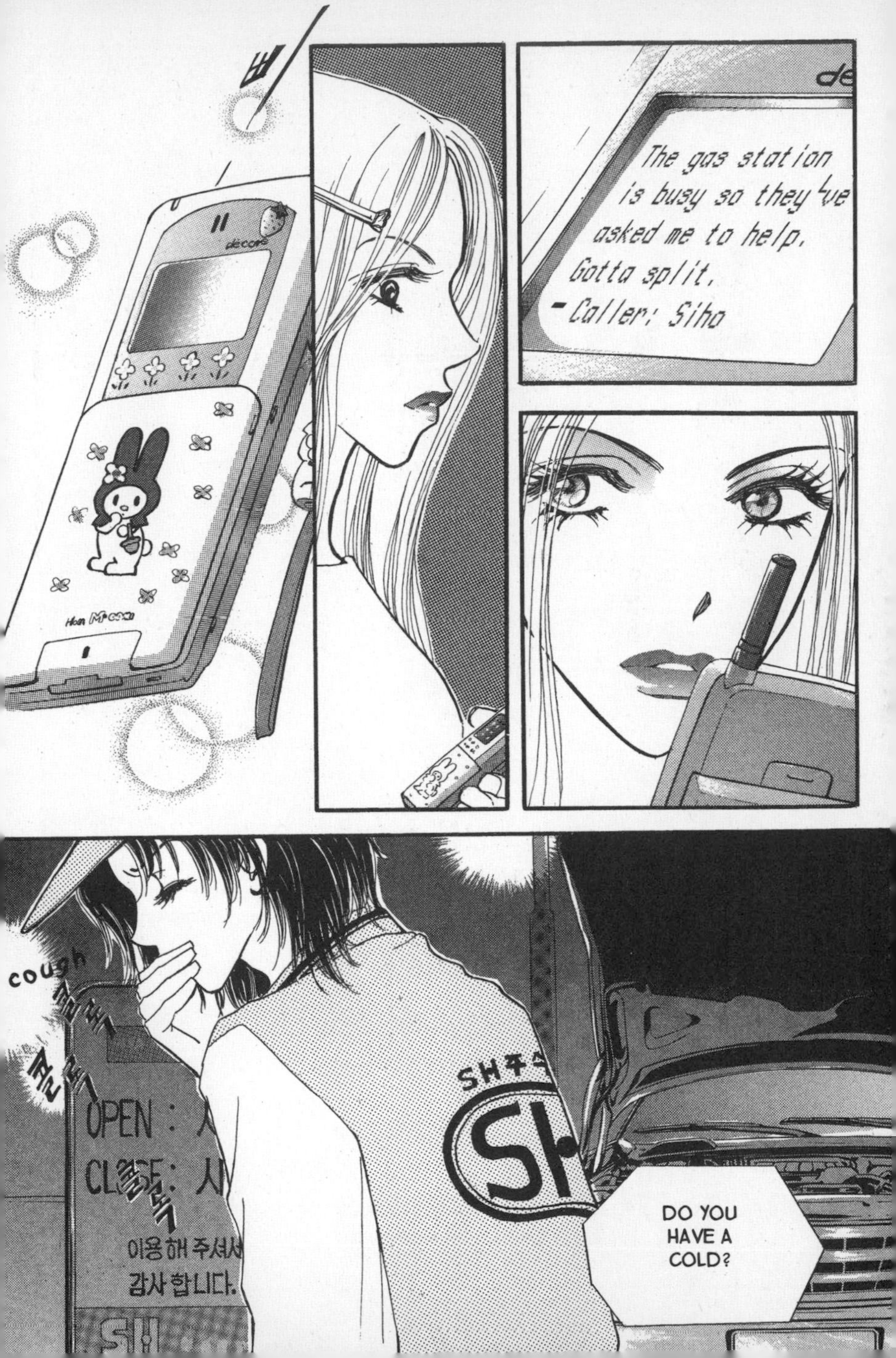
The gas station is busy so they've asked me to help. Gotta split.
- Caller: Siho
cough
OPEN :
CLOSE:
감사 합니다.
DO YOU HAVE A COLD?

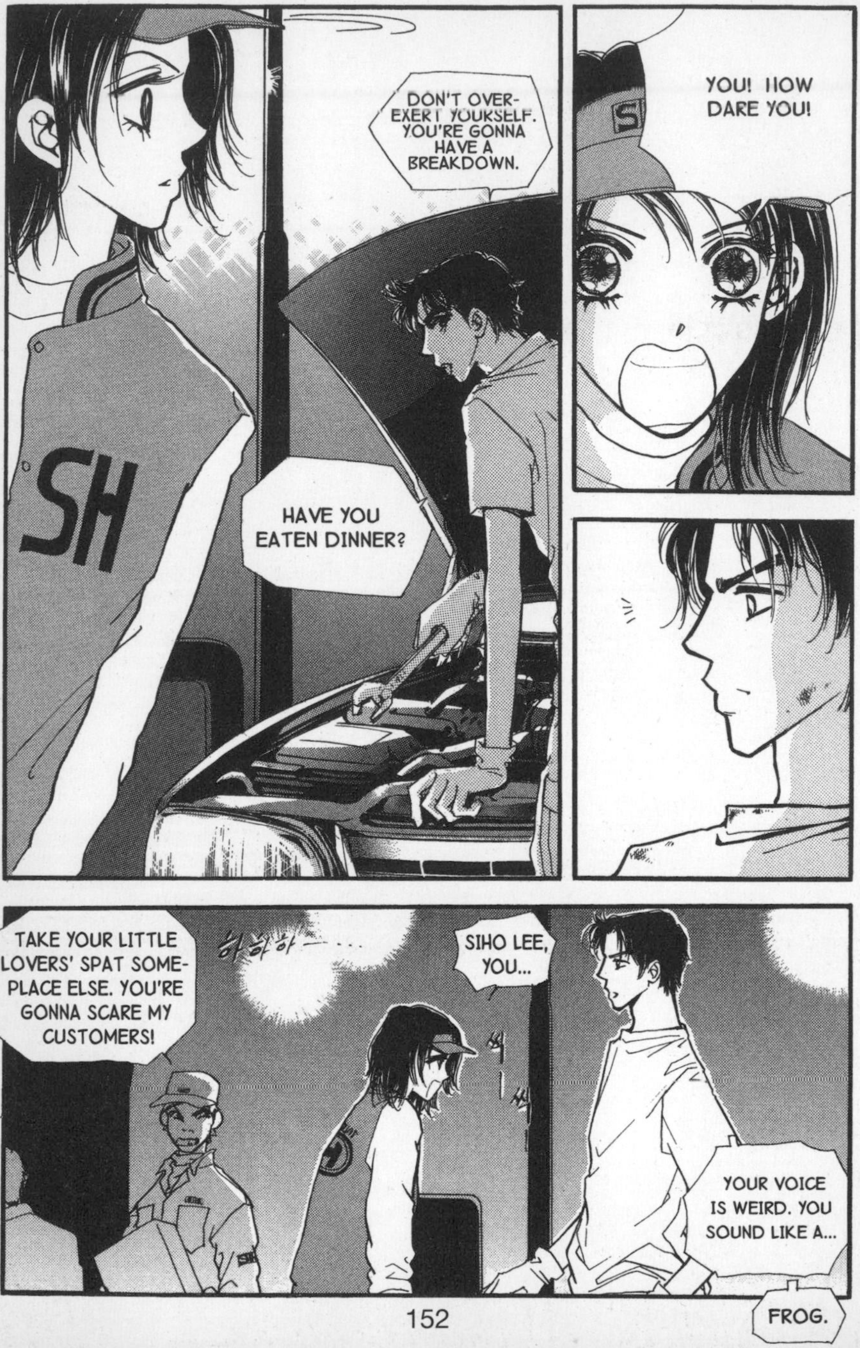
DON'T OVER-EXERT YOURSELF. YOU'RE GONNA HAVE A BREAKDOWN.
HAVE YOU EATEN DINNER?
YOU! HOW DARE YOU!
TAKE YOUR LITTLE LOVERS' SPAT SOME-PLACE ELSE. YOU'RE GONNA SCARE MY CUSTOMERS!
하하하—...
SIHO LEE, YOU...
YOUR VOICE IS WEIRD. YOU SOUND LIKE A...
FROG.

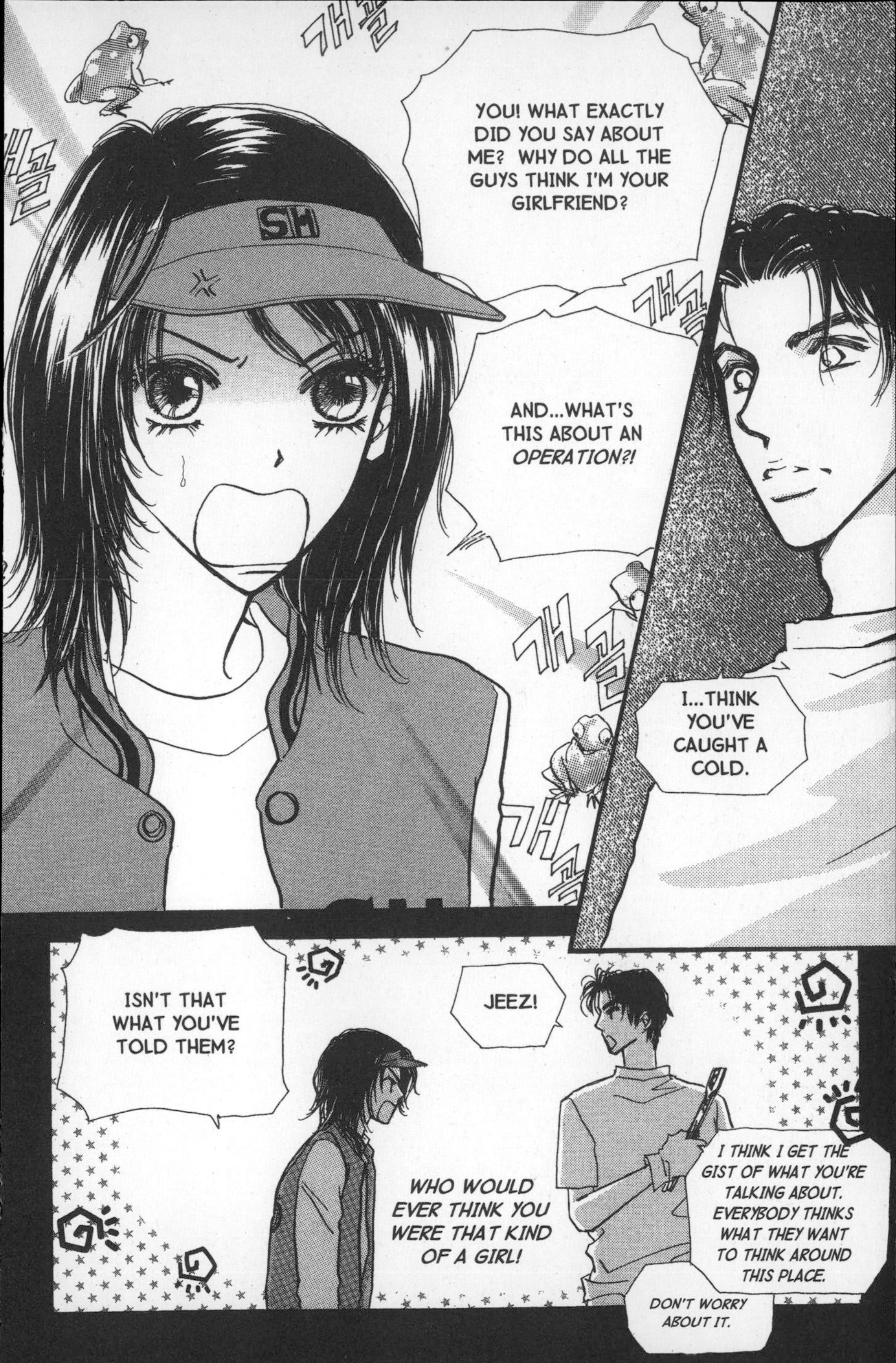
개골
개골
YOU! WHAT EXACTLY DID YOU SAY ABOUT ME? WHY DO ALL THE GUYS THINK I'M YOUR GIRLFRIEND?
개골
AND...WHAT'S THIS ABOUT AN *OPERATION?!*
개골
개골
I...THINK YOU'VE CAUGHT A COLD.
ISN'T THAT WHAT YOU'VE TOLD THEM?
JEEZ!
WHO WOULD EVER THINK YOU WERE THAT KIND OF A GIRL!
I THINK I GET THE GIST OF WHAT YOU'RE TALKING ABOUT. EVERYBODY THINKS WHAT THEY WANT TO THINK AROUND THIS PLACE.
DON'T WORRY ABOUT IT.

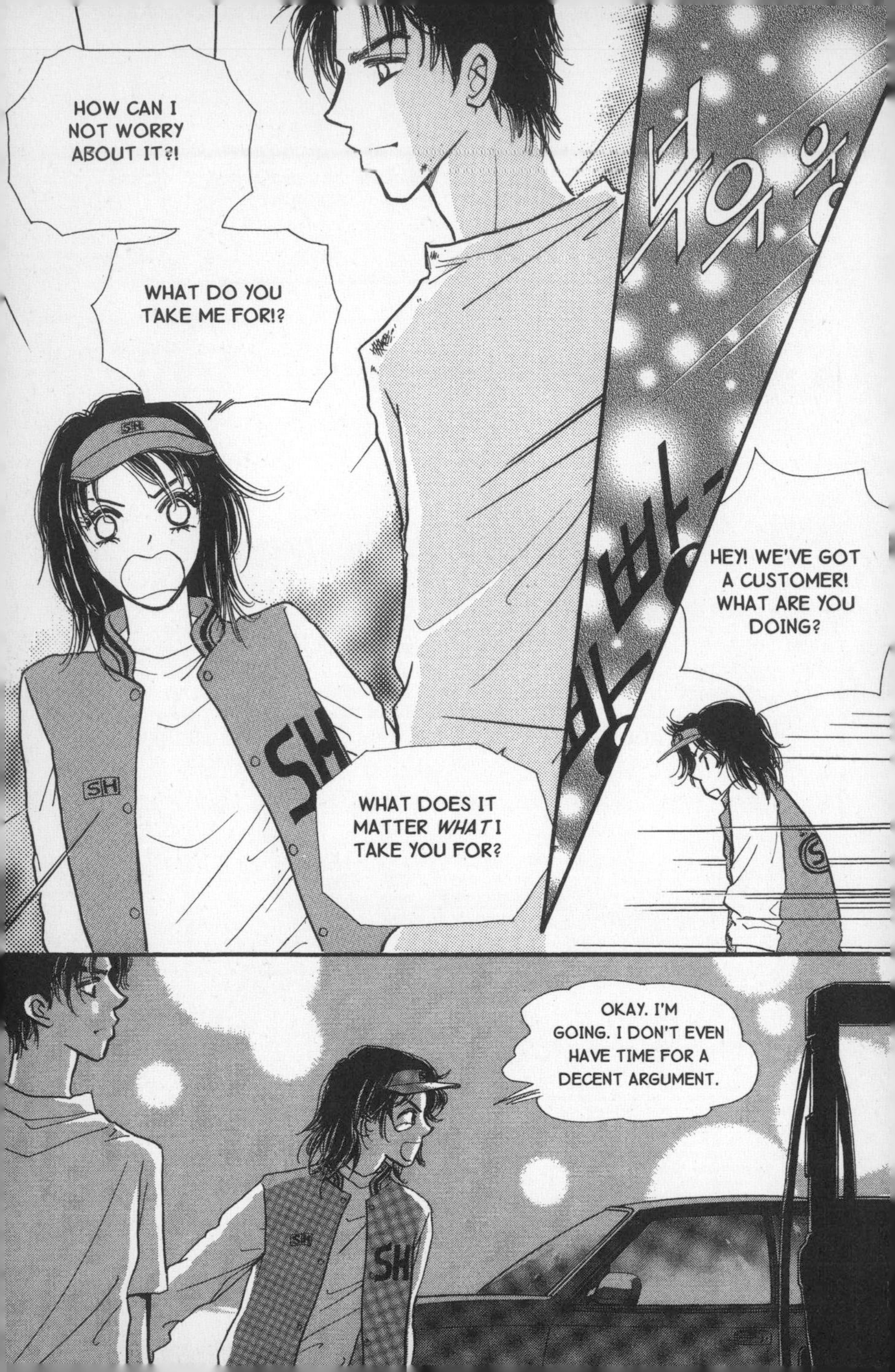
HOW CAN I NOT WORRY ABOUT IT?!
WHAT DO YOU TAKE ME FOR!?
WHAT DOES IT MATTER *WHAT* I TAKE YOU FOR?
HEY! WE'VE GOT A CUSTOMER! WHAT ARE YOU DOING?
OKAY. I'M GOING. I DON'T EVEN HAVE TIME FOR A DECENT ARGUMENT.

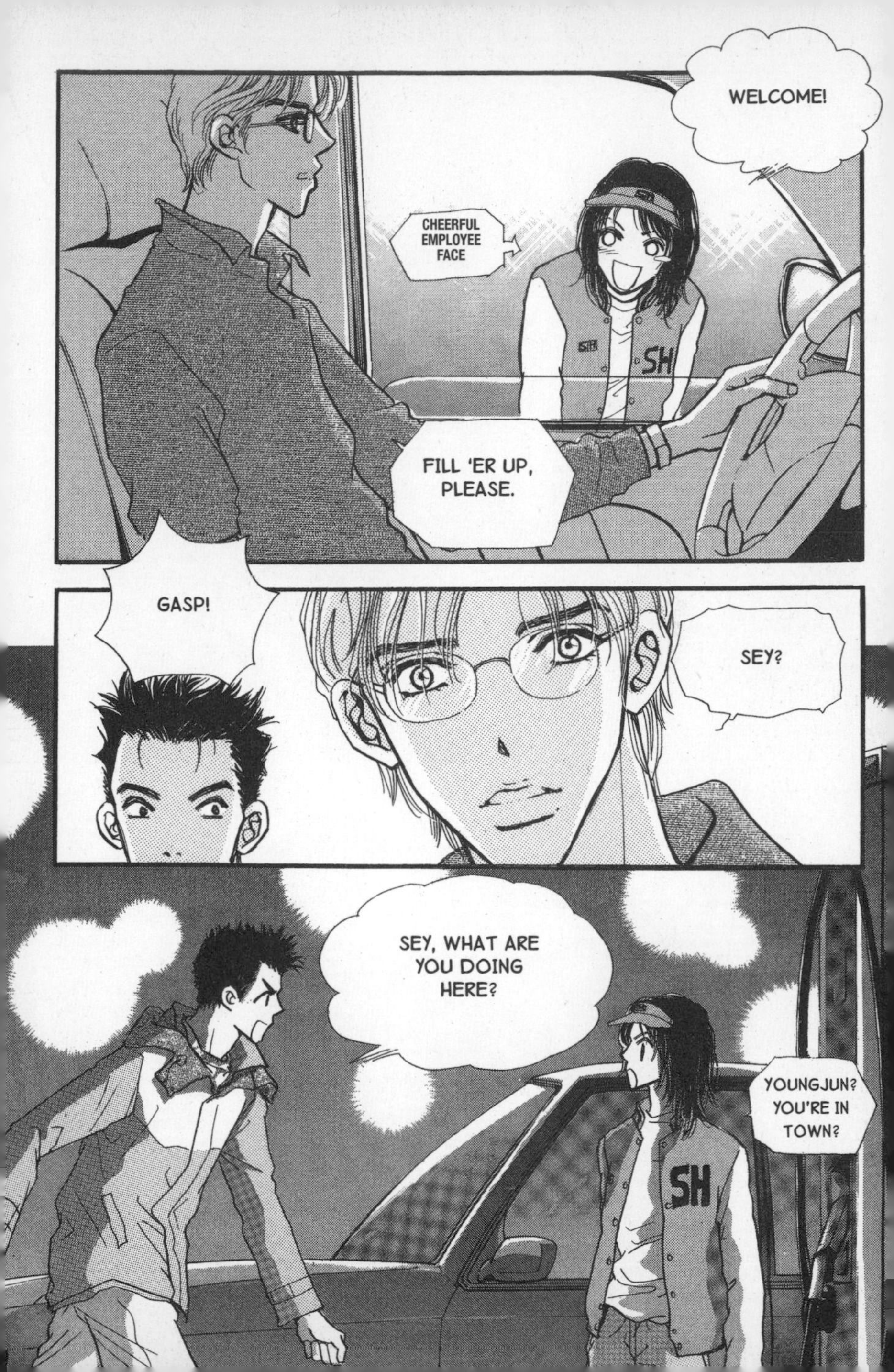
CHEERFUL EMPLOYEE FACE
WELCOME!
FILL 'ER UP, PLEASE.
GASP!
SEY?
SEY, WHAT ARE YOU DOING HERE?
YOUNGJUN? YOU'RE IN TOWN?

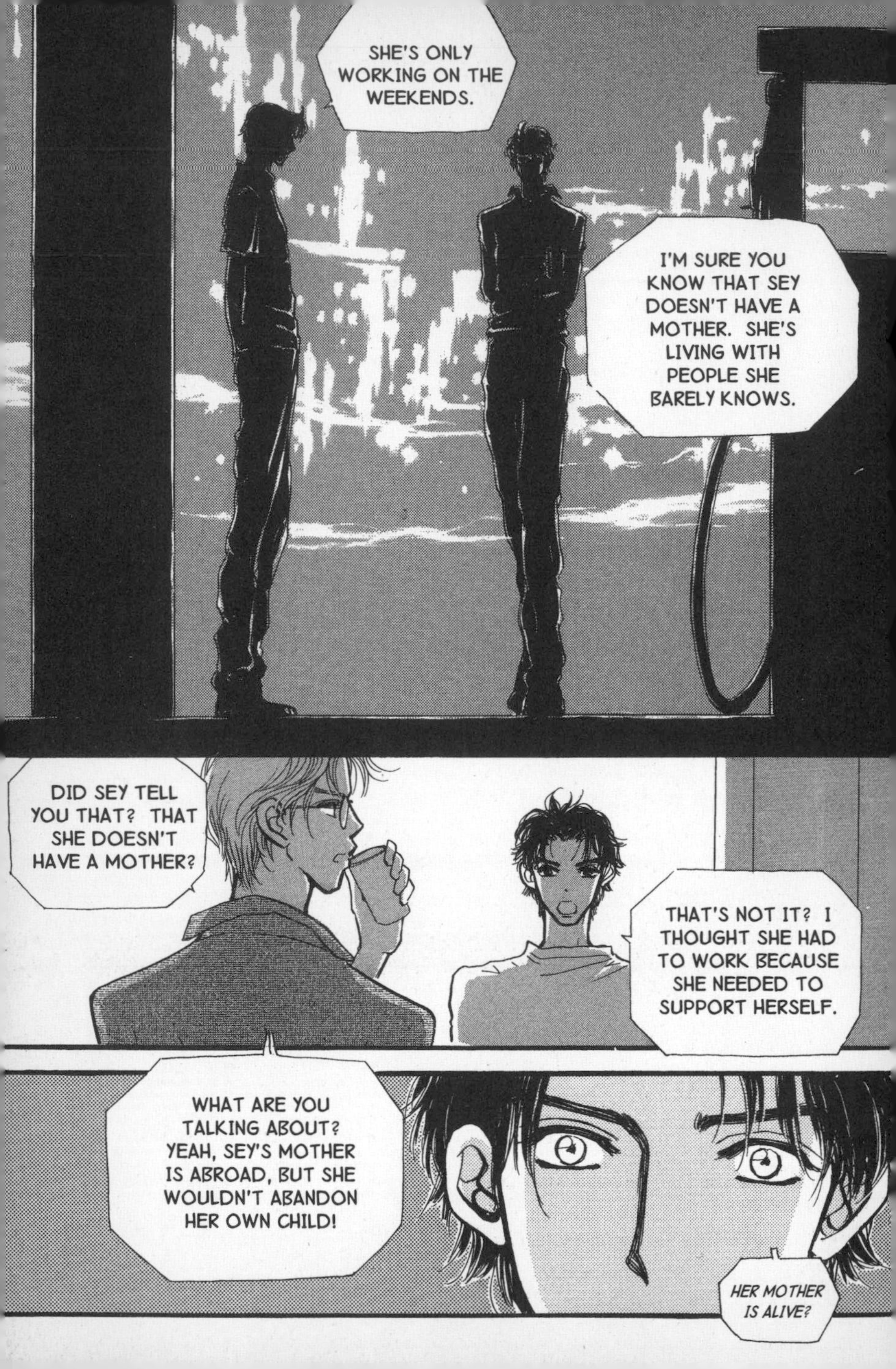
SHE'S ONLY WORKING ON THE WEEKENDS.
I'M SURE YOU KNOW THAT SEY DOESN'T HAVE A MOTHER. SHE'S LIVING WITH PEOPLE SHE BARELY KNOWS.
DID SEY TELL YOU THAT? THAT SHE DOESN'T HAVE A MOTHER?
THAT'S NOT IT? I THOUGHT SHE HAD TO WORK BECAUSE SHE NEEDED TO SUPPORT HERSELF.
WHAT ARE YOU TALKING ABOUT? YEAH, SEY'S MOTHER IS ABROAD, BUT SHE WOULDN'T ABANDON HER OWN CHILD!
HER MOTHER IS ALIVE?

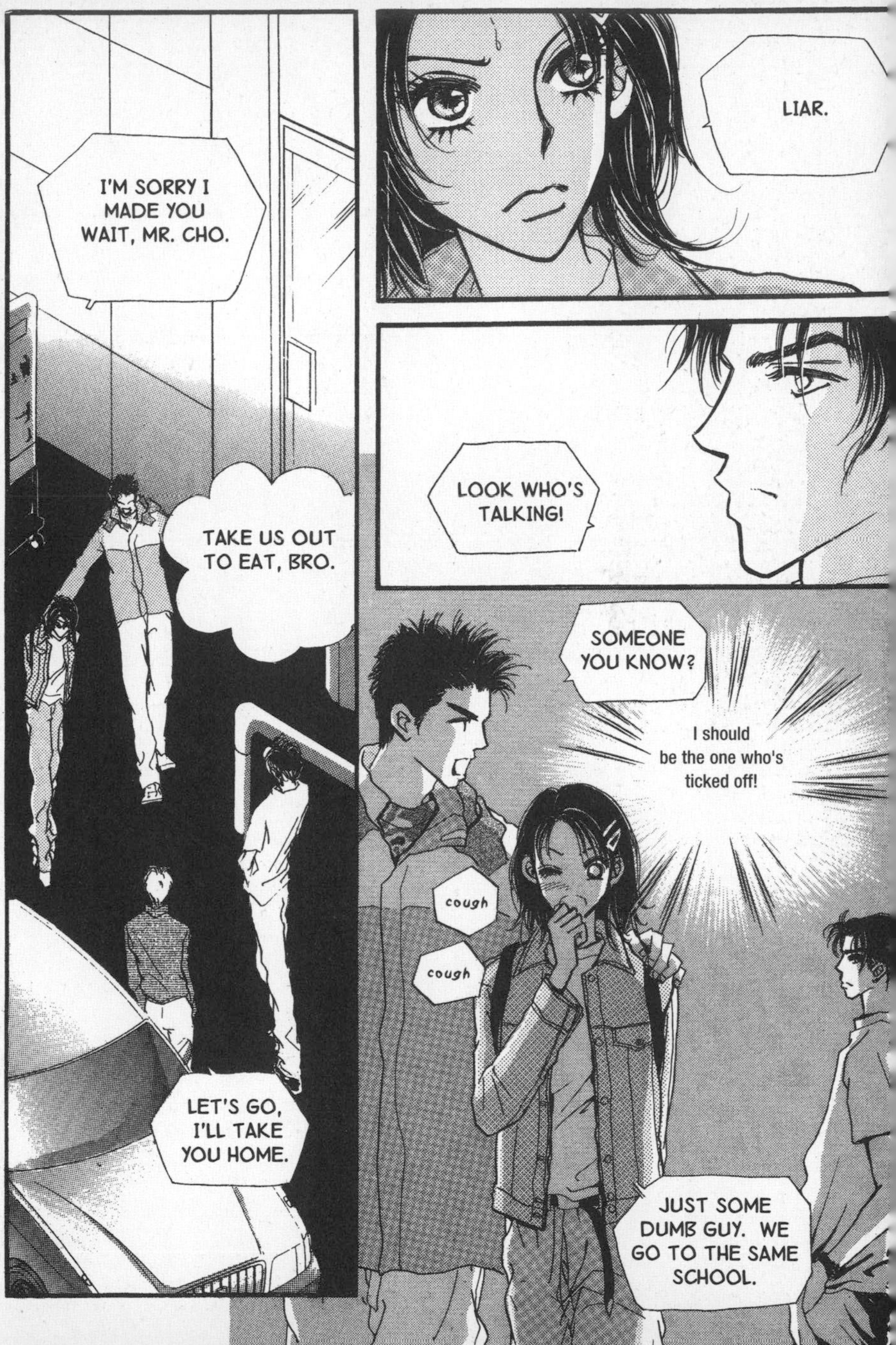
I'M SORRY I MADE YOU WAIT, MR. CHO.
TAKE US OUT TO EAT, BRO.
LET'S GO, I'LL TAKE YOU HOME.
LIAR.
LOOK WHO'S TALKING!
SOMEONE YOU KNOW?
I should be the one who's ticked off!
cough
cough
JUST SOME DUMB GUY. WE GO TO THE SAME SCHOOL.

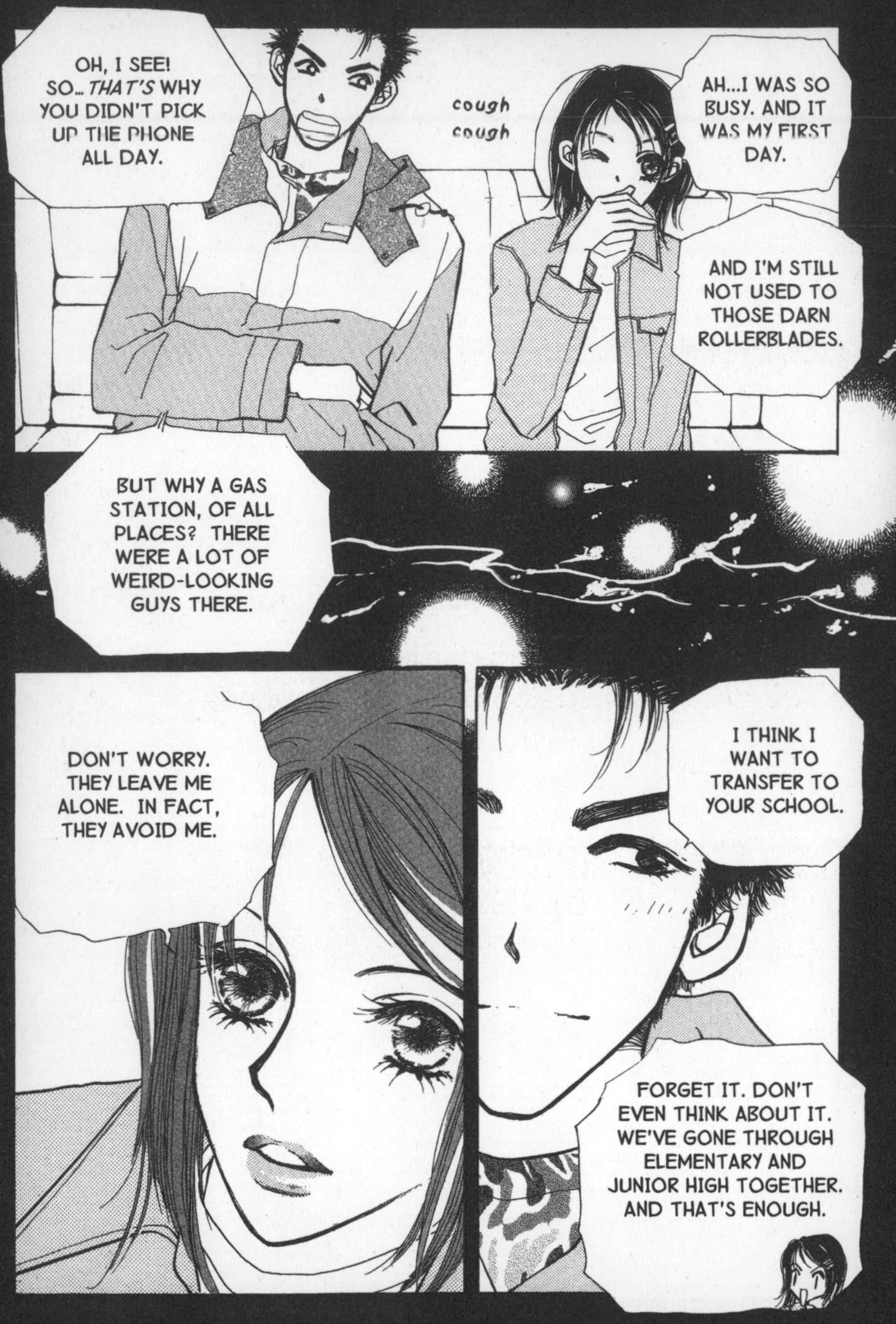
OH, I SEE! SO... THAT'S WHY YOU DIDN'T PICK UP THE PHONE ALL DAY.
cough cough
AH...I WAS SO BUSY. AND IT WAS MY FIRST DAY.
AND I'M STILL NOT USED TO THOSE DARN ROLLERBLADES.
BUT WHY A GAS STATION, OF ALL PLACES? THERE WERE A LOT OF WEIRD-LOOKING GUYS THERE.
DON'T WORRY. THEY LEAVE ME ALONE. IN FACT, THEY AVOID ME.
I THINK I WANT TO TRANSFER TO YOUR SCHOOL.
FORGET IT. DON'T EVEN THINK ABOUT IT. WE'VE GONE THROUGH ELEMENTARY AND JUNIOR HIGH TOGETHER. AND THAT'S ENOUGH.

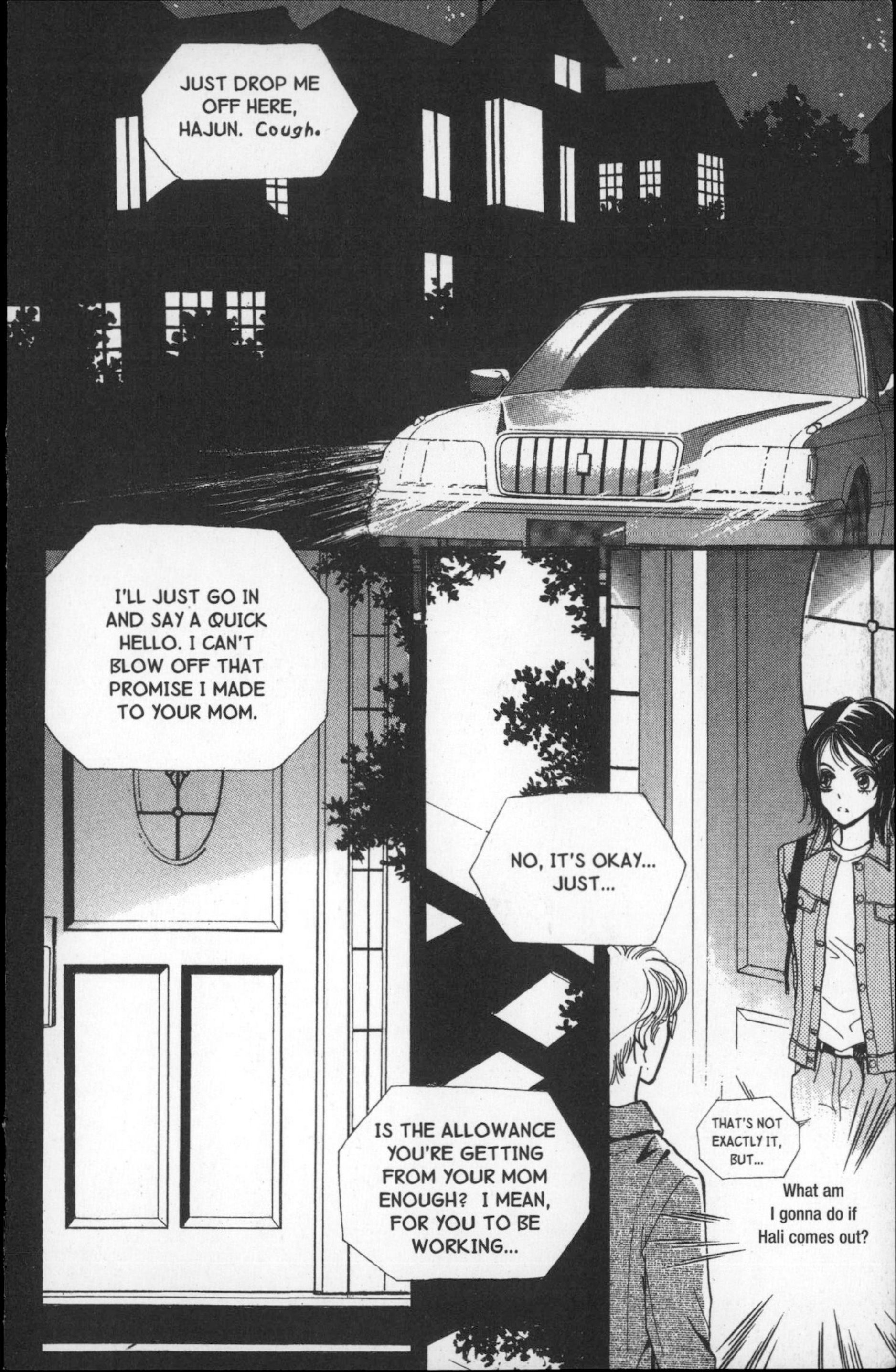
JUST DROP ME OFF HERE, HAJUN. Cough.
I'LL JUST GO IN AND SAY A QUICK HELLO. I CAN'T BLOW OFF THAT PROMISE I MADE TO YOUR MOM.
NO, IT'S OKAY... JUST...
IS THE ALLOWANCE YOU'RE GETTING FROM YOUR MOM ENOUGH? I MEAN, FOR YOU TO BE WORKING...
THAT'S NOT EXACTLY IT, BUT...
What am I gonna do if Hali comes out?

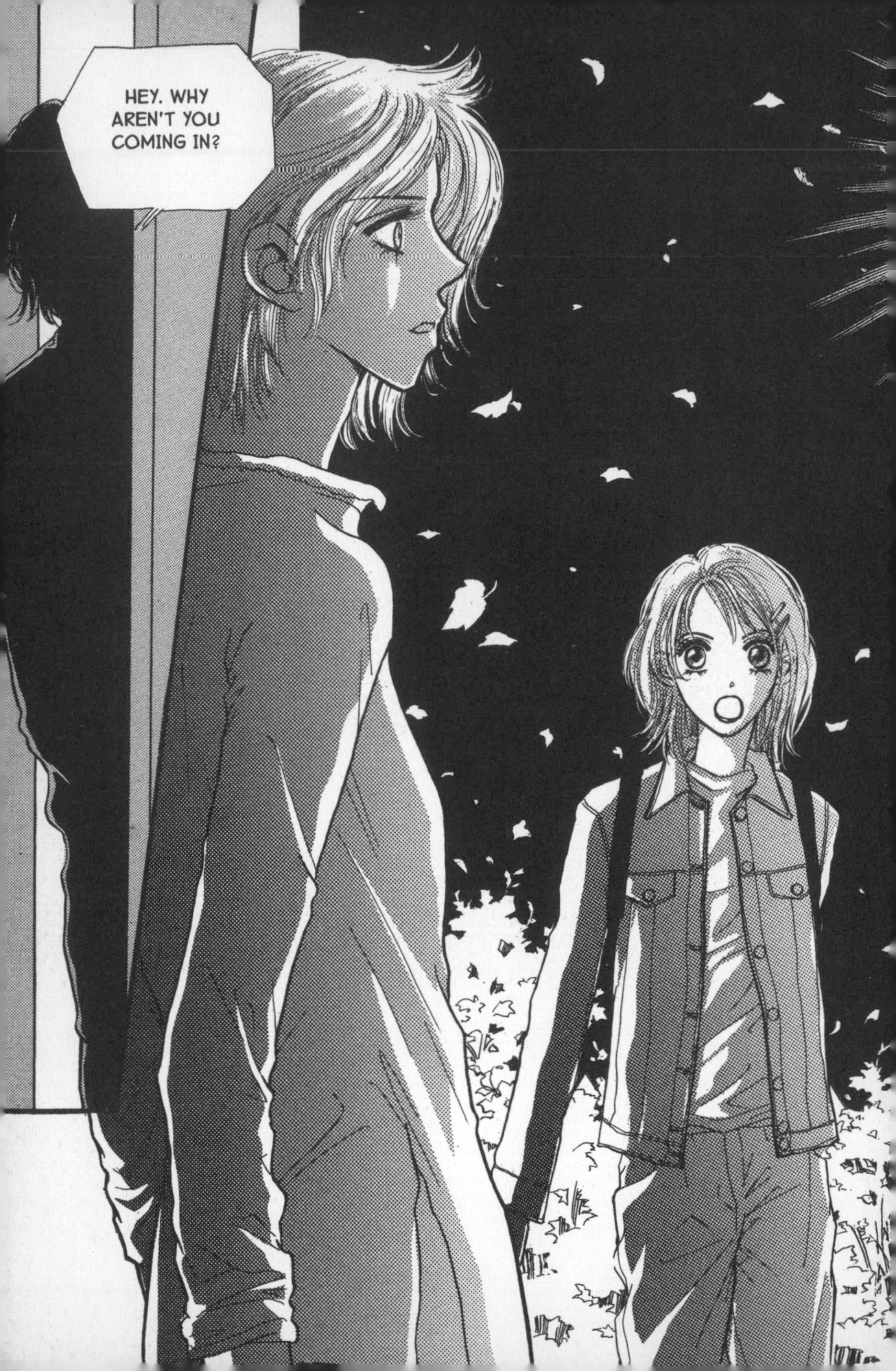
HEY. WHY AREN'T YOU COMING IN?

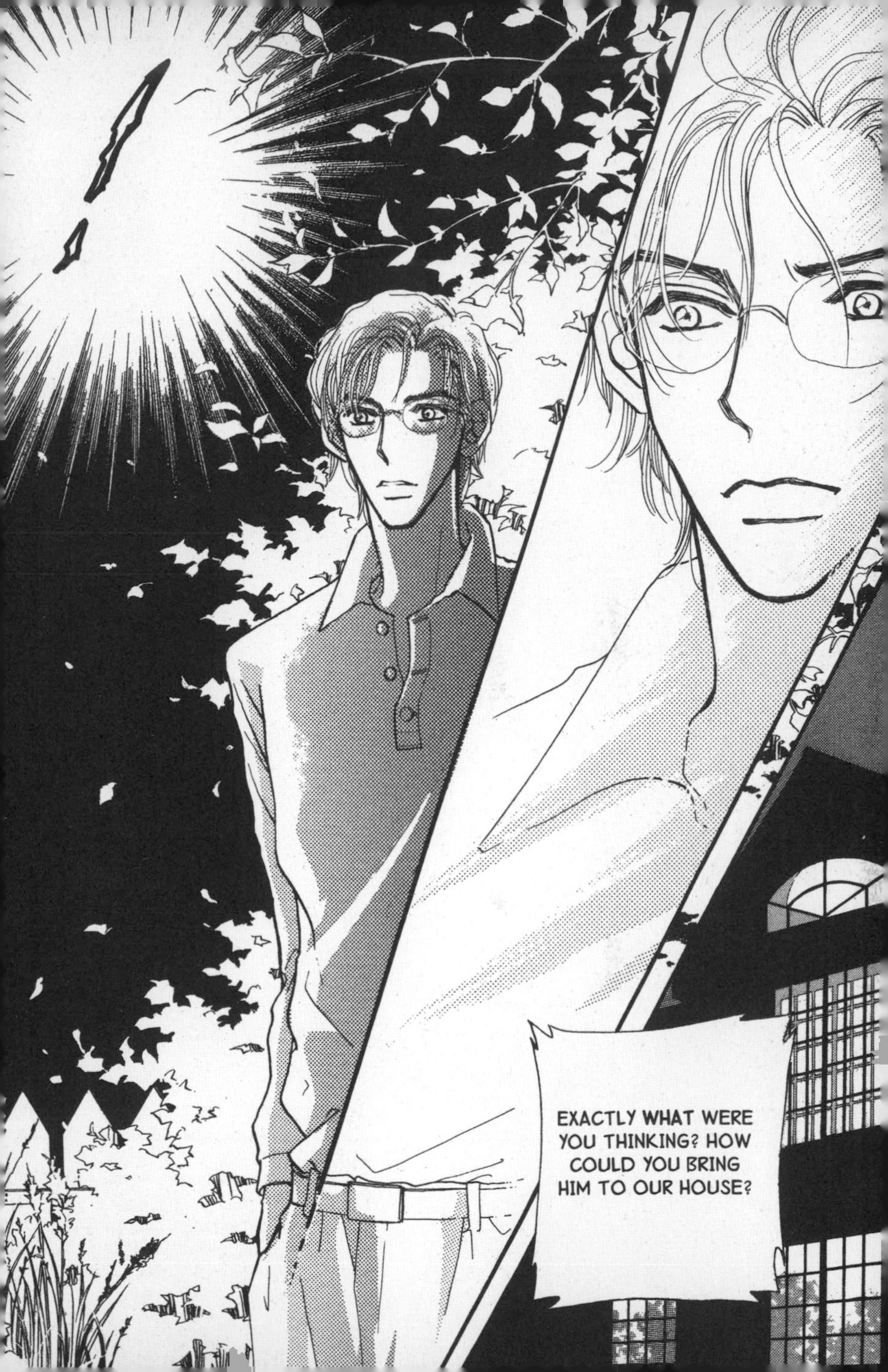
EXACTLY WHAT WERE YOU THINKING? HOW COULD YOU BRING HIM TO OUR HOUSE?

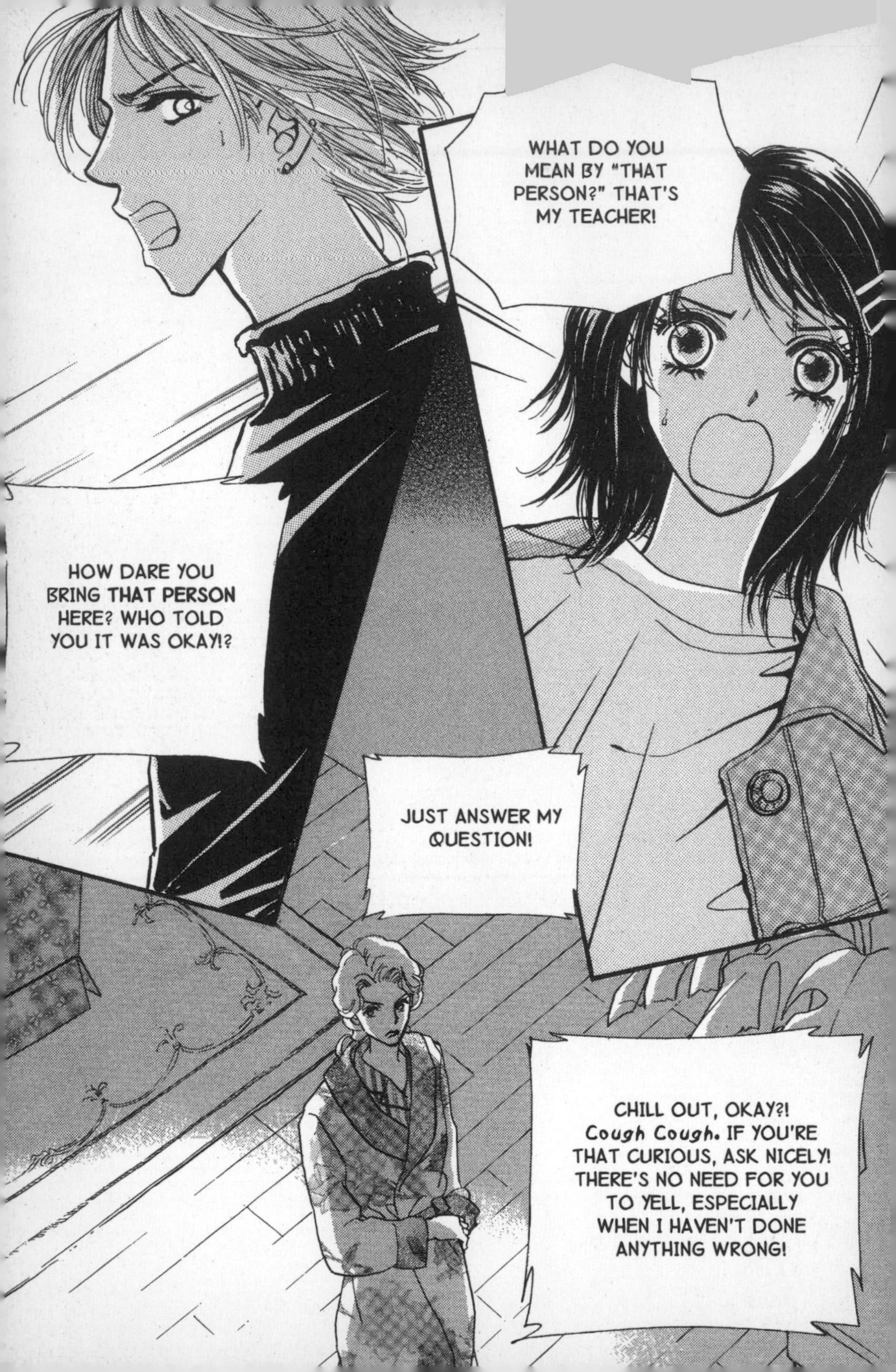
HOW DARE YOU BRING THAT PERSON HERE? WHO TOLD YOU IT WAS OKAY!?
WHAT DO YOU MEAN BY "THAT PERSON?" THAT'S MY TEACHER!
JUST ANSWER MY QUESTION!
CHILL OUT, OKAY?! *Cough Cough.* IF YOU'RE THAT CURIOUS, ASK NICELY! THERE'S NO NEED FOR YOU TO YELL, ESPECIALLY WHEN I HAVEN'T DONE ANYTHING WRONG!

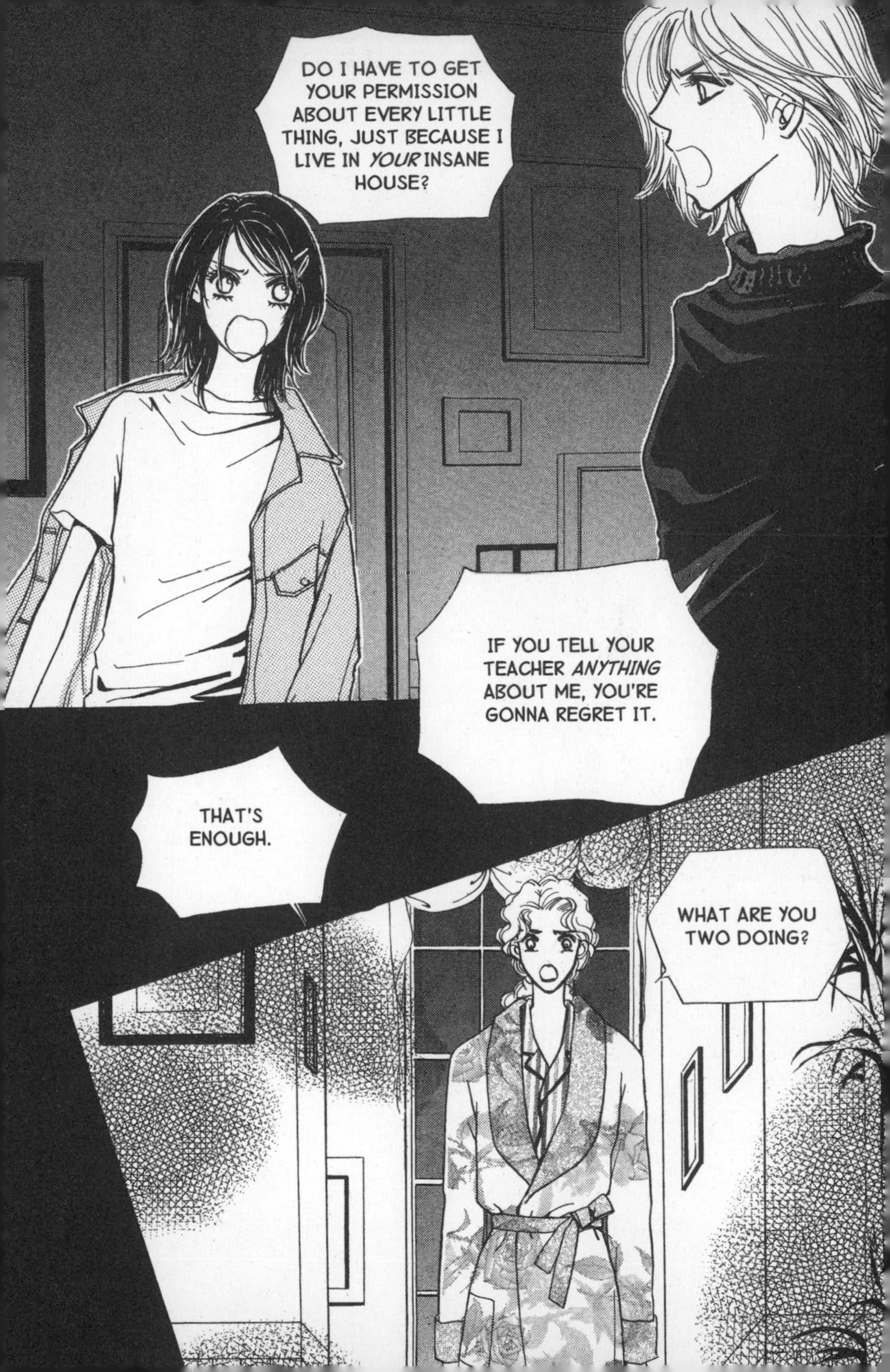
DO I HAVE TO GET YOUR PERMISSION ABOUT EVERY LITTLE THING, JUST BECAUSE I LIVE IN *YOUR* INSANE HOUSE?
IF YOU TELL YOUR TEACHER *ANYTHING* ABOUT ME, YOU'RE GONNA REGRET IT.
THAT'S ENOUGH.
WHAT ARE YOU TWO DOING?

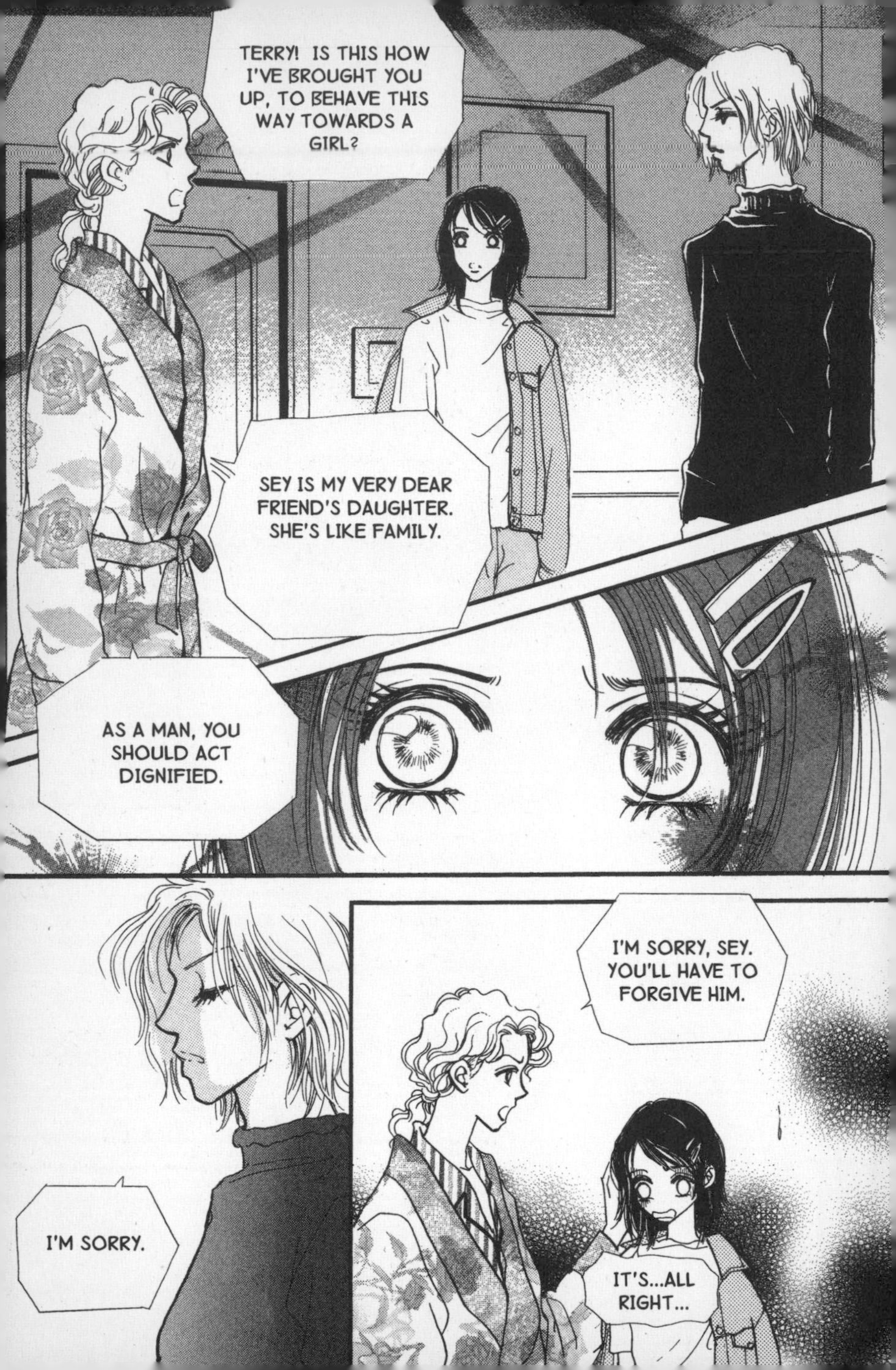
TERRY! IS THIS HOW I'VE BROUGHT YOU UP, TO BEHAVE THIS WAY TOWARDS A GIRL?
SEY IS MY VERY DEAR FRIEND'S DAUGHTER. SHE'S LIKE FAMILY.
AS A MAN, YOU SHOULD ACT DIGNIFIED.
I'M SORRY.
I'M SORRY, SEY. YOU'LL HAVE TO FORGIVE HIM.
IT'S...ALL RIGHT...

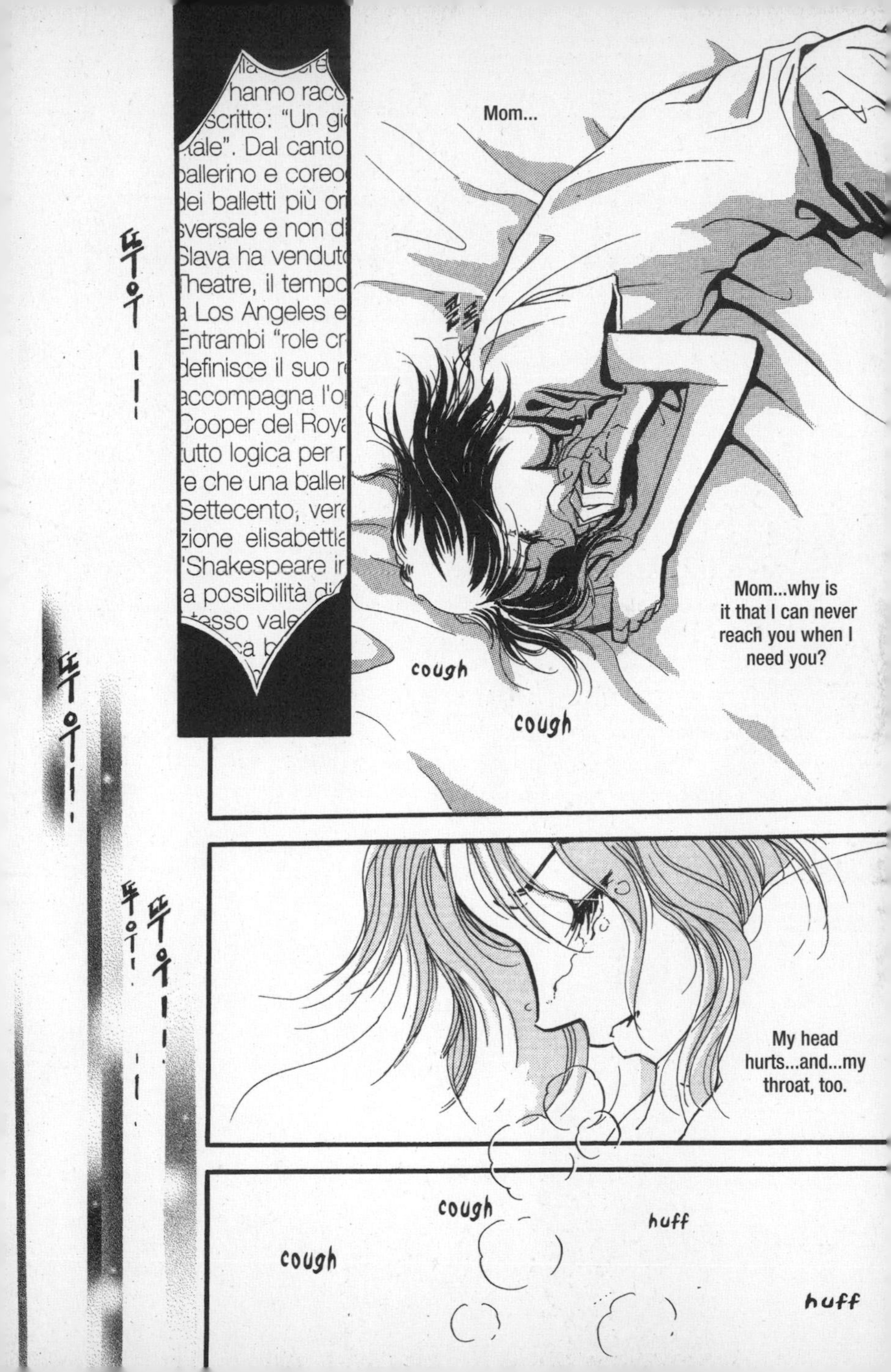

hanno racc
scritto: "Un gi
tale". Dal canto
ballerino e coreo
dei balletti più or
sversale e non d
Slava ha vendut
Theatre, il tempo
a Los Angeles e
Entrambi "role cr
definisce il suo r
accompagna l'o
Cooper del Roya
tutto logica per r
re che una baller
Settecento, vere
zione elisabettia
'Shakespeare i
a possibilità d
tesso vale
뚜우ㅡ
뚜우ㅡ
뚜우ㅡ
뚜우ㅡ
Mom...
콜록
cough
cough
Mom...why is it that I can never reach you when I need you?
My head hurts...and...my throat, too.
cough
cough
huff
huff

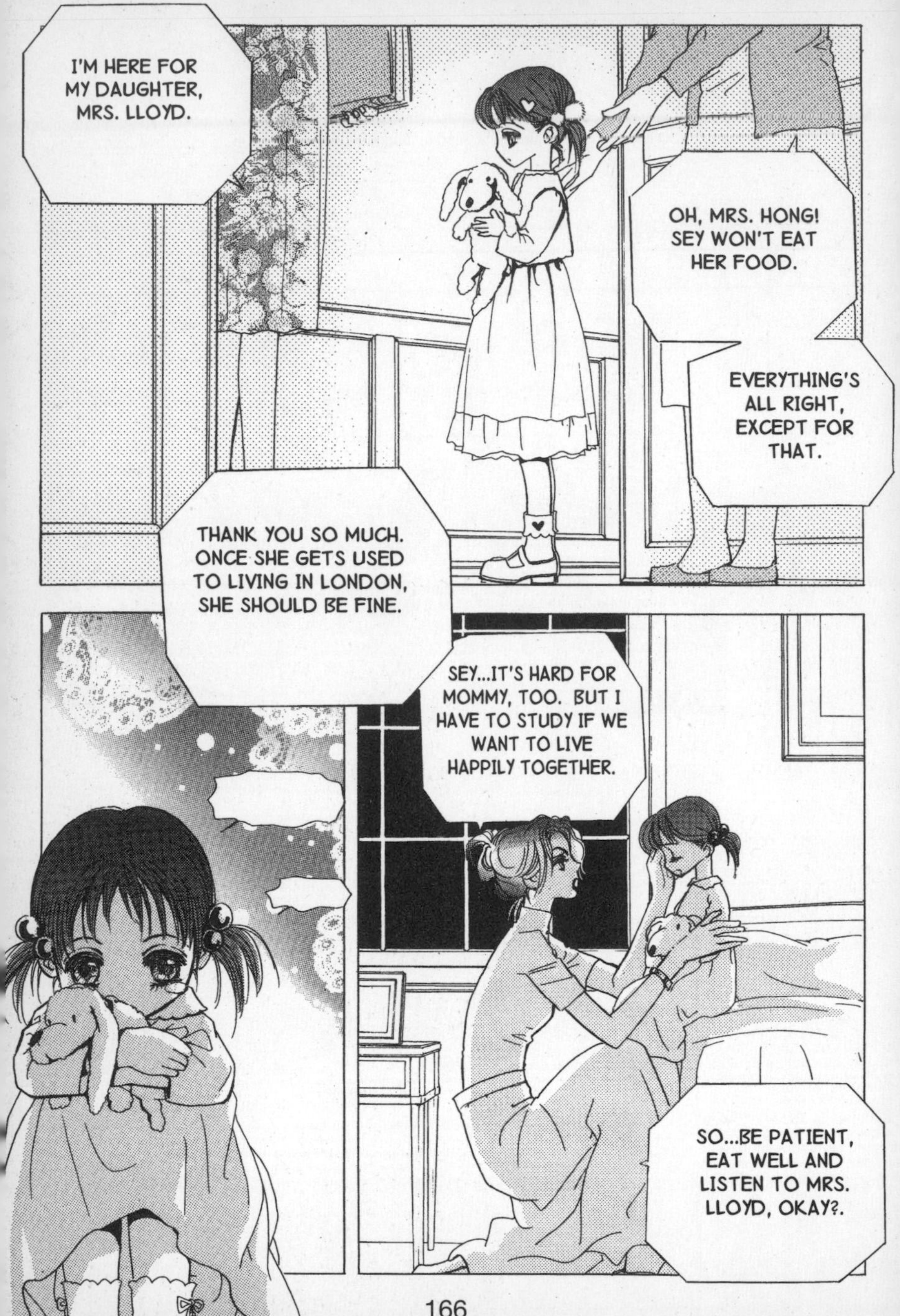
I'M HERE FOR MY DAUGHTER, MRS. LLOYD.
OH, MRS. HONG! SEY WON'T EAT HER FOOD.
EVERYTHING'S ALL RIGHT, EXCEPT FOR THAT.
THANK YOU SO MUCH. ONCE SHE GETS USED TO LIVING IN LONDON, SHE SHOULD BE FINE.
SEY...IT'S HARD FOR MOMMY, TOO. BUT I HAVE TO STUDY IF WE WANT TO LIVE HAPPILY TOGETHER.
SO...BE PATIENT, EAT WELL AND LISTEN TO MRS. LLOYD, OKAY?.

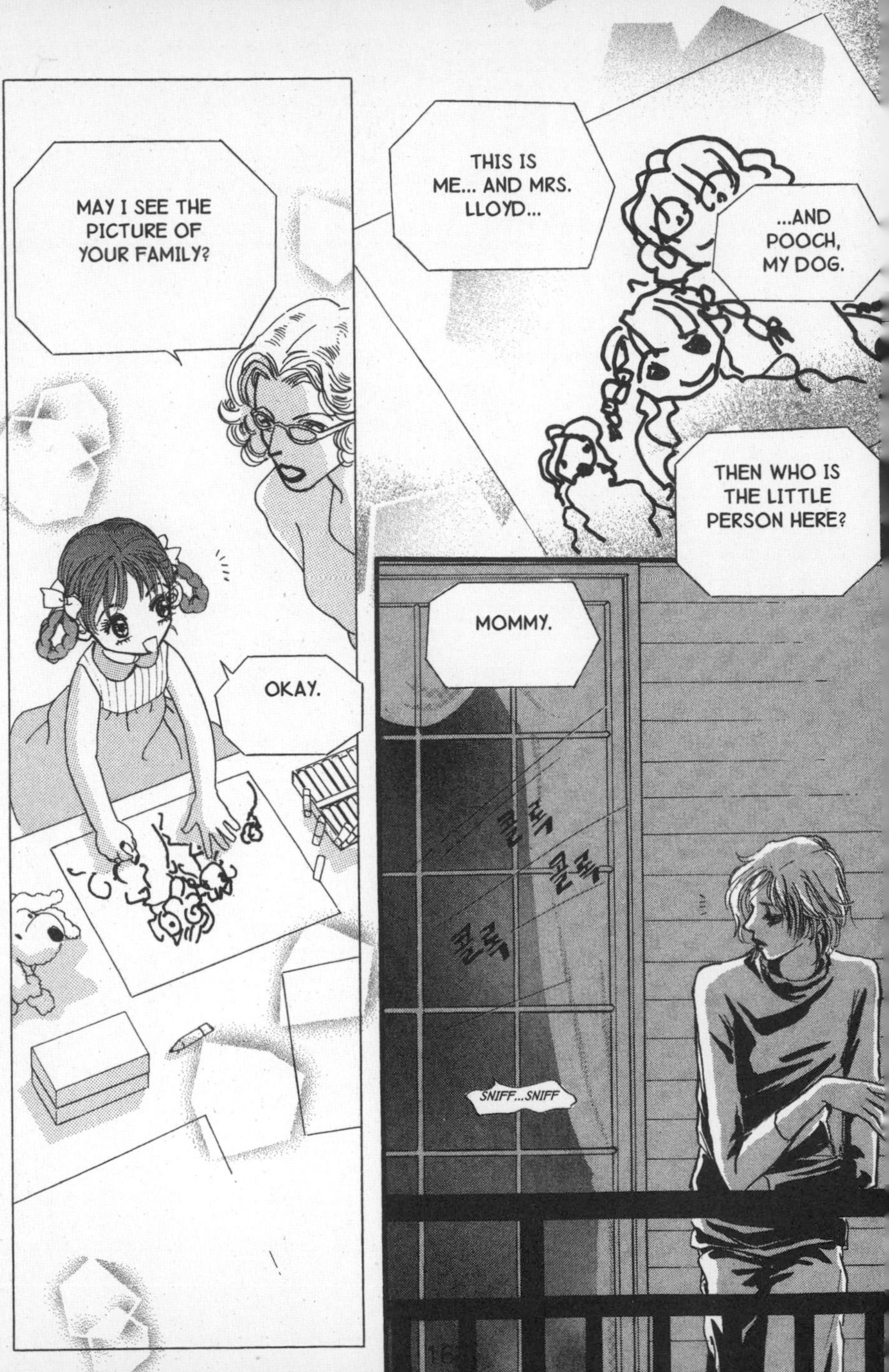
MAY I SEE THE PICTURE OF YOUR FAMILY?
OKAY.
THIS IS ME... AND MRS. LLOYD...
...AND POOCH, MY DOG.
THEN WHO IS THE LITTLE PERSON HERE?
MOMMY.
콜록
콜록
콜록
SNIFF...SNIFF

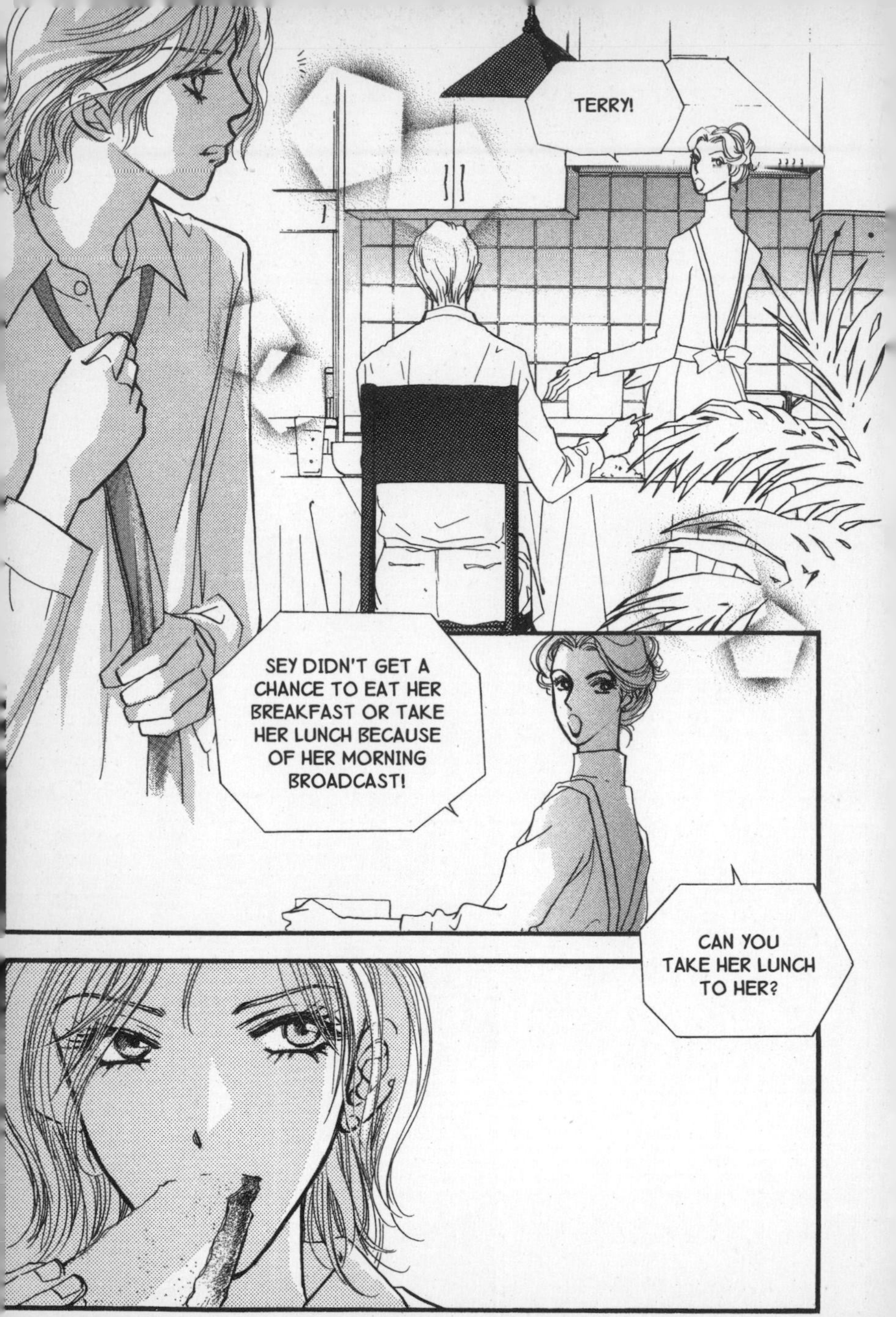
TERRY!
SEY DIDN'T GET A CHANCE TO EAT HER BREAKFAST OR TAKE HER LUNCH BECAUSE OF HER MORNING BROADCAST!
CAN YOU TAKE HER LUNCH TO HER?

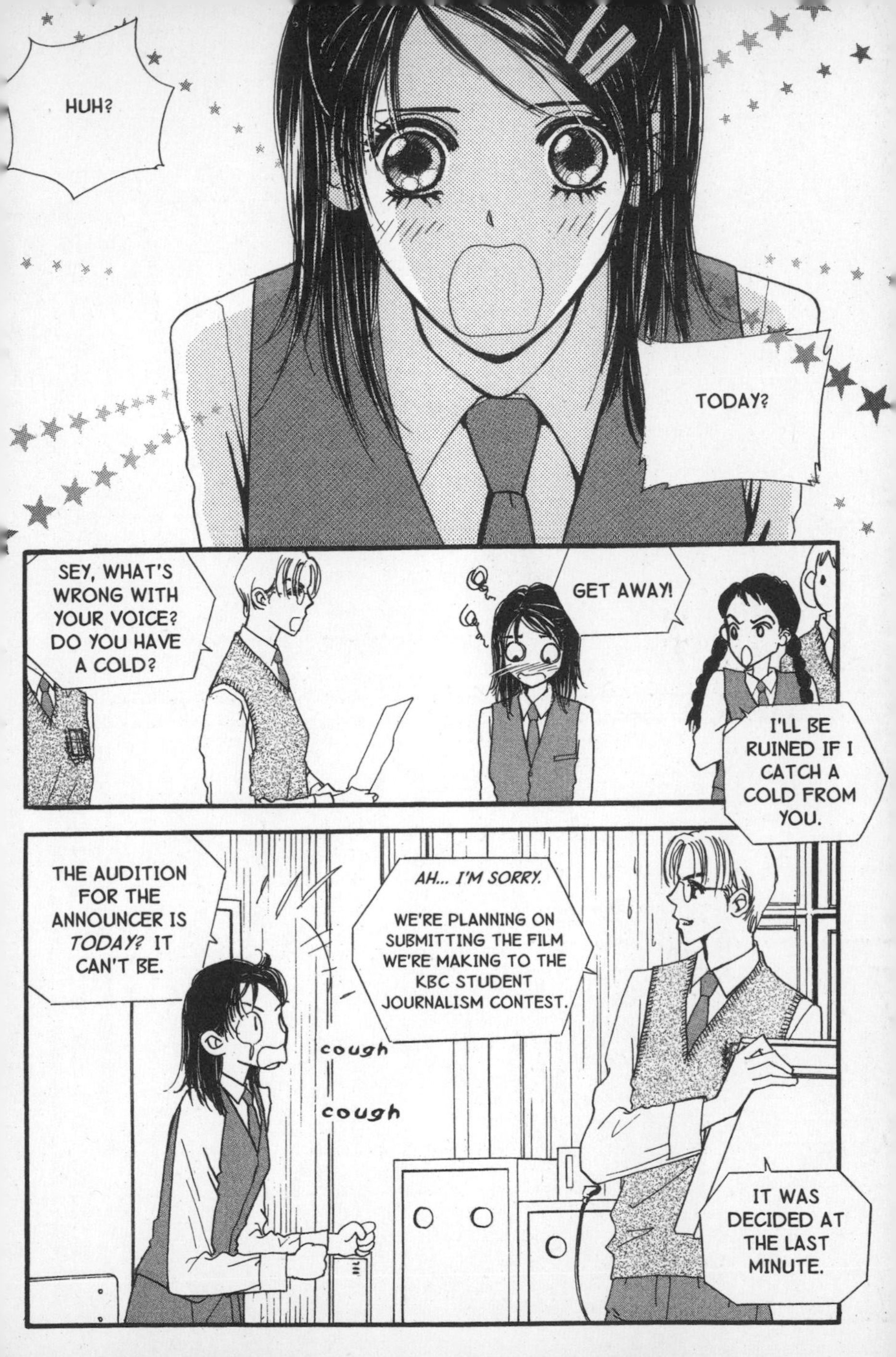
HUH?
TODAY?
SEY, WHAT'S WRONG WITH YOUR VOICE? DO YOU HAVE A COLD?
GET AWAY!
I'LL BE RUINED IF I CATCH A COLD FROM YOU.
THE AUDITION FOR THE ANNOUNCER IS *TODAY?* IT CAN'T BE.
AH... I'M SORRY.
WE'RE PLANNING ON SUBMITTING THE FILM WE'RE MAKING TO THE KBC STUDENT JOURNALISM CONTEST.
cough
cough
IT WAS DECIDED AT THE LAST MINUTE.

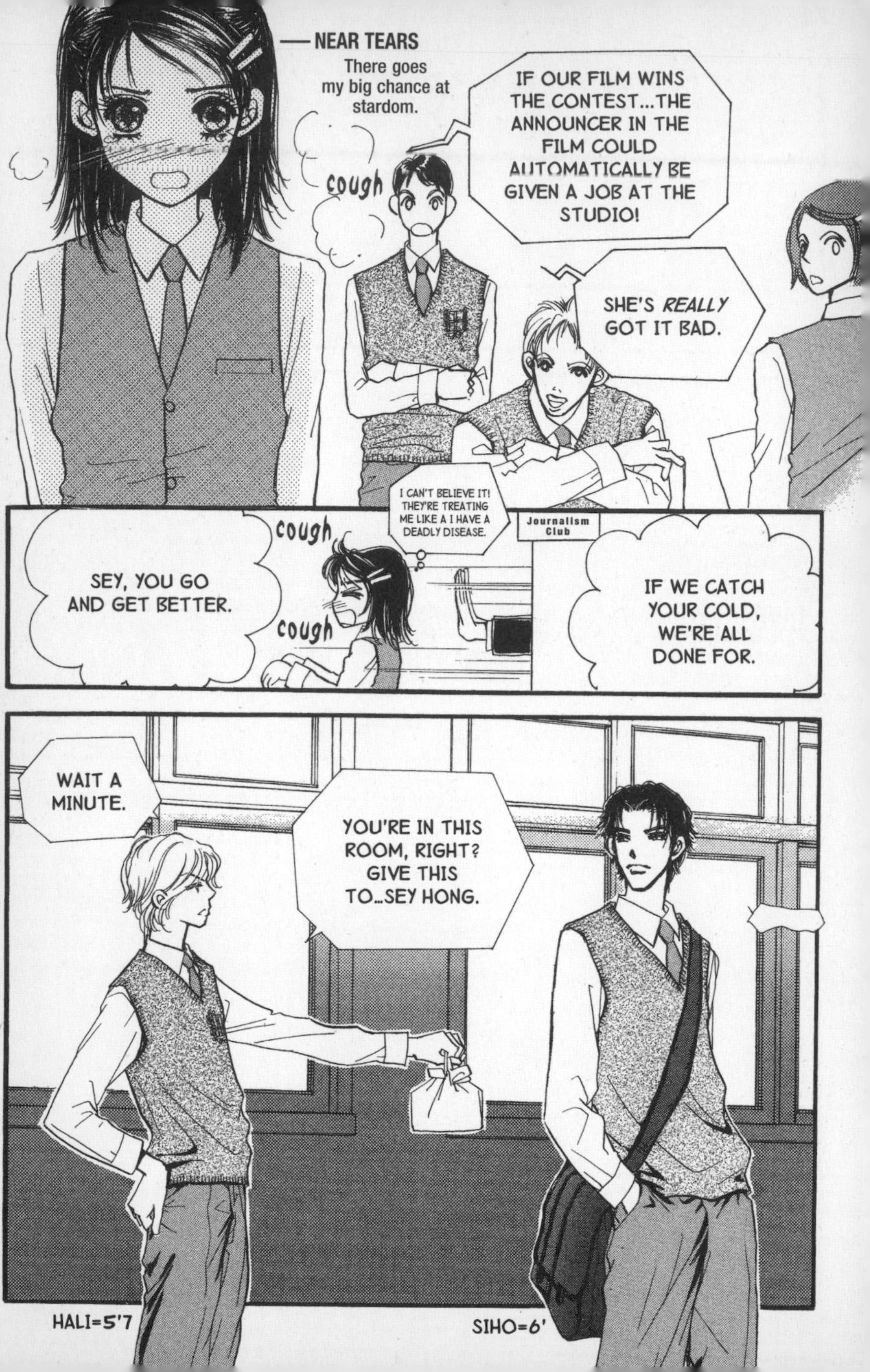

—NEAR TEARS
There goes my big chance at stardom.
cough
IF OUR FILM WINS THE CONTEST...THE ANNOUNCER IN THE FILM COULD AUTOMATICALLY BE GIVEN A JOB AT THE STUDIO!
SHE'S *REALLY* GOT IT BAD.
SEY, YOU GO AND GET BETTER.
cough
I CAN'T BELIEVE IT! THEY'RE TREATING ME LIKE A I HAVE A DEADLY DISEASE.
cough
Journalism Club
IF WE CATCH YOUR COLD, WE'RE ALL DONE FOR.
WAIT A MINUTE.
YOU'RE IN THIS ROOM, RIGHT? GIVE THIS TO...SEY HONG.
HALI=5'7
SIHO=6'

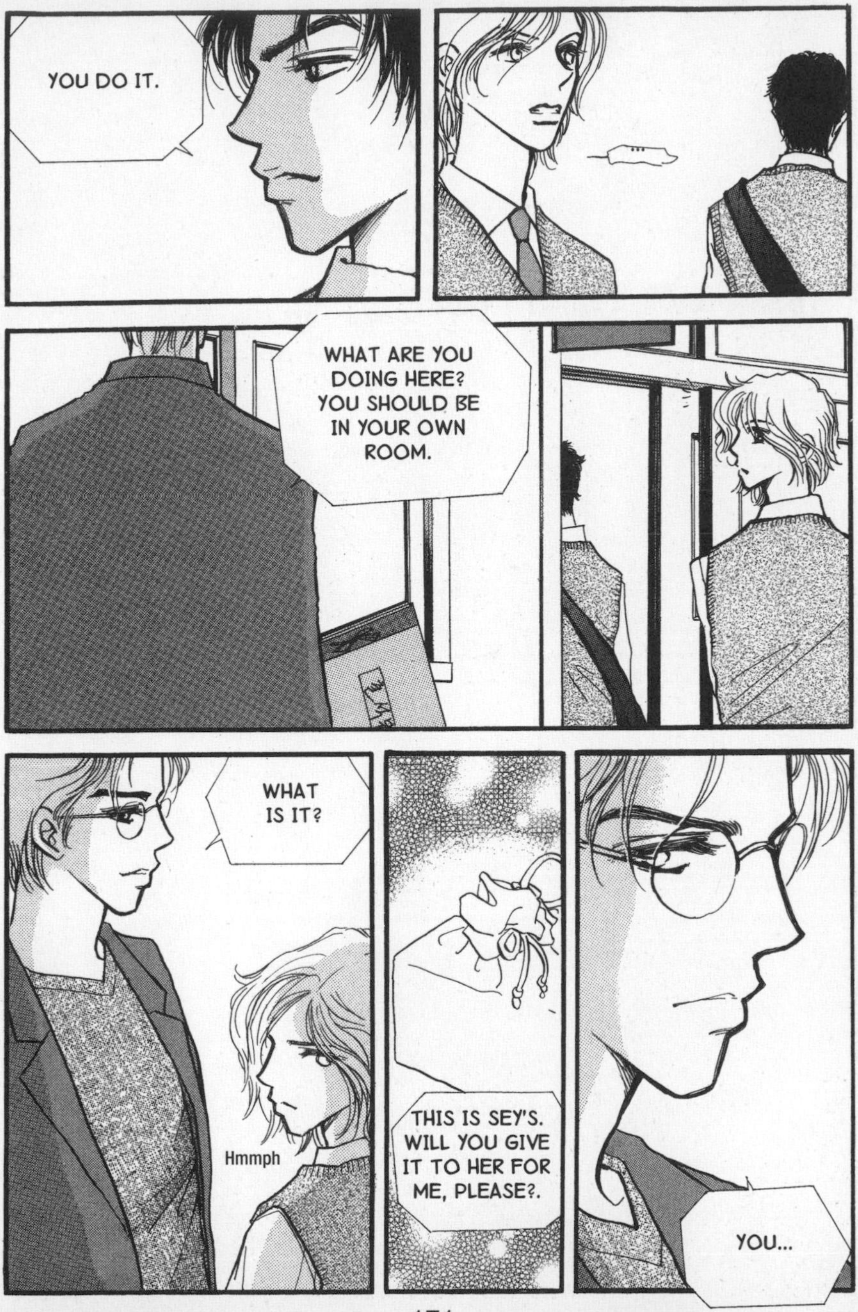
YOU DO IT.
...
WHAT ARE YOU DOING HERE? YOU SHOULD BE IN YOUR OWN ROOM.
WHAT IS IT?
Hmmph
THIS IS SEY'S. WILL YOU GIVE IT TO HER FOR ME, PLEASE?.
YOU...

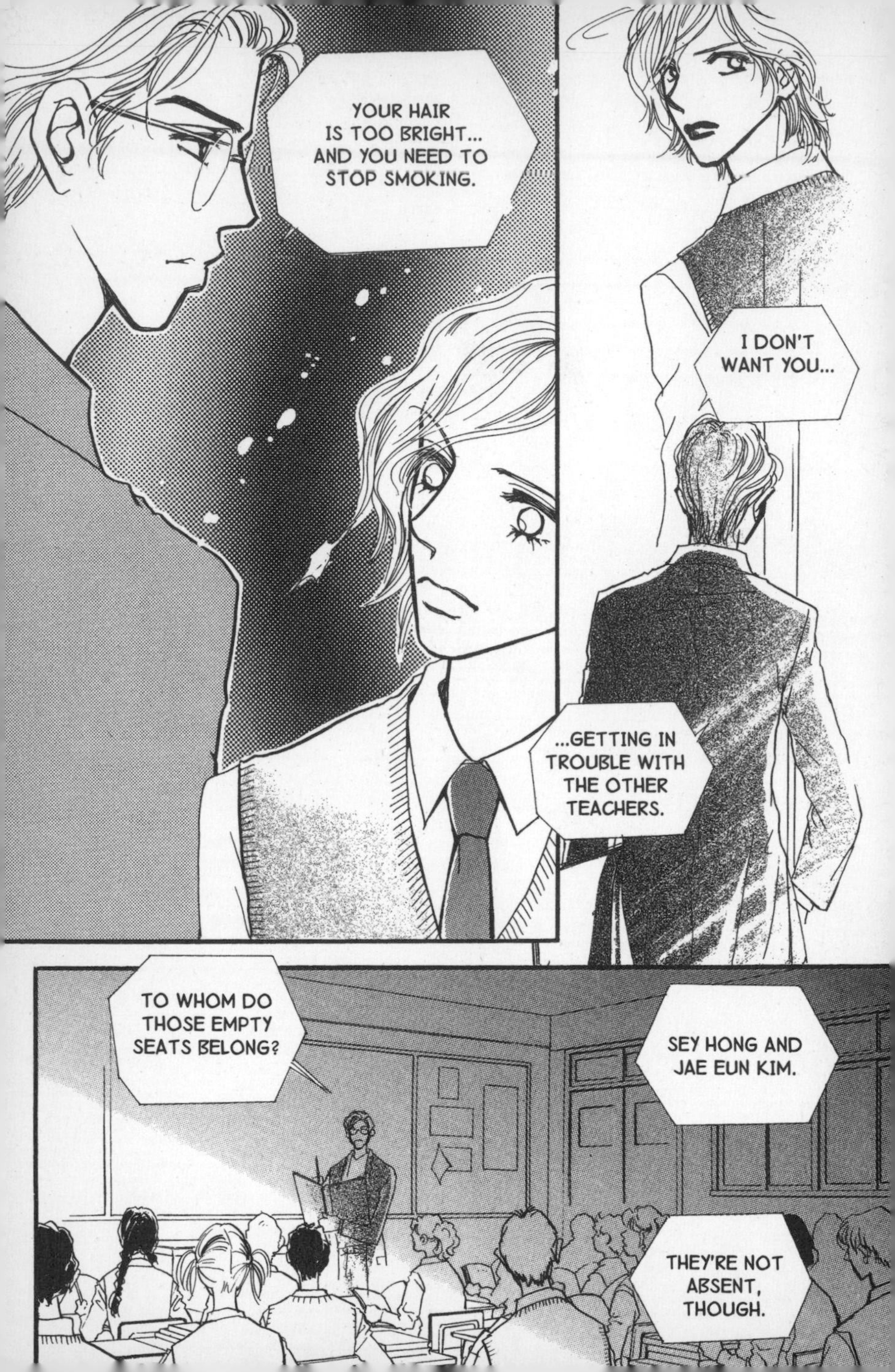
YOUR HAIR IS TOO BRIGHT... AND YOU NEED TO STOP SMOKING.
I DON'T WANT YOU...
...GETTING IN TROUBLE WITH THE OTHER TEACHERS.
TO WHOM DO THOSE EMPTY SEATS BELONG?
SEY HONG AND JAE EUN KIM.
THEY'RE NOT ABSENT, THOUGH.

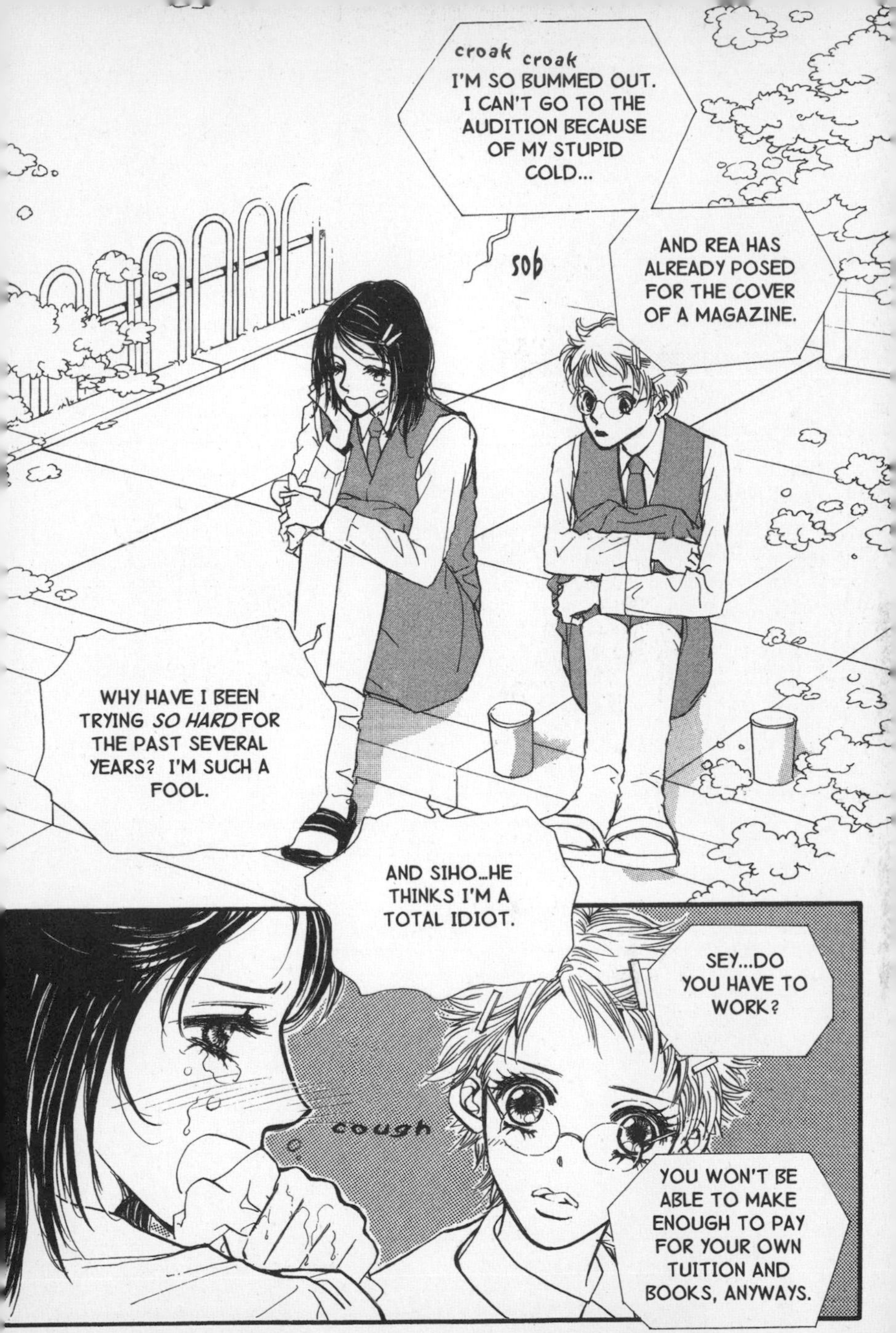
croak croak
I'M SO BUMMED OUT. I CAN'T GO TO THE AUDITION BECAUSE OF MY STUPID COLD...
sob
AND REA HAS ALREADY POSED FOR THE COVER OF A MAGAZINE.
WHY HAVE I BEEN TRYING *SO HARD* FOR THE PAST SEVERAL YEARS? I'M SUCH A FOOL.
AND SIHO...HE THINKS I'M A TOTAL IDIOT.
cough
SEY...DO YOU HAVE TO WORK?
YOU WON'T BE ABLE TO MAKE ENOUGH TO PAY FOR YOUR OWN TUITION AND BOOKS, ANYWAYS.

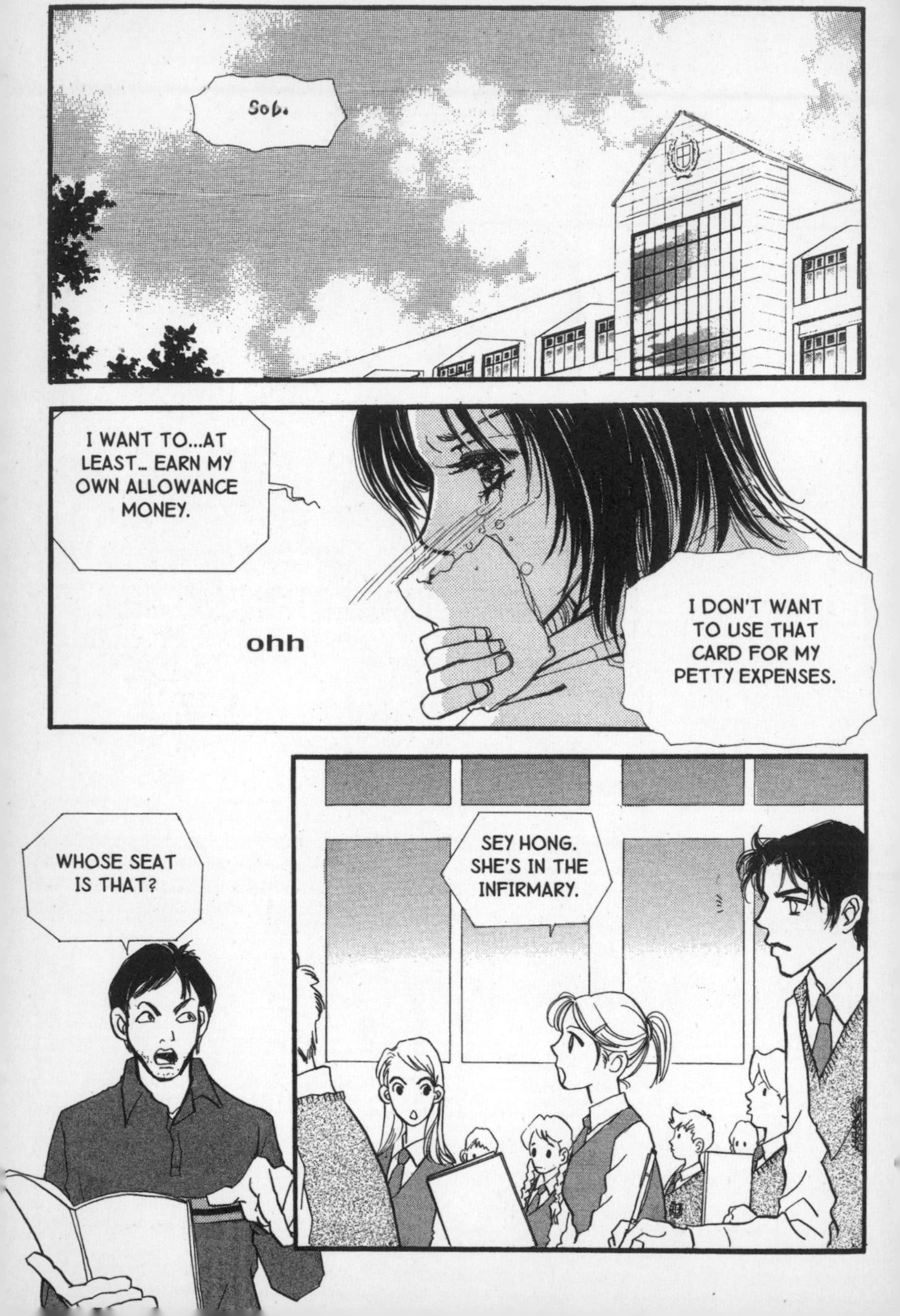

Sob.
I WANT TO...AT LEAST... EARN MY OWN ALLOWANCE MONEY.
ohh
I DON'T WANT TO USE THAT CARD FOR MY PETTY EXPENSES.
WHOSE SEAT IS THAT?
SEY HONG. SHE'S IN THE INFIRMARY.

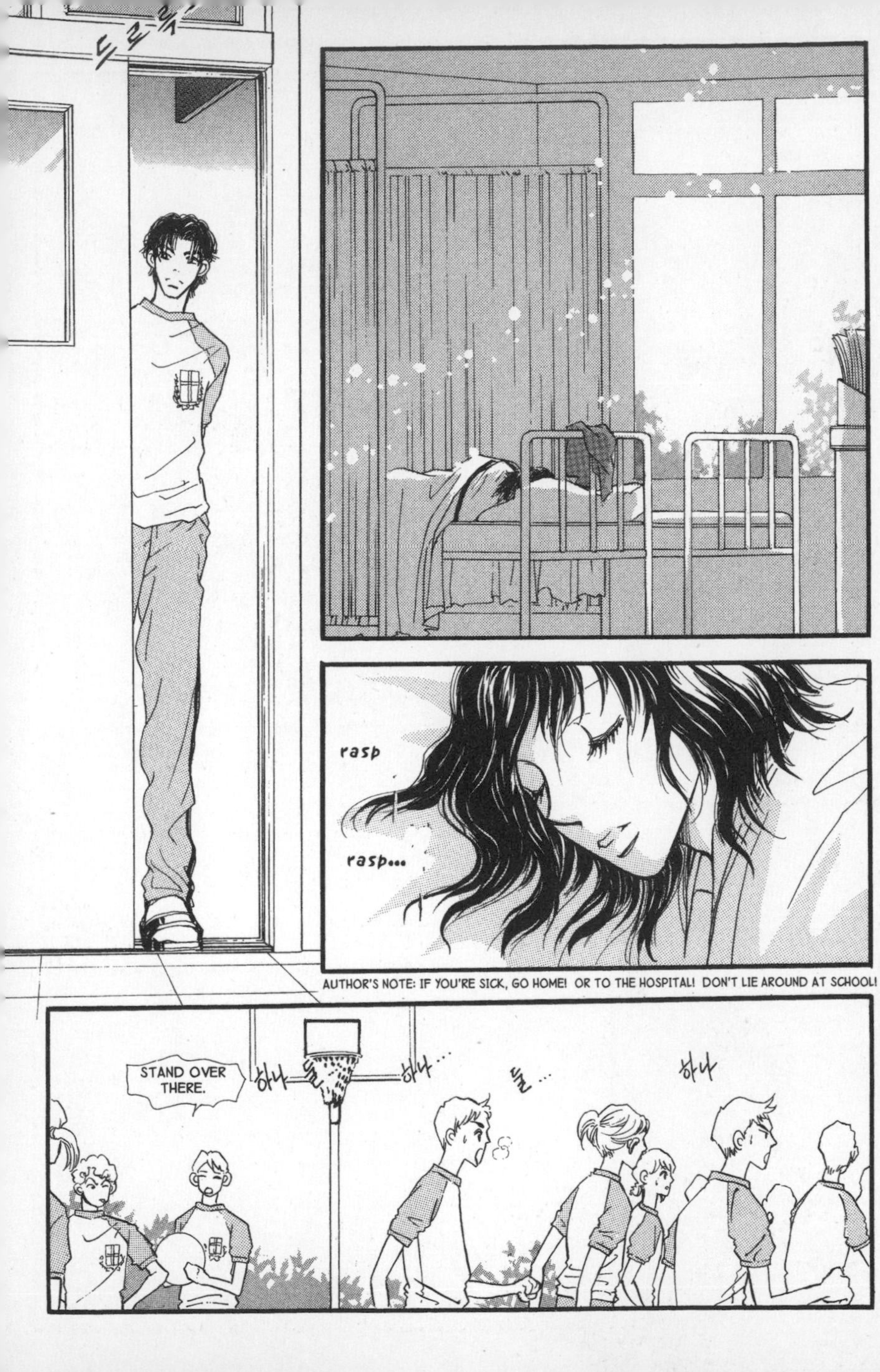

드르륵
rasp
rasp...
AUTHOR'S NOTE: IF YOU'RE SICK, GO HOME! OR TO THE HOSPITAL! DON'T LIE AROUND AT SCHOOL!
STAND OVER THERE.
하나 둘
하나...
둘...
하나

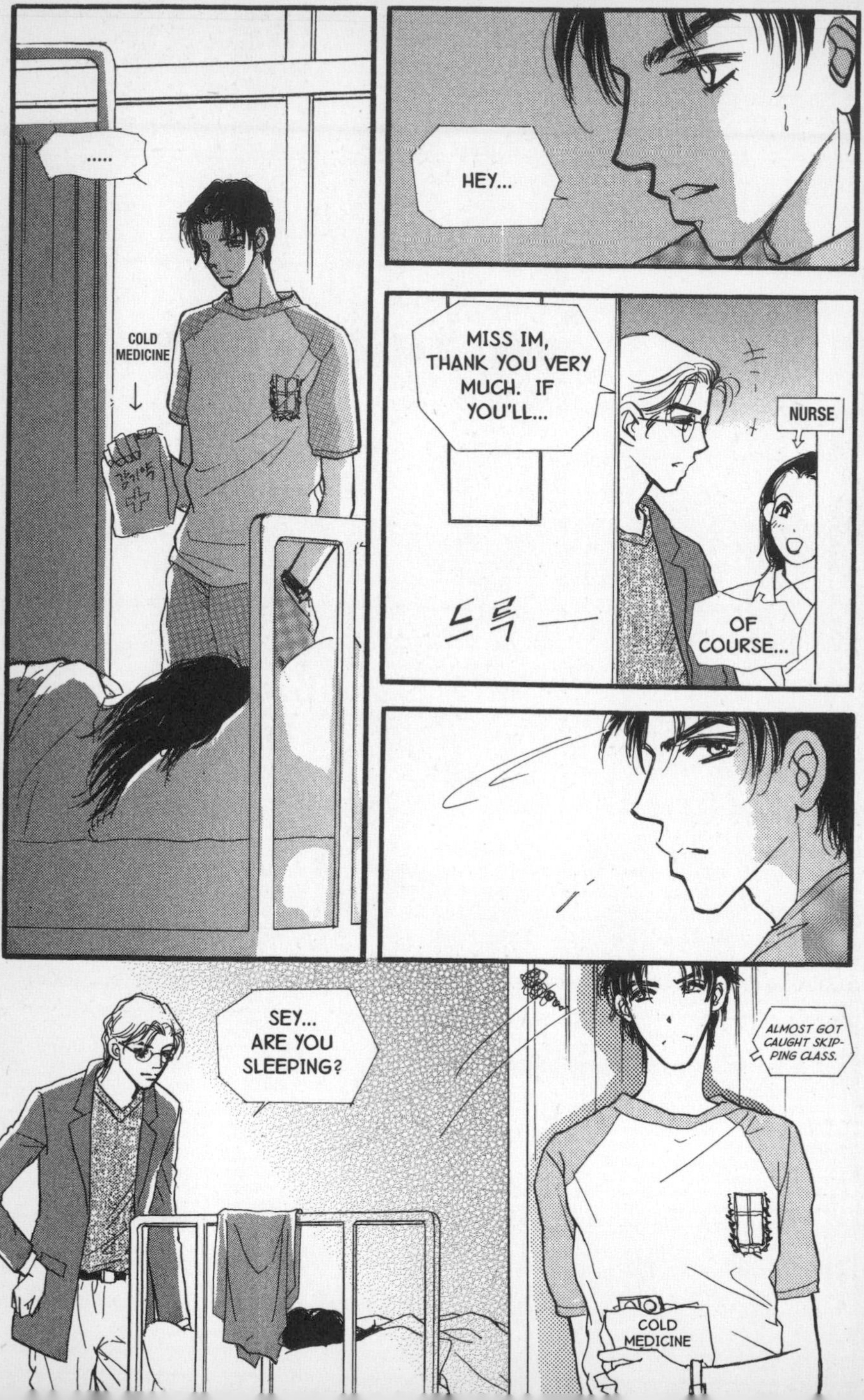
......
COLD MEDICINE
HEY...
MISS IM, THANK YOU VERY MUCH. IF YOU'LL...
NURSE
드륵
OF COURSE...
SEY... ARE YOU SLEEPING?
ALMOST GOT CAUGHT SKIP-PING CLASS.
COLD MEDICINE

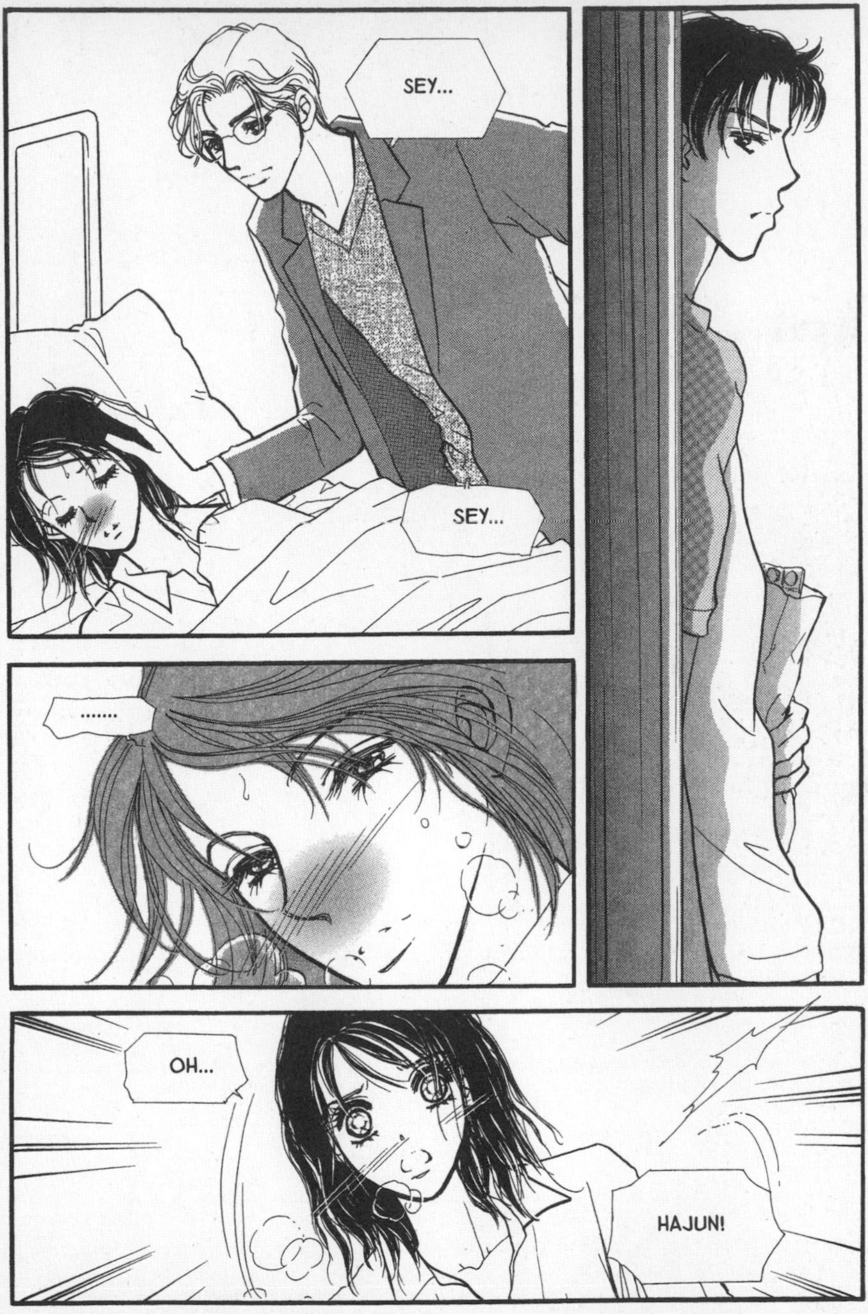
SEY...
SEY...
....
OH...
HAJUN!

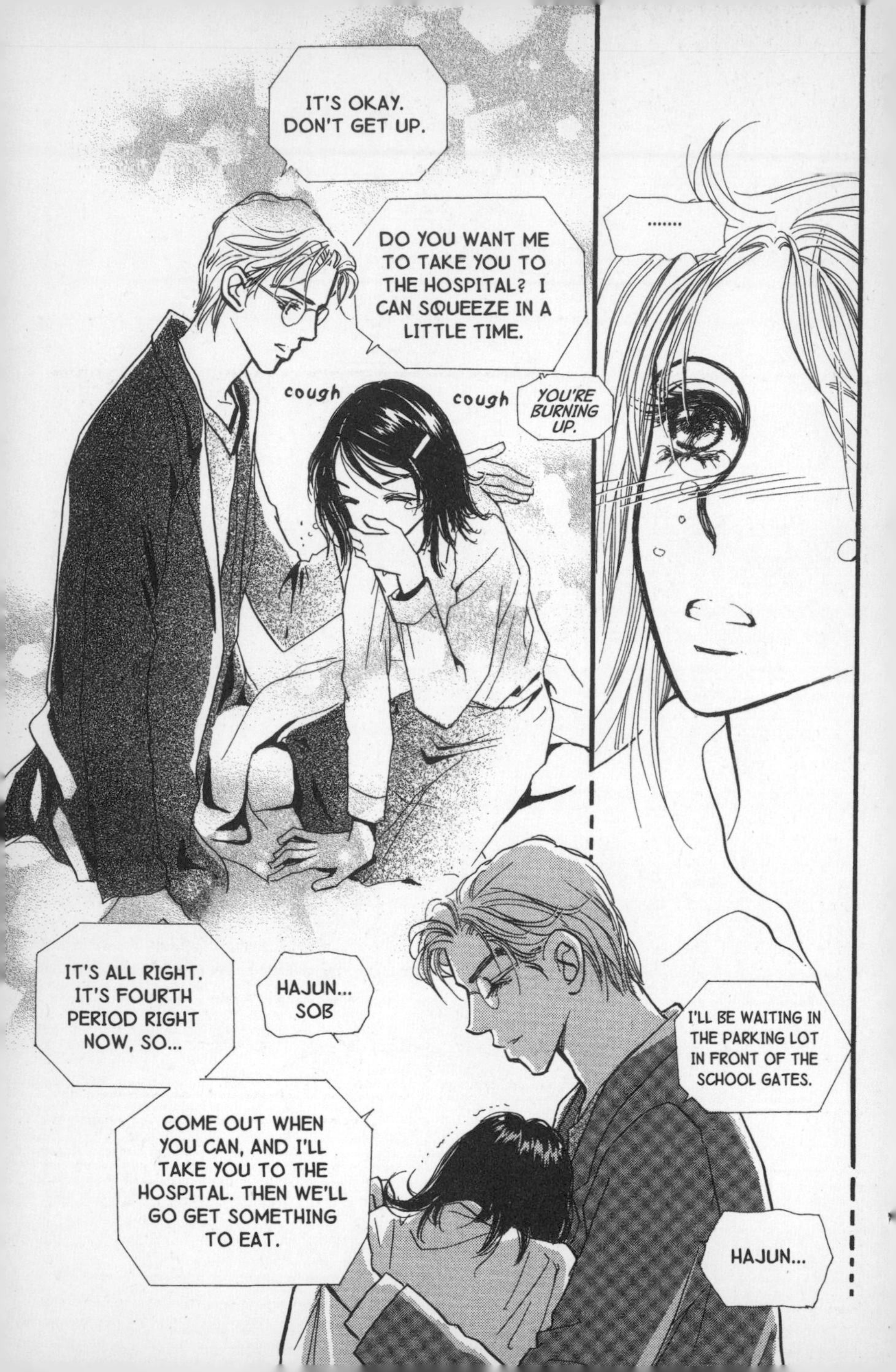
IT'S OKAY. DON'T GET UP.
DO YOU WANT ME TO TAKE YOU TO THE HOSPITAL? I CAN SQUEEZE IN A LITTLE TIME.
cough
cough
YOU'RE BURNING UP.
....
IT'S ALL RIGHT. IT'S FOURTH PERIOD RIGHT NOW, SO...
HAJUN... SOB
COME OUT WHEN YOU CAN, AND I'LL TAKE YOU TO THE HOSPITAL. THEN WE'LL GO GET SOMETHING TO EAT.
I'LL BE WAITING IN THE PARKING LOT IN FRONT OF THE SCHOOL GATES.
HAJUN...

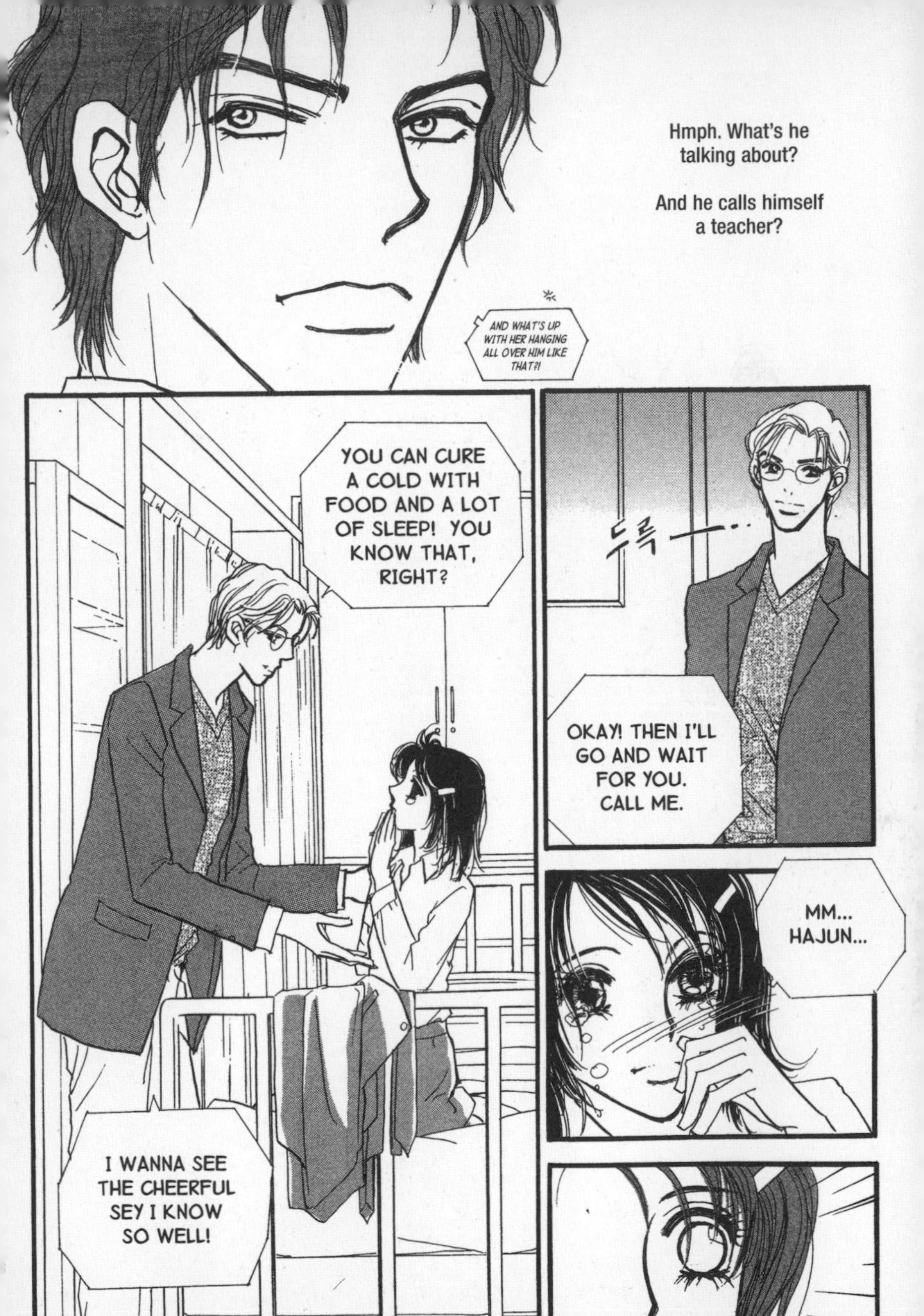
Hmph. What's he talking about?
And he calls himself a teacher?
AND WHAT'S UP WITH HER HANGING ALL OVER HIM LIKE THAT?!
YOU CAN CURE A COLD WITH FOOD AND A LOT OF SLEEP! YOU KNOW THAT, RIGHT?
I WANNA SEE THE CHEERFUL SEY I KNOW SO WELL!
드륵—...
OKAY! THEN I'LL GO AND WAIT FOR YOU. CALL ME.
MM... HAJUN...

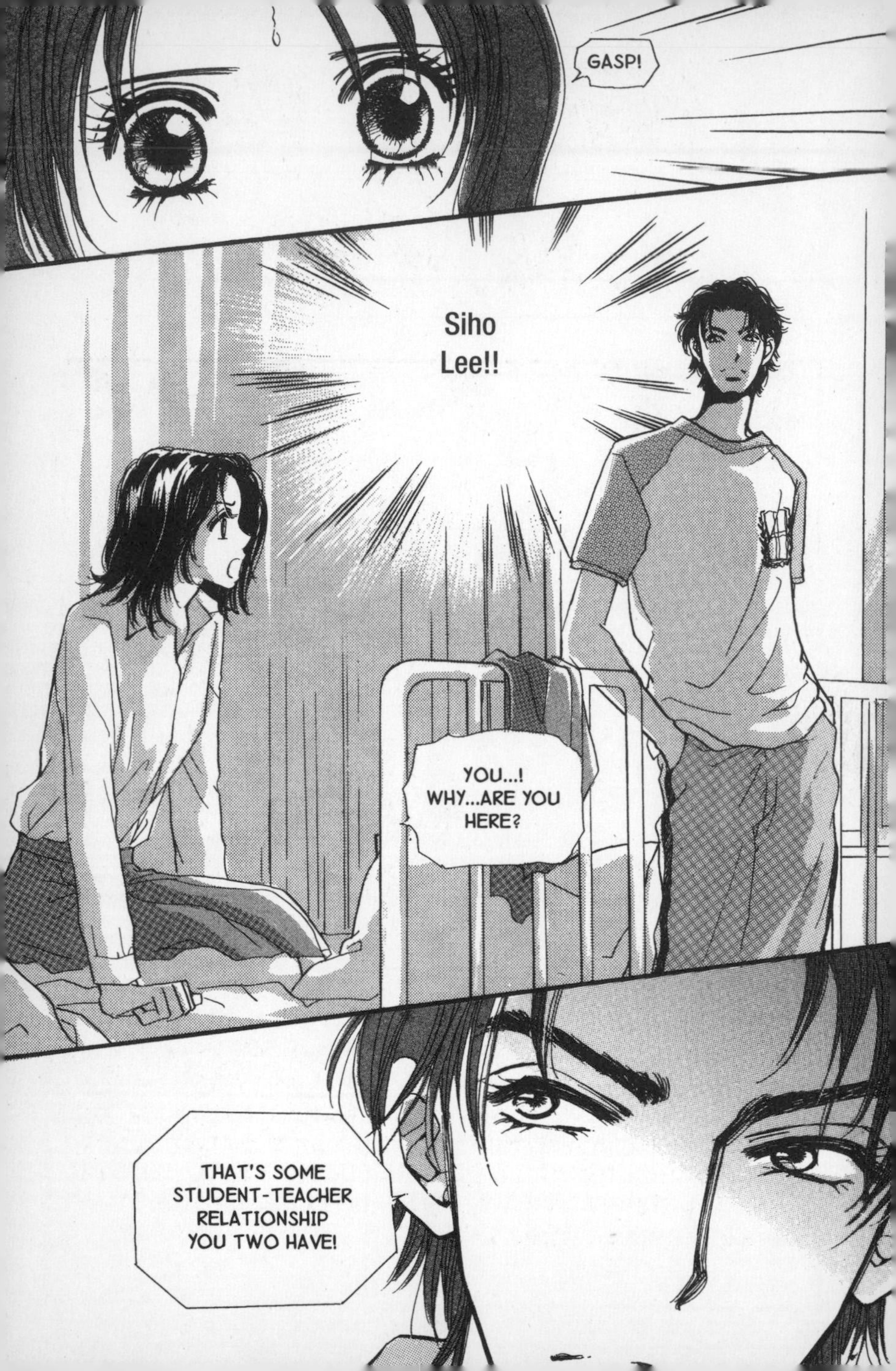
GASP!
Siho Lee!!
YOU...! WHY...ARE YOU HERE?
THAT'S SOME STUDENT-TEACHER RELATIONSHIP YOU TWO HAVE!

NEXT IN I.N.V.U.

Is bad boy Siho falling for Sey? Is Mr. Cho falling for Sey? Terry-- or Hali-- contemplates show biz mover-and-shaker Taegi Kwon's proposal and we find out how a high school kid like Siho pays his rent and what kind of woman heartthrob teacher Hajun Cho really wants. But how much longer will Hali have to impersonate her dead brother? And why doesn't Sey like boys? The answers to these questions and many more can be found in the next gender-bending issue of I.N.V.U.!

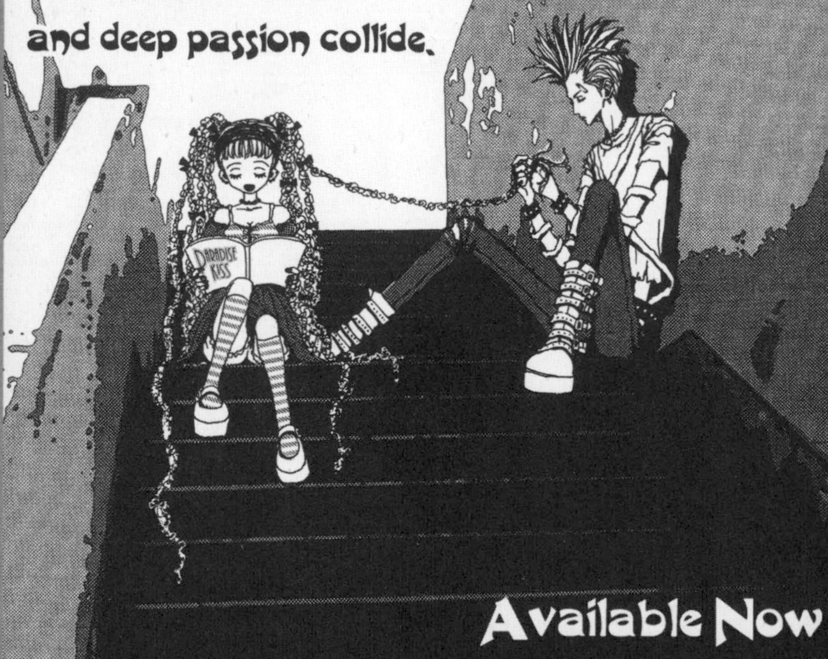
PARADISE KISS